One in Christ Jesus

One in Christ Jesus

Essays on Early Christianity and "All That Jazz," in Honor of S. Scott Bartchy

Edited by

David Lertis Matson

and

K. C. Richardson

☙PICKWICK *Publications* • Eugene, Oregon

ONE IN CHRIST

Essays on Early Christianity and "All that Jazz," in Honor of S. Scott Bartchy

Copyright © 2014 Wipf and Stock Publishers. All rights reserved. Except for brief quotations in critical publications or reviews, no part of this book may be reproduced in any manner without prior written permission from the publisher. Write: Permissions. Wipf and Stock Publishers, 199 W. 8th Ave., Suite 3, Eugene, OR 97401.

Cascade Books
An Imprint of Wipf and Stock Publishers
199 W. 8th Ave., Suite 3
Eugene, OR 97401

www.wipfandstock.com

ISBN 13: 978-1-62564-174-8

Cataloguing-in-Publication Data

One in Christ : essays on early Christianity and "all that jazz," in honor of S. Scott Bartchy / edited by David Lertis Matson and K. C. Richardson.

xx + 288 p. ; 23 cm. Includes bibliographical references.

ISBN 13: 978-1-62564-174-8

1. Bartchy, S. Scott. 2. Bartchy, S. Scott—Bibliography. 3. Bible. Galatians—Criticism, interpretation, etc. 4. Paul, the Apostle, Saint. I. Matson, David Lertis. II. Richardson, K. C.

BS2655.J4 O55 2014

Manufactured in the U.S.A.   12/10/2014

Contents

Sort of Like Jazz: A Tribute to S. Scott Bartchy | vii
Publications of S. Scott Bartchy | xi
Contributors | xv
Abbreviations | xviii

Part 1 "There Is No Longer..."

1 Galatians 3:28 beyond Status and Role: Living Anti-Structurally within Structure / *A. Sue Russell* | 1

2 Hierarchisierung und Relativierung multipler Identitäten in Galater 3:28 / *Wolfgang Stegemann* | 20

Part 2 "Jew or Greek..."

3 Social-Scientific Comments on "Neither Judean nor Greek" (Gal 3:28) / *Dennis C. Duling* | 35

4 Should Ἰουδαῖος Be Translated "Judean"? The Challenge of 1 Thessalonians 2:14 / *David Lertis Matson* | 69

5 "For our Lord was pursued by the Jews...": The (Ab)Use of the Motif of "Jewish" Violence against Jesus on a Greek Amulet (P. Heid. 1101) / *Joseph Emanuel Sanzo* | 86

6 "One in Christ": The View from Torah and Shoah / *Zev Garber* | 99

Part 3 "Slave or Free..."

7   To Serve as Slave: Footwashing as Paradigmatic Status Reversal / *Mark A. Matson* | 113

8   Trouble in the Hood: A Multidimensional Contextualization of Romans 13:1–7 / *Rick F. Talbott* | 132

9   1 Corinthians 7:17–24: Considering Stoic Argumentation and the Ἀδιάφορα of Slavery and Freedom / *Rollin A. Ramsaran* | 150

10 "Do Not Exploit a Brother or Sister": Slavery and Sexual Ethics in 1 Thessalonians 4:1–8 / *K. C. Richardson* | 165

11 Galatians 3:28 and the African Story / *J. Ayodeji Adewuya* | 184

12 Preaching Δοῦλος: Hard Saying or Stumbling Block? / *Bruce E. Shields* | 199

Part 4 "Male and Female"

13 Constructing Euodia and Syntyche: Philippians 4:2–3 and the Informed Imagination / *Robert F. Hull Jr.* | 209

14 Galatians 3:28: An Aspect of Eschatological Asceticism in Paul / *Robert James Mason* | 222

15 Fresh Screwtape Revelations: How to Bash Gays with the Bible / *John H. Elliott* | 240

Part 5 "You Are One in Christ Jesus"

16 A House or a Tower? Honor, Precedence, and the Contrasting Visions of 1 Peter and *The Shepherd of Hermas* / *Drake Levasheff* | 260

17 Sibling Rivalries: On the Reception of *1 Clement* in Corinth / *Cavan W. Concannon* | 273

Sort of Like Jazz
A Tribute to S. Scott Bartchy

"Pay to all what is due them," the apostle Paul once wrote to the Roman house churches, including "honor to whom honor is due" (Rom 13:7, NRSV). How appropriate that this volume pay honor to a man and scholar who has spent much of his life talking about honor, but certainly differently from the way the ancient Romans would have talked about it! As a worshiper of the community-forming God of Israel revealed in Jesus the Messiah, S. Scott Bartchy does not need to compete for the honor of this *Festschrift*, nor would he seek it. He would simply say that there is plenty of honor to go around from a God of endless supply.

This *Festschrift* comes on the occasion of our honoree's retirement from the University of California at Los Angeles after 34 years of teaching. Some of the contributors to this volume are former doctoral students, some are colleagues, but all are friends who have been impacted by the life, teaching, and scholarship of Scott Bartchy. Each of these essays represents a small but heartfelt effort to "give honor to whom honor is due." Scott Bartchy is worthy of such honor.

Some scholars excel in the art of teaching, others excel in research and writing. Very few excel in both. Our honoree is in that rare category of teacher-scholar whose influence has been deeply felt both in the classroom and in the wider academy. Scott was born and raised in Canton, Ohio, where his interest in religion was first awakened by his father, a famous tenor in the area, who sang for various Christian congregations and Jewish synagogues in the city. Scott was baptized (1952) and later ordained into the Christian ministry (1958) at the historic First Christian Church of Canton, a church associated with the wider Stone-Campbell fellowship, also known as the Restoration Movement.

Following his graduation with honors from Milligan College (Tennessee) where he double-majored in Religion and Social Science, Scott attended Harvard Divinity School, earning a Master of Theological Knowledge (Master of Divinity equivalent) in 1963. Later that year he began work on his Ph.D. at Harvard University, majoring in Christian Origins, New Testament Studies, and Early Christian History, along with a minor in the History of Religion. During his time at Harvard, Scott had the opportunity to study with several luminaries in the fields of biblical studies and ancient history, most notably Amos Wilder, Krister Stendahl, Helmut Koester, and Glen Bowersock. A 1963 seminar in the sociology of religion conducted by Talcott Parsons and Robert Bellah forever changed his perspective on the relationship among religion, culture, and society and awakened an interest in the social history of the early Christians that would inform his scholarship and teaching for the rest of his career.

Scott's dissertation, *Mallon Chresai*, was published by the Society of Biblical Literature in 1973 and quickly established Scott as the foremost authority on Greco-Roman slavery in early Christianity. Scott's expertise in this field led to invitations to contribute definitive articles on slavery to all of the major reference works published in the decades which followed. Along with his work on slavery, Scott's scholarship has dealt with related aspects of early Christian social relations, including the role of women within the early Christian movement, the early Christian critique of traditional views of male honor, and table fellowship within the Jesus community.

Following an appointment as Professor of Biblical Hermeneutics at Emmanuel School of Religion from 1974–1977 and as *Gastprofessor* in New Testament Studies at the University of Tübingen from 1977–1979, Scott became the Resident New Testament Scholar for the newly established Westwood Christian Foundation. In this position, Scott began a long and fruitful relationship with UCLA where he would earn the Distinguished Lecturer Award from the UCLA Department of History in 1987 and the university-wide Distinguished Lecturer Award the following year. Through his popular courses on the early Christians, his work as the co-founder and director for the Center for the Study of Religion at UCLA, and his tireless effort as adviser to numerous undergraduate and doctoral students, Scott helped establish the academic study of religion at UCLA and has left a lasting legacy with the university and beyond. Upon his retirement from UCLA in 2013, Scott was honored by his appointment as Professor Emeritus of the History of Religion. Throughout his academic career, Scott has also regularly lectured to both popular and church audiences, impacting important public discourse on religion.

Scott is married to Nancy L. Breuer with whom he lives in the "earthship," a state-of-the-art environmentally friendly home in the hills northwest of Los Angeles. Scott has a daughter, Beth, and a son, Christopher, with his first wife, Diane Walker. Scott is also an accomplished jazz pianist, performing regularly with the Scott Bartchy Quartet. The pencil-sketch that graces the cover of this *Festschrift* in fact features Scott playing with his quartet at a concert at the Westwood Hills Christian Church in Westwood, California.

The editors decided upon Gal 3:28 as an overall theme for this collection of essays for two primary reasons. First, Scott has always been a strong voice for non-hierarchical, egalitarian relationships within the body of Christ. In an early (and influential) essay affirming the giftedness of women for ministry in his own religious tradition, Scott could appeal to Gal 3:28 as one of the "normative" texts of the New Testament: "This programmatic statement is clearly normative in what it implicitly *rejects*: pride in maleness, in racial background, and in social-legal status. It is also clearly normative in what it explicitly *affirms*: neither sexual, ethnic, nor social-legal distinctions are valid for determining the status or true identity of anyone within the 'in Christ' community."[1]

Second, the three sets of binary relationships in Gal 3:28 provide the broad conceptual categories for arranging the diverse contents of this volume. Whereas many *Festschriften* often lack a coherent organizing principle, this volume has sought to provide some degree of structural unity while allowing each author to contribute from his or her own scholarly interest to the overall piece. As a jazz aficionado, Scott would appreciate this unity-in-diversity in the context of honoring his life's work. We cannot think of a more apt description of our honoree than the breath-taking eschatological vision of Gal 3:28.

The editors have allowed as much freedom as possible to the respective contributors of this volume, both in substance and style. We take no responsibility for the content of any essay except our own. As the reader will no doubt discern, a rich variety of styles, approaches, and perspectives exist in this volume, and a few essays go beyond the confines of first-century Christianity, Scott's area of expertise. Each author has been allowed to "improvise" in varying degrees, yet each contributing to the whole—sort of like jazz.

—The Editors

1. Bartchy, "Power, Submission, and Sexual Identity," in *Essays on New Testament Christianity: A Festschrift in Honor of Dean E. Walker*, edited by C. Robert Wetzel (Cincinnati, OH: Standard, 1978), 58–59 [50–80].

S. Scott Bartchy

Publications of S. Scott Bartchy

Gender Formation and Sex Roles

"Power, Submission, and Sexual Identity among the Early Christians." In *Essays on New Testament Christianity in Honor of Dean E. Walker*, edited by C. Robert Wetzel, 50–80. Cincinnati: Standard, 1978.
>   **Revised and translated into German**: "Machtverhältnisse, Unterordnung und sexuelles Selbstverständnis im Urchristentum." In *Die Bibel als politisches Buch: Beiträge zu einer befreienden Christologie*, edited by Dietrich Schirmer, 109–46. Urban-Taschenbücher 655. Stuttgart: Kohlhammer, 1982.
>   **Translated into Spanish**: *El Poder, La Sumission y La Identidad Sexual entre Los Christianos Primitivos*. Monterrey, Mexico: Comañerismo Estudiantil, 1989.

"Jesus, Power, and Gender Roles." *Theological Students Fellowship Bulletin* 7.3 (1984) 2–4.

"'Issues of Power and a Theology of the Family': Exegesis of Ephesians 5:18–31 and Analysis of Contemporary Culture." *Mission Journal* 21 (1987) no. 1:3–15; no. 2:3–11; no. 3:8–12.

"The Lasting Contributions of Greece and Rome to Our Thinking about Families." In *The Family Handbook*, edited by Herbert Anderson et al., 282–86. Family, Religion and Culture. Louisville: Westminster John Knox, 1998.

"Who Should Be Called 'Father'? Paul of Tarsus between the Jesus Tradition and *Patria Potestas*." In *The Social World of the New Testaments: Insights and Models*, edited by Jerome H. Neyrey and Eric C. Stewart, 165–80. Peabody, MA: Hendrickson Publishers, 2008. Reprint from *Biblical Theology Bulletin* 33 (2003) 135–47.

"Jesus, the Pharisees, and Mediterranean Manliness." In *Teaching the Historical Jesus: Issues and Exegesis*, edited by Zev Garber. New York: Routledge, forthcoming.

Historical Jesus

"Table Fellowship." In *Dictionary of Jesus and the Gospels*, edited by Joel B. Green and Scot McKnight, 796–800. Downers Grove, IL: InterVarsity Press, 1992.

"The Historical Jesus and Honor Reversal at the Table." In *The Social Setting of Jesus and the Gospels*, edited by Wolfgang Stegemann, Bruce J. Malina, and Gerd Theissen, 175–83. Minneapolis: Fortress, 2002.

German translation: "Der historische Jesus und die Umkehr der Ehre am Tisch." In *Jesus in neuen Kontexten: Sozialwissenschaftliche Perspektiven der Jesusforschung*, edited by Wolfgang Stegemann, Bruce Malina, and Gerd Theissen, 224–29. Stuttgart: Kohlhammer, 2002.

"Table Fellowship, Gospels." In the *Dictionary of the New Testament: A One-Volume Compendium of Contemporary Biblical Scholarship*, edited by Daniel G. Reid, 1063–67. Downers Grove, IL: InterVarsity Press, 2005. Repr. from *Dictionary of Jesus and the Gospels* (1992).

"Where Is the History in Mel Gibson's *The Passion of the Christ?*" *Pastoral Psychology* 53 (2005) 313–28.

Revision of "Where Is the History in Mel Gibson's *The Passion of the Christ?*" In *Mel Gibson's Passion: The Film, the Controversy, and Its Implications*, edited by Zev Garber, 76–92. Shofar Supplements 23. West Lafayette, IN: Purdue University Press, 2005.

"Jesus, the Pharisees, and Mediterranean Manliness." In *Teaching the Historical Jesus: Issues and Exegesis*, edited by Zev Garber. New York: Routledge, forthcoming.

Paul of Tarsus

"Undermining Ancient Patriarchy: The Apostle Paul's Vision of a Society of Siblings." *Biblical Theology Bulletin* 29 (1999) 68–78.

"Who Should Be Called 'Father'? Paul of Tarsus between the Jesus Tradition and *Patria Potestas*." *Biblical Theology Bulletin* 33 (2003) 135–47.

"'When I'm Weak, I'm Strong': A Pauline Paradox in Cultural Context." In *Kontexte der Schrift Band II: Kultur, Politik, Religion, Sprache, Text. Wolfgang Stegemann zum 60. Geburtstag*, edited by Christian Strecker, 49–60. Stuttgart: Kohlhammer, 2005.

"The Domestication of a Radical Jew: Paul of Tarsus." In *Maven in Blue Jeans: A Festschrift in Honor of Zev Garber*, edited by Steven L. Jacobs, 7–16. West Lafayette, IN: Purdue University Press, 2009.

"Foreword" to Rick F. Talbott, *Jesus, Paul, and Power: Rhetoric, Ritual and Metaphor in Ancient Mediterranean Christianity*, ix–xiv. Eugene, OR: Cascade Books, 2010.

"'Stickless' in Corinth: How Paul Sought to Recover His Authority." In *To Set at Liberty: Essays on Christianity and Its Social World in Honor of John H. Elliott*, edited by Stephen K. Black, 27–44. The Social World of Biblical Antiquity, 2/6. Sheffield: Sheffield Phoenix, 2014.

"Paulus hat nicht gelehrt: 'Jeder soll in seinem Stand bleiben': Luthers Fehlübersetzung von κλῆσις in 1 Korinther 7." In *Alte Texte in neuen Kontexte: Wo steht die sozialwis-senschaftlich Bibelexegese?*, edited by Wolfgang Stegemann and Richard DeMaris, 222–41. Stuttgart: Kohlhammer, 2014.

Luke-Acts

"Community of Goods in Acts: Idealization or Social Reality?" In *The Future of Early Christianity: Essays in Honor of Helmut Koester*, edited by Birger A. Pearson, 309–18. Minneapolis: Fortress, 1991.

"The Credibility Factor: How Chrsitain Practice Affected the Persuasiveness of Early Christian Preaching." In *Faith and Practice: Studies in the Book of Acts*, edited by David A. Fiensy and William D. Howden, 151–81. Atlanta: College Press, 1995.

"*Agnostos Theos*: Luke's Message to the 'Nations' about Israel's God." In *Society of Biblical Literature 1995 Seminar Papers*, edited by Eugene J. Lovering Jr., 304–20. Atlanta: Scholars, 1995.

"Narrative Criticism." In *Dictionary of the Later New Testament and Its Developments*, edited by Ralph P. Martin and Peter H. Davids, 787a–92a. Downers Grove, IL: InterVarsity, 1997.

"Divine Power, Community Formation, and Leadership in the Acts of the Apostles." In *Community Formation in the Early Church and in the Church Today*, edited by Richard N. Longenecker, 89–104. Peabody, MA: Hendrickson, 2002.

Greco-Roman Slavery

ΜΑΛΛΟΝ ΧΡΗΣΑΙ: First-Century Slavery and the Interpretation of 1 Corinthians 7:21. Society of Biblical Literature Dissertation Series 11. Missoula, MT: Scholars, 1973. Reprinted, Eugene, OR: Wipf & Stock, 2003.

"Slavery in the New Testament." In the *International Standard Bible Encyclopedia*, edited by Geoffrey W. Bromily, 4:543a–546b. 4 vols. Grand Rapids: Eerdmans, 1988.

"Servant/Slave in the New Testament." In the *International Standard Bible Encyclopedia*, edited by Geoffrey W. Bromiley, 4:420a–421b. 4 vols. Grand Rapids: Eerdmans, 1988.

"Slavery in the New Testament." In the *Mercer Dictionary of the Bible*, edited by Watson Mills, 831. Macon, GA: Mercer University Press, 1990.

Review of Dale B. Martin, *Slavery as Salvation: the Metaphor of Slavery in Pauline Christianity*. *Journal of Biblical Literature* 111 (1992) 345–47.

"Slavery (Greco-Roman and New Testament)." In the *Anchor Bible Dictionary*, edited by David Noel Freedman, 6:65–73. 6 vols. New York: Doubleday, 1992.

"Philemon, Epistle to." In the *Anchor Bible Dictionary*, edited by David Noel Freedman, 5:305–310. 6 vols. New York: Doubleday, 1992.

"Slavery in the New Testament." In the *HarperCollins Bible Dictionary*. Rev. ed. Edited by Paul J. Achtemeier, 1030–31. New York: Harper & Row, 1996.

"Slave, Slavery." In the *Dictionary of the Later New Testament and Its Developments*, edited by Ralph P. Martin and Peter H. Davids, 1098–102. Downers Grove, IL: InterVarsity Press, 1997.

"Response to Keith Bradley's Scholarship on Slavery." *Biblical Interpretation* 21 (2013) 524–32.

"Slaves and Slavery in the Roman World." In *The World of the New Testament: Cultural, Social, and Historical Contexts*, edited by Joel B. Green and Lee Martin McDonald, 169–78. Grand Rapids: Baker Academic, 2013.

"Paulus hat nicht gelehrt: 'Jeder soll in seinem Stand bleiben': Luthers Fehlübersetzung von κλῆσις in 1 Korinther 7." In *Alte Texte in neuen Kontexte: Wo steht die sozialwissenschaftlich Bibelexegese?*, edited by Wolfgang Stegemann and Richard DeMaris, 222–41. Stuttgart: Kohlhammer, 2014.

Table Fellowship

"Table Fellowship with Jesus and the 'Lord's Meal' at Corinth." In *Increase in Learning: Essays in Honor of James G. Van Buren*, edited by Robert J. Owens and Barbara E. Hamm, 45–61. Manhattan, KS: Manhattan Christian College, 1979.

"Table Fellowship." In the *Dictionary of Jesus and the Gospels*, edited by Joel B. Green and Scot McKnight, 796–800. Downers Grove, IL: InterVarsity Press, 1992.

"Table Fellowship, Gospels." In the *IVP Dictionary of the New Testament: A One Volume Compendium of Contemporary Biblical Scholarship*, edited by Daniel G. Reid, 1063–67. Reprint from *Dictionary of Jesus and the Gospels* (1992).

"The Historical Jesus and Honor Reversal at the Table." In *The Social Setting of Jesus and the Gospels*, edited by Wolfgang Stegemann, Bruce J. Malina, and Gerd Theissen, 175–83. Minneapolis: Fortress, 2002.

German translation: "Der historische Jesus und die Umkehr der Ehre am Tisch." In *Jesus in neuen Kontexten: Sozialwissenschaftliche Perspektiven der Jesusforschung*, edited by Wolfgang Stegemann, Bruce Malina, and Gerd Theissen, 224–29. Stuttgart: Kohlhammer, 2002.

"Personalized Eating and Community in Christ." *Leaven: A Journal of Christian Ministry* 20 (2012) 12–13.

Popular Publications

"The Second Generation of Christianity." In *These Were God's People: A Bible History*, edited by William C. Martin, 483–500. Nashville: Southwestern, 1966.

"Parental Equivocation and Student Moral Standards." In *Youth in Crisis*, edited by Peter C. Moore, 83–90. New York: Seabury, 1966.

"How Much Freedom Can you Stand? Identity Crisis and 'Life in the Spirit' in the First Century A.D." *Radix* 9 (1977) 21–22.

"Jesus, Power, and Gender Roles." *Theological Students Fellowship Bulletin* 7.3 (1984) 2–4.

"Can You Imagine Paul Telling Priscilla Not to Teach?" *Leaven: A Journal of Christian Ministry* 4.2 (1996) 19–23.

"The Sibling Secret (Revealed)." *Leaven: A Journal of Christian Ministry* 9.1 (2001) 18–22.

"Secret Siblings." *Sojourners* 33.11 (2004) 32–36.

"It's the Verb, Not the Noun!" (co-author with Nancy L. Breuer). *Voices Newsletter* no. 6 (2005) 1–3.

"Personalized Eating and Community in Christ." *Leaven: A Journal of Christian Ministry* 20.1 (2012) 12–13.

Book Reviews

Review of Rudolf Schnackenburg, *The Moral Teaching of the New Testament*. *Mission Journal* 1 (1968) 295–96, 345–47.

Review (co-author Frederick W. Norris) of G. C. Berkouwer, *Holy Scripture: Studies in Dogmatics*. *The Journal of Religion* 57 (1977) 96–98.

Review of Dale B. Martin, *Slavery as Salvation: the Metaphor of Slavery in Pauline Christianity*. *Journal of Biblical Literature* 111 (1992) 345–47.

Review of Laura Salah Nasrallah, *"An Ecstasy of Folly": Prophecy and Authority in Early Christianity*. *Bulletin of the Royal Institute for Inter-Faith Studies* 7.2 (2005) 255–58.

Contributors

J. Ayodeji Adewuya
Ph.D., University of Manchester
Professor of New Testament
Pentecostal Theological Seminary

Cavan W. Concannon
Ph.D., Harvard University
Assistant Professor of Religion
University of Southern California

Dennis C. Duling
Ph.D., University of Chicago
Professor Emeritus, Religious Studies and Theology
Canisius College

Rev. Dr. John H. Elliott
Dr. Theol., Westfälische Wilhelms-Universität, Münster, Germany
Professor Emeritus, Theology and Religious Studies
University of San Francisco

Zev Garber
Ph.D., University of Southern California
Emeritus Professor of Jewish Studies and Philosophy
Los Angeles Valley College

Robert F. Hull Jr.
Ph.D., Princeton Theological Seminary
Professor of New Testament, Emeritus
Emmanuel Christian Seminary

Drake Levasheff
Ph.D., University of California, Los Angeles
Director, Orange County Regional Center
Azusa Pacific University

Robert James Mason
Ph.D., Candidate, Claremont Graduate University
Adjunct Professor of Religious Studies
California State University, Northridge

David Lertis Matson
Ph.D., Baylor University
Professor of Biblical Studies
Hope International University

Mark A. Matson
Ph.D., Duke University
Associate Professor of Bible
Milligan College

Rollin A. Ramsaran
Ph.D., Boston University
Academic Dean and Professor of New Testament and Christian Origins
Emmanuel Christian Seminary

K. C. Richardson
Ph.D., University of California, Los Angeles
Associate Professor of Biblical Studies
Hope International University

A. Sue Russell
Ph.D., University of California, Los Angeles
Associate Professor of Missions and Contextual Studies
Asbury Theological Seminary

Joseph Emanuel Sanzo
Ph.D., University of California, Los Angeles
Postdoctoral Research Fellow
The Hebrew University of Jerusalem

Bruce E. Shields
Dr. Theol., Eberhard-Karls Universität, Tübingen, Germany
Russell and Marian Blowers Professor of Christian Ministries, Emeritus
Emmanuel Christian Seminary

Dr. Wolfgang Stegemann
Dr. Theol. habil. University of Heidelberg
Professor of New Testament Studies
Augustana Hochschule Neuendettelsau, Germany

Rick F. Talbott
Ph.D., University of California, Los Angeles
Professor of Religious Studies and Department Chair
California State University, Northridge

Abbreviations

AB	Anchor Bible
ABD	*The Anchor Bible Dictionary*. 6 vols. Edited by David Noel Freedman. Garden City, NY: Doubleday, 1992
BibIntSer	Biblical Interpretation Series
BTB	*Biblical Theology Bulletin*
BZNW	Beihefte zur Zeitschrift für die neutestamentliche Wissenschaft
ERS	*Ethnic and Racial Studies*
ESV	English Standard Version
HTR	*Harvard Theological Review*
JBL	*Journal of Biblical Literature*
JECS	*Journal for Early Christian Studies*
JSHJ	*Journal for the Study of the Historical Jesus*
JSNT	*Journal for the Study of the New Testament*
JSNTSup	Journal for the Study of the New Testament Supplement Series
LCL	Loeb Classical Library
LNTS	Library of New Testament Studies
NovT	*Novum Testamentum*
NovTSup	Novum Testamentum Supplements
NTS	*New Testament Studies*
PCritCon	Paul in Critical Contexts
SBL	Society of Biblical Literature

SBLDS	Society of Biblical Literature Dissertation Series
TDNT	*Theological Dictionary of the New Testament*. Edited by Gerhard Kittel and Gerhard Friedrich. Translated by Geoffrey W. Bromiley. Grand Rapids: Eerdmans, 1966–
TSAJ	Texts and Studies in Ancient Judaism
WBC	Word Biblical Commentary
WUNT	Wissenschaftliche Untersuchungen zum Neuen Testament
ZNW	*Zeitschrift für die neutestamentliche Wissenschaft*
ZPE	*Zeitschrift für Papyrologie und Epigraphik*

1

Galatians 3:28 beyond Status and Role
Living Anti-Structurally within Structure

A. Sue Russell

Introduction

One of S. Scott Bartchy's many important contributions to the study of early Christianity is his emphasis on the social aspect of being a follower of Christ, in his words, the radical way in which followers of Christ were to treat one another. In his classes and writing he emphasizes the contrast between first-century values for social interaction and the values in the Jesus and Paul tradition.[1] However, within the Pauline corpus there appears to be a contradiction between writings that promote and affirm equality of persons within Pauline communities and those that seem to reinforce societal expectations of role relationships, particularly ones reinforcing traditional hierarchical structures of Greco-Roman society. While the majority of writings affirm equality and mutuality in Christ, some writings in the Pauline corpus seem to condone the institution of slavery and reinforce traditional hierarchical

---

1. Bartchy, *Call No Man Father*. In one of his seminars in which he presented a comparison of first-century values for social interaction and the values in the Jesus and Paul tradition, I realized I had seen a similar chart in Victor Turner's discussion of liminality. When I presented this idea in a class, we both realized that these concepts provided a framework for the contrasts that he emphasized. He enthusiastically encouraged me to continue to explore this idea. This idea germinated to become my dissertation from which this paper is written. Bartchy's thought is reflected throughout this paper and I am grateful for his contribution to my scholarly development.

roles of husband and wife. However, this contradiction is resolved by understanding the social dimension of Paul's inaugurated eschatology.

Pauline theology is marked by a distinct understanding that the cross marks a change in the eons—the new has dawned in the present age. There are three parallel yet distinct aspects to this inaugurated eschatology in Pauline theology. First are the temporal aspects. In Pauline theology, the cross brought an "already/not yet" experience for the early Christian communities—one of living in a new age while still participating in the old. The second is the individual aspect. In Pauline writings, the individual is a new creation indwelt with the Spirit but still living within the old body. The third parallel is the social aspect. Early Christian communities were to live "in-Christ" relationships within the structures of the society. The contradictions between the equality expressed in Gal 3:28, "There is neither Jew nor Gentile, there is neither slave nor free, there is no male and female,"[2] and the writings that reinforce hierarchical structures reflect the social dimension of Pauline inaugurated eschatology.[3]

In order to demonstrate the social parallel of inaugurated eschatology, Victor Turner's concepts of liminality, structure, and anti-structure are used as a consistent hermeneutical framework for all three aspects of inaugurated eschatology: temporal, individual, and social. This framework reconciles the conflict between Gal 3:28 and those passages that seem to reinforce social structure within the Pauline corpus.

Understanding the Framework-Defining Structure and Anti-Structure

Three aspects of Victor Turner's work are important in creating a consistent hermeneutical framework for Pauline inaugurated eschatological, particularly for the social dimension. The first is concepts related to social structure. The second is the characteristics of liminality and people in liminality. And the third is the quality of relationships found in the liminality.

---

2. Unless otherwise noted, all New Testament quotes are from English Standard Version, 2001.

3. This paper is revised from my recent dissertation, "In the World But Not of the World."

Structure

Structure, according to Turner, is the working arrangements of society and the process of ordering of actors and relations in reference to given social ends.[4] Structures are the more stable aspects of actor-to-actor relationship based on the perception of the rules and meanings of the social roles.[5] Structural ties are those organized by social bonds of caste, class, rank or positions which creates a hierarchical system in which there is political-legal and economic separation between people in terms of more and less.[6] In structure people behave in ways clearly defined by norms and standards based on position or status. There are usually corporate rights based on membership, status, and role which define a person's access to resources and people from whom resources can be obtained. The social body influences, defines, and constrains the actions of individuals. As social beings, people cannot live outside of the social body, except as hermits.

Liminality and Anti-structure

In contrast to structure, anti-structure was originally used to describe the social relationships within the liminal phase of rites of passage. The concept of liminality was first articulated in Arnold Van Gennep's study of rites of passage which were ceremonies when people were making a transition from one status to another, such as child to adult, single to married, living to dead. He noted that many cultures had ceremonies that marked these transitions. They varied in detail but these rites of passages had three stages: separation, liminality, and reincorporation.[7] For instance, in many initiation rites, children are separated from their parents and are secluded in a special place for a period of time with other children of the same age. During this liminal phase they are neither child nor adult but are taught how to live as an adult. The liminal period ends with a ceremony in which the person is reincorporated into society as an adult.

Turner expanded the study of the liminal phase of rites of passage. He noted that one of the distinctive features of liminality was that people no longer related to one another according to their structural statues and roles. The liminal phase is characterized by what Turner calls anti-structure.[8] In

---

4. Turner, *Dramas, Fields, and Metaphors*, 34.
5. Ibid.
6. Turner, *Ritual Process*, 96.
7. Van Gennep, *Rites of Passage*.
8. Turner, *Ritual Process*, 106.

contrast to structure, anti-structure is the absence of social statuses and roles. In liminality, people are between and betwixt the positions in the structural arrangements of society. The person in liminality is classified, yet not classified, and is often referred to as dead or at least not a part of a structural category.[9] Individuals within the liminal phase are ambiguous because they are outside the normal structural status and classifications.

Although people in liminality do not have structural status and roles, they are richly represented by symbols. They are often likened to being dead, being in the womb, being invisible, bisexual, or in a wilderness.[10] People in liminality are often defined by a special name and set of symbols, such as initiate, neophyte, or in other cases prophet, trickster, etc.[11] They are represented as having nothing that is of value in structure; they have no status, property, insignia, rank, or role in a kinship system. Since sex distinctions are an important component of structural states, they do not apply in the structureless realm of liminality. They often exhibit properties of homogeneity, equality, anonymity, and absence of property.[12] Turner also noted that these anti-structural characteristics of the liminal experience were not confined to rites of passage but could be found in other groups such as millenarian groups, pilgrims, and monastic movements.

The characteristics of structure and anti-structure are listed in Table 1.1. The anti-structural nature of liminality affects both the characteristics of the people within it and the relationships between them.

Table 1.1.

Turner's contrasts of characteristics of structure and anti-structure[13]

Structure	Anti-Structure
State	Transition
Partiality	Totality
Heterogeneity	Homogeneity
Structure	Communitas
Inequality	Equality

9. Ibid., 95.
10. Ibid.
11. Turner, *Forest of Symbols*, 96.
12. Turner, *Ritual Process*, 111.
13. Ibid., 106.

Structure	Anti-Structure
Systems of nomenclature	Anonymity
Property	Absence of property
Status	Absence of status
Distinctions of clothing	Nakedness/uniform clothing
Sexuality	Sexual continence
Maximization of sex distinctions	Minimization of sex distinctions
Distinctions of rank	Absences of rank
Just pride of possession	Humility
Care for personal appearance	Disregard for personal appearance
Distinctions of wealth	No distinctions of wealth
Selfishness	Unselfishness
Secularity	Sacredness
Technical instruction	Sacred instruction
Speech	Silence
Kinship rights and obligations	Suspension of kinship rights and obligations
Intermittent reference to mystical powers	Continuous reference to mystical powers
Sagacity	Foolishness
Complexity	Simplicity
Avoidance of Pain and suffering	Acceptance of pain a suffering
Degrees of autonomy	Heteronomy

Quality of Relationships in Liminality-Communitas

Another important aspect of liminality is the quality of relationships of people in the liminal phase. People in the liminal phase relate to each other as people without structural differentiation, not according to structured roles of the broader society. The formal social obligations of structure are exchanged for personal relationships.[14] They form what Turner has referred to as communitas. Communitas is a "mode of relationship" and involves "the whole person in relation to other whole human beings."[15] It is the instant mutuality when each person experiences the being of another without the structural social differentiations.[16] "Communitas is when individuals although differing in mental and physical endowment are nevertheless regarded as equal in terms of shared humanity."[17] It describes the intense comradeship and egalitarianism in liminality in which personal structural distinctions of rank and status disappear.[18] Communitas is often expressed by people referring to each other as siblings or comrades of one another. Those in communitas support each other through the suffering and pain that they endure in the liminal phase.[19] Communitas can cross ethnic boundaries as well as national and tribal divisions.

Although communitas was originally used to describe social relationships within rites of passage, it has been expanded to other social relationships of groups in liminality. Whereas many groups may experience communitas for a short period of time while separated from society, early Christian communities lived in liminality and experienced communitas within the structures of society. This is the social dimension of inaugurated eschatology. The concepts of liminality, structure and anti-structure provide a way of integrating all three dimensions of Paul's eschatological theology within a single interpretive framework.

Liminality and Pauline Communities

Pauline inaugurated eschatology has three dimensions: temporal, individual, and social. Each of these can be expressed in a framework of liminality. The first is a temporal liminality; early followers of Christ were living between the times. The second is the embodied liminality of individuals. And finally are the anti-structural social dimensions of the in-Christ community. Each of these contributes to understanding the character of early Christian communities and provides a consistent framework for interpreting Pauline writing on social relationships within these communities.

---

14. Ibid., 112.
15. Bowie, *Anthropology of Religion*, 170.
16. Turner, *Ritual Process*, 134.
17. Ibid., 177.
18. Ibid., 93.
19. Ibid., 112.

Temporal Liminality: The Change in the Eons

The first dimension of liminality in Paul's inaugurated eschatology is a temporal liminality which sets the eschatological framework for life within Pauline communities. In Pauline theology, the cross marked the change of the eons and formed the basis of living in Christ.[20] It marked the start of the new age in which God's rule had broken into the present age and the new creation had begun.[21] T. Ryan Jackson notes that, "In contrast to the eschatology of Jewish traditions which influenced him, Paul shifts the eschatological focus from the strictly future to a view which has incorporated the past so that the Christ event becomes God's decisive incursion into the world."[22]

For Paul, the cross marked a change in dominion—God's rule had now begun in the present age.[23] The follower of Christ had been delivered from his past and was living in a new age while still in the present age.[24] Although God's rule had broken into the present and the new age had begun, in Paul's understanding it was not completed until the *parousia*.[25] The new age overlapped the old.[26] The overlapping time in which the new age had been inaugurated into the present, and the new dominion which had begun but was not yet complete, created a temporal liminality. In Pauline theology, the cross brought about an already/not yet experience that produced a tension of living in the new age reality while still in the present age. This understanding of temporal liminality is found throughout the Pauline writings and was the motivation and reason for a new way of living.

Embodied Liminality: New Creations in Christ

Not only did the cross inaugurate the new age within the present age and in doing so transformed time, the new age was also marked by the Spirit,

---

20. Fee, *Paul, the Spirit, and the People of God*, 49–59; Jackson, *New Creation in Paul's Letters*, 91–113; Pate, *End of the Age*, 44; Sampley, *Walking between the Times*, 7–24; Witherington, *Jesus, Paul, and the End of the World*, 23–35.

21. Strecker, *Die liminale Theologie des Paulus*, 222; Sampley, *Walking between the Times*, 247; Fee, *Paul, the Spirit and the People of God*, 51; 1 Cor 5:17.

22. Jackson, *New Creation in Paul's Letters*, 99.

23. Strecker, *Die liminale Theologie des Paulus*, 234–5; see Rom 6:19–23.

24. Ladd, *Theology of the New Testament*, 597; Donfried, *Paul, Thessalonica, and Early Christianity*, 243; Pate, *End of the Age*, 45; Fee, *Paul, the Spirit and the People of God*, 49; see 2 Cor 2:16; Gal 6:8; Col 1:13; 1 Cor 15:50; Eph 2:5; Rom 6:41; 1 Thess 5:2; 2 Thess 2:2; 1 Cor 1:8; 2 Cor 1:14; Phil 1:6.

25. Donfried, *Paul, Thessalonica, and Early Christianity*, 234.

26. Lee, *Cosmic Drama of Salvation*, 30.

which indwelt those who were in Christ, thus transforming individuals. Individuals not only lived in liminal time, but they also embodied that liminality. For Paul, those who were in Christ embodied the eschaton, the end of the age, through the indwelling of the Spirit.[27] Paul used several images to capture the essence of the change that happened with the indwelling of the Spirit, including the Adam/Christ analogy, the extended image between old/new self, outer/inner self, and physical/spiritual person.[28]

Although the Spirit was embodied in Christ followers, Paul also understood that they embodied the Spirit within their physical bodies and literally became liminal people. They embodied this already/not yet in the transition between a fleshly body and a spiritual/immortal body. Just as in the temporal aspects of liminality in which the new age had broken into the present age, Paul understood that Christ followers were still bound to the world through their physical body.[29] They were still part of the untransformed world, and the body was still subject to the attacks of the old power.[30] Paul emphasized that followers of Christ could not be saved apart from their bodies. However, they were to use their bodies in accordance with their new life in Christ. They were not to live as if they were still under the dominion of sin and death.[31] Paul wanted his communities to understand that although they had bodies of flesh they had the capacity to live as children of God because of God's Spirit in them. Therefore as liminal people, they were not to do the deeds of the flesh but to do the deeds of the Spirit.[32] They were to actively present their bodies for acts of righteousness, thus reflecting their change of allegiance to God and the new domain in which they lived.[33]

The final part of the embodied liminality in Pauline writing was the reintegration to a new status "with Christ." Paul argued that the reintegration to this new status was at the death of the followers of Christ or at the return of Christ.[34] Paul used the hope of this reintegration to encourage followers of Christ to endure their "slight momentary affliction."[35] For Paul,

---

27. Pate, *End of the Age*, 153; Campbell, *Paul and Union with Christ*, 408.

28. Kreitzer, "Eschatology," 257; see Rom 5; 6:6; 7:22; 1 Cor 15; 2 Cor 2:14–16; 4:16; Eph 2:15; 3:15; 4:22–24; Col 3:9–10.

29. Tannehill, *Dying and Rising with Christ*, 79.

30. Gorman, *Cruciformity*, 56.

31. Russell, *Flesh/Spirit Conflict in Galatians*, 2.

32. Gal 5:15–16.

33. Ladd, *Theology of the New Testament*, 528.

34. 2 Cor 4:14.

35. 2 Cor 4:6.

present life was only temporary, a liminal phase prior to his true life in Christ. Paul wrote, "But our citizenship is in heaven and from it we await a Savior, the Lord Jesus Christ, who will transform our lowly bodies to be like his glorious body by the power that enables him even to subject all things to himself."[36] These three different stages: flesh, spirit/flesh, and spirit/new body are similar to the three states in an extended rite of passage in which those who are "in Christ" are in the liminal phase until their death or the *parousia* as seen below in Table 1.2.

Table 1.2
Rites of Passage and Dimensions of Inaugurated Eschatology

	Old State	Transition	Liminality	Transition	New State
Temporal	Old Age	Separation / Cross / Holy Spirit/Baptism	New Age in Old Age	Reintegration / Death or Parousia / Resurrection	New Age
Embodied	Flesh		Spirit in the Flesh		Spirit in a New Body
Social	Status (Structure)		In-Christ in Status (Anti-Structure in Structure)		In-Christ (Anti-Structure)

In-Christ Community: Liminal Social Body—Communitas

The third and parallel dimension of liminality in Pauline inaugurated eschatology is the liminal community of those in Christ (see Table 1.2). There was a distinct transformation of social relationships for those who were followers of Christ. Pauline theology not only describes the salvation of the individual but also outlines the new corporate community in which individuals became embedded when they became a follower of Jesus. In Paul's writing, the Spirit not only created liminal individuals but also created a new liminal community, the body of Christ. For Paul, the individual and community were vitally interconnected.[37] Volker Rabens states, "It is not difficult to demonstrate the centrality of relationships in the writings of Paul and the traditions on which he draws."[38] Paul's writing was permeated by

---

36. Phil 3:20–21.
37. Dunson, *Individual and Community*, 166.
38. Rabens, *Holy Spirit and Ethics*, 33.

the concepts related to the community of Christ followers.[39] It is this social dimension that is often missing in discussions of inaugurated eschatology. Turner's framework of liminality, structure, and anti-structure provides concepts to highlight the social aspects of inaugurated eschatology.

Paul uses "in Christ" to mark the identity of the individual as a member of the new community and also to articulate the expected actions of people within the new liminal community.[40] In Paul's teaching, people in the community were not differentiated by structural criteria, but all in the community had the same anti-structural status as being in Christ. Paul made it clear that structural characteristics did not qualify someone to become a part of the community of Christ followers. Someone became a member of the community through the anti-structural criteria of obedience to Jesus.[41] Paul wrote, "For I am not ashamed of the gospel for it is the power of God for salvation to everyone who believes, to the Jew first and also to the Greek."[42] People in Christ had the same identity that transcended ethnic, status, economic, and gender differences. This in-Christ identity not only marked membership in the community but also defined the way members of the community were to interact with one another.[43] Baptismal statements in the Pauline corpus were intended not only to reflect an ontological equality in Christ but also to make apparent the anti-structural identity of people in the community of Christ followers.[44] This new anti-structural identity did not erase the status differences of people in the community, but people within their structural status were to relate to each other according to the same overarching status of "in Christ." This is the overarching hermeneutical framework for interpreting Paul's teachings concerning interpersonal relationships within the community.

Rather than structural identity markers, the Spirit was the common identity marker of Christ followers in the Pauline communities. Paul wrote, "You, however, are not in the flesh but in the Spirit, if in fact the Spirit of God dwells in you. Anyone who does not have the Spirit of Christ does not belong to Him."[45] The Spirit was the common possession of all Christ followers and was the common identity marker for the new community in

---

39. Lohfink, *Jesus and Community*, 78.
40. Gorman, *Cruciformity*, 352.
41. Rom 4:13; 3:21–31; Gal 2:15–21.
42. Rom 1:15.
43. Hansen, *All of You Are One*, 6.
44. Gal 3:28; 1 Cor 12:13; Col 3:11.
45. Rom 8:9.

which social, gender, and ethnic barriers were eliminated.[46] According to Paul, people were "baptized by one Spirit into one body."[47] Gerhard Lohfink notes, "Only in the Spirit is it possible to dismantle national and social barriers, group interests, caste systems and domination of one sex over another . . . The people of God, the church as a Body of Christ, is a social reality."[48] Paul used several analogies based on their common anti-structural identity of being "in Christ" and being marked by the Holy Spirit to demonstrate the unity and solidarity that transcended but did not eliminate ethnic, social, economic, and gender differences, including body, sibling, and temple.[49]

Paul's use of these three images reflected the anti-structural character of the corporate community of Christ followers. Although they came from different backgrounds, they had the same common identity—in Christ indwelt by the Spirit. Like other communities in liminality, these images reflected the uniting together in one corporate community people of different ethnic, social, economic, and gender statuses with a common identity. Unlike other liminal communities which separate themselves from structure, or erase social distinctions, the in-Christ identity marked by the Spirit transcended but did not erase these social differentiations. Despite social differentiation, interpersonal relationships within the community were to be characterized by communitas, reflecting their transcendent anti-structural identity. However, these anti-structural relationships were to be lived in the structural statuses and roles, reflecting the social dimensions of inaugurated eschatology and living anti-structurally within structure.

Living Anti-Structurally within Structure

The anti-structural relationships in the in-Christ communities reflected the salient social identity of being "in Christ."[50] As described above, Paul used several metaphors—temple, family, and body—to strengthen and reinforce the value of unity in the diversity of the early Christian communities. Relationships of mutuality, siblinghood, humility, and love reinforced the equality of all being "in Christ." However, their in-Christ identity, their liminal identity, did not erase social distinctions, nor was the liminal identity just an ontological spiritual reality as some have suggested.[51] Paul's exhortations

46. Lohfink, *Jesus and Community*, 88.
47. 1 Cor 12:13.
48. Lohfink, *Jesus and Community*, 93.
49. Pate, *End of the Age*, 170; Fee, *God's Empowering Presence*, 874.
50. Tucker, *Remain in Your Calling*, 49.
51. Hogan, "No Longer Male and Female," 7.

make it clear that within the in-Christ community behavior and interpersonal interaction were to be characterized by communitas in which they related as persons not according to their social statuses and roles. However, these interactions were lived out in their statuses in a society in which hierarchy and power were the norm.[52] They had to live in family-like mutuality, unity, and love within their distinct structural statuses.[53] For instance, within the Corinthian community, Paul elaborated how he envisioned social distinctions of sexuality, gender, slave/free, Jew and Gentile ethnicity, dietary practices, and economic differences could be lived out in solidarity and mutuality within the in-Christ community.[54] Paul did not ignore these distinctions nor reject them. Instead, he provided guidelines for how they were to live out their in-Christ identity within these social distinctions.

However, some writings in the Pauline tradition seem to reinforce structural values, particularly in the case of the household code. Paul's vision of the in-Christ community in Gal 3:28, namely, "There is neither Jew nor Gentile, there is neither slave nor free, there is no male and female, for you all are one in Christ Jesus," is not just an ontological spiritual reality nor an attempt to define a utopian ideal. Rather, Gal 3:28 represented the anti-structural, in-Christ identity that was to be lived out within these structural statuses and, in doing so, transform followers. This dialectic of anti-structure within structure of inaugurated eschatology provides the interpretive framework for understanding the relationship between the mutuality in the community and the hierarchy within structural statuses of the society in which they are embedded. I address each of these structural categories in the order presented in Gal 3:28.

Neither Jew nor Gentile

In Pauline communities, people from different ethnic identities were incorporated "in Christ" and marked by the Spirit with a common identity. Bruce Hansen argues that becoming a part of the in-Christ community did not fundamentally change people's ethnic categories, but the in-Christ communities were free of cultural domination and exclusion.[55] In second temple Judaism and in Greco-Roman culture, ethnic differences were a part of the discourse of exclusion, hierarchy, and domination. Kathy Ehrensperger ob-

---

52. Tucker, *Remain in Your Calling*, 59.

53. Hansen, *All of You Are One*, 86; see 1 Corinthians 5–7; 8–10; 7:18–19; 7:21–23; 9:19; 11:17–34.

54. Ibid., 156.

55. Ibid., 84.

serves, "To be a member of a people other than Greeks or Romans, and to adhere to another culture and value system meant to be despised as uncivilized, barbaric, even born to be slaves."[56] To become a member of the dominant culture, people had to become Romanized or Hellenized and lose the distinction of their ethnolinguistic particularity. There was no equality for people of a different ethnic background. The hierarchy of peoples was absolutely clear in Greco-Roman culture, and it justified domination of others.[57]

Within Paul's writings, although Jews and Gentiles are one in Christ, they still retained their ethnolinguistic distinctions.[58] Paul did not ignore ethnic differences; however, people were to live as one within their ethnic particularity.[59] The mutuality and solidarity between people of different ethnicities in Christ challenged the hierarchical Greco-Roman world filled with the dominating and dominated. In both cases, the Jewish exclusion of Gentiles and the Roman domination of others, the common in-Christ identity challenged both exclusion and domination based on ethnolinguistic identity. Members of the early Christian communities did not have to change their ethnic identity or have a common ethnic identity, but they were to be united in their diversity. They were to express their anti-structural identity of "in Christ" within their ethnolinguistic particularity.

Neither Slave Nor Free

Just as Paul did not encourage Jews and Gentiles to change their ethnicity, neither did he encourage slaves to change their condition. However, what Paul advocated was the inclusion and equality of all statuses "in Christ," just as he did for economic status, marital status, and gender. Paul welcomed slaves into the community as equals within the body of Christ, and they shared in the common identity of "in Christ." According to Bartchy, Paul saw religious, social, or legal status as neither a hindrance nor an advantage with respect to living according to their calling.[60] God had not called them out of their previous statuses, but into Christ.[61] For Paul, the statuses of slave and free were meaningless for those "in Christ." Obedience to Christ's commands, in other words living anti-structural lives within the structures

---

56. Ehrensperger, *Paul and the Dynamics of Power*, 192.
57. Ibid.
58. Hansen, *All of You Are One*, 166.
59. Tucker, "Baths, Baptism, and Patronage," 177.
60. Bartchy, *ΜΑΛΛΟΝ ΧΡΗΣΑΙ*, 151.
61. Ibid.

of their society, was what mattered.⁶² However, this did not mean Paul was prohibiting them from changing their status.⁶³

Although Paul did not directly challenge the institutions of slavery, he did change the perception of the slave. Within the in-Christ community, the slave was no longer a thing but rather a person, a fellow brother or sister in Christ.⁶⁴ In his letter to Philemon, Paul acknowledged the institution of slavery and the right of Philemon to own Onesimus. Although Paul would have liked to have kept Onesimus with him, he left the decision to Philemon. He wrote, "but I preferred to do nothing without your consent . . ."⁶⁵ Although there was implicit acknowledgment of the slave/master relationship, Paul appealed more strongly to the new anti-structural relationship of mutual membership in the body of Christ. Paul wrote to Philemon that he returned Onesimus to him no longer a slave, but more than a slave, as a dear brother, a member of the in-Christ community.⁶⁶ Finally, Paul asked that Philemon welcome Onesimus as he would Paul himself, reflecting that in Christ there was no difference between free and slave.⁶⁷ What is interesting is that Paul did not demand that Philemon free Onesimus but rather encouraged him to treat Onesimus as he would any member in the body of Christ—even while Onesimus remained a slave. However, implied in Paul's letter is the desire that Onesimus would become socially what he was in Christ.⁶⁸

No Male and Female

The hermeneutical framework of the Pauline tradition of living anti-structurally "in Christ" while in structure applies to statements in Pauline tradition on gender roles, particularly in marriage.⁶⁹ These statements redefined how men and women, particularly husbands and wives, were to live as brothers and sisters within their culturally defined roles.⁷⁰ The in-Christ identity and mutual submissions relativized the hierarchical arrangement of statuses in marriage. Distinct passages about the relationships of husbands

---

62. 1 Cor 7:18.
63. Ibid.
64. Ehrensperger, *Paul and the Dynamics of Power*, 195.
65. Phlm 14a.
66. Phlm 16.
67. Hogan, *"No Longer Male and Female,"* 32; see Phlm 17.
68. Ibid.
69. An overview of the scholarly discussion can be found in Pierce, "Contemporary Evangelicals for Gender Equality," 58–78.
70. Hansen, *All of You Are One*, 135.

and wives illustrate their consistency with other Pauline instructions of living anti-structurally within structural status.

In 1 Corinthians 7, Paul wrote extensively about issues of marriage, sexuality, and divorce, addressing both men and women in a balanced way. There were three distinct aspects of marriage that Paul addressed. Within marital rights, the structural expectations of marriage were that women belonged to their husbands.[71] It was the structural role of a wife to fulfill her duty to her husband because her body did not belong to her but to her husband.[72] However, in the new community (the body of Christ) mutuality was expressed within these structural roles. Not only were wives to fulfill their duties to their husband, but husbands were mutually responsible for fulfilling their duties to their wives because their bodies belonged to their wives.[73] The mutual responsibilities—the "one another" of the in-Christ community—was demonstrated in marital relationships between husbands and wives.

The second way that Paul demonstrates this same kind of mutuality within marriage was in the marital responsibility and choice within mixed marriages—marriages in which one spouse was a follower of Christ and the other was not.[74] In these passages, Paul spoke about divorce, particularly about divorce and choices in mixed marriages. A wife who had an unbelieving husband was instructed not to divorce her husband. In the same way, men were not to force their wives to stay married or convert to Christianity. Once again, Paul expressed the mutuality of the in-Christ community by making the same demands on men as on women. Men were not to divorce their wives, and they were instructed to stay married to unbelievers should the unbelieving spouse desire it. Both men and women had the same obligation to their marital partners. This even-handed mutuality stood in contrast to what might have been expected from other writers living in the first century.[75]

Finally, Paul addressed marital choices and service to the Lord.[76] Both men and women were given the choice whether to marry or remain single in their service to Christ. As with ethnicity and slavery, they were to pursue living the cruciform life in the context of their present status.[77] Once

---

71. 1 Cor 7:1–7.

72. Hogan, "No Longer Male and Female," 38; Witherington, *Conflict and Community in Corinth*, 175.

73. Hogan, "No Longer Male and Female," 32; Paget, *As Christ Submits to the Church*, 69.

74. 1 Cor 7:8–16.

75. Ciampa and Rosner, *First Letter to the Corinthians*, 296.

76. 1 Cor 7:25–35.

77. Hansen, *All of You Are One*, 138.

again, in a society that gave only men the choice in regard to marriage or celibacy, in the in-Christ community there was no difference in choices given to men and women. Both were allowed to determine what was best for them in regard to marriage and service to Christ. As Gilbert Bilezikian notes, "This text indicates that the early church did not perpetuate in its life the functional differentiations between male and female that were prevalent in its ambient patriarchal society. Men and women were treated as equals in their service in the church."[78]

The final passage examined here is the description of a new way of living as husband and wife within the household code.[79] Some argue that in these passages the writer is reinforcing the hierarchy and domination of the *pater* (father) over the household.[80] However, this passage must be interpreted using the same hermeneutical framework of living anti-structurally (in Christ) within the structures of society. In this passage, the author addresses the mutual submission of those in Christ in three different role relationships within the social body: husband/wife, father/child, and master/slave. The structural obligations within the Greco-Roman society were for wives to submit to their husbands, children to obey their fathers, and slaves to obey their masters. However, the emphasis of the passage is how in-Christ members were to live anti-structural exemplary lives within that structure.

The writer made two fundamental changes to the expectations of the traditional household code for husbands and wives that reflect this emphasis. First, he provided a new motivation for societal expectations. Wives were not to submit to husbands because of societal expectations and obligations, but rather submission was based on mutual submission and respect of members in the in-Christ body.[81] For a wife who was a Christ follower, especially if married to someone who was not, this provided a way for her to please Christ within the structural obligations of her household. As a member of the in-Christ community, her conduct toward her husband, whether Christian or non-Christian, was to be Christ-like.

Second, the writer outlined reciprocal submission for a man in his structural role as husband. He does not deny that a hierarchy exists but instead reinforces the in-Christ community expectations that those in the

---

78. Bilezikian, *Beyond Sex Roles*, 134.

79. Eph 5:22—6:9.

80. O'Brien argues that Paul is reinforcing the natural order of subordination of wife, children, and slave. Some form of this argument is used by those who argue that Paul or the writer of Ephesians is reverting back to more conservative views of gender relationships within the household (*Ephesians*, 409–38). See also Hoehner, *Ephesians*, 720–84; Arnold, *Ephesians*, 363–410.

81. Keener, *Paul, Women, and Wives*, 185.

superordinate position were to serve and use their status for the benefit of others.[82] As a Christ follower, a man was to express those relationships not in power and authority but in love and service.[83] Mutual love and submission were actions expected of every in-Christ member, not just husbands and wives.[84] The actions of husbands and wives toward each other were to reflect the mutuality of members of the in-Christ community and in doing so relativized the hierarchical structural role relationships between husband and wife. The siblinghood of fellowship was thus embedded in the household structures and transformed them. Within the structural arrangements of the hierarchy, the relationship between husband and wife was to reflect the anti-structural characteristics of communitas. They were to live anti-structurally within structure.

Conclusion

Placing the social dimension of Pauline writings into Turner's framework of liminality, structure, and anti-structure provides a way of interpreting seemingly contradictory statements as a consistent social parallel to the other two dimensions of inaugurated eschatology: temporal and embodied. The hermeneutical framework of living anti-structurally within the structures of society allows a consistent interpretation of what Paul meant in Gal 3:28 and how it was lived out in Pauline communities. In the Pauline communities, followers of Christ did not ignore or renounce their statuses, rather they were to live and to relate to one another as if there were no status differences. People did not stop being women or men; it did not change their status as Jew or non-Jew, slave or free; nor did it disengage them from the hierarchical structures of the Greco-Roman society. However, it redefined how people were to relate to one another within those statuses. They were to relate to one another in love, humility, and mutuality rather than in power and hierarchy.

The uniqueness of the Pauline communities was not that its members were living in liminality. Many communities experience this phenomenon. The unique aspect of the liminality of the in-Christ communities was that it did not eliminate the structures of society, but it redefined how people were to relate to one another within those structures. Bartchy concludes, "The person who had been called was no longer defined as a Jew or Greek, as a male or female, as a slave or a freeman, but as a saint; this 'holiness of Christ'

82. Fee, "Hermeneutics and the Gender Debate," 364–81.
83. Ibid., 379.
84. Eph 5:21.

was not a status but a new way of existing in the world under the grace and the command of God."[85] Followers of Christ were to be in the world, but not of the world; they were to live anti-structural lives within structure.

Works Cited

Arnold, Clinton E. *Ephesians: Exegetical Commentary on the New Testament.* Grand Rapids: Zondervan, 2010.

Bartchy, S. Scott. *ΜΑΛΛΟΝ ΧΡΗΣΑΙ: First-Century Slavery and 1 Corinthians 7:21.* SBLDS 11. Missoula, MT: Society of Biblical Literature, 1973. Reprinted, Eugene, OR: Wipf & Stock, 2003.

———. *Call No Man Father.* Grand Rapids: Baker Academic, forthcoming.

Bilezikian, Gilbert G. *Beyond Sex Roles.* Grand Rapids: Baker, 2006.

Bowie, Fiona. *The Anthropology of Religion.* Oxford: Blackwell, 2000.

Burke, Trevor J. *Family Matters: A Socio-Historical Study of Kinship Metaphors in 1 Thessalonians.* JSNTSup 247. London: T. & T. Clark, 2003.

Campbell, Constantine R. *Paul and Union with Christ.* Grand Rapids: Zondervan, 2012.

Ciampa, Roy E., and Brian S. Rosner. *The First Letter to the Corinthians.* Grand Rapids: Eerdmans, 2010.

Donfried, Karl Paul. *Paul, Thessalonica, and Early Christianity.* Grand Rapids: Eerdmans, 2002.

Dunson, Ben C. *Individual and Community in Paul's Letter to the Romans.* WUNT 2/332. Tübingen: Mohr/Siebeck, 2012.

Ehrensperger, Kathy. *Paul and the Dynamics of Power: Communication and Interaction in the Early Christ-Movement.* LNTS 325. New York: T. & T. Clark, 2007.

Fee, Gordon D. *God's Empowering Presence: The Holy Spirit in the Letters of Paul.* Peabody, MA: Hendrickson, 1994.

———. "Hermeneutics and the Gender Debate." In *Discovering Biblical Equality*, edited by Ronald W. Pierce and Rebecca Merrill Groothuis, 364–81. Downers Grove, IL: IVP Academic, 2005.

———. *Paul, the Spirit, and the People of God.* Peabody, MA: Hendrickson, 1996.

Gorman, Michael J. *Cruciformity: Paul's Narrative Spirituality of the Cross.* Grand Rapids: Eerdmans, 2001.

Hansen, Bruce. *All of You Are One: The Social Vision of Galatians 3:28, 1 Corinthians 12.13 and Colossians 3.11.* LNTS 409. New York: T. & T. Clark, 2010.

Hoehner, Harold W. *Ephesians: An Exegetical Commentary.* Grand Rapids: Baker Academic, 2002.

Hogan, Pauline Nigh. *"No Longer Male and Female": Interpreting Galatians 3.28 in Early Christianity.* LNTS 380. New York: T. & T. Clark, 2008.

Jackson, T. Ryan. *New Creation in Paul's Letters.* WUNT 2/272. Tübingen: Mohr/Siebeck, 2010.

Keener, Craig S. *Paul, Women, and Wives: Marriage and Women's Ministry in the Letters of Paul.* Grand Rapids: Baker Academic, 1993.

Kreitzer, L. J. "Eschatology." In *Dictionary of Paul and His Letters*, edited by Gerald F. Hawthorne and Ralph P. Martin, 253–69. Downers Grove, IL: InterVarsity Press, 1993.

---

85. Bartchy, *ΜΑΛΛΟΝ ΧΡΗΣΑΙ*, 153.

Ladd, George Eldon. *A Theology of the New Testament*. Grand Rapids: Eerdmans, 1974.
Lee, Sang Meyng, *The Cosmic Drama of Salvation*. WUNT 2/276. Tübingen: Mohr/Siebeck, 2010.
Lohfink, Gerhard. *Jesus and Community: The Social Dimension of Christian Faith*. Translated by John P. Galvin. Philadelphia: Fortress, 1982.
O'Brien, Peter T. *The Letter to the Ephesians*. Pillar New Testament Commentary. Grand Rapids: Eerdmans, 1999.
Paget, Alan G. *As Christ Submits to the Church: A Biblical Understanding of Leadership and Mutual Submission*. Grand Rapids: Baker Academic, 2011.
Pate, C. Marvin. *The End of the Age Has Come*. Grand Rapids: Zondervan, 1995.
Pierce, Ronald W. "Contemporary Evangelicals for Gender Equality." In *Discovering Biblical Equality*, edited by Ronald W. Pierce and Rebecca Merrill Groothuis, 58–78. Downers Grove, IL: IVP Academic, 2005.
Rabens, Volker. *The Holy Spirit and Ethics in Paul*. WUNT 2/283. Tübingen: Mohr/Siebeck, 2010.
Russell, A. Sue. "In the World But Not of the World: The Liminal Life of Pre-Constantine Christian Communities." PhD diss., UCLA, 2013.
Russell, Walter Bo. *The Flesh/Spirit Conflict in Galatians*. New York: University Press of America, 1997.
Sampley, J. Paul. *Walking between the Times: Paul's Moral Reasoning*. Minneapolis: Fortress, 1991.
Strecker, Christian. *Die liminale Theologie des Paulus: Zugänge zur paulinischen Theologie aus kulturanthropologischer Perspektive*. Forschungen zur Religion und Literatur des Alten und Neuen Testaments 185. Göttingen: Vandenhoeck & Ruprecht, 1999.
Tannehill, Robert C. *Dying and Rising with Christ: A Study in Pauline Theology*. BZNW 32. 1967. Reprinted, Eugene, OR: Wipf & Stock, 2006.
Tucker, J. Brian. "Baths, Baptism, and Patronage: The Continuing Role of Roman Social Identity in Corinth." In *Reading Paul in Context: Explorations in Identity Formation*, edited by Kathy Ehrensperger and J. Brian Tucker, 173–188. LNTS 428. London: T. & T. Clark, 2010.
———. *Remain in Your Calling: Paul and the Continuation of Social Identities in 1 Corinthians*. Eugene, OR: Pickwick Publications, 2011.
Turner, Victor. *Dramas, Fields, and Metaphors: Symbolic Action in Human Society*. Ithaca: Cornell University Press, 1974.
———. *The Forest of Symbols: Aspects of Ndembu Ritual*. Ithaca: Cornell University Press, 1967.
———. *The Ritual Process: Structure and Anti-Structure*. Ithaca: Cornell University Press, 1969.
———. *From Ritual to Theater: The Human Seriousness of Play*. New York: Performing Arts Journal Publications, 1982.
Turner, Victor, and Edith Turner. *Image and Pilgrimage in Christian Culture*. New York: Columbia University Press, 1978.
Van Gennep, Arnold. *The Rites of Passage*. Translated by M. B. Vizedom and G. L. Caffee. Chicago: University of Chicago Press, 1960.
Witherington, Ben. *Jesus, Paul, and the End of the World*. Downers Grove, IL: InterVarsity, 1992.
———. *Conflict and Community in Corinth: A Socio-Rhetorical Commentary on 1 and 2 Corinthians*. Grand Rapids: Eerdmans, 1995.

2

Hierarchisierung und Relativierung multipler Identitäten in Galater 3:28

Wolfgang Stegemann

Einleitung

Ich habe Scott Bartchy im Jahr 1977 kennen gelernt. Wir trafen uns auf einer Tagung der damals noch kleinen Gruppe von exegetischen Sozialgeschichtlern, die ihr neues Konzept der Bibelauslegung miteinander teilen wollten. Scott war zusammen mit John H. (Jack) Elliott gekommen. Für uns—d.h. für mich und Willy und Luise Schottroff, meinen Bruder Ekkehard Stegemann, Frank Crüsemann, Hans Kippenberg und andere Kolleginnen und Kollegen—war die Begegnung mit Scott und Jack eine willkommene Unterstützung und Erweiterung unserer eigenen Arbeit. Da waren zwei US-Amerikaner, die genauso wie wir einen neuen Ansatz in der Bibelexegese vertraten, der sich darum bemühte, die sozialen Kontexte der biblischen Texte für deren Verstehen zu berücksichtigen. Wir kannten Scotts Doktorarbeit: *ΜΑΛΛΟΝ ΧΡΗΣΑΙ: First-Century Slavery and the Interpretation of 1 Corinthians 7:21*, die 1973 erschienen war, und wir wussten sofort, dass wir mit ihm und Jack Bundesgenossen gefunden hatten, die wie wir leidenschaftlich daran interessiert waren, der Bibelexegese, ja der Theologie insgesamt einen neuen Akzent zu geben. Sozialgeschichte—das war das Zauberwort.

Wir interessierten uns dafür, in welchen sozialen und politischen Kontexten die biblischen Texte entstanden waren. Scotts Doktorarbeit hatte in unserer Sicht eines der wichtigen Themen aufgegriffen, nämlich die Frage, wie sich der Apostel Paulus zur antiken Sklaverei verhalten hatte.

Scott hatte dazu die antike Sklaverei insgesamt erforscht. Es ist ein Kennzeichen der exegetischen Arbeit von Scott geblieben, dass er sich nicht zufrieden gibt mit der Rezeption der Oberfläche biblischer Texte, sondern zum Verständnis ihrer Signalwörter in die Tiefe geht, und Tiefe heißt hier: die Erkundung der sozialen und kulturellen Wirklichkeiten, in denen die Kommunikation der Autoren und Adressaten der biblischen Texte stattfand. Es sind manchmal einzelne Wörter—wie etwa das Wort *klēsis*—denen er mit einer leidenschaftlichen Akribie nachgeht.[1] Sie machen nicht selten den entscheidenden Unterschied aus, d.h. von ihrem Verständnis hängt die Interpretation ganzer Textzusammenhänge, ja die Auffassung der Konzeption ihrer Autoren ab. Auf den Punkt gebracht: Wir verstehen Paulus erst dann, wenn wir jedes einzelne, sinntragende Wort seiner Briefe verstanden haben. Diese sozialgeschichtliche Tiefenhermeneutik hat Scott dann in Zusammenarbeit mit anderen amerikanischen Kolleginnen und Kollegen um Fragen der kulturellen Dimensionen biblischer Texte erweitert. Es gibt seit dieser kulturgeschichtlichen Horizonterweiterung keinen Aufsatz oder Vortrag von Scott, der nicht die sozialen und kulturellen Gegebenheiten der antiken mediterranen Kulturen beachten würde, in deren Kontext auch die Texte des Neuen Testaments entstanden sind.

Nun ist es eines, dass wir die Tiefendimensionen biblischer Texte in ihrem *gesellschaftlichen* Kontext angemessen berücksichtigen, ein anderes, in welchem Maße wir begreifen und erkennen können, ob biblische Texte in diesen Kontexten kritische und neue Akzente setzen, die den *mainstream* verlassen, überschreiten oder gar kritisch überholen. Es ist der Auftrag der historischen Wissenschaft, dass sie auch den der allgemeinen Mentalität widersprechenden oder sich zumindest von ihnen unterscheidenden Welterfahrungen Raum gibt, sie überhaupt als solche erkennt und einzuschätzen weiß. Wir wollen wissen, was das Besondere der „christlichen" Diskurse war, wie sie in den neutestamentlichen Texten geführt werden, und natürlich auch, ob und in welcher Hinsicht das Leben der Christusglaubenden sich von dem Leben anderer unterschieden hat. In seinem erwähnten Aufsatz zu 1. Korinther 7:20–21 bietet Scott Bartchy ein treffendes Beispiel. So lesen wir als Resümee seiner Analyse:

> Um es klar zu sagen: Paulus wie seine Zeitgenossen konnte sich offensichtlich nicht vorstellen, dass die Sklaverei als solche aus ihrer Welt eliminiert werden könnte. Nichtsdestoweniger wollte Paulus nicht, dass eine Sklavin oder ein Sklave, die oder der zur Nachfolgegemeinschaft Christi hinzugekommen waren, denken, dass ihr rechtlicher und sozialer Status ihre Beziehung zu

---

1. Bartchy, „Paulus hat nicht gelehrt."

Gott und ihr herzliches Willkommen im Leib Christi negativ beeinflussen könnte. Die entscheidende Frage war: Für wen hielten sie sich? Dies ist eine Frage primärer Identität. Für Paulus übertrumpft das Sein in Christus alle anderen Bestimmungen ... Es war dieser neue Status und diese neue Identität, die sie aufgaben, worin sie nicht verblieben, wenn sie zurückfielen und sich durch ihren sozialen, religiösen oder rechtlichen Status, den ihre Familien, Ehegatten ihre Kollegen und Eigentümer unhinterfragt als die wirkliche Wahrheit über sich selbst betonten, identifizierten. Zum Beispiel: Ein Vater spricht: „Du bist mein Sohn, und ich bin sehr dagegen, dass Du mit einer Lehre zu tun hast, die die Autorität des Vaters, meine *potestas*, in Frage stellt. Oder: Du bist meine Frau und Du solltest meine Götter ehren. Aber stattdessen hast Du die Ehre unserer Familie schwer verletzt, als Du eine Person, die gekreuzigt wurde, wie einen Gott verehrtest." Wie konnte aus der Teilnahme an dieser neuen Art von Christusgruppe, die ein Surrogat für die familiäre Gruppe von Geschwistern war, sich aber nicht auf Blutsverwandtschaft und Loyalität, nicht auf sozialen Status, nicht auf Geschlechtszugehörigkeit und nicht auf religiöses Erbe gründete, etwas Gutes werden? Der Druck der Familien, Freunde, Gleichgestellten, nicht in ihrer Berufung durch und in Christus zu bleiben, muss enorm gewesen sein. Deswegen ermunterte Paulus sie: Jeder/jede soll in seiner/ihrer Berufung in Christus bleiben, in der er/sie berufen worden sind."[2]

Dieses Resümee enthält auch einen Beitrag zu dem biblischen Text, mit dem ich mich hier beschäftige. Denn Bartchy spielt an auf Gal 3:28, wenn er schreibt: „Für Paulus übertrumpft das Sein in Christus alle anderen Bestimmungen." Dies gilt auch für den folgenden Satz (man muss die „familiäre Gruppe" nur zur *ethnischen* Abstammungsgemeinschaft erweitern): „Wie konnte aus der Teilnahme an dieser neuen Art von Christusgruppe, die ein Surrogat für die familiäre Gruppe von Geschwistern war, sich aber *nicht* auf Blutsverwandtschaft und Loyalität, *nicht* auf sozialen Status, *nicht* auf Geschlechtszugehörigkeit ... gründete, etwas Gutes werden?" Ich habe die Negationen bewusst hervorgehoben, denn mir scheint, dass Bartchy damit einen entscheidenden Aspekt von Gal 3:28 benannt hat: die *Nicht-Differenz*. Ich beginne mit einem kurzen Überblick über vier Deutungsmodelle von Gal 3:28, in die ich meine eigene Deutung einordne.

---

2. Ibid.

Vier grundsätzliche Deutungsmodelle von Galater 3:28

Galater 3:28 gehört zu den umstrittensten Texten des Neuen Testaments. Die vielen unterschiedlichen ja zum Teil gegensätzlichen Auslegungen, die dieser Vers allein in den letzten drei Jahrzehnten hervorgerufen hat, lassen sich hier nicht annähernd darstellen. Hinsichtlich der Bedeutung des Verses unterscheide ich vier Auffassungen, die ich hier in aller Kürze benenne:[3]

1. Der Vers formuliert einen radikalen Egalitarismus, der (für die christlichen Gemeinschaften) alle ethnischen, sozialen und geschlechtlichen Unterschiede aufhebt. Für die Glaubenden in Christus sind diese Differenzen abgeschafft.

2. Die Aufhebung der ethnischen, sozialen und geschlechtlichen Differenzen gilt nur in Beziehung zu Gott und hat einen soteriologischen bzw. „religiösen" Sinn, sie gilt nicht für das Leben der Glaubenden in der christlichen Gemeinschaft oder im Alltag der Welt.

3. Gal 3:28 steht im Kontext einer Aussage über die Taufe, sie bezieht sich damit auf die außerordentliche Erfahrung eines rituellen Aktes, hier eines Passageritus. Eine Auswirkung dieser rituellen Erfahrung auf das alltägliche Leben der Christusglaubenden ist nicht ausgeschlossen, aber auch nicht zwingend.

4. Es geht in Gal 3:28 nicht um die Aufhebung oder Abschaffung ethnischer, sozialer und geschlechtlicher Unterschiede, sondern um deren Relativierung und Unterordnung unter die im Glauben bzw. in der Taufe neu gewonnene Leitidentität: das In-Christus-Sein.

Paulus' hierarchische Strukturierung der multiplen Identitäten der Christusglaubenden

Ich favorisiere das 4. Deutungsmodell, das insbesondere von Caroline Johnson Hodge ausgearbeitet und auf Gal 3:28 angewendet wurde.[4] Dieses Modell setzt voraus, dass auch in der Antike Menschen durch multiple Identitäten geprägt waren, wobei in bestimmten Situationen die einen betont und die anderen relativiert werden konnten: „A model of multiple identities offers an alternative to the notion that individuals and groups might embody several ethnic or other identities, situationally emphasizing

---

3. Dazu auch Strecker, *Liminale Theologie*, 354–58. Ich füge seinen drei genannten Modellen ein viertes hinzu.

4. Hodge, *If Sons, Then Heirs*.

one while downplaying others. This interpretative framework helps us understand Paul's careful construction of Jews and gentiles, now descended from the same founding ancestor and belonging to the same God, but not collapsed into one group."[5]

Dem entspricht auch die moderne Ethnologieforschung, die zumal durch die Arbeiten des norwegischen Ethnologen Frederik Barth geprägt sind.[6] Er hat darauf aufmerksam gemacht, dass ethnische Identität sich insbesondere über *Abgrenzungen* von anderen Gruppen entwirft. Dabei ergeben sich die jeweiligen Identifizierungen aus der Situation, d.h. insbesondere aus dem aktuellen Gegenüber, von dem sich eine ethnische Gruppe in ihrem Wir-Bewusstsein unterscheidet. Sein Beispiel ist das Volk der Pathanen im afghanisch-pakistanisch-iranischen Grenzgebiet.

Die *Pathanen* verstehen sich gegenüber den Iranern als *Afghanen*, d.h. sie beziehen sich in dieser Situation auf ihre Zugehörigkeit zum afghanischen Staat. In der Interaktion mit Hindus überwiegt die Selbstdefinition als *Muslime*, d.h. in diesem Kontext mobilisieren die Pathanen ihre Zugehörigkeit zum Islam. Gegenüber Schiiten, also innerhalb des Islam, identifizieren sie sich als *Sunniten*. Gegenüber den Angehörigen der benachbarten Ethnie der Belutschen identifizieren sie sich als *Pathanen*. Innerhalb des eigenen Stammes existieren dann weitere Unterdifferenzierungen, vor allem nach Klanzugehörigkeit.

Ethnische Identität scheint also eine dynamische und multiple Möglichkeit zu sein. Ethnische Grenzen konstituieren sich in einem Prozess wechselseitiger Selbst- und Fremdzuschreibungen. Über Zugehörigkeit und Solidarität entscheidet das jeweilige Gegenüber.

Für antike Beispiele außerhalb des Neuen Testaments verweist Johnson Hodge u.a. auf die Rede des Hermokrates in Thukydides' *Geschichte des Peleponnesischen Kriegs*.[7] Als ein überzeugendes Beispiel für Paulus nennt sie 1 Kor 1:22–24:

> [22] Und da Juden/Judäer Zeichen fordern und Griechen Weisheit suchen, [23] verkündigen wir (*hemeis*) Christus als gekreuzigt, den Juden/Judäern ein Ärgernis und den Völkern eine Torheit, [24] ihnen aber, den Berufenen (*klētoi*), Juden/Judäern wie Griechen, Christus, Gottes Kraft und Gottes Weisheit."

In diesem Text repräsentieren Juden/Judäer und Griechen zwei unterschiedliche ethnische Gruppen, die hier auch durch zwei spezifische

---

5. Ibid., 117.
6. Barth, ed., *Ethnic Groups*.
7. Hodge, *If Sons, Then Heirs*, 118–20.

kulturelle Kennzeichen (Zeichenforderung/Weisheit) unterschieden werden. Diese Merkmale der beiden ethnischen Gruppen sind offenkundig *situationsgebunden* formuliert, weil sie im Argumentationszusammenhang eine unterschiedliche Reaktion auf die Verkündigung des gekreuzigten Christus vorbereiten sollen: Der Zeichenforderung der Juden/Judäer entsprechend wird ihre negative Reaktion auf den gekreuzigten Messias als Ärgernis (*skandalon*) auf den Begriff gebracht, der Weisheit der Griechen (bzw. der nichtjüdischen Völker; *ethnē*) entspricht ihre Deutung des gekreuzigten Christus als Torheit (*moria*). Die Christusglaubenden Juden/Judäer und Griechen bekommen durch den übergeordneten Begriff „Berufene" (*klētoi*) eine beide ethnische Gruppen überspannende gemeinsame *Leitidentität*, die sie von jenen Mitgliedern ihrer ethnischen Gruppen unterscheidet, die diese „Berufung" nicht teilen. D.h. aber auch: Es bestehen zwischen den Juden/Judäern, die zu den Christusglaubenden gehören (also zu den *klētoi*), und denen, die nicht dazu gehören, *keine ethnischen* Unterschiede (gleiches gilt entsprechend für die Gruppe der Griechen)! Sie unterscheiden sich allerdings durch ihre Reaktion auf die Verkündigung des gekreuzigten Christus, den sie als Gottes Kraft (*dynamis*), so die berufenen Juden/Judäer, und Gottes Weisheit (*sophia*), so die berufenen Griechen/Völker, verstehen. Ich finde es bemerkenswert, dass trotz der ihnen von Paulus zugeschriebenen neuen Leitidentität, die die jeweiligen griechischen und judäischen Christusglaubenden (als *klētoi*) verbindet, dennoch ihre Reaktionen auf die Berufung (*klēsis*; 1 Kor 1:26; 7:20) entlang der vorher den Juden/Judäern und Griechen zugeschriebenen kulturellen Spezifika (Zeichenforderung/Weisheit) differenziert wird. Dies ist ein starker Hinweis darauf, dass trotz der gemeinsamen neuen Leitidentität der Christusglaubenden aus den Juden und den Völkern deren genuine ethnische Identität nicht verschwindet.

Johnson Hodge kommt in ihrer Auslegung dieser Verse zu folgendem Fazit: "Although Paul superimposes another identity—„those who are called"—over the ethnic identities of *Ioudaios*, gentile and Greek, these ethnic identities do not disappear . . . For Paul, being called or being in-Christ cuts across ethnic identities, including both *Ioudaioi* and non-*Ioudaioi*."[8]

Vergleichbares trifft nach Johnson Hodge auch auf Gal 3:28 zu. Nach ihrer Deutung gilt:

> Paul does not advocate a liberationist, egalitarian interpretation of Galatians 3:28. Nor is Paul concerned with erasing difference in this verse. Instead, Galatians 3:28 is an integral component of Paul's argument that the God of Israel has called the gentiles to

---

8. Hodge, *If Sons, Then Heirs*, 126.

> a specific, embodied existence as gentiles-in-Christ. The model of multiple identities that I have developed here—plural, overlapping, flexible, hierarchical, situationally relevant—suggests that we can read Galatians 3:28 in terms of ethnic discourse and not against it. Thus *Ioudaioi* and Greeks, slaves and free, male and female can all be "one in Christ" without abandoning other identities.[9]

Johnson Hodge betont, dass die in Gal 3:28 benannten ethnischen, sozialen und geschlechtlichen Identitäten nicht aufgegeben, sondern einer neuen leitenden Identität untergeordnet werden. Diese wird in Gal 3:28 mit der Wendung „denn ihr alle seid einer in Christus Jesus" umschrieben. Die weiterhin bestehenden (ethnischen, sozialen und geschlechtlichen) Identitäten werden einer neuen hierarchischen Ordnung (*hierarchical order*) unterworfen, an deren Spitze „the unitary good" steht: die Zugehörigkeit zu Christus, oder, wie man auch etwa mit Verweis auf 1 Korinther 12 sagen könnte, die Zugehörigkeit zum „Leib/Körper Christi" (*soma Christou*). Die Argumentation von Johnson Hodge geht allerdings noch einen Schritt weiter, da sie diese neue Top-Identität—„in Christus"—nicht als ethnisch neutral versteht. Vielmehr ist nach ihrer Deutung des Textzusammenhangs von Gal 3:28 der unmittelbar folgende Vers, also Gal 3:29 (und zwar in Verbindung mit Gal 3:16) der Clou der paulinischen Argumentation. Hier zunächst die beiden Verse, Gal 3:16, 29:

> 16 Dem Abraham aber wurden die Verheißungen zugesagt und seiner Nachkommenschaft (*sperma*). Er spricht nicht: „und seinen Nachkommen" wie bei vielen, sondern wie bei einem: „und deinem Nachkommen", *und* der ist Christus . . .
> 29 Wenn ihr aber des Christus seid, so seid ihr damit Abrahams Nachkommenschaft (*sperma*) und nach Verheißung Erben.

Johnson Hodge vertritt folgende These: "More important, this highest good, being in-Christ, is not ethnically neutral; it is grounded in Jewish identity. As the seed of David and the son of God (Rom 1:3–4), Christ is the link for gentiles to the lineage of Abraham. For a gentile to be in-Christ means that he or she has secured a place within the larger network of Israel."[10]

Dieses Ergebnis ist nicht ohne Bedeutung. Denn es gibt in diesem Zusammenhang durchaus auch andere Auffassungen, etwa die von John M.

---

9. Ibid. 129.
10. Ibid., 131.

G. Barclay, auf die ich jetzt kurz eingehe. Vor allem wäre diese Deutung für das Selbstverständnis der Christinnen und Christen aus den Völkern (*gentile Christians*) von großer Bedeutung.

Ist ethnische Identität in den paulinischen Gemeinden „simply irrelevant"?

In seinem kenntnisreichen Buch über Jews in the Mediterranean Diaspora: From Alexander to Trajan (323 BCE—117 CE) stellt John M. G. Barclay folgende Behauptung auf: „Paul explicitly describes his aim as the creation of communities in which there is neither Jew nor Greek' (Gal 3.28). In the context of their new community, the ethnic identity of Paul's converts was simply irrelevant: they were to choose their mates, for instance ‚in the Lord' (1 Cor 7.39) regardless of their ethnic origin..."[11]

Barclay glaubt, dass Paulus „multi-ethnic Christian communities" gebildet hat.[12] Auch in einem Aufsatz, der im selben Jahr veröffentlicht wurde, nennt er Paulus einen „*fashioner* of multiethnic and multicultural communities."[13] Für Barclay scheint also die Formation multiethnischer und multikultureller Gruppen kein zufälliges Ergebnis der Gründung christlicher Gemeinschaften durch Paulus zu sein, sondern sie war ausdrücklich intendiert. Barclay ist übrigens der Meinung, dass die sog. *new perspective on Paul* die Frage nach der Bedeutung von Ethnizität überhaupt erst auf die Agenda der Paulusexegese gesetzt hat:

> the new perspective (on Paul) suggests that Paul could serve as a valuable resource in our struggles to fashion a harmonious but multicultural society. It reads Paul as the fashioner of multiethnic and multicultural communities, which function not to erase but to moderate between differing cultural specificities... A cautious use of our Pauline heritage could equip us to undertake that long and difficult search for a polity which both respects ineradicable difference and enables meaningful community.[14]

Barclay weiß natürlich selbst, dass seine Interpretation durch soziale und kulturelle Erfahrungen unserer eigenen Gegenwart beeinflusst ist, was im Übrigen für die Paulusinterpretationen zu allen Zeiten gilt: „The history of the interpretation of Paul shows the different modes in which Paul's

---

11. Barclay, *Jews in the Mediterranean Diaspora*, 385 (Kursivierung von mir).
12. Ibid., 386–87.
13. Barclay, „Neither Jew nor Greek."
14. Ibid., 213–14.

theology has been construed ... (and) reflect(s) the social and cultural questions dominant in the interpreter's environment."[15]

Ich stimme Barclay darin zu, dass innerhalb der Diskurse der neuen Paulusperspektive vor allem James Dunn die fundamentale Bedeutung der Ethnizität für die paulinische Theologie in den Fokus gerückt hat. Dunn ist wichtig, dass Paulus nicht (wie dies vor allem in der sog. *old perspective* angenommen wurde) mit dem Judentum *gebrochen* hat, vielmehr habe er sein Judentum vor allem wegen dessen (angeblichen) Ethnozentrismus kritisiert:

> The decisive corollary which Paul saw, and which he did not hesitate to draw, was that the covenant is no longer identified or characterized by such distinctively Jewish observances as circumcision, food laws and Sabbath. Covenant works had become too closely identified as Jewish observances, covenant righteousness as national righteousness ... God's purposes and God's people have now expanded beyond Israel according to the flesh, and so God's righteousness can no longer be restricted in terms of works of the law which emphasize kinship at the level of the flesh.[16]

Dunns Argumentation setzt implizit ein Verständnis des Judentums als einer *Religion* voraus, die die Mitgliedschaft ethnisch einschränkt, indem sie sie an die Zugehörigkeit zum jüdischen *Volk* bindet. Jedenfalls gelte dies für das Judentum zur Zeit des Paulus. Auf diesem Hintergrund kann Paulus dann leicht zum trans-ethnischen und multikulturellen Helden werden. Er öffnet die Beziehung zu dem einen Gott für alle Menschen, indem er den (angeblichen) ethnozentrischen *Partikularismus* des jüdischen Volkes und die mit ihm verbundenen *exkludierenden* Vorschriften der Mosetora—also zumal der „distinctive Jewish observances" wie Beschneidung, Speisegesetze und Sabbatheiligung—überwindet.

So interessant diese Deutung ist, sie geht von einer problematischen, inzwischen überholten Voraussetzung aus, wonach das, was wir „Judentum" (*Judaism*) nennen (in Analogie zum „Christentum"), eine (antike) *Religion* ist. Doch um es abgekürzt zu sagen: Umgekehrt wird ein Schuh daraus. Schon 1994 hat etwa Stanley Stowers (wie vorher und neben und nach ihm viele andere) darauf aufmerksam gemacht, dass das „Religionsmodell" vom Judentum anachronistisch ist. Er plädiert stattdessen dafür, das antike Judentum in Begriffen der *Ethnizität* zu interpretieren:

---

15. Ibid., 197.
16. Dunn, *Jesus, Paul and the Law*, 197, 200.

The modern version of the traditional reading trades heavily on the anachronistic concept of religion. The concept of religion was created in eighteenth-century European culture. Intellectual historians have shown that religion becomes the genus of which Christianity is a species only in the seventeenth century. The modern concept of religion as an essentially private sphere of personal belief and activity separate from politics, law, economic activity, and ethnicity is an even later development. When the high priest was the nation's ruler and the Roman emperor was the pontifex marximus and the law of the Judean people was their sacred writings it is easy to see that religion, politics, and ethnicity were inseparable. Yet exegetes of the New Testament constantly employ the anachronistic category of religion in reading Pauline texts. In fact, assuming the postindustrial organization of Western societies is one side of the universal address based on liberal individualism that modern interpreters find in Paul's letters.[17]

Bruce J. Malina hat schon vorher darauf aufmerksam gemacht,[18] dass in den antiken mediterranen Gesellschaften Religion „eingebettet" war (er spricht von „*embedded religion*") in die zwei zentralen Institutionen der antiken mediterranen Gesellschaften: Gemeinwesen (*polity*) und Familie/Verwandtschaft (*kinship*). Malina sieht darin einen fundamentalen Unterschied zum modernen Religionsverständnis, das Religion als „*disembedded*", also als einen eigenständigen Bereich sozialer Erfahrung—etwa neben den Sektoren Politik oder Ökonomie—versteht. Es gab in den antiken Gesellschaften im Prinzip keine *eigene* soziale Institution, die als „Religion" wahrgenommen wurde.

Auf dieser Grundlage kann noch einmal deutlicher werden, was es für antike Menschen bedeutet haben muss, wenn sich in „christlichen" Gemeinschaften in Städten des östlichen Teils des römischen Weltreichs bis hin nach Rom Angehörige verschiedener Ethnien (Juden/Judäer, Griechen, Galater, Römer usw.) versammelten. Dass die gemeinsame Verehrung des Gottes Israels von Juden/Judäern gemeinsam mit Angehörigen anderer Völker überhaupt möglich war, ist wohl dem Faktum zu verdanken, dass der Gott der Juden/Judäer als der einzige Gott zugleich auch als der Gott aller Völker verstanden wurde: „Oder ist Gott allein der Gott der Juden/Judäer (*Ioudaion*), nicht auch der Völker (*ethnon*)? Ja auch der Völker" (Röm 3:29). Diese Besonderheit bringt es mit sich, dass der Zugang zu Gott—jedenfalls

---

17. Stowers, *A Rereading of Romans*, 26–27.
18. Malina, „Religion"; vgl. auch Stegemann and Stegemann, *Urchristliche Sozialgeschichte*, 247. Ausführlicher W. Stegemann, *Jesus in seine Zeit*, 207–35.

für Paulus—nicht exklusiv an die Zugehörigkeit zum jüdischen Volk gebunden ist:

> ¹¹ Denn die Schrift sagt: „Jeder, der an ihn glaubt, wird nicht zuschanden werden." ¹² Denn es ist kein Unterschied (*diastole*) zwischen Juden/Judäer und Grieche, denn er ist Herr über alle, und er ist reich für alle, die ihn anrufen; ¹³ „denn jeder, der den Namen des Herrn anrufen wird, wird gerettet werden." (Röm 10:11–13)

Gerade aufgrund ihrer ethnischen Differenzierung bedurften die neuen „christlichen" Gemeinschaften aus Juden/Judäern und Völkern der *diskursiven Konstruktion* ihrer neuen kollektiven Identität. Paulus kannte zwar den später erfundenen Begriff „*Christianoi*" noch nicht (vgl. Apg 11:26; 26:28: 1 Petr 4:16). Doch er scheint diesen zumal mit dem Syntagma *en Christō* vorzubereiten. Ich stimme insofern der zitierten Aussage von Barclay zu, dass es Paulus nicht darum ging, ethnische oder kulturelle Unterschiede abzuschaffen bzw. auszulöschen (*erase*), sondern zwischen diesen Unterschieden zu vermitteln (*moderate*). Dies gelang ihm, indem er die multiplen Identitäten relativierte und einer neuen Leitidentität unterstellte: „in Christus".

In Gal 3:28 betont Paulus nachdrücklich die *Einheit* der Gemeinschaft der Christusglaubenden: „ihr seid aller einer (*heis*) in Christus".[19] Hier geht es ihm offensichtlich nicht um Abgrenzung nach außen, sondern um eine Bekräftigung des Bewusstseins der gemeinschaftlichen Identität *en Christō* nach innen, innerhalb der galatischen „christlichen" Gemeinschaft. Sie sind offenbar von Christusglaubenden Juden/Judäern unter Druck gesetzt worden und zum Teil auch dafür offen gewesen, sich unter das Dach der judäischen Ethnizität zu begeben. Dass Paulus dann schließlich auch den Christusglaubenden aus den Völkern (denn um *deren* Hinwendung zum judäischen Volk wird gestritten) eine Art Zugehörigkeit zu Israel (und zwar über die Zugehörigkeit zu Christus als dem verheißenen Nachkommen Abrahams) zuspricht (Gal 3:29), ließe sich von hierher „situationsbedingt" erklären, also als ein sekundäres oder sekundierendes Argument deuten. Doch muss dies hier nicht entschieden werden.

Die paulinische Relativierung der Ehe

Bisher ging es um ethnische Unterschiede zwischen Juden/Judäern und Griechen bzw. Angehörigen anderer (nicht-jüdischer) Völker. Doch was

---

19. Siehe dazu jetzt Campbell, *Unity and Diversity*.

ist mit den sozialen Differenzen zwischen Sklaven und Freien, was mit der Geschlechterdifferenz zwischen Männern und Frauen? Darum geht es ja auch in Gal 3:28: „Nicht ist Jude/Judäer und nicht Grieche, nicht ist Sklave und nicht Freier, nicht ist männlich und weiblich; denn alle seid ihr einer in Christus Jesus."

Ich habe bisher die These vertreten, dass es in Gal 3:28 um die *Relativierung* von ethnischen, sozialen und geschlechtlichen Identitätsdifferenzen geht, nicht um deren *Aufhebung* oder Abschaffung. Galater 3:28 ist also meiner Meinung nach keine *ontologische* Aussage über die Existenz oder Nichtexistenz von Juden/Judäern und Griechen, Sklaven und Freien, Männern und Frauen. Anders gesagt: „In Christus" werden die getauften Christusglaubenden judäischer oder griechischer Provenienz nicht ihrer ethnischen Herkunft *entkleidet*. Sie werden vielmehr neu *bekleidet*, d.h. sie ziehen Christus als ein neues Gewand an: „denn wieviele ihr in (*eis*) Christus hinein getauft wurdet, ihr habt Christus *angezogen (enedysasthe)*" (Gal 3:27). Die hier verwendet Vokabel für das Anziehen oder Überziehen eines Kleidungsstücks ruft übrigens nicht notwendig die Vorstellung von einem *Kleiderwechsel* hervor, wonach also ein bisheriges Kleidungsstück ausgezogen und durch ein anderes ersetzt wird. Den Vorgang des Kleiderwechsels formuliert Röm 13:12–14, doch geht er dort aus dem Kontext und nicht allein aus der Verwendung der Vokabel *endyo* hervor. Dagegen legt 1 Kor 15:53–54 die Vorstellung von einem Überziehen eines neuen Kleidungsstücks nahe. Am deutlichsten wird der semantische Gebrauch von *endyo* im Sinne von „überziehen über" in 1 Thess 5:8. Hier geht es darum, dass sich die Glaubenden den Brustpanzer des Glaubens und der Liebe anlegen. Auch dieses Bild würde dafür sprechen, dass nicht Identitäten abgeschafft, sondern einer neuen Leitidentität unterstellt werden.

Kurz: Es geht nicht um die ontische oder ontologische *Aufhebung* von Differenzkategorien, sondern um deren *Subordination* unter eine neu gewonnene Leitidentität. Diese Deutung ist nach meiner Überzeugung besonders anschaulich in der dritten Negation, der Differenz von „männlich und weiblich". Die Formulierung negiert ja gerade die *Differenz* „männlich und weiblich" (*ouk eni arsen kai thēly*), aber eben nicht die *Existenz* von Männern und Frauen. Wie auch? Es gibt in den christlichen Gemeinden nach wie vor Männer und Frauen, wie man allein schon aus einigen Texten des ersten Korintherbriefes entnehmen kann (1 Kor 11 und 1 Kor 7 bzw. 1 Kor 14), in denen deren Existenz in der korinthischen Gemeinschaft der Christusglaubenden vorausgesetzt und ihr Verhalten sogar punktuell kritisiert wird. Es gibt in der paulinischen *ekklesia* auch immer noch Sklaven und Freie (wie etwa aus dem Philemonbrief und auch dem 1. Korintherbrief hervorgeht). Der Fokus in Gal 3:28 liegt vielmehr auf der *Subordination* von

Identitätsmerkmalen (ethnisch, sozial, geschlechtlich) unter eine neu gewonnene Leitidentität: „in Christus".

Was heißt dies für die sog. „geschlechtliche" Differenz: „nicht ist männlich und weiblich" (*ouk eni arsen kai thēly*). Was wird hier negiert? Mir scheint, dass es um ein *Beziehungsverhältnis* zwischen männlichen und weiblichen Menschen geht, da sich die Negativpartikel *ouk* auf die Wortverbindung *arsen kai thely* bezieht. Es liegt nahe, diese Verbindung als Anspielung auf bzw. Zitat von Gen 1:27 zu verstehen, also jener Aussage über die Schöpfung der Menschen als männliche und weibliche Wesen, die gleich anschließend in Gen 1:28 als Voraussetzung der Reproduktion der Gattung Mensch verstanden wird. Möglich ist durchaus, dass Paulus Asexualität bzw. sexuelle Askese als Ideal (vgl. 1 Kor 7:1) vorschwebt.[20] Für Paulus ist Sexualität jedenfalls ein Aspekt ehelicher Gemeinschaft und auf diese beschränkt. Doch zunächst und vor allem: Das Zitat aus Gen 1:27 in Verbindung mit Gen 1:28 bezieht sich auf die gesellschaftlich anerkannte Institution der Reproduktion, nämlich auf die *Ehe*. Dafür spricht nicht zuletzt, dass auch in Mark 10:6 und Matt 19:4 das Zitat aus der Schöpfungsgeschichte als Argument für die prinzipielle Unauflöslichkeit der Ehe dient. Dann ginge es Paulus nicht um die Aufhebung der *geschlechtlichen* Differenz der Menschen. Es ginge ihm um die Relativierung der *Institution Ehe—und zwar hinsichtlich ihrer reproduktiven Funktion*. Deshalb könnte man vielleicht das *ouk eni arsen kai thely* sinngemäß mit: „nicht gibt es Ehemänner und Ehefrauen" wiedergeben.

Wenn diese Interpretation richtig ist, dann würde uns ein anderer Paulustext, nämlich 1 Kor 7, in die komfortable Lage versetzen, diese Deutung der paulinischen Teilaussage *ouk eni arsen kai thēly* von Gal 3:28 etwas näher zu erhellen, aber auch insgesamt die These von der *Relativierung* der Differenzen in Gal 3:28 und ihrer hierarchischen Subordination zu überprüfen. Das soll hier wenigstens in aller Kürze versucht werden. Paulus plädiert in 1 Kor 7:7 grundsätzlich für Ehelosigkeit und damit, wie aus dem Kontext hervorgeht, auch für sexuelle Askese, für einen *Lebensstil*, den er für sich selbst gewählt hat. Ehelosigkeit empfiehlt er auch den Unverheirateten und Witwen (1 Kor 7:8), doch wenn sie sich sexuell nicht enthalten können, sollen sie heiraten. Auch geschiedene Frauen sollen am besten nicht wieder heiraten (1 Kor 7:11). Kurz: Paulus will nicht die Ehe *abschaffen*, sondern er *relativiert* sie, er unterstellt sie der von ihm favorisierten *Ehelosigkeit* und *sexuellen Askese*; die Ehe repräsentiert demgegenüber einen „minderen" Lebensstil im Verhältnis zum höherwertigen asketischen Lebensstil der Christusglaubenden. Die Ehe scheint nahezu nur eine Konzession an das

---

20. So etwa Strecker, *Liminale Theologie*, 388–90.

sexuelle Begehren zu sein. Grundsätzlicher, d.h. unter Berücksichtigung der vorläufig noch andauernden Existenz der Institution Ehe, wünscht Paulus sich, angesichts der begrenzten Zeit, der Zeit, die noch übrig bleibt, eine Beziehung des „als ob nicht" (*hos mē*) zwischen Ehemännern und Ehefrauen: „Dies aber sage ich, Brüder: Die Zeit ist begrenzt: dass künftig die, die Frauen haben, seien, als hätten sie keine" (1 Kor 7:29).

Ich lasse dahingestellt, dass Paulus hier wie auch sonst aus der Sicht der (Ehe-) Männer argumentiert. Seine Favorisierung der Ehelosigkeit scheint allerdings ironischer Weise vor allem von Frauen und nicht von Männern begrüßt worden zu sein (man denke nur an die *Acta Pauli et Theclae*). Doch wichtiger im gegenwärtigen Zusammenhang ist mir die Erkenntnis: Sie bestätigt, dass es in Gal 3:28 um die *Relativierung* von Unterschieden geht, nicht um deren Aufhebung oder Abschaffung.

Works Cited

Barclay, John M. G. *Jews in the Mediterranean Diaspora: From Alexander to Trajan (323 BCE–117 CE)*. Berkeley: University of California Press, 1996.

———. "'Neither Jew nor Greek': Multiculturalism and the New Perspective on Paul." In *Ethnicity and the Bible*, edited by Mark G. Brett, 197–214. BibIntSer 19. Leiden: Brill, 1996.

Bartchy, S. Scott. *ΜΑΛΛΟΝ ΧΡΗΣΑΙ: First-Century Slavery and the Interpretation of 1 Corinthians 7:21*. SBLDS. Missoula, MT: Society of Biblical Literature, 1973. Reprinted, Eugene, OR: Wipf & Stock, 2003.

———. "Paulus hat nicht gelehrt 'Jeder soll in seinem Stand bleiben': Luthers Fehlübersetzung von *klēsis* in 1. Korinther 7." In *Alte Texte in neuen Kontexten: Wo steht die sozialwissenschaftliche Bibelexegese?*, edited by Wolfgang Stegemann and Richard E. DeMaris. Stuttgart: Kohlhammer, 2014.

Barth, Frederik, ed. *Ethnic Groups and Boundaries: The Social Organization of Culture Difference*. London: Allen & Unwin, 1969.

Campbell, William S. *Unity and Diversity in Christ: Interpreting Paul in Context: Collected Essays*. Eugene, OR: Cascade Books, 2013.

Dunn, James D. G. *Jesus, Paul and the Law: Studies in Mark and Galatians*. Louisville: Westminster John Knox, 1990.

Hodge, Caroline Johnson. *If Sons, Then Heirs: A Study of Kinship and Ethnicity in the Letters of Paul*. Oxford: Oxford University Press, 2007.

Malina, Bruce J. "Religion in the World of Paul." *BTB* 16 (1986) 92–101.

Stegemann, Ekkehard W., and Wolfgang Stegemann. *Urchristliche Sozialgeschichte: Die Anfänge im Judentum und die Christusgemeinden in der mediterranen Welt*. 2nd ed. Stuttgart: Kohlhammer, 1997. [ET = *The Jesus Movement: A Social History of Its First Century*. Translated by O. C. Dean Jr. Minneapolis: Fortress, 2000.]

Stegemann, Wolfgang. *Jesus und seine Zeit*. Biblische Enzyklopädie 10. Stuttgart: Kohlhammer, 2010.

Stowers, Stanley K. *A Rereading of Romans: Justice, Jews and Gentiles*. New Haven: Yale University Press, 1994.

Strecker, Christian. *Die liminale Theologie des Paulus: Zugänge zur paulinischen Theologie aus kulturanthropologischer Perspektive*. Forschungen zur Religion und Literatur des Alten und Neuen Testaments 185. Göttingen: Vandenhoeck & Ruprecht, 1999.

3

Social-Scientific Comments on "Neither Judean nor Greek" (Gal 3:28)
Dennis C. Duling

ABRAHAM, MOSES, THE PROPHETS, Jesus, Paul, and Mohammed were "improvisers." I dedicate this essay to my friend and colleague, Scott Bartchy, whose fictive family improvisations have fed my understanding of Paul's ethnicity, networking, and relation to social memory, and whose piano improvisations and pedagogy have fed my life.

In his impressive study of Paul as a radical Jew, Daniel Boyarin, drawing on John Gager, states this hermeneutical principle: "the choice of a starting point will to a large extent determine one's reading of Paul."[1] Boyarin's starting point, his "key for unlocking Paul," is Gal 3:28–29.[2] This chapter addresses only part of 3:28, "There is neither Judean[3] nor Greek . . . for you are all one in Christ Jesus." After a brief summary of the historical context of Gal 3:28, it takes up two alternative theological interpretations that suggest inconsistencies in Paul's comments, the second of which demonstrates the centrality of 3:28. The chapter then moves to three social-scientific theories—Ethnicity, Mar-

---

1. Boyarin, *A Radical Jew*, 5–6; Gager, *Origins*, 204–5; for the center/beginning point, see also Sanders, *Palestinian Judaism*, 434–42.

2. Ibid., 23.

3. Except when quoting others, this essay translates Ἰουδαῖος and Χριστιανός as "Judean" and "Christ believer," on which see Elliott, "Misleading Nomenclature"; Esler, *Conflict*, 67–68; and Hanson and Oakman, *Palestine*, 11. Bible translations are mainly from the NRSV, but are occasionally changed, as in this case.

ginality, and Structuration Theories—that can offer insights for understanding and explaining Paul's duality. The thesis is social psychological, that is, that Paul was a "cultural marginal" whose social location "in-between" ethnic Judeans and Gentiles and whose attempt to unify believers from these different camps led him to make occasional accommodations. I suggest, further, that these accommodating inconsistencies led to unintended consequences, namely, when the End did not come, the power and domination structure that he sought to dissolve maintained itself and that with respect to ethnicity tensions contributed to the "parting of the ways."

Historical Context

According to Paul, when Torah-observant Christ-believing Judeans ("men from James") arrived at Antioch from Jerusalem, Peter, a fellow Judean Christ-believer, stopped eating with uncircumcised Christ-believers and was joined by other Judean Christ-believers (Gal 2:11–14). Angered by this dissolution of unity, Paul claimed that he had charged Peter with hypocrisy and had maintained in opposition to the Jerusalemite "circumcision party" that neither circumcision nor food laws apply to "Greek" (Gentile)[4] believers. Employing family/kinship metaphors,[5] Paul claimed that the importance of Abraham was his belief[6] that Christ (not corporate Israel as a whole) is Abraham's true "seed"/descendant,[7] and that believers "in Christ," including Torah-free Gentiles, have inherited the status of "children of Abraham."[8] God had promised Abraham that he would become "the ancestor of a multitude of ἔθνη," a term that in Hellenistic Greek (LXX) can mean not only "peoples," but also "Gentiles,"[9] and therefore, argued Paul, Gentile

---

4. I do not agree with Stanley, "Neither Jew nor Greek," who rejects the common view that "Greeks" refers broadly to Gentiles. Paul's view (Rom 1:16; 2:9–10; 3:9; 10:12; 1 Cor 1:22, 24; 10:32; 12:13; Gal 3:28) has parallels with "circumcised"/"uncircumcised" (Rom 3:30; Gal 5:6; cf. Gal 2:9). He once uses a "Gentile" division, "Greek and barbarian" (Rom 1:14; cf. also deutero-Pauline "barbarian and Scythian," Col 3:11). See Stendahl, *Paul*, 1; Esler, *Galatians*, 82–88.

5. Bartchy, "Undermining Ancient Patriarchy"; "Who Should Be Called Father?"; "The Domestication of a Radical Jew."

6. Gal 3:6–9; Rom 4:3 (Gen 15:6). In Rom 4:9–12, Paul argues that Abraham's belief preceded his circumcision.

7. Gal 3:16; cf. Gen 12:2–3; 15:5; 17:8; 18:18; 22:17–18.

8. Gal 3:6–9, 29 (corporately!); cf. 4:5.

9. Gen 17:4 LXX; cf. Gal 3:8, 26, 29. See Esler, "Paul's Contestation.""Εθνη meant "nations," "peoples," but increasingly in Hellenistic Greek "Gentiles." See further below.

"children of Abraham" are adopted as "children of God."[10] Judeans and Gentiles must be unified as "one in Christ Jesus."[11]

Galatians 3:27–28 has parallels in 1 Cor 12:13 and Col 3:11, although the male/female contrast in Galatians is absent in the latter two passages.[12] All three passages stress not only unity,[13] but baptism,[14] a ritual that, as Wayne A. Meeks has demonstrated, had multivalent meanings based on Jesus' death/resurrection.[15] Baptism was almost certainly a triple-immersion ritual,[16] and this suggests that each of three cultural oppositions that Paul rejected was symbolically "removed" *seriatim* in three acts of dipping. Such an initiation rite signified entering a new community—even if the "new life" transformation remained incomplete until the End.

Theology

The usual starting point for interpreting Gal 3:28 in traditional Protestant Christianity is inherited from Martin Luther who, much stressed by his inability to experience forgiveness for his sins through confession or doing penance by good works, sought and finally found a gracious, forgiving God while he was meditating on Rom 1:17: "For in it [the gospel] the righteousness of God is revealed through faith for faith; as it is written, 'The one who is righteous will live by faith' [Hab 2:4]." Luther later recalled, "I felt that I was altogether born again and had entered paradise itself through open gates..."[17] Most Protestants, following Luther, have believed that the key to salvation in Paul is found in Rom 1:17 and passages like it, for example, Gal 2:16: "a person is justified not by the works of the law but through faith in

---

10. Gal 3:26; cf. 4:5; Johnson Hodge, *If Sons, Then Heirs.*

11. Gal 3:26 and 3:28d frame 3:27–3:28; see Betz, *Galatians*, 181.

12. The male-female contrast also has a different *form* from the other two oppositions, suggesting that it might have been added (ibid., 182); however, it might have been omitted in the parallels because they are found in letters less favorable to women (1 Cor 11:2–16; 14:33b–36 [if Pauline]; Col 3:18–4:1 [the Household Code]).

13. Gal 3:28: "one in Christ Jesus"; 1 Cor 12:13: "one body," "one Spirit"; Col 3:11: "Christ is all and in all." Unity is a major Pauline theme, e.g., 1 Cor 1:22, 24; 7:18–22; 8:8; 9:19–21; 10:32; 2 Cor. 3:14; Gal 2:11–12, 16; 3:7; 5:6; Rom 3:9, 20, 23, 27–28; 10:4, 12; 14:1–20. See Hansen, *All of You Are One*, 1; Cromhout, *Walking*, 73–78.

14. Gal 3:27; 1 Cor 12:13; Col 3:9–10.

15. Meeks, *Urban Christians*, 154–57.

16. BAGD, βαπτίζω, "I dip," "I immerse," "I plunge," "I sink"; also catacomb art. See Ferguson, *Baptism*, 164, 197–98; 205–206. On clothing/unclothing, see *Gos.Thom.* 37; *Did.* 7; Ferguson, *Baptism*, 453; Jensen, *Baptismal Imagery*, 16,158–60,167–72.

17. Luther, "Preface to the Latin Writings."

Jesus Christ . . . [N]o one will be justified by the works of the law." Therefore, the traditional Protestant "center" of Paul's thought has been justification by faith apart from "works of the law."[18] For Luther that meant "faith alone" (*sola fidei*).[19] Doing "works of the law" from this perspective has often been considered "legalism," the wrong path. "Neither Judean nor Greek, . . . but all are one in Christ Jesus" becomes a natural inference from "justification by faith." This traditional starting point is also the heart of Lutheran theology in the twentieth century. Its most influential New Testament scholar has been critic/theologian Rudolf Bultmann, who, with existentialist revisions, interpreted the Pauline view of human existence as the plight and solution of all humankind.[20]

However, there are passages in Paul, particularly in Romans, that do not seem to be consistent with Paul's comments about, and Luther's opposition to, "works of the law." Consider for example, "Do we then overthrow the law by this faith? By no means! On the contrary, we uphold the law" (Rom 3:31), or ". . . the law is holy, and the commandment is holy and just and good" (Rom 7:12). Paul also wrote that Judeans have priority over Greeks (Rom 1:16) and are privileged to the "oracles of God" (Rom 3:2). "Israel" is, finally, a cultivated olive tree onto which Christ-believing Gentile branches have been grafted that as a result of boasting can be cut off, just like non-Christ believing Judean branches (Rom 11:18).[21] These and similar passages have generated an alternative interpretation of Paul, namely, the "New Perspective on Paul" (NPP). Its most recent, influential scholars have been Krister Stendahl, E. P. Sanders, James Dunn, and N. T. Wright.[22]

Krister Stendahl set the stage in 1961 by arguing that Luther's interpretation of Paul's "works of the law" as "earning merits for salvation" was a misunderstanding rooted in late medieval Catholic theology and piety.[23] The pre-Augustinian Paul himself, said Stendahl, did not have Luther's introspective, guilt-ridden conscience. Paul says, "As to righteousness under

---

18. Luther, *Disputation of the Year 1516* ("Ninety-five Theses"); Calvin, *Institutes* 2.38.

19. Luther added "alone" to his German translation of "justification by faith" in Rom 3:28, arguing from context and precedent (Luther, "Open Letter on Translating"); Swan, "Luther Added."

20. Bultmann, *Theology*.

21. Esler, "Ancient Oleiculture."

22. See, e.g., Watson, *Paul*, 1–18; Hagner, "Paul and Judaism," 111–30; Esler, *Galatians*, 141–59; Cromhout, *Walking*, 73–106. Schweitzer once held that Luther's "justification" was a "subsidiary crater" in Paul's thinking; see *Mysticism*, 225; there were other predecessors (Hagner, "Paul and Judaism," 113).

23. Stendahl, "Introspective Conscience." Stendahl notes forerunners to his view, particularly Moore, "Christian Writers on Judaism" (201, n. 1).

the law *I was blameless*" (Phil 3:6).[24] Thus, the center of Pauline thought was not justification by faith but "the place of the Gentiles in the Church and in the plan of God, with the problem of Jew/Gentiles or Jewish Christians/Gentile Christians."[25] This view shifted the center of Paul's thought toward "neither Judean nor Greek" in Gal 3:28.

In 1977 E. P. Sanders seconded Stendahl's critiques of Luther and Lutheran-influenced Protestant exegesis, including that of Bultmann.[26] Most importantly, Sanders made an intensive study of "Palestinian Judaism" and, summarizing it as "covenantal nomism," defined it as a "religious system" in which "... *obedience [to the law] maintains one's position in the covenant, but it does not earn God's grace as such.*"[27] "Getting in" was by God's grace and not merits; however, works of the law (and repentance) were still necessary for "staying in." What about Paul? For Sanders, "... Paul presents an *essentially different type of religiousness from any found in Palestinian Jewish literature.*"[28] Paul "explicitly denies that the Jewish covenant can be effective for salvation, thus consciously denying the basis of Judaism."[29] In short, Paul made a total break with "Judaism."[30] "What is distinctive about Paul's view of the law—and in fact about his theology—was ... [that] ... Christ saves Gentiles as well as Jews."[31] Again, the center of Paul's thought was "neither Judean nor Greek" in Gal 3:28.

James D. G. Dunn agreed with Stendahl and coined the expression "the new perspective on Paul" (NPP) on the basis of Sanders's work,[32] but he did *not* agree with Sanders's view of Paul.[33] Dunn observed that right before Paul's first statement of "justification by faith" (Gal 2:16 [quoted above]),

24. Paul's only regret was having persecuted the church: Gal 1:13-14; Phil 3:6; Cor 15:9. Other texts for Paul's more positive view of his past are 1 Cor 4:4; 9:27; 15:10; 2 Cor 1:12; 5:10.

25. Stendahl, "Introspective Conscience," 204. This point had been made by Schweitzer and Wrede.

26. Sanders, *Palestinian Judaism*, 443; cf. 474. Sanders also cited predecessors, e.g., Moore ("Christian Writers") and Jewish writers who critiqued German Lutheran scholars Ferdinand Weber, Wilhelm Bousset, Emil Schürer, and Rudolf Bultmann and students (1-59).

27. Ibid., 420.

28. Ibid., 543.

29. Ibid., 551.

30. Sanders, *Law*, 47, 207-10.

31. Sanders, *Palestinian Judaism*, 496-97.

32. Dunn, "New Perspective," 120. Dunn also honored his Jewish and Christian forerunners. Hagner, "Paul and Judaism," 112, thinks that the NPP is "new" only in the sense that Sanders's work was written after the Holocaust.

33. Dunn, "New Perspective," 103-5.

Paul contrasted *"we Judeans by birth"* with "sinners from the Gentiles" (Gal 2:15). Paul therefore included himself as one of the *"Jews* whose Christian faith is but an extension of their *Jewish* faith in a graciously electing and sustaining God."[34] Paul did not disparage "doing the [whole] law," but only select *"works* of the law"—circumcision, food laws, and "special days" (Gal 4:10), particularly the Sabbath—because [for "Jews"] such works ". . . had become the expression of a too narrowly *nationalistic* and *racial* conception of the covenant, . . . a badge not of Abraham's faith but of Israel's boast."[35] According to Dunn, such Judean "badges of covenant membership" (cf. Genesis 17; 1 Macc 1:60–63) had the sociological function of "boundary markers" that separated Judeans and Greeks,[36] and Paul sought to remove them. "Faith in Christ" was "the primary identity marker" in the "time of fulfillment."[37] The Judean/Gentile issue of Gal 3:28 is, again, the center of Paul's theology.[38]

Not to be outdone, N. T. Wright claimed that he had already developed a similar position in 1976 (before Sanders!).[39] He agreed with Sanders's and Dunn's critique of Luther, with most of Sanders's "Judaism,"[40] and most of Dunn's Paul;[41] however, said Wright, Dunn "has not, I think, got to the heart of Paul," nor had most other NPP scholars. He therefore spoke of "new perspectives" (plural) and called his own view a "fresh [not new] perspective."[42] Yes, the NPP had been correct "that every time Paul discusses justification he seems simultaneously to be talking about Gentile inclusion—but [it] ha[d] not, usually, shown how this integrates with the traditional view that he [Paul] is talking about how sinners are put right with God." Shades of

---

34. Ibid., 108. Dunn acknowledged that Sanders' subsequent view in *Paul, the Law, and the Jewish People* was broader, but that Sanders still maintained that Paul was not aligned with "covenantal nomism" because it could not fulfill God's purpose to save the whole world.

35. Dunn, "New Perspective," 19 (italics mine).

36. Ibid., 108–111; Dunn, "Works of the Law"; Dunn, *Jesus, Paul, and the Law*, ch. 8.

37. Dunn, "New Perspective, 113, 114.

38. Dunn, "Works of the Law," 140.

39. Wright, "New Perspectives." Wright had rejected the traditional Lutheran interpretation of Romans 10:4 ("Christ is the end of the law").

40. Not "solution to plight," but Paul's rethinking of the plight of Israel and the world in the light of his gospel of Jesus' crucifixion and resurrection.

41. Wright, "New Perspectives"; Wright, *Paul: In Fresh Perspective*, ch. 2. Dunn and Wright, "Evening Conversation," agree that the NPP might not have been necessary if Reformed/Calvinistic rather than Lutheran theology had dominated biblical criticism in the late nineteenth and early twentieth century.

42. Wright, "New Perspectives."

Luther![43] Furthermore, in Wright's view Paul must be understood in terms of the narrative structure of his thought (e.g., Romans 9–11), covenant renewal, and new creation. Paul is in continuity and discontinuity with "Judaism."

These very cursory descriptions in no way do justice to these scholars who have intensely labored on this subject, but hopefully my comments demonstrate at least two major points: first, that "neither Judean nor Greek . . . but all are one in Christ Jesus" in Gal 3:28 was indeed central to Paul's thinking, and that the two major theological alternatives to interpret Paul, the Lutheran/traditional Protestant one and the NPP, demonstrate that Paul made different kinds of comments about the law and his mission strategy that were at times accommodations that led him to be inconsistent; and second, that a critical issue in these inconsistencies was the issue of ethnic boundaries between Judeans and Gentiles. Both need some attention.

Inconsistencies

It is difficult to deny that there are inconsistencies in Paul's letters. The Lutheran and NPP alternatives above indicate theological attempts to deal with this problem by claiming that some texts are primary (the center) and some are secondary (the periphery). An alternative suggestion is that Paul's ideas evolved, especially from his angry letter to the Galatians—for Brown, Paul's "mistake"[44]—to his "masterpiece," the more moderate, accommodating letter to the Romans. In contrast to these solutions, Sanders's early view was that Paul had a "participationist theology" resulting in "conflicting convictions . . . better left asserted than explained."[45] Yet, Sanders argued that Paul was "a coherent thinker, despite the unsystematic nature of his thought and the variations in formulation,"[46] and later he expanded this perspective by being open to the possibility of "organic growth" in Paul's later letters of "incipient ideas" in his earlier letters.[47] John Gager maintained more sharply that Paul's letters betray an "embarrassment of contradiction and inconsistency,"[48] and to illustrate this point, he contrasted seven "Anti-Israel" passages with eight

---

43. Wright, *Paul: In Fresh Perspective*, 36 (italics mine).
44. Brown in Brown and Meier, *Antioch and Rome*, 115.
45. Sanders, *Law*, 198.
46. Sanders, *Palestinian Judaism*, 433.
47. Sanders, "Did Paul's Theology Develop?" 333.
48. Ibid.; Gager, *Reinventing Paul*, 11.

"Pro-Israel" passages.[49] Yet, following Stendahl and others,[50] he argued that Paul wrote only to Gentile believers and offered them a special way (*Sonderweg*), belief in Christ, while he allowed the Judean believers a different way, the way of law (cf. Gal 5:3, 11; Rom 3:1–2). This "two ways" helped to explain, but not dispense with, Paul's inconsistencies.

An illustration of Paul's inconsistent comments about Judeans/Gentiles is the contrast between Gal 2:9 and 1 Cor 9:19–23. In his account of the Jerusalem Assembly (Gal 2:1–10) that led up to the Antioch Incident (Gal 2:11–14), Paul recalled that a compromise mission strategy was reached: "*we* should go to the Gentiles, and *they* [Peter and the Judean missionaries] to the circumcised" (Gal 2:9). However, Paul's mission strategy appeared to be quite different if one takes 1 Cor 9:19–23 at face value.

A 19) For though I am *free* with respect to *all*, I have made myself a *slave* to *all*, so that I might win more of them.

  B 20) To the *Judeans* I became as a Judean, in order to win Judeans.

    C To *those under the law* I became as one under the law (though I myself am not under the law) so that I might win those under the law.

    C′ 21) To *those outside the law* I became as one outside the law (though I am not free from God's law but am under Christ's law) so that I might win those outside the law.

  B′ 22) To *the weak* I became weak, so that I might win the weak.

A′ I have become *all things* to *all people*, that I might by all means save some.

23) I do it for the sake of the gospel, so that I may share in its blessings. (1 Cor 9:19–23, NRSV [slight changes]).

The chiastic form of this passage indicates that Paul was serious and thoughtful and that he was quite conscious that his attempt to win recruits among both Judeans and Gentiles required a dual missionary strategy.[51] Scholars do not agree on how to interpret this inconsistency. In the first

---

49. Gager, *Reinventing Paul*, 5–7, 11. "Anti-Israel [law]": Gal 3:10, 11; 6:15; Rom 3:20; 9:31; 11:28; 1 Cor 3:14–15; "Pro-Israel" [law]: Gal 3:21; Rom 3:1–2, 31; 7:7, 12; 9:4; 11:1, 26). He notes 2 Pet 3:16: Paul is "hard to understand" (δυσνόητά).

50. Ibid., 146; Stendahl, "Introspective Conscience"; Stowers, *A Rereading of Romans*.

51. See above, note 13. The passage implies only two of the three oppositions in Gal 3:28, and in that regard is like the 1 Cor 12:13 and Col 3:11.

place, it overlaps other debated questions: whether Paul first went to Judeans (Acts) or not (implied from the letters [apart from this passage]); and whether his comments and frequent use of Scripture imply the presence of Judeans in his churches or not. Moreover, there is a problem about Paul's character, that is, whether the duplicity in 1 Cor 9:19–23 implies that Paul was deceitful and hypocritical, thus unethical—or not. Günther Bornkamm argued that 1 Cor 9:19–23 was indeed Paul's real mission strategy because he would not have missed the opportunity to recruit Judeans in the cities he visited, which Bornkamm supported with Paul's comment that he was beaten with thirty-nine stripes, a synagogue punishment (2 Cor 11:24).[52] Sanders, however, concluded that there is "no clear solution" to Paul's real missionary strategy ("[w]e just do not know"), yet he opted for the probability that the divided mission in Gal 2:9 was more probable, suggesting that 1 Cor 9:19–23 was hyperbolic and that Acts was a distortion.[53] Peter Richardson argued that in 1 Cor 9:19–23, which has as its larger context Paul's attempt to solve the "meat offered to idols" conflict (1 Corinthians 8–10), Paul was opportunistically prepared to abandon the law. The problem for Richardson was that Paul did not grant the same accommodation principle to Peter at Antioch, who had been willing initially to eat with Gentiles; thus, Paul's charge that Peter was a hypocrite was not justified. Richardson concluded that this was really a turf war: Peter was operating on Paul's territory.[54] D. A. Carson attempted to counter Richardson's solution by arguing that Paul's "principle of accommodation" was not a "license for unlimited flexibility" since Paul was "subject to the law of Christ" (1 Cor 9:21) and this made some of his commands non-negotiable. The impression of inconsistencies arose because of Paul's self-denying voluntary servanthood, a "third ground."[55] Finally, Mark D. Nanos argued that Paul in 1 Cor 9:19–23 was not talking about his *behavior*, which would have made him deceptive (by misleading the Judeans), but rather was a matter of his "*argumentative behavior*," that is, his evangelistic strategy of "rhetorical adaptation" to the convictional propositions of his audience, just as a teacher is willing for the sake of argument to accept the alternative position of students, but not to actually lead their lifestyle.[56]

52. Bornkamm, "Missionary Stance"; see also Vielhauer, "'Paulinism.'"
53. Sanders, *Law*, 186–90.
54. Richardson, "Pauline Inconsistency."
55. Carson, "Pauline Inconsistency."
56. Nanos, "Paul's Relationship."

I am inclined to agree with Sanders's early view and Gager's position that Paul's many contradictions should be left standing.[57] Heikki Räisänen held this same view when he argued that an evolution from Galatians to Romans will not work since Paul's inconsistency is also found within Romans itself![58] In Räisänen's words, Paul is

> wrestling with an impossible task, his attempting to "square the circle." He tries to hold together two incompatible convictions: 1) God has made with Israel an irrevocable covenant and given Israel his law which invites the people to a certain kind of righteous life, and 2) this righteousness is not true righteousness, as it is not based on faith in Jesus.[59]

I shall return to the issue of Paul's inconsistencies, but now take up the second NPP point that Paul saw Judean "works of the law" as sociological, as "boundary markers" that separated Judeans and Gentiles.

Ethnicity Theory

Dunn usually called the boundary markers of the law "nationalistic" and "racial," although he occasionally used as an equivalent the term "ethnic."[60] Wright had also used the expression "national righteousness" to describe Judean covenant separatism (election), but more consistently used the expressions "ethnic Israel," "ethnic status," or "ethnic origin,"[61] and he interpreted Paul's unity vision of the church as a "single multi-ethnic family."[62] I think that the terms "nationalistic" and "racial" were unfortunate, as I shall indicate, but the NPP did energize a methodological turn toward Ethnicity Theory in Pauline scholarship. This can be illustrated from several recent studies.

Philip F. Esler agrees that for Paul "justification by faith" was subsidiary to the problem of Gentile inclusion,[63] and he explains strong Judean/Gentile group boundaries with the aid of Ethnicity Theory and Social Identity

---

57. Räisänen, *Paul and the Law*, especially 268–69. For a list of Räisänen's view of Paul's many contradictions, see Watson, *Paul*, 18.

58. Räisänen, "Paul's Conversion," 405, contrasting Romans 9 and Romans 11, or even Rom 11:10 and 11:11.

59. Ibid., 410; "Square the Circle" comes from Walker, "Interpolations," 176.

60. Duling, "Ethnicity and Paul's Letter to the Romans," 69–70.

61. Wright, *Paul*, 126.

62. Wright, "Paul in Different Perspectives"; *Paul: In Fresh Perspective*.

63. Esler, *Galatians*, 153, citing Schweitzer, who offered the metaphor, but also Wrede.

Theory.⁶⁴ John M. G. Barclay insightfully surveys the NPP and Boyarin's rich contribution, and in relation to Paul's partially "dejudaized Judaism,"⁶⁵ describes Paul's view as a "multicultural" and "multiethnic" ideology in which ". . . Jews and Gentiles are simultaneously *affirmed* as Jews and Gentiles and *humbled* in their cultural pretensions."⁶⁶ Bruce Hansen builds on what David G. Horrell called Paul's Christological "renegotiation" of Israel's covenant identity⁶⁷ and argues that Paul used "ethnic discourse," including a religious communal myth that appeals to ancestors,⁶⁸ a "vertical-demotic *ethnie*" that appeals to more inclusive political or religious communities, and an assimilation model of two extant groups that combine to form a new group (A + B → C).⁶⁹ Caroline Johnson Hodge argues that Paul used kinship, ethnicity, and adoption language to show that Gentile Christ-believers remained Gentiles but had nonetheless become "children of Abraham" and adopted "sons of Israel," thus relatives of the Israelites and heirs of Israel's ancestors.⁷⁰ Joshua D. Garroway pushes Johnson Hodge's thesis further by contending that Paul believed that his Gentile believers had become Judeans, that is, he proposes a Gentile/Judean hybrid identity, a sort of "third race" theory (I use traditional language) in which the alternative may indeed be called "Christian."⁷¹ Finally, Markus Cromhout's informed and informative treatment considers Paul's inconsistency in terms of Israelite ethnic identity and Gentile inclusion, but he asks whether Paul's hope for Israel's final inclusion was not "perhaps too little too late."⁷²

These scholars focus on the Judean/Gentile issue of Gal 3:28 in terms of ethnicity. I follow this path, but want to clarify my position by sketching a few points about Ethnicity Theory.

The English adjective "ethnic" and related terms are derived from the ancient Greek adjective ἐθνικός, and thus on the noun ἔθνος and its plural

---

64. Barth, "Introduction," (see further, below); Esler, *Galatians*, 86–92, using Tajfel, *Differentiation*.

65. The expression is taken from Theissen, *Social Reality*, 205.

66. Barclay, "Neither Jew nor Greek," 211.

67. Hansen, *All of You Are One*; Horrell, "Theological Ideology." Hanson stresses Paul's ideology, not "reality," in contrast to Esler, *Galatians*. I am closer to Esler's perspective.

68. Boyarin had made this point about Diaspora Judeans, but Hansen rejects Boyarin's emphasis on Platonic universalism as missing Paul's social-communal dimension.

69. See Smith, *Ethnic Origins*; Barclay, "Neither Jew nor Greek"; Horowitz, "Ethnic Identity."

70. Johnson Hodge *"If Sons, Then Heirs."*

71. Garroway, *Paul's Gentile-Jews*, 2–3.

72. Cromhout, *Sandals*, 99–106.

ἔθνη."Ἔθνος has evolved from referring to almost any human or animal collectivity (Homeric Greek), to use of the plural for the "peoples" of the world (Hellenic Greek), to mostly "*foreign* peoples" (Hellenistic Greek), thus to the adjectival meaning "pagan" or "heathen" (Middle English), and finally to its more neutral Hellenic sense of "peoples" or "nations" (modern English).[73] In the social-scientific literature of early twentieth-century United States, the language "ethnic group" began to replace the term "race," in part because "race" centered primarily on physical features, particularly skin color, which was too narrow for describing "white" immigrants from western and northern Europe,[74] in part because Euro-American evolutionary theories of racial superiority/inferiority were increasingly judged by scholars to be pseudo-scientific.[75] In 1942 W. Lloyd Warner and Paul Lunt coined the noun "ethnicity" to describe "white" immigrants to New England and in 1953 this neologism appeared in the *Oxford English Dictionary*.[76] These language developments are also the major reason why "ethnicity" rather than "race" is more appropriate to describe the Judean/Gentile problematic.

A similar point can be made about "nationalism." Sociologist Anthony Smith distinguishes between "*ethnic* nationalism" and "*civic* nationalism."[77] Ethnic nationalism bases group membership on ethnic differences and is more exclusionary and separatist; "*civic* nationalism" is based on the Western concept of loyalty to a physically bounded nation state and is more inclusive and integrative. The term "nationalism" alone usually means "*civic* nationalism," which became so powerful in the nineteenth century, although Fascist nationalism also had strong "ethnic" and "racial" overtones. Yet, ethnic groups are generally considered to be "*pre*-nationalistic"[78] and they often impede nation-state building.[79] Smith made this important observation about Mediterranean antiquity and Paul: "It is *ethnie* [ethnic groups] rather than nations, ethnicity rather than nationalism, that pervades the social and

---

73. Liddell-Scott-Jones, *A Greek-English Lexicon*, τὸ ἔθνος, online at *http://www.perseus.tufts.edu/hopper/text?doc=Perseus%3Atext%3A1999.04.0057%3Aentry%3De)%2Fqnos*). Sollors, "Ethnic, Ethnical, Ethnicity, *Ethnie, Ethnique*" based on the *Oxford English Dictionary* of 1961 and 1972 in Sollors, *Theories of Ethnicity*, ch. 1 ("Etymology").

74. Largely because of North American quota laws between 1890 and 1924.

75. Sorokin, *Contemporary Sociological Theories*, 482, n. 8; Huxley and Haddon, *We Europeans*, 91–92.

76. Warner and Lunt, *Status System*, 72–73. The frequent claim that the neologism "ethnicity" was invented by David Riesman in 1953 and the frequent claim that "ethnicity" first appeared in the *Oxford English Dictionary* in 1972 are both inaccurate.

77. Smith, *Ethnic Origins*.

78. Armstrong, *Nations Before Nationalism*; Smith, *Ethnic Origins*.

79. Geertz, "Integrative Revolution."

cultural life of antiquity and the early Middle Ages in Europe and the Near East."[80]

Credit for advancing "ethnic group" theory is usually given to Max Weber.[81] Weber initially wrote that "[t]he whole conception of ethnic groups is so vague that it might be good to abandon it altogether,"[82] but he went on to offer this definition:

> We shall call "ethnic groups" [*ethnische Gemeinschaften*] those human groups that entertain a subjective belief [*subjektiven Glauben*] in their *common descent* because of similarities of *physical type* or of *custom* or both, or because of *memories of colonization and migration*; this belief must be important for the propagation of *group formation*; conversely *it does not matter whether or not an objective blood relationship* [*Blutsgemeinsamkeit objektiv*] *exists* . . . ethnic membership does not constitute a group [*Gemeinschaft*]; it only facilitates group formation [*Vergemeinschaftung*] of any kind, particularly in the *political sphere*. On the other hand it is primarily *the political community*, no matter how artificially organized [*künstlichen Gliederungen*], that inspires the belief in common ethnicity [*ethnischen Gemeinsamkeitsglauben*].[83]

Weber mentioned phenotypical features, but his main emphasis was on cultural features: common language, customs, religion, etiquette, values (what is "honorable"), morality, aspects of daily life (food preferences, gender divisions), shared political motives, and political solidarity vis-à-vis other groups.[84] Yet, he also emphasized that pervasive ideas about blood and descent are "subjective beliefs" in ethnic groups. These two emphases—ethnic features and subjective beliefs—laid the groundwork for the two major theories of ethnicity since the 1960s, "Primordialism" and "Constructionism."

---

80. Smith, *Ethnic Origins*, 89.

81. Weber, "Ethnic Groups." "Ethnic groups" is Ferdinand Kolegar's translation of *ethnische Gemeinschaften* in Weber's untitled draft (1911), posthumously published and titled as *Ethnische Gemeinschaften* in Weber, *Wirtschaft und Gesellschaft* (1922). This English translation first appeared in Parsons, et al., *Theories of Society*, 1961 (see 305–9) and then in Roth and Wittich, *Community and Society* (385–98; 1968, reprint 1978). See Mommsen, "Max Weber's 'Grand Sociology'"; Banton, "Max Weber."

82. Weber, "Ethnic Groups" in *Economy and Society*, 385.

83. Ibid., 389 (italics mine); for the German see http://www.textlog.de/7776.html.

84. Swedberg, "Ethnic Groups"; Cohen, "Ethnicity," 385; Verkuyten, *Social Psychology*.

First, Primordialism. In a survey of small group research in 1957, sociologist Eduard A. Shils opposed Interactionist Theory[85] by arguing that small group members relate to each other on the basis of "especially 'significant relational' *qualities*," one of which is the "*ineffable*" quality that families attribute to the "*ties of blood*."[86] He called such qualities "*primordial*." A few years later Clifford Geertz described the group-binding qualities of "ethnic" (formerly "tribal"[87]) communities that were resisting the development toward national/civic statehood.[88] Geertz borrowed Shils's small group concepts to describe Weberian-type ethnic qualities as "overpowering," "ineffable," and "unaccountable," and as based on "*primordial* attachments."[89] He also added a shared past or putative "common history."[90] Shils and Geertz are now recognized as the "fathers" of Primordialism.

There is another kind of Primordialism, Sociobiological Primordialism, which defends a "natural selection" approach to kinship-oriented ethnic groups;[91] but the major alternative to cultural Primordialism is the social-scientific approach called "Constructionism." In 1969 sociologist Fredrik Barth acknowledged the importance of what he called "cultural stuff" (Weberian-type ethnic characteristics), which he subdivided into "basic value orientations" and "overt signals and signs."[92] However, echoing Weber's "subjective beliefs," he emphasized a major theoretical shift to *how* and *why* ethnic groups develop and maintain their boundaries, stressing their "we"-versus-"they" mentality in concrete situations. "The critical focus of investigation . . . [should be] the ethnic *boundary* that defines the [ethnic]

---

85. Homans, *The Human Group*, believed that small group relations are based on members' approval or disapproval of one another, an interaction, cost/benefit model.

86. Shils, "Primordial," 142. See Duling, "Social-Scientific Small Group Research."

87. In a Post-colonial era "tribal" is often considered to be ethnocentric; see Cohen, "Ethnicity," 384.

88. Weber had noted (social) memories of colonialism and immigration; Isajiw, "Definitions of Ethnicity," says that the European analysis of ethnicity has focused more on colonialism than immigration.

89. Geertz, "Innovative Revolution," 259, citing Shils, "Primordial."

90. Ibid., 261.

91. Van den Berghe, *The Ethnic Phenomenon*. Sociobiological Primordialists, observing that certain characteristics—altruism, aggression, war, criminality—tend to recur in family groups, argue for a Darwinian-style "natural selection," that is, that humans attempt to maximize their "fitness" by selecting mates from their own kin group. In general, see Wilson, *On Human Nature*; *Sociobiology*. Sociobiological Primordialism is quite controversial; see Wilson, "For Sociobiology"; Gould et al., "Against Sociobiology."

92. Barth, "Introduction," 14.

group, *not the cultural stuff* that it encloses."⁹³ Thus, "the *social organization* of cultural difference"⁹⁴ is more important than the differences themselves. From this perspective, cultural features are constructed and reconstructed over time; indeed, so are ethnic identities, ethnic memberships, ethnic locations, subsistence patterns, and political forms and allegiances.⁹⁵

Barthian Constructionism has been supplemented, revised, refined, and critiqued.⁹⁶ Variant emphases include self-interested, rational choices that promote political or economic advantage;⁹⁷ power-conflict relations;⁹⁸ analysis of symbols, myths, values, and traditions;⁹⁹ and marginality, enculturation, and assimilation theories (more on this later). Popular themes are simultaneous multiple ethnic identities "nested" inside each other,¹⁰⁰ freely chosen ethnic identities used in different situations ("hybridity"; "Situationalism"),¹⁰¹ "imagined communities,"¹⁰² social mobility, interethnic marriage, ethnic stratification, and multiculturalism.¹⁰³ Constructionists in general emphasize that ethnicity is not natural or inherent, but freely chosen; not imposed by outsiders ("ascribed"), but elected by insiders ("self-ascribed"); not moving toward assimilation, but to exclusion. Ethnic identity is therefore not essential, but situational; not ontological, but contextual, not fixed, but fluid.¹⁰⁴ The common theme is that ethnic identity is *constructed depending on the social context or immediate situation*.

Barthian-influenced Constructionism has come to dominate Ethnicity Theory, but Primordialism is showing signs of resilience.¹⁰⁵ Geertz, for example, can be understood as engaging in social description of *others'* views, as describing *emic* (native) perspectives,¹⁰⁶ thus as characterized

93. Barth, "Introduction," 15 (italics mine); in his "Enduring and Emerging Issues," Barth thinks that he has anticipated Postmodernism.

94. The subtitle of *Ethnic Groups and Boundaries*.

95. Ibid.

96. Scott, "A Resynthesis"; Yang, *Ethnic Studies*, 47–56.

97. Varshney, *Ethnic Conflict*. An example in the United States would be minority support for affirmative action legislation.

98. Horowitz, *Ethnic Groups*.

99. Armstrong, *Nations Before Nationalism*; Smith, *Ethnic Origins*.

100. Esler, *Conflict*, 60–61; Duling, "Ethnicity and Paul's Letter to the Romans," 74.

101. Ratcliffe, "Ethnic Group," 3; Back, *New Ethnicities*.

102. Anderson, *Imagined Communities*.

103. Gans, "Symbolic Ethnicity"; "Symbolic Religiosity."

104. Thompson, *Theories*; Yang, *Ethnic Studies*, 47–56. See, however, Buell, *Why This New Race?*

105. Bayer, "Reconsidering Primordialism."

106. Jenkins, "Ethnicity, Anthropological Aspects." See Headland, Pike, and Harris,

by what Anthony Smith calls a "weak" or "participant" Primordialism, as contrasted with "strong" Primordialism.[107] Some theorists attempt to combine Primordialism and Constructionism, whether "dialectically" or "synthetically";[108] this is a combination of "fixity" and "fluidity."[109] I take such a mediating position.[110] Elsewhere, I have created ethnicity models that are Constructionist, yet incorporate "cultural stuff," the cultural features or characteristic mentioned by Weber, Shils, and Geertz, but also by Richard Schermerhorn,[111] John Hutchinson and Anthony Smith,[112] Martin Bulmer,[113] and others.[114]

Pauline Ethnicity Discourse

John Hutchinson and Anthony D. Smith state: "[Al]though the term 'ethnicity' is recent, the sense of kinship, group solidarity, and common culture to which it refers is as old as the historical record. Ethnic communities have been present in every period and continent and have played an important role in all societies."[115] This statement has been amply demonstrated and confirmed for the ancient Circum-Mediterranean[116] and in studies of Paul, as amply noted previously. Here I look at four of Paul's most explicit ethnicity comments.[117]

In Rom 9:4-5 Paul constructs Judean ethnicity with this statement:

Emics and Etics.

107. Smith, "Politics of Culture," 707; cf. Brett, "Interpreting Ethnicity," 12–13, n. 29. Sociobiological Primordialism is "strong" Primordialism.

108. McKay, "An Exploratory Synthesis"; Scott, "Resynthesis."

109. Buell and Johnson Hodge, "Politics"; Buell, *Why This New Race?* 6–8, 37–41.

110. See Duling, "'Whatever Gain I Had . . . ,'" 223–28; "Ethnicity and Paul's Letter to the Roman," 72–77.

111. Schermerhorn, *Comparative Ethnic Relations*, 12.

112. Smith, "Politics of Culture," 708; Hutchinson and Smith, *Ethnicity*, 6.

113. Bulmer, "Race and Ethnicity," 54.

114. Duling, "Ethnicity and Paul's Letter to the Romans," 73; "Ethnicity, Ethnocentrism, and the Matthean Ethnos," 128 (reprinted in *A Marginal Scribe*, 295); "'Whatever Gain I Had' . . ." 240 (reprint 16–17). For elaboration of the latter, see Cromhout *Jesus and Identity*, 81–107; *Sandals*, chs. 2, 3.

115. Hutchinson and Smith, *Ethnicity*, 3.

116. E.g., Malkin, *Ancient Perceptions*; Buell, *Why This New Race?*; Brett, *Ethnicity*; Cromhout, *Jesus and Identity*.

117. Duling, ibid. Hansen's comprehensive *All of You Are One* focuses on the parallels (Gal 3:28; 1 Cor 12:13; and Col 3:11) and ideology; I, like Esler, want to emphasize reality.

4) They are Israelites (Ἰσραηλῖται), and to them belong the sonship (ἡ υἱοθεσία), the glory (ἡ δόξα), the covenants (αἱ διαθῆκαι), the giving of the law (ἡ νομοθεσία), the worship (ἡ λατρεία), and the promises (αἱ ἐπαγγελίαι); 5) to them belong the patriarchs (οἱ πατέρες), and "out of them" according to the flesh (ἐξ ὧν ὁ κατὰ σάρκα), is the Christ. God who is over all be blessed forever. Amen. (NRSV, slightly altered)

This statement contains most of the features of ethnicity:[118] an ancestor-based name (Jacob/Israel), myths of common ancestry (the patriarchs), kinship relationships (the sonship), common religion and customs (the giving of the law; worship), and shared historical memories (all of the above plus the glory and promises). Paul intentionally chooses to describe "Israelites," not "Judeans,"[119] and introduces that description with "my brothers, my kinsmen" "according to the flesh" (Rom 9:3), which recalls Dunn's and Wright's observations about Paul's including himself among Judean believers (Gal 2:15; Rom 10:3). But Paul has reservations. He says that *some* "children of the flesh" are *not* among the "children of the promise" (Rom 9:2-3, 6-13; 10:1-4); are *not* the true "seed"/children of Abraham, Isaac, and Jacob/Israel; are *not* among the faithful remnant who believe in the Messiah (9:27). For Paul, ethnic descent is no guarantee of inclusion: "[N]ot all of Abraham's children are his true descendants" (Rom 9:7). Moreover, he offers a parallel to the Galatians "neither Judean nor Greek" (Gal 3:28): ". . . there is *no distinction between Judean and Greek*; the same Lord is Lord of all and bestows his riches upon *all who call upon him*" (Rom 10:12). Paul claims that "in Christ Jesus," who is the dying and resurrected "Lord" (Christology/ecclesiology), the "fictive kinship" family trumps the real ethnic family.

In a second example Paul again plays the ethnicity card, now in more direct reference to himself. In Rom 11:1 he says: "I ask, then, has God rejected his people. By no means! I myself am an Israelite (Ἰσραηλίτης), a descendant of Abraham (σπέρματος Ἀβραάμ), a member of the tribe of Benjamin (φυλῆς Βενιαμίν)." In diatribe fashion, Paul argues in this context that God keeps his promises to Israel, for although they are a "disobedient and contrary people" (10:21), there is a faithful remnant (11:2-10). He includes himself.

A third example comes from 2 Cor 11:21b-23a where, defending himself, he constructs his ethnic identity as equivalent to that of rival Judean Christ-believing missionaries.[120]

---

118. For righteousness as "privileged identity" among ancient Judeans and Paul, see Esler, *Galatians*, 141-77.

119. Dunn, *Romans*, 2:635; Roetzel, "*Ioudaioi* and Paul," 13.

120. For details and literature, see Duling, "2 Corinthians 11:22" (esp. 73-76;

> But whatever any one dares to boast of—I am speaking as a fool—I also dare to boast of that. Are they Hebrews (Ἑβραῖοί)? So am I. Are they Israelites (Ἰσραηλῖται)? So am I. Are they descendants ["seed"] of Abraham (σπέρμα Ἀβραάμ)? So am I. Are they servants of Christ? I am a better one . . .

In this example Paul employs the rhetorical devices of irony, self-praise, and comparison,[121] as well as the image of "the Fool," a stock comic figure who entertained at banquets and on stage at the theater.[122] His dramatic "boast" appeals to descent from Jacob/Israel and Abraham (instead of Benjamin), but reversing himself in the following verses, he claims, as Cromhout says, that his honor is not based on his real ethnicity (ascribed honor), but on the evidence of his apostolic sufferings (acquired honor).[123]

A final example is Phil 3:4b-6, the literary context for Stendahl's assertion that Paul had a "robust conscience."[124] Paul's situation is conflict (again!): rival Judean missionaries are said to have come to Philippi to circumcise his recruits.[125] Paul angrily labels them "dogs" and "cutters" who "do evil" (Phil 3:2-3). Once again he plays the ethnicity card and defends himself by boasting of his higher status as a Judean:

> If anyone else has reason to be confident in the flesh, I have more: circumcised (περιτομῇ) on the eighth day, a member of the people (γένους) of Israel, of the tribe of Benjamin (φυλῆς Βενιαμίν), a Hebrew born of Hebrews (Ἑβραῖος ἐξ Ἑβραίων); as to the law (κατὰ νόμον), a Pharisee; as to zeal, a persecutor of the church (ἐκκλησίαν); as to righteousness under the law (νόμῳ), blameless. (NRSV)[126]

Paul's ethnic self-identity statement in this passage is twice as long as those in Rom 11:1 and 2 Cor 11:21b-23a. He lists not three, but six, primordial features of the model: names (Israel; Hebrews); an external sign (circumcision); descent from real or mythical ancestors (Israel; Benjamin);

---

reprint, 824-28).

121. Forbes, "Comparison."

122. Lambrecht, "The Fool's Speech."

123. Cromhout, *Sandals*, 99; Fitzgerald, *Cracks*. "Catalogues of Sufferings" distinguished true and false philosophers.

124. Duling, "'Whatever Gain I Had' . . ."

125. For the connection of circumcision in Phil 3:4b-9 with the centrality of circumcision in Galatians 1-2, see Räisänen, "Paul's Conversion," 410.

126. Cromhout, *Sandals*, 98-99, observes that the first four features are ascribed honor and the last three features are acquired honor.

perhaps a hint at language (Hebrew);[127] religion (the law; a Pharisee); and political motivation (his persecuting zeal). Again, however, Paul rejects his ethnic credentials: "But whatever gain I had, I counted as loss for the sake of Christ" (Phil 3:7). While he considers the features of his Judean ethnic status to be irreproachable, they amount to nothing, or, in his language, σκύβαλα (3:8: "refuse," "animal scats," "human excrement," or one might perhaps translate with more literal vulgarity, "shit").[128]

In summary, whether Paul compared himself positively to Judean "brothers" and "kinsmen," or defended himself against Judean opponents, he could cite his impeccable ethnic heritage, which included what Fredrik Barth called "basic value orientations" and "overt signals and signs." He saw himself as a circumcised "Israelite," a descendant of Abraham, a member of the tribe of Benjamin, a Hebrew, and a Pharisee, with the advantages that accrue to all Israelites: sonship, glory, covenants, the law, worship, the promises, and the patriarchs. He often used family and ethnic language. Yet, he claimed that his impeccable ethnic qualifications were mere σκύβαλα; that the significance of Abraham was his faith-based righteousness prior to circumcision; that Gentile Christ believers were also the true "children of Abraham" and adopted "children of God" and should live in unity and harmony with Judean Christ believers. The family/kinship language in this instance was *fictive*, thus pointing to *fictive* ethnicity.[129] Most importantly, he rejected as necessary for Gentiles the key ethnic boundary markers that privileged ethnic Israel enjoyed as the chosen, covenant people. His "basic value orientation" meant transcending traditional ethnic status and the outward signs of it, particularly circumcision, purity at table fellowship, and calendrical ritual, while at the same time his letters are full of "ethnic reasoning."[130] I have written elsewhere,

> Paul believed that he had entered another ἔθνος, which had its own boundaries, its own values, and its own symbols . . . It was a different sort of ἔθνος. This was the true γένος ["people"/"ancestry"] from Abraham, a σῶμα ("body") of the new life of Christ, [with] a more inclusive language and culture, the norms of a different kind of γνῶσις ["knowledge"], the

127. The identification "Hebrew" is found in grave and synagogue inscriptions at Rome and elsewhere; Schürer, Vermes, and Millar, *History*, 3:83, 29.

128. BAGD, 759; Watson, *Paul*, 78: "What Paul renounces according to Phil. 3.7ff is his whole covenant-status as a Jew . . ."; also Räisänen, "Paul's Conversion," 410.

129. Bartchy, footnote 5 above. Fictive kin language also characterized social relations in synagogues and "voluntary associations"; see Duling, *Marginal Scribe*, chs. 7, 8; Harland, *Dynamics*, chs. 3, 4.

130. Buell, *Why This New Race?*

model of suffering slavery, and the rite of baptism. This was a new family. While the boundaries were still somewhat fluid—the goal had not been attained—they were sharp enough to know who was in and out.[131]

Yet, this description does not yet fully address Paul's inconsistencies. I turn to a second social-scientific theory, Marginality Theory.

Cultural Marginality

As noted previously, John Gager accepts the view that Paul is inconsistent. He also lists four ways that scholars have used to interpret Paul's inconsistencies:[132] subordination of one set of passages to another; additions by ecclesiastical redactors;[133] psychology (powerful personal factors made it impossible for Paul to fully disengage from his past);[134] and abandonment of any resolution.[135] I have accepted the last option and have elaborated its ethnicity dimension. Now I turn to a version of Gager's third option: psychology, but—this is critical—social psychology, specifically the concept of "cultural marginality."[136]

At least four distinct kinds of marginality are found in the social-scientific literature.[137] "*Ideological* marginality" can refer to voluntary, alternative, mainly "anti-structure" life-style groups.[138] Sociologist Janet Mancini

---

131. Duling, "'Whatever Gain I Had' . . . ," 240.

132. Gager, *Reinventing*, 7–10.

133. O'Neill, *Recovery*; Walker, *Interpolations*, supports some of O'Neill's interpolations, e.g., Rom 1:29–2:29, which, he argues, is not only non-Pauline, but anti-Pauline.

134. Hamerton-Kelly, *Sacred Violence*, 11–12, citing Paul's anguish for his ethnic brothers in Rom 9:1–5; also Räisänen, *Paul*, 82–83; 232–33, who casts doubt on Stendahl's view of Paul's "robust conscience" because Paul's "personal experience of liberation" as it related to ecstatic experiences implies something of his own struggles.

135. Sanders, *Law*, 198: "conflicting convictions . . . better left asserted than explained."

136. Duling, *Marginal Scribe*, especially chs. 5, 9. The social psychological approach has been influenced by Malina, "Normative Dissonance"; see further the notions of the "coexistence of contradictions" and the "contextual nature of values and behavior" in Sinha and Tripathi, "Individualism"; for a critique in relation to Paul, Bertone, *The Law of the Spirit*, 21–33.

137. Ibid., 251–59. Billson, "No Owner of Soil," describes and categorizes these three involuntary ethnicity types for an anniversary of the "Marginal Man" theory.

138. Turner, *Ritual Process*, 94–95. This option, an extension of Turner's view of "liminal" marginality, or *communitas*, in rites of passage could inform Paul's quasi-structured communities (see Duling, *Marginal Scribe*, 64–65), but it better fits the anti-structure of Johannine communities; see Malina and Rohrbaugh, *Social-Science*

Billson describes three other kinds, all involuntary. "*Structural* marginality" refers to those at the margins of society who correspond roughly (although not exclusively) to the bottom strata of the social ladder.[139] "*Social role* marginality" is "the product of failure to belong to a [desired] positive reference group,"[140] for example, women or minorities hindered in their desire to enter professions previously not available to them. The most relevant kind of marginality for interpreting Paul's inconsistency, however, is the fourth kind (Billson's third), "*cultural* marginality." This is Billson's gender inclusive language for the social psychological concept "Marginal Man" developed by Robert Park in the late 1920s to describe immigrants to the United States.[141] The "Marginal Man" is reputedly "caught" between the "old world" and the "new world," thus "condemned" to live between two competing cultures without completely belonging to either. For Park, such a person experiences "acceptance or rejection, belonging or isolation, in-group or out-group" tensions, "ambiguities of status and role," and "isolation, identity confusion, and alienation." In a later study Park extended his concept to "races" that never fully assimilate.[142] Everett V. Stonequist enlarged Park's concept by defining the "Marginal Man" as "unwittingly initiated into two *or more* historic traditions, languages, political loyalties, moral codes, or religions, one of which is more dominant."[143] Cultural marginals are thus *perpetually* "*in-between.*" Although negative psychological views of the early concept have been criticized as academic ethnocentrism,[144] the "in-between" experience of ambiguity is not denied. Also, some negative psychological effects are still taken into consideration in comparable ethnological descriptions of

---

Commentary on the Gospel of John.

139. Germani, *Marginality*, 49–54, incorporates Billson's "social role marginality" (following note). For the overlap of center-periphery and hierarchical models, see Duling, *Marginal Scribe*, 249–50; for stratified social conditions related to recent archaeological study of spaces where poor, urban dwellers in Paul's churches might have lived, see Duling, "Strength."

140. Billson, "No Owner of Soil," 184, draws on "reference group theory." It might offer some insight on upward social mobility in Paul's new *ethnos* communities. Germani, *Marginality*, incorporates "social role marginality" within "structural marginality."

141. Park, "Human Migration"; "Personality"; Antonovsky, "Refinement," 56; Schermerhorn, "Marginal Man."

142. Park, *Race and Culture*. See further, below.

143. Stonequist, *Marginal Man*, 3.

144. Lee, *Marginality*, 48, 58, 62–63 admits that cultural marginality may have psychologically damaging results, but rejects negative "maladjustment" interpretations (e.g., "identity confusion," "cultural schizophrenia"), arguing that marginal persons are "liberated" and "truly free." Billson, "No Owner Soil," 190 n. 4 also rejects negative psychology.

indigenous peoples who are caught between their native culture and "white" culture, who are said to experience "ethnostress."¹⁴⁵ I illustrate cultural marginality with a Venn diagram.

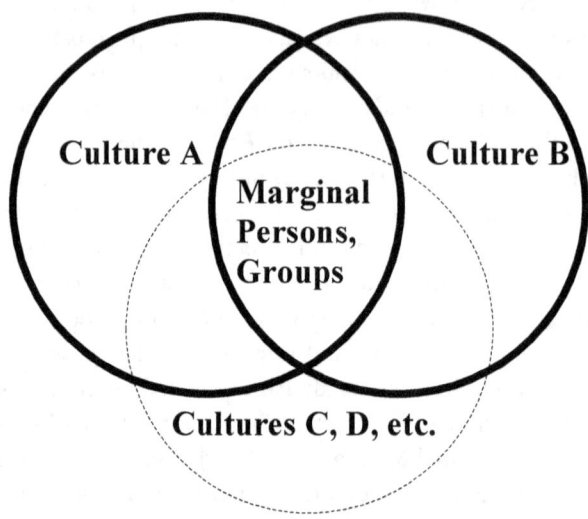

*A Venn Diagram of Culturally Marginal Persons and Groups*¹⁴⁶

Robert E. Park also developed a "race relations cycle" (pre-"ethnicity" language) in which immigrants potentially pass through four possible stages—contact, conflict, accommodation, and assimilation.¹⁴⁷ Again, Park's "Marginal Man" does not reach the last, or assimilation, stage.¹⁴⁸ His social psychological theory has a correspondence with the theories of cross-cultural psychologist John W. Berry and Assimilation Theorist Adam Weisberger.¹⁴⁹ Both are instructive interpretations of "in-betweenness" in cultural marginality.

---

145. Hill, "Ethnostress." See Wallace, *Tuscarora*, ch. 5. A concrete example is forced enculturation in boarding schools. Ethnostress ". . . can be traced to a loss of faith and belief in one's self and in one's culture" (Hill, quoted by Wallace, 108).

146. Duling, *Marginal Scribe*, 254.

147. Park, "Personality." Park's "race relations cycle" has been too simplistically dubbed "straight line assimilation"; clearly he thought that "Marginal Man" was not fully assimilated.

148. For the generational generation, "what the son wishes to forget the grandson wishes to remember" (Marcus Hanson); see Malina, *Timothy*, 23–24.

149. Alba and Nee, "Rethinking Assimilation Theory," especially 863–65.

Berry, who studies psychological, sociocultural, and economic adaptations of immigrants, refugees, and indigenous peoples to dominant or "host" societies, has proposed four degrees of "acculturation" (his umbrella concept): "integration" and "separation" are collective; "assimilation" is individual; and "marginalization" can be either individual or collective. These four degrees of acculturation can be set within a five stage, temporal sequence, an advance on Park's "race relations cycle."[150]

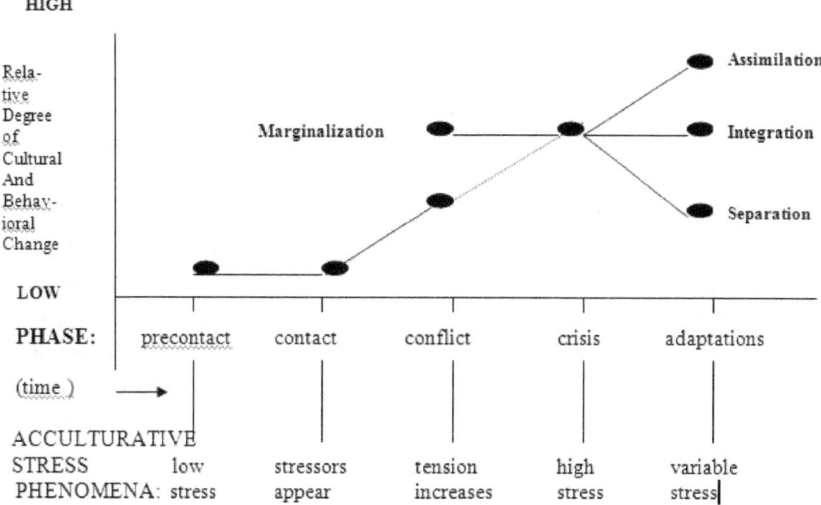

Degree of Cultural and Psychological Change as a Function of Phases and Varieties of Acculturation (John Berry)

Berry's main point is that cultural marginals ("Marginalization") do not place high value on strong ties with other groups in the "larger society," but they are nonetheless willing to abandon *to some degree* their native cultural identity in order not to be totally separate or segregated. In short, cultural marginals remain stranded "in-between" initial precontact/contact and crisis/final adaptation stages, thus in a continual state of conflict and increased tension, of "acculturative stress."

Weisberger attempts to update Park's "Marginal Man" concept with a theory about *doubly* ambivalent cultural marginalization:

---

150. See Berry, "Psychology of Acculturation," 201; Berry's view is discussed in Duling, *Marginal Scribe*, 255–57. See also Boyarin, *Radical Jew*; Roetzel, "*Ioudaioi* and Paul."

> The marginal person is not only unable to sever ties with his or her own culture and to merge into the new one, *but also is unable to return to the native culture or shrug off the influence of the new one*. Park understands the former relationship, but misses the latter. His image of being betwixt and between is unidirectional, whereas the marginal person is caught in a cross-current, located within a *structure of double ambivalence*. This person is ambivalent toward his or her own culture, wants to return but cannot, wants to leave but cannot do that either; and is ambivalent toward the new culture, wants to assimilate but cannot, and wants to reject it but cannot.[151]

John J. Collins has allowed for the possibility that some Judeans became assimilated into Gentile culture, including the possibility that they abandoned the necessity of circumcising their male children.[152] Paul, a cultural marginal, certainly did not require circumcision for Gentile believers, but indications of his "in-betweenness" suggests that he allowed it to remain intact for Judean believers. Barclay, in his study "Neither Jew nor Greek," without discussing Cultural Marginality or Acculturation Theory, distinguished between "acculturation" and "assimilation," and suggested that in the Mediterranean world the former might have meant the "adoption of Hellenistic speech, literary forms, values and philosophies," while the latter might have referred to "social integration into Hellenistic society."[153] In Barclay's view, Paul could have been acculturated without being fully assimilated.

All this points to the social-scientific theory that Paul was a culturally marginal figure, indeed perhaps a "doubly cultural marginal" figure, a Diaspora Judean who stood on the boundary between ethnic Judeans and Gentiles, thus one who was "in-between." From this perspective, it is not surprising that Paul's letters contain unresolved ambiguities and inconsistencies, or that Pauline studies are loaded with attempts to explain, resolve, or apologize for his inconsistencies, and that two major theological orientations to Paul based on contrasting passages have appeared.

One might conclude this study at this point, but it seems to me important to add a social-scientific comment about the historical implications of Paul's cultural marginality.

---

151. Weisberger, "Marginality," 429.

152. Collins, *Between Athens and Jerusalem*.

153. Barclay, "Neither Jew nor Greek," 209; for virtual assimilation of Judeans into Gentile culture, see Collins, "Between Athens and Jerusalem."

Structuration Theory and the "Parting of the Ways"

Paul wrote "occasional letters" to local congregations in his network. Although he undoubtedly had a reputation in his churches, there was no modern mass communication that could have allowed recipients of letters to make instantaneous comparisons with what he said orally in a different setting or in other letters at the time that he wrote them. He could scarcely have imagined that his letters would be gathered in a collection, carefully arranged, incorporated into a Christian canon, and microscopically examined to find a systematic center. To reiterate, one might expect that a Judean Christ believer who stood on the boundary between Judeans and Greeks, who was "caught" between the promises to Israel and his gospel of Gentile inclusion, between his own impeccable ethnicity and his inclusive non-ethnic ethnos ideology, would not be always totally consistent, or that total consistency on his part was even culturally necessary.[154] His cultural marginality led him to make accommodations from situation to situation, from context to context. This had consequences that he did not foresee.

David G. Horrell has explored unforeseen consequences by calling attention to Anthony Giddens's Structuration Theory, which states that there is a dialectical relationship between social structures that limit possibilities for individual agents on the one hand and individual agents who contribute to altering social structures on the other. This duality points to "the essentially recursive character of social life: the structural properties of social systems are both medium and outcome of the practices that constitute those systems."[155] Giddens's (and Horrell's) analogy for this duality is language, that is, speaking is limited by the structure ("rules and resources") of a language system (*the medium*), but speaking the language also contributes to changing its structure over time (*the outcome*). A crucial point is that agents who have influence also have greater power to shape signification and in the process develop an ideology of domination and legitimation. It is important here to see that, as Horrell, following Giddens, says, "*human agents do not always, or even generally, understand fully the conditions upon which their action is based; nor do they intend, or foresee, all of its consequences.*"[156] Horrell applies Structuration Theory to the unintended consequences of Paul's ambiguities, namely, Paul's challenge to structural domination and legitimation included occasional accommodations that allowed his follow-

---

154. For New Testament applications of "sociological ambivalence" theories (Robert Merton *et al*) and related concepts, see Malina, "Normative Dissonance and Christian Origins."

155. Giddens, *Profiles*, 36–37; Horrell, *Social Ethos*, 47; "Development," 224.

156. Horrell, *Social Ethos*, 52; "Development," 226 (italics mine).

ers an understanding of his letters that contributed to the resurgence of domination and legitimation. As is well known, this understanding appears in the deutero-Pauline literature. "Neither slave nor free" and "no male and female" in Gal 3:28 was transformed into a structure of domination and legitimation of masters over slaves and males over females in the Household Codes. Thus, Paul was not able to overcome a domination and legitimation structure that was considered to be the very foundation of domestic and political stability in the ancient Mediterranean world. I would add that in the wake of his situational accommodations and inconsistencies about Judeans and Gentiles, neither was his Judean/Gentile ideology in Gal 3:28 ultimately able to overcome the traditional boundary markers that Paul as agent sought to counter. If so, Paul's cultural marginality was a contributing factor in the "parting of the ways" between Judeans and Christ believers, thus Jews and Christians.[157]

Conclusion

Boyarin makes a telling point about Paul's "diasporized identity" that I call "the Boyarin paradox":

> What will appear from the Christian perspective as tolerance, namely Paul's willingness—indeed insistence—that within the Christian community all cultural practice is equally to be tolerated, from the rabbinic Jewish perspective is simply an eradication of the entire value system which insists that our cultural practice is our task and a calling in the world and must not be abandoned or reduced to a matter of taste.[158]

Cromhout expressed "the Boyarin's paradox" this way: "Paul's 'tolerance' of cultural difference actually turns out to be intolerant of those for whom the practices of their cultural traditions are at the very core of their identity."[159]

To this paradox another should be added: Paul's "in-between" location as a cultural marginal, which involved him in statements about the law and Judeans that were situational and accommodating, was not always fully consistent with his ideal of "neither Judean nor Gentile," which meant "the end of the law." An Instrumentalist might conjecture that Paul was very aware of, and even used to his advantage, his cultural marginality when he said that he became as one under the law to those under the law and one outside the

---

157. Dunn, *Jews and Christians*; Wilson, *Related Strangers*.
158. Boyarin, *Radical Jew*, 32; cf. Barclay, "Neither Jew nor Greek," 208.
159. Cromhout, *Walking*, 105.

law to those outside the law "for the sake of the gospel." A less critical view of Paul's character is that he was well aware that he was a Judean living in a larger Gentile world—after all, he was a the "apostle to the Gentiles"—and wrestled with the ambiguity. It is more likely that his inconsistencies in general, which had included his specific statements about his mission strategy, were part of his culturally marginal "in-betweenness." These inconsistencies were also related to his use of familial and ethnic discourse which had the potential to subtly work against his fictive "multi-ethnic" family ideology. Such inconsistencies had unintended consequences. In the post-Pauline churches they could have been interpreted in such a way that they lent support to the developing structure of institutional power and the domination of masters over slaves, males over females, and one should therefore add, Gentiles over Judeans—thus contributing to the "parting of the ways."

Works Cited

Alba, Richard, and Victor Nee. "Rethinking Assimilation Theory for a New Era of Immigration." *International Migration Review* 31 (1997) 826–74.

Anderson, Benedict. *Imagined Communities: Reflections on the Origin and Spread of Nationalism*. Rev. ed. New York: Verso, 2006.

Antonovsky, Aaron. "Toward a Refinement of the 'Marginal Man' Concept." *Social Forces* 35 (1956) 57–62.

Armstrong, John. *Nations before Nationalism*. Chapel Hill: University of North Carolina Press, 1982.

Back, Les. *New Ethnicities and Urban Culture: Racisms and Multiculture in Young Lives*. Race and Representation 2. London: UCL Press, 1996.

Banton, Michael. "Max Weber on 'Ethnic Communities': a Critique." *Nations and Nationalism* 13 (2007) 19–35.

Barclay, John M. G. "'Neither Jew nor Greek': Multiculturalism and the New Perspective on Paul." In *Ethnicity and the Bible*, edited by Mark G. Brett, 197–214. BibIntSer 19. Leiden: Brill, 1996. Paperback reprint, Boston: Brill Academic, 2002.

Bartchy, Scott S. "The Domestication of a Radical Jew." In *Maven in Blue Jeans: A Festschrift in Honor of Zev Garber*, edited by Steven Leonard Jacobs, 7–16. Shofar Supplements in Jewish Studies. West Lafayette, IN: Purdue University Press, 2009.

———. "Undermining Ancient Patriarchy: The Apostle Paul's Vision of a Society of Siblings." *BTB* 29 (1999) 68–78.

———. "Who Should Be Called Father? Paul of Tarsus between the Jesus Tradition and *Patria Potestas*." *BTB* 33 (2003) 135–47.

Barth, Fredrik. "Enduring and Emerging Issues in the Analysis of Ethnicity." In *The Anthropology of Ethnicity: Beyond "Ethnic Groups and Boundaries*, edited by Hans Vermeulen and Cora Govers, 11–32. Amsterdam: Het Spinhuis, 1994.

———. "Introduction." In *Ethnic Groups and Boundaries: The Social Organization of Cultural Difference*, edited by Hans Vermeulen and Cora Govers, 9–38. 1969. Reprinted, Long Grove, IL: Waveland, 1998.

Bayer, Murat. "Reconsidering Primordialism: An Alternative Approach to the Study of Ethnicity." *ERS* 32 (2009) 1–20.

Beggars All. "Luther Added the Word 'Alone' to Romans 3:28?" http://beggarsall-reformation.blogspot.com/2006/02/luther-added-word-alone-to-romans-328.html.

Berry, John W. "Psychology of Acculturation." In *Nebraska Symposium on Motivation, 1989*, Volume 37: *Cross Cultural Perspectives*, edited by John J. Berman, 201–34. Lincoln: University of Nebraska Press, 1990.

Bertone, John Anthony. *The Law of the Spirit: Experience of the Spirit and Displacement of the Law in Romans 8:1–16*. Studies in Biblical Literature 86. New York: Lang, 2005.

Betz, Hans Dieter. *Galatians: A Commentary on Paul's Letter to the Churches in Galatia*. Hermeneia. Philadelphia: Fortress, 1979.

Billson, Janet Mancini. "No Owner of Soil: The Concept of Marginality Revisited on its Sixtieth Birthday." *International Review of Modern Sociology* 18 (1988) 183–204.

Bornkamm, Günther. "The Missionary Stance of Paul in 1 Corinthians 9 and in Acts." In *Studies in Luke-Acts: Essays Presented in Honor of Paul Schubert*, edited by Leander E. Keck and J. Louis Martyn, 194–207. Nashville: Abingdon, 1966.

Boyarin, Daniel. *A Radical Jew: Paul and the Politics of Identity*. Berkeley: University of California Press, 1997. Online: http://ark.cdlib.org/ark:/13030/ft7w10086w.

Brett, Mark G., ed. *Ethnicity and the Bible*. BibIntSer 19. Leiden: Brill, 1996. Paperback reprint, Boston: Brill Academic, 2002.

———. "Interpreting Ethnicity: Method, Hermeneutics, Ethics." In *Ethnicity and the Bible*, edited by Mark G. Brett, 3–22. BibIntSer 19. Leiden: Brill, 1996.

Brown, Raymond E., and John P. Meier. *Antioch and Rome: New Testament Cradles of Catholic Christianity*. New York: Paulist, 1983.

Buell, Denise Kimber. "Ethnicity and Religion in Mediterranean Antiquity and Beyond." *Recherches de science religieuse* 26 (2000) 243–49.

———. "The Politics of Interpretation: The Rhetoric of Race and Ethnicity in Paul." *JBL* 12 (2004) 235–52.

———. *Why This New Race? Ethnic Reasoning in Early Christianity*. New York: Columbia University Press, 2005.

Buell, Denise Kimber, and Caroline Johnson Hodge. "The Politics of Interpretation: The Rhetoric of Race and Ethnicity in Paul." *JBL* 123 (2004) 235–51.

Bulmer, Martin. "Race and Ethnicity." In *Key Variables in Social Investigation*, edited by R. G. Burgess, 54–75. New York: Routledge, 1986.

Bultmann, Rudolf. *Theology of the New Testament*. Translated by Kendrick Grobel. New York: Scribner, 1951–55. Republished with a New Introduction by Robert Morgan. Waco: Baylor University Press, 2007.

Calvin, John. *Institutes of the Christian Religion*. Translated by Henry Beveridge. 1845–46. Reprinted, Grand Rapids: Eerdmans, 1989.

Carson, Donald A. "Pauline Inconsistency: Reflections on 1 Corinthians 9.19–23 and Galatians 2.11–14." *Churchman* 100 (1986) 6–45.

Cohen, Ronald. "Ethnicity: Problem and Focus in Anthropology." *Annual Review of Anthropology* 7 (1978) 379–403.

Collins, John J. *Between Athens and Jerusalem: Jewish Identity in the Hellenistic Diaspora*. New York: Crossroad, 1986.

Cromhout, Markus. *Jesus and Identity: Reconstructing Judean Ethnicity in Q*. Matrix: The Bible in Mediterranean Context 3. Eugene, OR: Cascade Books, 2007.

———. *Walking in Their Sandals: A Guide to First-Century Israelite Ethnic Identity*. Eugene, OR: Cascade Books, 2010.

Duling, Dennis C. "2 Corinthians 11:22: Historical Context, Rhetoric, and Ethnic Identity." In *The New Testament and Early Christian Literature in Greco-Roman Context: Studies in Honor of David E. Aune*, edited by John Fotopoulos, 65–91. NovTSup 122. Leiden: Brill, 2006. Reprinted in *Hervormde Theological Studies* 64 (2008) 819–43. Online, http://www.hts.org.za/index.php/HTS/article/view/57/54.

———. "Ethnicity and Paul's Letter to the Romans." In *Understanding the Social World of the New Testament*, edited by Dietmar Neufeld and Richard E. DeMaris, 68–89. New York: Routledge, 2010.

———. "Ethnicity, Ethnocentrism, and the Matthean *Ethnos*." *BTB* 35 (2005) 125–43. Revised in Duling, *A Marginal Scribe*, 288–328. http://academic.shu.edu/btb/vol35/4/04%20Duling.pdf.

———. *A Marginal Scribe: Studies in the Gospel of Matthew in a Social-Scientific Perspective*. Matrix: The Bible in Mediterranean Context 7. Eugene, OR: Cascade, 2012.

———. "Paul's Aegean Network: The Strength of Strong Ties." *BTB* 43 (2013) 135–154.

———. "Small Groups: Social Science Research Applied to Second Testament Study." *BTB* 25 (1995) 179–93.

———. "'Whatever Gain I Had . . .': Ethnicity and Paul's Self-Identification in Philippians 3:3–5." In *Fabrics of Discourse: Essays in Honor of Vernon K. Robbins*, edited by David B. Gowler, L. Gregory Bloomquist, and Duane F. Watson, 222–41. Harrisburg, PA: Trinity, 2003. Reprinted in *Hervormde Theological Studies* 64 (2008) 799–818. Online, http://www.ajol.info/index.php/hts/article/view/41305.

Dunn, James D. G. *Jesus, Paul, and the Law: Studies in Mark and Galatians*. London: SPCK, 1990.

———. *Jews and Christians: The Parting of the Ways A.D. 70 to 135*. Grand Rapids: Eerdmans, 1999.

———. "The New Perspective on Paul." *Bulletin of the John Rylands Library* 65 (1983) 95–122. Reprinted in Dunn, *Jesus, Paul, and the Law: Studies in Mark and Galatians*, 183–214. London: SPCK, 1990; Dunn, *The New Perspective on Paul*, 99–120. Rev. ed. Grand Rapids: Eerdmans, 2005.

———. *Romans*. 2 vols. WBC 38A, 38B. Dallas: Word, 1988.

———. "Works of the Law and the Curse of the Law (Galatians 3.10–14)." *NTS* 31 (1985) 523–42. Reprinted in *The New Perspective on Paul*, 121–40. Rev. ed. Grand Rapids: Eerdmans, 2005.

Dunn, James D. G., and N. T. Wright. "An Evening Conversation on Paul with James D. G. Dunn and N. T. Wright." http://www.thepaulpage.com/Conversation.html.

Elliott, John H. "Jesus the Israelite Was Neither a 'Jew' nor a 'Christian': On Correcting Misleading Nomenclature." *JSHJ* 5 (2007) 119–55.

Esler, Philip F. "Ancient Oleiculture and Ethnic Differentiation: The Meaning of the Olive-Tree Image in Romans 11." *JSNT* 26 (2003) 103–124.

———. *Conflict and Identity in Romans: The Social Setting of Paul's Letter*. Minneapolis: Fortress, 2003.

———. *Galatians*. New Testament Readings. New York: Routledge, 1998.

———. "Group Boundaries and Intergroup Conflict in Galatians: A New Reading of Galatians 5:13—6:10." In *Ethnicity and the Bible*, edited by Mark G. Brett, 215–40. BibIntSer 19. Leiden: Brill, 1996. Paperback reprint Brill Academic, 2002.

———. "Paul's Contestation of Israel's (Ethnic) Memory of Abraham in Galatians 3." *BTB* 36 (2006) 23–34.

Ferguson, Everett. *Baptism in the Early Church: History, Theology, and Liturgy in the First Five Centuries*. Grand Rapids: Eerdmans, 2009.

Fitzgerald, John T. *Cracks in the Earthen Vessel: An Examination of the Catalogues of Hardships in the Corinthian Correspondence*. SBLDS 99. Atlanta: Scholars, 1988.

Forbes, Christopher. "Comparison, Self-Praise, and Irony: Paul's Boasting and the Conventions of Hellenistic Rhetoric." *NTS* 32 (1986) 1–30.

Gager, John. *Reinventing Paul*. New York: Oxford University Press, 2000.

Gans, Herbert J. "Symbolic Ethnicity: The Future of Ethnic Groups and Cultures in America." *ERS* 2 (1979) 1–20. http://dx.doi.org/10.1080/01419870.1979.9993248

———. "Symbolic Ethnicity and Symbolic Religiosity: Towards a Comparison of Ethnic and Religious Acculturation." *ERS* 17 (1994) 577–92.

Garroway, Joshua D. *Paul's Gentile-Jews: Neither Jew nor Gentile, but Both*. New York: Palgrave MacMillan, 2012.

Geertz, Clifford. "The Integrative Revolution. Primordial Sentiments and Civil Politics in the New States." In *Old Societies and New States*, edited by Clifford Geertz, 105–57. New York: Free Press, 1963. Reprinted in Geertz, *The Interpretation of Cultures: Selected Essays*, 255–310. New York: Basic Books, 1973.

———. "Thick Description: Toward an Interpretative Theory of Culture." In Geertz, *The Interpretation of Cultures: Selected Essays*, 3–30. New York: Basic Books, 1973.

Germani, Gino. *Marginality*. New Brunswick, NJ: Transaction, 1980.

Giddens, Anthony. *Profiles and Critiques in Social Theory*. Berkeley: University of California Press, 1982.

Gould, Stephen J., Richard Lewontin, Elizabeth Allen, et al. "Against Sociobiology." *New York Review of Books* 22 (November 13, 1975). Online, http://libcom.org/library/against-sociobiology.

Hagner, Donald A. "Paul and Judaism. The Jewish Matrix of Early Christianity: Issues in the Current Debate." *Bulletin for Biblical Research* 3 (1993) 111–30.

Hamerton-Kelly, Robert. *Sacred Violence: Paul's Hermeneutic of the Cross*. Minneapolis: Fortress, 1992.

Hansen, Bruce. *All of You Are One: The Social Vision of Galatians 3.28, 1 Corinthians 12.13 and Colossians 3.11*. LNTS 409. London: T. & T. Clark, 2010.

Hanson, K. C., and Douglas E. Oakman. *Palestine in the Time of Jesus: Social Structures and Social Conflicts*. 2nd ed. Minneapolis: Fortress, 2008.

Harland, Philip A. *Dynamics of Identity in the World of Early Christians: Associations, Judeans, and Cultural Minorities*. New York: T. & T. Clark, 2009.

Headland, Thomas N., Kenneth L. Pike, and Marvin Harris. *Emics and Etics: The Insider/Outsider Debate*. Frontiers in Anthropology 7. New York: Sage, 1990.

Hill, Diane. "Ethnostress: The Disruption of the Aboriginal Spirit." Tribal Sovereignty Associates (August, 1992). Online, http://www.oninjuryresources.ca/downloads/SLS/2007/SLS-2007F-Ethnostress-handout.pdf

Homans, George C. *The Human Group*. 1950. Reprint with Introductions by A. Paul Hare and R. B. Polley. New Brunswick, NJ: Transaction, 1992.

Horowitz, Donald L. *Ethnic Groups in Conflict*. Berkeley: University of California Press, 1985. Republished with a New Preface, 2000.

Horrell, David G. "The Development of Theological Ideology in Pauline Christianity. A Structuration Theory Perspective." In *Modelling Early Christianity: Social-Scientific Studies of the New Testament in its Context*, edited by Philip F. Esler, 224–36. London: Routledge, 1995.

———. "'No Longer Jew or Greek': Paul's Corporate Christology and the Construction of Christian Community." In *Christology, Controversy, and Community: New Testament Essays in Honour of David R. Catchpole*, edited by David G. Horrell and Christopher M. Tuckett, 321–44. NovTSup 99. Leiden: Brill, 2000.

———. *The Social Ethos of the Corinthian Correspondence: Interest and Ideology from 1 Corinthians to 1 Clement*. Studies of the New Testament World. Edinburgh: T. & T. Clark, 1996.

Hutchinson, John, and Anthony D. Smith, eds. *Ethnicity*. Oxford Reader. Oxford: Oxford University Press, 1996.

Huxley, Julian, and A. C. Haddon, with Alexander Carr-Saunders and Charles Singer. *We Europeans. A Survey of "Racial" Problems, with a Chapter on Europe Overseas*. London: Cape, 1935.

Isajiw, Wsevolod W. "Definitions of Ethnicity." *Ethnicity* 1 (1974) 111–24.

Jenkins, Richard. "Ethnicity, Anthropological Aspects." In *International Encyclopedia of the Social and Behavioural Sciences*, edited by Nathan J. Smelser and P. B. Baltes, 4824–28. Oxford: Pergamon, 2001.

Jensen, Robin M. *Baptismal Imagery in Early Christianity: Ritual, Visual, and Theological Dimensions*. Grand Rapids: Baker Academic, 2012.

Hodge, Caroline Johnson. *"If Sons, Then Heirs": A Study of Kinship and Ethnicity in Paul's Letter to the Romans*. Oxford: Oxford University Press, 2007.

———. "Olive Trees and Ethnicities: Judeans and Gentiles in Romans 11:17–24." In *Christians as a Religious Minority in a Multicultural City: Modes of Interaction and Identity Formation in Early Imperial Rome*, edited by Jürgen Zangenburg and Michael Labahn, 77–89. JSNTSup 243. London: Continuum, 2008.

Lambrecht, Jan. "The Fool's Speech and Its Context: Paul's Particular Way of Arguing in 2 Cor 10–13." *Biblica* 82 (2001) 305–24.

Lee, Jung Young. *Marginality: The Key to Multicultural Theology*. Minneapolis: Fortress, 1995.

Liddell, Henry George, Robert Scott, Henry Stuart Jones, and Roderick McKenzie. *A Greek-English Lexicon*. 9th ed. Oxford: Oxford University Press, 1996. Online, http://www.perseus.tufts.edu/hopper/text?doc=Perseus%3Atext%3A1999.04.0057%3Aentry%3De)%2Fqnos.

Luther, Martin. "Disputation of Doctor Martin Luther on the Power and Efficacy of Indulgences (Ninety-Five Theses, 1517)." In Adolph Spaeth, *Works of Martin Luther*, edited by L. D. Reed et al., 1: 29–38. Philadelphia: Holman, 1915). Online, http://www.iclnet.org/pub/resources/text/wittenberg/luther/web/ninetyfive.html.

———. "Open Letter on Translating." http://www.gutenberg.org/cache/epub/272/pg272.html

McKay, James. "An Exploratory Synthesis of Primordial and Mobilizationist Approaches to Ethnic Phenomena." *ERS* 5 (1982) 395–420.

Malina, Bruce J. "Normative Dissonance and Christian Origins." In *Semeia* 35: *Social-Scientific Criticism of the New Testament*, edited by John H. Elliott, 35–39. Decatur, GA: Scholars, 1995.

———. *Timothy: Paul's Closest Associate. Paul's Social Network: Brothers and Sisters in Faith*. Collegeville, MN: Glazier/Liturgical, 2008.

Malina, Bruce J., and Richard L. Rohrbaugh. *Social-Science Commentary on the Gospel of John*. Minneapolis: Fortress, 1998.

Malkin, Irad, ed. *Ancient Perceptions of Greek Ethnicity*. Vol. 5. Cambridge: Harvard University Center for Hellenic Studies, 2001.

Meeks, Wayne A. *The First Urban Christians: The Social World of the Apostle Paul*. New Haven: Yale University Press, 1983.

Mommsen, Wolfgang J. "Max Weber's 'Grand Sociology': The Origins and Composition of *Wirtschaft und Gesellschaft Soziologie*." *History and Theory* 39 (2000) 364–83.

Moore, George Foote. "Christian Writers on Judaism." *HTR* 14 (1921) 199–215.

Nanos, Mark D. "Paul's Relationship to Torah in Light of His Strategy 'to Become Everything to Everyone' (1 Corinthians 9:19–22)." In *Paul and Judaism: Crosscurrents in Pauline Exegesis and the Study of Jewish-Christian Relations*, edited by Reimund Bieringer and Didier Pollefeyt, 106–40. LNTS 463. London: T. & T. Clark, 2012. Web version: http://www.marknanos.com/1cor9-leuven-9-4-09.pdf.

O'Neill, J. C. *The Recovery of Paul's Letter to the Galatians*. London: SPCK, 1972.

Park, Robert E. "Human Migration and the Marginal Man." *American Journal of Sociology* 33 (1928) 881–93.

———. "Personality and Cultural Conflict." *Publication of the American Sociological Society* 25 (1931) 95–110. Reprinted in *Park, Race and Culture*, edited by E. C. Hughes et al., 357–71. Glencoe, IL: Free Press, 1950.

———. *Race and Culture*. Glencoe, IL: Free Press, 1950.

Parsons, Talcott, Edward Shils, Kaspar D. Naegele, and Jesse R. Pitts, eds. *Theories of Society*. New York: Free Press, 1961.

Räisänen, Heikki. *Paul and the Law*. 2nd ed. Philadelphia: Fortress, 1987.

———. "Paul's Conversion and the Development of His View of the Law." *NTS* 33 (1987) 404–19.

Ratcliffe, Peter. "Ethnic Group." *Sociopedia.isa*, 2010. Online, http://www2.warwick.ac.uk/fac/soc/sociology/pg/current/programmes/ma/modules/quantitativemethods/home/week4a/ethnic_group_-_sociopedia.pdf

Richardson, Peter. "Pauline Inconsistency: 1 Corinthians 9:19–23 and Galatians 2:11–14." *NTS* 26 (1979–1980) 347–62.

Roetzel, Calvin J. "*Ioudaioi* and Paul." In *The New Testament and Early Christian Literature in Greco-Roman Context: Studies in Honor of David E. Aune*, edited by John Fotopoulos, 3–15. NovTSup 122. Leiden: Brill, 2006.

Sanders, E. P. "Did Paul's Theology Develop?" In *The Word Leaps the Gap: Essays on Scripture and Theology in Honor of Richard B. Hays*, edited by C. Ross Wagner, C. Kaven Rowe, and A. Katherine Grieb, 325–50. Grand Rapids: Eerdmans, 2008.

———. *Paul and Palestinian Judaism: A Comparison of Patterns of Religion*. Philadelphia: Fortress, 1977.

———. *Paul, the Law, and the Jewish People*. Minneapolis: Fortress, 1983.

Schermerhorn, Richard Alonzo. *Comparative Ethnic Relations: A Framework for Theory and Research*. New York: Random House, 1970.

———. "Marginal Man." *Dictionary of the Social Sciences*, 406-7. New York: Free Press, 1964.
Schürer, Emil, Geza Vermes, and Fergus Millar. *The History of the Jewish People in the Age of Jesus Christ (175 B.C.–A.D. 135)*. 3 vols. Edinburgh: T. & T. Clark, 1973.
Schweitzer, Albert. *The Mysticism of Paul the Apostle*. London: A. & C. Black, 1931.
Scott, George M., Jr. "A Resynthesis of the Primordial and Circumstantial Approaches to Ethnic Group Solidarity: Towards an Explanatory Model." *ERS* 13 (1990) 147-71.
Shils, Edward A. "Primordial, Personal, Sacred and Civil Ties." *British Journal of Sociology* 8 (1957) 130-145.
Sinha, Durganand and Rama Charan Tripathi. "Individualism in a Collectivist Culture: A Case of Coexistence of Opposites." In *Individualism and Collectivism: Theory, Method, Applications*, edited by Uichol Kim, Harry C. Triandis, Çiğdem Kâğitçibaşi, Sang-Chin Choi, and Gene Yoon, 123-136. Cross-Cultural Research and Methodology 18. Thousand Oaks, CA: Sage, 1994.
Smith, Anthony D. *The Ethnic Origins of Nations*. Malden, MA: Basil Blackwell, 1986.
———. "The Politics of Culture: Ethnicity and Nationalism." In *Companion Encyclopedia of Anthropology*, edited by Timothy Ingold, 706-33. London: Routledge, 1994.
Sollors, Werner. *Theories of Ethnicity: A Classical Reader*. Basingstoke, UK: Macmillan, 1996.
Sorokin, Pitirim. *Contemporary Sociological Theories*. New York: Harper, 1928. Online, http://www.google.com/url?sa=t&rct=j&q=&esrc=s&frm=1&sourc e=web&cd=2&ved=0CDUQFjAB&url=http%3A%2F%2Fwww.markfoster. net%2Fstruc%2Fcontemporary_sociological_theories.pdf&ei=OO9SUpjrLcWs4 AO1sIHYDw&usg=AFQjCNFg5ecEJJytG8e7F2qMBRti1qb3TQ.
Stanley, Christopher D. "'Neither Israelite nor Greek': Ethnic Conflict in Graeco-Roman Society [Gal 3:28]." *JSNT* 64 (1998) 101-24.
Stendahl, Krister. "The Apostle Paul and the Introspective Conscience of the West." *HTR* 56 (1963) 199-215. Reprinted in *Paul Among Jews and Gentiles*, 78-96.
———. *Paul among Jews and Gentiles*. Philadelphia: Fortress, 1976.
Stonequist, Everett V. *The Marginal Man*. New York: Scribner, 1937.
Stowers, Stanley. *A Rereading of Romans: Justice, Jews and Gentiles*. New Haven: Yale University Press, 1994.
Swan, James. "Luther Added the Word 'Alone' to Romans 3:28?" *Beggars All: Reformation Apologetics*. Online: http://beggarsallreformation.blogspot.com/2006/02/luther-added-word-alone-to-romans-328.html.
Swedberg, Richard. "Ethnic Groups (*ethnische Gruppen*)." In *The Max Weber Dictionary: Key Words and Central Concepts*, 91-92. Stanford: Stanford University Press, 2005.
Tajfel, Henri, ed. *Differentiation between Social Groups: Studies in the Social Psychology of Intergroup Relations*. London: Academic Press, 1978.
Theissen, Gerd. *Social Reality and the Early Christians: Theology, Ethics, and the World of the New Testament*. Translated by Margaret Kohl. Minneapolis: Fortress, 1992.
Thompson, Richard H. *Theories of Ethnicity. A Critical Appraisal*. Contributions in Sociology 82. Westport, CT: Greenwood, 1989,
Turner, Victor. *The Ritual Process: Structure and Anti-Structure*. Chicago: Aldine, 1969.
Van den Berghe, Pierre L. *The Ethnic Phenomenon*. New York: Praeger, 1987.

Varshney, Ashutosh. *Ethnic Conflict and Rational Choice: A Theoretical Engagement.* Cambridge: Harvard Center for International Affairs, 1995.
Verkuyten, Maykel. *The Social Psychology of Ethnic Identity.* New York: Routledge, 2005.
Walker, William O., Jr., *Interpolations in the Pauline Letters.* JSNTSup 213. Sheffield: Sheffield Academic, 2001.
Wallace, Anthony F. C. *Tuscarora: A History.* Tribal Worlds: Critical Studies in American Indian Nation Building. Albany: SUNY Press, 2012.
Warner, W. Lloyd, and Paul S. Lunt. *The Status System of a Modern Community.* Yankee City Series, Vol. 2. New Haven: Yale University Press, 1942. Excerpt from pp. 72–73 titled "Ethnicity" in Werner Sollors, ed. *Theories of Ethnicity: A Classical Reader,* 13–14. Basingstoke, UK: Macmillan, 1996.
Watson, Francis. *Paul, Judaism, and Gentiles: A Sociological Approach.* Society for New Testament Studies Monograph Series 56. Cambridge: Cambridge University Press, 1986.
Weber, Max. *Economy and Society: An Outline of Interpretive Sociology.* Edited by Günther Roth and Claus Wittich. New York: Bedminster, 1968. Reprinted, Berkeley: University of California Press, 1978.
———. "Ethnic Groups." In *Theories of Society,* edited by Talcott Parsons, Edward Shils, Kaspar D. Naegele, and Jesse R. Pitts, 1:305–309. New York: Free Press, 1961.
———. "Ethnic Groups." In *Max Weber, Economy and Society: An Outline of Interpretive Sociology,* edited by Günther Roth and Claus Wittich, 385–98. Berkeley: University of California Press, 1968.
———. "Ethnische Gemeinschaften." In Max Weber, *Wirtschaft und Gesellschaft: Grundriss der verstehenden Soziologie,* edited by Marianne Weber and Melchior Palyi. 1922. Edited also by Johannes Winckelmann, 5th ed. Tübingen: Mohr/Siebeck, 1973 (=WuG 5). Online: http://www.textlog.de/7748.html.
Welborn, Laurence L. "The Runaway Paul." *HTR* 92 (1999) 115–63.
Weisberger, Adam. "Marginality and Its Directions." *Social Forum* 7 (1992) 425–47.
Wilson, Edward O. *On Human Nature.* Cambridge: Harvard University Press, 1978.
———. "For Sociobiology." *New York Review of Books* 22 (December, 1975). Online, http://www.nybooks.com/articles/archives/1975/dec/11/for-sociobiology/?pagination=false
———. *Sociobiology: The New Synthesis.* 1975. Anniversary Reprint. Cambridge: Harvard University Press, 2000.
Wilson, Stephen G. *Related Strangers: Jews and Christians 70–170 C.E.* Minneapolis: Fortress, 1995.
Wright, N. T. "The Messiah and the People of God: A Study in Pauline Theology with Particular Reference to the Argument of the Epistle to the Romans." PhD diss., Oxford University, 1980.
———. "New Perspectives on Paul." Edinburgh Conference Lecture, 2003. Online, http://ntwrightpage.com/Wright_New_Perspectives.htm.
———. "Paul in Different Perspectives." Lecture at Auburn Avenue Presbyterian Church, Monroe, Louisiana, 2005. Online, http://ntwrightpage.com/Wright_Auburn_Paul.htm
———. *Paul: In Fresh Perspective.* Minneapolis: Fortress, 2005.
———. *What Paul Really Said.* Grand Rapids: Eerdmans, 1997.
Yang, Philip Q. *Ethnic Studies: Issues and Approaches.* Albany: SUNY Press, 2000.

4

Should Ἰουδαῖος Be Translated "Judean"?
The Challenge of 1 Thessalonians 2:14[1]

David Lertis Matson

ALTHOUGH I WAS NEVER a full-time student of Professor S. Scott Bartchy, the coursework that I took with him at UCLA and our continued dialogue and friendship over the years have shaped my life and scholarship in ways that he will probably never know. In addition to teaching me the importance of good writing (to this day I cannot split an infinitive!), he taught me to read carefully, think clearly, and advocate passionately. His enthusiasm for teaching and desire for understanding the Scriptures in their first-century historical and social context made quite an impression on me as a young biblical student. He continues to be a catalyst of many creative thoughts and ideas, including first challenging me to re-think the translation of Ἰουδαῖος in the New Testament, the topic of this paper. While Scott may or may not agree with my conclusions, I do hope that this essay reflects in some small way those things that he has taught me so well.

Translating the term Ἰουδαῖος as "Judean" has become increasingly commonplace in some quarters of the scholarly guild, particularly among social-scientific interpreters of the New Testament.[2] Their justification is

---

1. An earlier form of this paper was presented to the Society of Biblical Literature Pacific Coast Region, Santa Clara University, 2012.

2. This usage has dominant associations with the international team of biblical

essentially three-fold: 1) "Judean" reflects the nearly ubiquitous practice in antiquity of naming ethnic groups after their land of origin; 2) "Judean" is the most appropriate term to describe members of the house of Israel in the Second Temple period; 3) "Judean" distinguishes first-century members of the House of Israel from later Talmudic Judaism and thus precludes anti-Judaism (and European anti-Semitism) from creeping into interpretation. Commenting, for example, on "those who say that they are Jews [Ἰουδαίους] and are not" (Rev 2:9; 3:9), Bruce J. Malina and John J. Pilch write: "Both here and in all of the other New Testament instances where the term *Judeans* (in Greek Ἰουδαῖοι) appears, there is nothing of the modern connotation of 'Jew' or 'Jewishness' . . . Rather *Judean* meant 'a person belonging to a group called "Judeans,"' situated geographically and forming a territory taking its name from its inhabitants, 'Judea.'"[3]

Social-scientific interpreters are right to call attention to the territorial significance of Ἰουδαῖος in antiquity.[4] In the Hebrew Bible, יְהוּדִי (LXX Ἰουδαῖος) refers specifically to a member of the tribe of Judah living in the land or in exile.[5] Josephus likewise remarks that the name Ἰουδαῖοι derived from the tribe of Judah and, "as this tribe was the first to come to those parts, both the people themselves and the country have taken their name from it" (*Ant.* 11.173). For non-Israelite Greek writers, an Ἰουδαῖος was anyone with presumed origins in Judea; as early as 300 BCE, for example, Hecataeus of Abdera speaks of the Ἰουδαῖοι as a people who came out of Egypt and settled in Ἰουδαία (cited by Diodorus Siculus, *Bibliotheca Historica* 40.3), and Clearchus of Soli, a disciple of Aristotle cited by Josephus, quotes his

---

scholars known as the Context Group, of which Professor Bartchy is a member, and has become the editorial practice of the *Biblical Theology Bulletin*, a journal dedicated to social-scientific perspectives on the Bible. For a recent *apologia*, see Elliott, "Jesus the Israelite," 119–54, based on an earlier paper presented at the international meeting of the Context Group in Prague, Czech Republic, May 22, 1997. That a fair number of New Testament scholars still do not employ this terminology indicates that the matter is still a live issue, and a particularly controversial one in the case of a document like the Gospel of John.

3. Malina and Pilch, *Revelation*, 64, emphasis original. One convert to this linguistic practice is David Rhoads, who in his work on Mark uses the term *Judean* for "anyone in the ancient Mediterranean world who belonged ethnically to the people of Israel, whether inside or outside the land of Israel" (*Mark and Method*, 259–60 n. 1).

4. As social-scientific interpreters are fond of pointing out, Ἰουδαῖος means "of, or pertaining to, Judea" (e.g., Pilch, "No Jews or Christians in the Bible," 3). Etymologically, Ἰουδαῖος and Ἰουδαία are the same term, the latter being the singular feminine of the former. The feminine form of the word can even refer to a female member of the House of Israel, such as in Sus 22 (LXX; omitted by Theodotion).

5. The earliest geographical meaning of Ἰουδαῖοι appears at 4 Kgdms 16:6 where it signifies the people of Judea.

master as saying that "the district which they inhabit is known as Judea ['Ἰουδαία]" (*Ag. Ap.* 1.179).[6] Shaye J. D. Cohen summarizes that at least before the middle of the first century BCE, Ἰουδαῖος in secular Greek authors always denotes the ethnic inhabitants of Judea; only with the growth of the Jewish diaspora does the term begin to be used for Judeans living outside of the homeland.[7]

The arguments linking Ἰουδαῖος to territory are powerful and compelling, and receive an extended justification in Philip F. Esler, a more recent advocate of this view.[8] He considers the translation of Ἰουδαῖος as "Jew" not only intellectually indefensible but morally questionable: "To honor the memory of these first-century people it is necessary to call them by a name that accords with their own sense of identity. 'Jews' does not suit this purpose, both because it fails to communicate the territorial relationship they had with the land of Judea and its temple and because it inevitably imposes on them associations derived from the troubled, indeed, often terrible history of the Jews."[9]

Like King Agrippa in Protestant hymnology, I am "almost persuaded." My own hesitation in adopting such a position mirrors the original position of Esler, who considered the translation of "Judean" potentially misleading in English and feared "losing a distinctive way of referring to an inhabitant of the geographic region of Judea."[10] Yet in advocating "Judean" as the translation of choice in any and all cases, Esler and other social-scientific interpreters fail to appreciate a special case like 1 Thess 2:14-16, which arguably contains the earliest historical reference to the death of Jesus and one that expressly attributes responsibility for that death to the Ἰουδαῖοι. Here social-scientific interpreters are right to insist on translating Ἰουδαῖος as "Judean," yet by insisting on a uniform translational practice elsewhere they inevitably weaken the territorial force of the term precisely when it is needed most. The problem, to re-paraphrase Kierkegaard, is that when everyone is a Judean, no one is a Judean.

6. The term seems initially to have been used exclusively by outsiders (so Elliott, "Jesus the Israelite," 130–37) though over time appears to have become an Israelite self-designation as well (e.g., Acts 22:3; Rom 2:17; Gal 2:14–15; Rev 2:9; 3:9). Dunn's remarks are instructive in this regard (*Romans 1–8*, 109). Unless otherwise noted, all citations of classical authors come from the LCL.

7. Cohen, *Beginnings*, 94. See especially the evidence cited in his footnotes 76 (93) and 80 (94). The *Letter of Aristeas* uses the term for Judeans living throughout the world (11–12, 22–24, 35–36, 38, 308, 310).

8. Esler, *Conflict and Identity*, 62–74. See the beginnings of his shift in his earlier commentary on Galatians (*Galatians*, 3–4).

9. Esler, *Conflict and Identity*, 68.

10. Ibid., 67.

Lexical and Syntactical Considerations

This passage from Paul's earliest letter[11] has evoked no little consternation for interpreters sensitive to their post-Shoah situation, leading some to seek a solution in a possible interpolation.[12] Yet the need to appeal to such desperate measures would largely disappear if the geographical meaning of Ἰουδαῖος were correctly assessed. The text reads in the NRSV as follows:

> For you, brothers and sisters, became imitators of the churches of God in Christ Jesus that are in Judea [ἐν τῇ Ἰουδαίᾳ], for you suffered the same things from your own compatriots as they did from the Jews [ὑπὸ τῶν Ἰουδαίων], who killed both the Lord Jesus and the prophets and drove us out; they displease God and oppose everyone by hindering us from speaking to the Gentiles so that they may be saved. Thus they have constantly been filling up the measure of their sins; but God's wrath has overtaken them at last.[13]

Here the close juxtaposition of Ἰουδαία and Ἰουδαῖοι clearly identifies the latter as the inhabitants of the former: the churches of "Judea" suffered at the hands of the "Judeans."[14] Why Paul invokes the example of the churches of Judea or where he locates them exactly within Judea[15] is of

---

11. I am tentatively assuming a date in the mid-fifties for Galatians, another candidate for that distinction (but see footnote 31, where an early date for Galatians potentially figures into the argument in an important way). While I am becoming increasingly sympathetic to an early date for James (mid-to-late forties), the fact that James does not allude to the death of Jesus (5:6 is unlikely) makes the letter a moot point in this regard.

12. So Pearson, "1 Thessalonians 2:13–16," 79–94, followed by Boers, Beck, Keck, and others. Baur considered the passage thoroughly un-Pauline and based his estimate of 1 Thessalonians as inauthentic partly on this passage.

13. Unless otherwise indicated, all biblical quotations come from the New Revised Standard Version.

14 Lowe ("Who Were the Ἰουδαῖοι?" 104–5) suggests that one obvious way of recognizing a distinct geographical sense to οἱ Ἰουδαῖοι is to note when it occurs in close proximity with ἡ Ἰουδαία (e.g., Jos. Ant. 11.60–61; 13.24; 15.406; 18.2; 19.366; J.W. 2.184–85; 187; 1 Macc 10:33; John 7:1). Also noted by Elliott, "Jesus the Israelite," 141.

15. Ἰουδαία is capable of at least three meanings in the New Testament: 1) Judea proper, distinct from Samaria, Galilee, Perea, and Idumea (e.g., Matt 2:1; Mark 3:8; Acts 8:1; 9:31); 2) Palestine as a whole—the kingdom of Herod the Great (Luke 1:5; 23:5; Acts 10:37; cf. Strabo *Geogr.* 16.2.34; Ptolemy *Geography* 5.16.1); 3) the procurate of Pontius Pilate (Luke 3:1 [Matt 2:22]; cf. Tacitus *Ann.* 2.42—"Iudaea provincial"). Paul's own usage seems to limit the term to the immediate environs of Jerusalem (see Rom 15:31; 2 Cor 1:16; and Gal 1:22, where Judea is practically synonymous with Jerusalem), though some attempt to separate Jerusalem from Paul's Judean purview in Gal 1:22 to avoid a potential conflict with Acts 9:26–28 (e.g., Ridderbos, *Epistle of Paul to the Churches of Galatia*, 73 n. 5).

no present concern; what matters is the geographical delimitation of the term, restricting culpability for the death of Jesus to Judeans who participated in some way in his execution.[16] The localized meaning of συμφυλέτης ("compatriot"), referring to a fellow resident of one's city or city-district,[17] adds force to this territorial understanding of Ἰουδαῖος and underscores the geographical comparison between the churches of Thessalonica, who suffered at the hands of their fellow-citizens,[18] and the churches of Judea, who suffered at the hands of theirs. In both geographical contexts, as Jon A. Weatherly observes, only a portion of the population is in view: "Both the persecutors and those persecuted in Judea are 'Judeans,' just as both the recipients of the letter and their persecutors are συμφυλέται."[19]

The lexical meaning of Ἰουδαῖος in 1 Thess 2:14 as "Judean" receives further support from certain syntactical considerations. A question of critical exegetical importance rarely asked by commentators is whether the participial phrase τῶν ... ἀποκτεινάντων (following τῶν Ἰουδαίων), which comes into English as a relative clause, is restrictive or non-restrictive in meaning.[20] Until recently, nearly all major English translations (not to mention the critical Greek editions of Tischendorf, Westscott-Hort, UBS, and Nestle-Aland) have understood the clause as non-restrictive and punctuate it accordingly.[21] The result, when combined with the lexical meaning of Ἰουδαῖος as "Jew," creates a certain generalizing effect that can potentially

---

16. Weatherly, "Authenticity," 84–86, notes that an unqualified use of Ἰουδαῖοι often appears in Josephus to specify only a portion of Israel rather than the nation as a whole (e.g., *J.W.* 3.28,471; 5.109,251).

17. So Weatherly, "Authenticity," 85, n. 3. Frame, *Critical and Exegetical Commentary*, 110 suggests συμπολίτης as a near synonym; contra Malherbe, *Letters to the Thessalonians*, 168, who opts for an ethnic sense of the term (hence "Gentiles").

18. Were the persecutors of the Thessalonian believers Jews or Gentiles? The predominant gentile character of the church (1:9; 4:5) and the contrast to τῶν Ἰουδαίων at 2:14 suggest that they were Gentiles (so the TNIV, which translates συμφυλετῶν as "Gentiles" [changed to "countrymen" in the 2011 NIV]; nothing in the term συμφυλέτης itself, however, rules out a Jewish presence, especially if evidence from Acts is taken into account (Acts 17:5–9).

19. Weatherly, "Authenticity," 86.

20. I wish to acknowledge my indebtedness to Fee, *First and Second Letters to the Thessalonians*, 94–100, for first acquainting me with the exegetical issues and scholarly discussion. At various points in this section I augment and build upon his insights.

21. Comma: RSV, NRSV, REB, NASB, NAB (missing in 1970 edition), NET, NCV, ESV, NIV (1984), TNIV, GNB; NJB, NKJV; semi-colon: ASV; period: HCSB, CEB. According to Gilliard, "Antisemitic Comma," 482, Tyndale's use of a stop (in this case a slash) set the stage for the punctuation history in the English translation of this verse (citing L. A. Weigle). Gilliard also observes that a slash appears in manuscripts of the Wycliffe versions from about 1400 onward.

mislead readers of the Bible today into assuming that all Jews are to blame for the death of Jesus.[22] Particularly jolting is the paraphrase by J. B. Phillips in his *New Testament in Modern English* (rev. 1972), which goes beyond the "fatal comma" of most English translations and punctuates Paul's words with a full stop:

> For when you suffered at the hands of your fellow-countrymen you were sharing the experience of the Judean Christian churches, who suffered persecution by the Jews. It was the Jews who killed their own prophets, the Jews who killed the Lord Jesus, and the Jews who drove us out. They do not please God, and are in opposition to all mankind. They refused to let us speak to the gentiles to tell them the message by which they could be saved. All these years they have been adding to the full record of their sins and finally the wrath of God has fallen upon them.[23]

Yet Paul's use of participial constructions elsewhere, especially in 1 Thessalonians, calls the non-restrictive interpretation into serious question. Paul uses the articular attributive participle seventeen times in 1 Thessalonians, and in all but perhaps two of those usages the participial phrase is arguably restrictive,[24] including two in the immediate vicinity (ὑμῖν τοῖς πιστεύουσιν [2:13b]; τῶν ἐκκλησιῶν . . . τῶν οὐσῶν ἐν τῇ Ἰουδαίᾳ [2:14a]). Thus it would go against the immediate context as well as Paul's predominant grammatical practice elsewhere in 1 Thessalonians and in his non-disputed writings as a whole[25] if a restrictive meaning were not in place at 1 Thess 2:15.

---

22. That 1 Thess 2:14-16 did not figure prominently in historic Christian polemic against Jews (e.g., John Chrysostom) should not de-sensitize us to its potential hermeneutical effects on modern readers of the Bible.

23. Noted and cited by Gilliard, "Antisemitic Comma," 483. He points out that Phillips was preceded in the use of a full stop by the Coverdale Bible (1535; also Matthew's Bible [1537]) and the Geneva Bible (1560), which were then succeeded by a colon (Bishop's Bible [1602]), semicolon (English Revised Version [1881]), and, in the modern period, a comma. Two recent versions (CEB and HCSB) revert to the period.

24. See the Appendix for a helpful listing of adjectival participial constructions of the second or third attributive position in which the article precedes the participle after the substantive or pronoun that the participial construction is modifying. This type of construction typically comes into English as a relative clause. Fee, *First and Second Letters to the Thessalonians*, 95, n. 35, notes most of these occurrences to which I would add 2:13; 4:13; and 5:10. Contra Verhoef, "Bedeutung," 42-43, who fails to reckon with all of the pertinent textual data in 1 Thessalonians and seems unduly influenced by the German linguistic heritage in his analysis of Greek participial constructions. The only question marks in my mind are 4:5 (τὰ ἔθνη τὰ μὴ εἰδότα τὸν θεόν) and 4:13 (οἱ λοιποὶ οἱ μὴ ἔχοντες ἐλπίδα), both of which are arguably restrictive. Fee contradicts himself on his estimate of the latter (cf. 95, n. 35 and 168).

25. Fee notes that Paul's use of the participial construction in question "is rarely, if

Noteworthy in this regard is the 2011 New International Version's deletion of the comma at the end of verse 14 (a change from the TNIV and 1984 NIV), resulting in a restrictive clause modifying "the Jews." Such a decision is certainly an advance over other English translations, both historic and modern. Yet the translators of the 2011 NIV fail to perceive the lexical impact of their decision on Ἰουδαῖος, which the restrictive syntax now argues in favor of "Judean."[26] Thus I would propose to translate: "For you yourselves, brothers *and sisters*, became imitators of the churches of God that are in Judea in Christ Jesus, because you yourselves also suffered the same things by your own fellow citizens as also they did by the Judeans who killed both the Lord Jesus and the prophets . . ." Gordon D. Fee, one of the few commentators to see the essential connection, speculates "whether this comma could ever have happened if it were not for the (unfortunate) verse numbers that have been inserted into the text."[27]

Understanding 1 Thess 2:14–15 in restrictive terms allows us to limit more narrowly the objects of Paul's heated condemnation and, in contrast to Phillips, locate them squarely in the region of Judea:[28] 1) the Judeans "killed both the Lord Jesus and the prophets." Against the commonly held view that "prophets" in v. 15a is a reference to Old Testament prophets, the order of Paul's compound object (τὸν κύριον . . . Ἰησοῦν καὶ τοὺς προφήτας)[29] suggests that Paul has Christian prophets in mind,[30] some of

---

ever, nonrestrictive in Paul's letters" (*First and Second Thessalonians*, 95). After identifying sixty-eight attributive participles in the non-disputed writings of Paul, Gilliard "Antisemitic Comma," 492, remarks on its use in 1 Thess 2:15: "It would have been quite irregular, if not unique, for Paul to have used that participial phrase non-restrictively—and the burden of proof rests on anyone who wishes so to interpret it."

26. The only English translations of which I am aware to use "Judeans" for τῶν Ἰουδαίων at 1 Thess 2:14 is Fenton Farrar's *The New Testament in Modern English* (7th ed., 1908) and the NKJV (1982), though both miss the restrictive nature of the sentence by punctuating it with a colon and comma respectively (but see footnote 57). Gilliard notes that the punctuation issue is peculiar to English and the major Western Romance languages, which are able to distinguish restrictive from non-restrictive clauses with the use of a comma, unlike German and Russian, for example ("Antisemitic Comma," 483).

27. Fee, *First and Second Letters to the Thessalonians*, 95, n. 35.

28. For the following, I am indebted to ibid., 97–98.

29. On the existence of Christian prophets, see Q 11:49; Acts 11:27; 13:1; 15:32; 21:10. A similar sequence appears with "apostles" in 1 Cor 12:28–29; Eph 2:20; 3:5; 4:11; and Rev 18:20, most likely with Christian prophets in view (so Barth, *Ephesians*, 315–16). In the Phillips translation of 1 Thess 2:14–16 cited above, Phillips reverses the order without justification.

30. Some later scribes added ἰδίους before προφήτας in keeping with their understanding of the verse as non-restrictive. But the textual evidence lacking this adjective is early and widespread. Interestingly, Gilliard proposes to understand the article τοὺς as a possessive pronoun—"his" (the Lord Jesus') prophets, including John the Baptist

whom, like Stephen and James, suffered martyrdom (ironically, in Stephen's case, at the hands of Paul!) in Judea (Acts 8:58-60; 12:1-3); 2) the Judeans "drove us out," which, whether as a reference to persecution or expulsion (or both), can conceivably and not unreasonably find its place within the purview of Paul's Judean experiences now largely lost to us;[31] 3) the Judeans "displease God and oppose everyone by hindering us from speaking to the Gentiles so that they may be saved." The shift here from aorist participles (ἀποκτεινάντων, ἐκδιωξάντων) to present participles (ἀρεσκόντων, κωλυόντων) has led some to posit a shift in Paul's thought from Judeans in particular to "the Jews" more generally.[32] But the single article (τῶν) governing the succession of participles in vv. 15-16a suggests that Paul has the same group in mind and is now using polemical hyperbole to describe the fate of culpable Judeans.[33]

Source and Receptor Language Considerations

Kurt and Barbara Aland have reminded us that even the smallest matters of punctuation can affect the meaning of a biblical text.[34] Few passages offer a more cogent example than 1 Thess 2:14-16. The etymological connection of Ἰουδαία and Ἰουδαῖος combined with a restrictive participial construction argues strongly in favor of "Judeans," not "Jews" more generally, as the special objects of Paul's stinging condemnation. In this case the social-scientific interpreters are right in their insistence to translate Ἰουδαῖοι as "Judeans." Thus Malina and Pilch write of this passage: "The Judeans in question seem to have

and Stephen ("Antisemitic Comma," 499).

31. We must keep in mind our ignorance of many of the events of Paul's career, including the five times he was flogged by "Judeans" (2 Cor 11:24). Bockmuehl, "1 Thessalonians 2:14-16 and the Church in Jerusalem," 1-31, sees evidence for three key periods of Christian persecution in Judea: 1) mid-30s (Acts 8:1b); 2) early 40s (Acts 12:1-3); and late 40s (Gal 4:29; 6:12). He believes that the last, combined with certain political and economic misfortunes in Judea, forms the essential backdrop to Paul's words in 1 Thess 2:14-16.

32. So, e.g., Richard, *First and Second Thessalonians*, 120; Bruce, *1 and 2 Thessalonians*, 46. See also Hagner, "Paul's Quarrel with Judaism," 134, who thinks that "the polemical words in vv. 15-16 quickly broaden in their application . . . to include all the Jews who were unreceptive to the gospel and who opposed Paul's missionary work." He sees Paul expressing a Deuteronomistic "in-house" condemnation against other Jews.

33. So Fee, *First and Second Letters to the Thessalonians*, 99. Schlueter, *Filling Up the Measure*, 111-23, sees "polemical hyperbole" as part of Paul's overall rhetorical strategy in the letter. That she fails to consider "Judeans" as a viable translation of Ἰουδαίων in 1 Thess 2:14 is a serious weakness in her argument.

34. Kurt and Barbara Aland, *Text of the New Testament*, 287. Rom 9:5 and Eph 4:12 are two examples that come readily to mind.

been those who previously supported Paul in his Pharisaic zeal to put down Jesus groups. When Paul took on his new charge from the God of Israel to proclaim the gospel of God, that group turned to suppress Paul as well."[35]

Yet translating Ἰουδαῖος uniformly as "Judean" throughout the Second Temple period and in the New Testament is problematic for at least two reasons. First, from the standpoint of the source language, Ἰουδαῖος does not always retain its strong territorial associations throughout this entire time period. Stephen G. Wilson, relying partly on the work of Cohen, contends that Ἰουδαῖος changes from being primarily an ethno-geographic term (up to 100 BCE) to being primarily a religio-cultural term thereafter.[36] In 2 Macc 6:6, for example, a text typically dated between the late-second and mid-first century BCE, those subjects suffering under the persecution of Antiochus could not so much as "confess [ὁμολογεῖν] themselves to be Jews [Ἰουδαῖον]." Cohen remarks: "Ἰουδαῖοι [sic] cannot mean 'Judeans' here, because why should Antiochus care if people identify themselves as Judeans? Ethnic-geographic identity seems to be irrelevant."[37] Rather, the context of the passage indicates that adherence to Jewish laws was uppermost in the mind of the epitomist, particularly Sabbath observance and circumcision. In another important passage, 2 Macc 9:17 portrays a repentant Antiochus begging the God of Israel for mercy and vowing in turn to "become a Jew [Ἰουδαῖον ἔσεσθαι]." Here, Cohen observes, "We may presume that Antiochus is offering God a theological conversion, not a change in domicile or political affiliation . . . He promises that he will become a Jew, a worshiper of the true God, but he does not intend to become a Judean, a member of the house of Israel living on God's holy land. After all, Antiochus is a Macedonian king and intends to remain one."[38]

The weakening of territorial associations in the term should not be missed. Cohen contends that what we are seeing here is the emergence of

---

35. Malina and Pilch, *Letters of Paul*, 41.

36. Wilson, "'Jew' and Related Terms," 157-71.

37. Cohen, "Beginnings," 91. Cohen sees the emergence of a "religious" meaning of Ἰουδαῖος among Greco-Roman authors in the late first-century, for example in Epictetus (*Dissertations* 2.19-21), who identifies an Ἰουδαῖος with anyone who worships the god of the Judeans (60-61, 96). Detection of a religious meaning should not be taken as evidence of normative Jewish belief and practice, a situation that would not be achieved until after 70 CE.

38. Cohen, *Beginnings*, 92-93. Cohen believes that the "harbingers" of gentile conversion to Judaism appear in the Persian period, with "the destruction of the temple, the disappearance of the tribal system, the emergence of a diaspora, *the weakening of the connection between the people and the land*, and the gradual elaboration of non-temple-oriented forms of religiosity" (122, emphasis mine).

a distinctly "religious" or cultural meaning of Ἰουδαῖος,[39] which, along with a political dimension,[40] arose during the persecutions of Antiochus and subsequent Hasmonean conquests (notably John Hyrcanus and Aristobulus I) when it was now possible to apostatize from or convert to the God of the Judeans.[41] Thus it should come as no surprise that 2 Maccabees witnesses the earliest usage of the cognate noun Ἰουδαϊσμός (NRSV "Judaism" or "Jewish faith" [2:21; 8:1; 14:38(2x); cf. 4 Macc 4:26]) to describe the religious practices and beliefs of the Judeans, though whether the term bears a sole religious meaning at this early stage is uncertain.[42] That the

---

39. Paul himself encroaches on this meaning on at least two occasions, once in Rom 2:28-29, where he re-defines an Ἰουδαῖος in terms of an inner spiritual disposition (see Wilson, "'Jew' and Related Terms," 160-61), and once in 1 Cor 9:20, where he speaks of becoming ὡς Ἰουδαῖος. On the latter passage, Barrett, *First Epistle to the Corinthians*, 211, remarks, "He could *become* a Jew only if, having been a Jew, he had ceased to be one and become something else. His Judaism was no longer of his very being, but a guise he could adopt or discard at will" (emphasis his). The "guise" of which Barrett speaks can only be religious or cultural in nature rather than ethnic unless, of course, one wants to posit that changing one's religion in the ancient world also meant changing one's ethnicity (so Denise Kimber Buell, *Why This New Race?*). Regrettably, I discovered Buell's book too late to interact with her notion of ethnicity as both fluid and fixed in the ancient world. Suffice it here to point out that the "Christian" Paul can still identify himself as an Ἰουδαῖος (Acts 22:3) and an Ἰσραηλίτης (Rom 11:1; 2 Cor 11:22) many years after his conversion and can still speak of the Israelites as "my kindred according to the flesh" (Rom 9:3; cf. Phil 4:5). Thus the extent to which the Christian Paul saw himself as changing religions is not entirely clear. He can certainly continue to emphasize his Jewish ethnic identity when it serves his rhetorical purposes. In Barrett's terms, what was that "something else" that Paul could ethnically become? On Paul's so-called "liminality," see the essays by Duling and Russell in this volume.

40. According to Cohen, the Hasmoneans's acceptance of a Greek conception of πολιτεία allowed for the separation of ethnicity from citizenship and thus the incorporation of Gentiles into the Judean state (*Beginnings*, 127).

41. Cohen, *Beginnings*, 105-106. Josephus, for example, tells how the descendants of the Herodian Alexander abandoned τῶν Ἰουδαίοις ἐπιχωρίων and went over πρὸς τὰ Ἕλλησι πάτρια (*Ant.* 18.141). Cohen sees incipient evidence of a religious meaning in Bel and the Dragon 28 where Cyrus is declared to have "become a Jew" (Ἰουδαῖος γέγονεν) but still believes that the ethnic-geographic meaning is paramount here (ibid., 86-87). See also Lowe, "Who Were the Ἰουδαῖοι?" 108-9. Of the Hasmonean conquests, Meier, *Marginal Jew*, 616, observes: "For the first time since the reign of King Solomon in the 10th century B.C., the northern regions of Israel had been reintegrated with the rump state in the south (Judea in the narrow sense) into one Israel, one kingdom of the Jews (Judea in the wider sense), with its capital in the temple-city of Jerusalem."

42. Cohen, *Beginnings*, 106. Cohen remarks, "The creation of the word Ἰουδαϊσμός is an important moment in the development of Jewish identity and in the birth of Jewishness..." (ibid). Elliott, "Jesus the Israelite," 136, thinks that the term arose in reaction to Ἑλληνισμός (2 Macc 4:13; NRSV "Hellenization"). Ἰουδαϊσμός has an undeniable religious meaning in Ignatius, where it appears in juxtaposition with Χριστιανισμός (*Magn.* 8:1; 10:1,3; *Phld.* 6:1).

term can bear a distinctly religious meaning by the mid-first century is clear from Paul, who speaks of his *former* (ποτε) manner of life "in Judaism" (ἐν τῷ Ἰουδαϊσμῷ, Gal 1:13; KJV: "the Jews' religion"), which he closely identifies with "the traditions of my ancestors" (τῶν πατρικῶν μου παραδόσεων, Gal 1:14).[43] Esler strongly objects to Cohen's separation of religion from ethnicity as anachronistic and faults Cohen's use of ethnic theory but unfortunately offers no rebuttal to important diachronic developments observable in 2 Maccabees to which Cohen traces the beginnings of Jewishness as early as 100 BCE.[44]

Nor does Esler deal with the notable example of the conversion of the royal house of Adiabene as reported by Josephus, "the most conspicuous instance of proselytization known to us from this period."[45] When the gentile King Izates desires to embrace the Jewish religion, he realizes his need to be circumcised in order to become "thoroughly a Jew [εἶναι βεβαίως Ἰουδαῖος]" (*Ant.* 20.38); when his mother Helena learns of it, she warns that his subjects "would never bear to be ruled over by a Jew [Ἰουδαῖος] . . . by a man who was so zealous in another religion" [ἑτέροις ζηλωτὴν ἐθῶν] (*Ant.* 20.39, 47). Here Ἰουδαῖος clearly transcends its original territorial connotations. Izates was not born in Judea, was not born to Judean parents, did not live in Judea, and had no plans to immigrate there.[46] Rather, his being an Ἰουδαῖος

---

43. Only a religio-cultural meaning of Ἰουδαϊσμός is possible in Gal 1:14 since Paul speaks of it as something characterizing him in the past. Martyn, *Galatians*, 154, fully recognizes the religious meaning of the term: "Galatians is thus the letter in which Paul speaks directly and explicitly and repeatedly about Judaism as a *religion*" (emphasis his).

44. See Esler's complete critique of Cohen's position in *Conflict and Identity*, 68–74. Actually, there may be more to the debate here than meets the eye. For some antiimperial interpreters, the admission of a religious dimension separate from economics and politics means the possibility of a Jesus who is "merely" religious and apolitical. As Horsley, *Jesus and Empire*, 5–6, contends, "The Jesus who defers to empire . . . is rooted in a Jesus who has been reduced to merely a religious figure. Since by definition empire is political, a Jesus who is merely religious has no relevance to or implications for empire."

45. Bruce, *Paul: Apostle of the Heart Set Free*, 128. Bruce dates this notable conversion to ca. 40 CE.

46. Izates and his mother would be buried in Jerusalem, however (Jos. *Ant.* 20.95). Esler, *Conflict and Identity*, 72–74, appeals to the notion of "dual ethnicity" to explain how a person might belong to more than one ethnic group at the same time. But neither Antiochus nor Izates meets the criteria that Esler lays out in his examples, which seem to depend on a combination of birth, descent, or residence (49). Moreover, the notion of dual ethnicity is dubious in the case of Herod the Great since Herod feels compelled to have his court historian Nicolas of Damascus invent a Judean pedigree for him to allay suspicions that Herod was a "half-Judean" (ἡμιουδαῖος) (cf. Jos. *Ant.* 14.9,403; Cohen, *Beginnings*, 16–18). Kokkinos distinguishes Herod as Phoenician by descent, Idumean by place of birth, and Jewish by official religion, among other nuances (in

had to do with adopting the tenets of Jewish law, as Josephus repeatedly emphasizes (*Ant.* 20.17, 35, 38, 41). At best, as in the case of Antiochus, a geographical meaning is remotely present in that a gentile convert had become attached to a god whose temple was located in a particular area.[47] Thus it is at least questionable whether "Judean" can account for the various nuances of the term beginning to emerge in the late Second Temple period, beginning with Antiochus's persecution and Hasmonean conquests and running through the destruction of the Jerusalem temple, reflected particularly in a post-70 document like the Gospel of John.[48]

Second, from the standpoint of the receptor language, Esler's original objection still stands: "Judean" to the English mind signifies one hailing from the geographic region of Judea. Thus to translate all instances of Ἰουδαῖος in the territorial sense of "Judean" hinders the English reader from perceiving critical contexts when actual inhabitants of Judea may be in view—such as in 1 Thess 2:14. The situation is somewhat analogous to the problem in Josephus who, as Malcolm Lowe observes, sometimes uses Ἰουδαῖος in *different* senses in the *same* passage, supposing his reader to be able to fill in the correct sense in any given context.[49] Ironically, the failure to differentiate between a religious or cultural meaning ("Jew") and an ethnic-geographic one ("Judean") may actually contribute to the anachronism and anti-Judaism that social-scientific interpreters try so ardently to avoid.

So how ought we to translate Ἰουδαῖος in the New Testament? The proposal simply to transliterate the term is really no answer as the word

---

Jensen, *Herod Antipas in Galilee*, 42).

47. Lowe, "Who Were the Ἰουδαῖοι?" 109. In Josephus's account, Helena later determines to visit the temple in Jerusalem "so very famous among all men" (*Ant.* 20.49), but her desire seems to stem more from curiosity than any symbolic attachment to Judea. Izates never expresses his desire to visit Jerusalem and accompanies his mother only part-way. As for Antiochus, his desire was not to go to Judea but to "visit every inhabited place to proclaim the power of God" (2 Macc 9:17). Cohen terms him "a wandering Jew" (*Beginnings*, 130).

48. Much of the debate with respect to Ἰουδαῖος has focused on the Gospel of John, most recently in Sheridan, "Issues," 671–95. Sheridan recognizes "a broad associative range" of οἱ Ἰουδαῖοι in the Gospel of John and rejects the translation "Judeans" as too "underdifferentiated" (in linguistic theory), unable to account for the complexity of the data (690). Whereas Malina and Rohrbaugh, *Gospel of John*, 45, insist on "Judean" as a uniform translation of Ἰουδαῖος in John, other connotations are clearly present, including the Jerusalem leadership (1:19), Pharisees (1:19, 24; 9:18), Galileans (6:41, 52), and hostile opponents of Jesus (9:22). Thus Kostenberger, *John*, 59, is right to assert that "no single proposal explains all instances of the term in John's Gospel," opting for a connotative meaning supplied by the context. The TNIV reflects this connotative translation philosophy to some degree, translating οἱ Ἰουδαῖοι as "Jewish leaders" in certain contexts (e.g., 1:19; 18:36; 19:12, 31, 38; 20:19).

49. Lowe, "Who Were the Ἰουδαῖοι?" 104–5. Emphasis his.

is too frequent and too important to leave the English reader guessing.[50] Using a circumlocution like "Israelite," certainly an acceptable designation for members of the House of Israel in the Second Temple period,[51] does not really offer a lexical solution. Esler, taking his cue from a passage in Josephus, opts for the use of periphrasis when actual inhabitants of Judea are in view, such as when Josephus employs the phrase "genuine Judeans" (ὁ γνήσιος ἐξ αὐτῆς Ἰουδαίας λαός, J.W. 2.43) to differentiate those Ἰουδαῖοι living in Judea from those Ἰουδαῖοι living in Galilee, Idumea, and Perea.[52] Yet Josephus's far more consistent practice is to distinguish the inhabitants of Judea from Galileans, who differed from their counterparts in dialect, language and customs.[53] Moreover, the use of periphrasis by Malina and Pilch at Acts 2:9 results in the rather tautological "Judean Judeans," which the English reader is likely to find unhelpful and confusing.[54]

A problematic text like 1 Thess 2:14-16 has shown the wisdom of respecting the connotative meaning of Ἰουδαῖος in any given context. To strait-jacket the term throughout the New Testament not only ignores important diachronic developments but runs the risk of muting the geographical connection where English readers need to perceive it most. Despite the problems, then, we may need to continue to employ the term "Jew" when Ἰουδαῖος may have stronger and broader associations than the land.[55] After

50. Proposed by Sloyan, *John*, xiii–xiv; also Efroymson, "Let *Ioudaioi* Be *Ioudaioi*," 5. Ἰουδαῖος occurs 194 times in the New Testament. Pronunciation for an English audience is potentially a problem as well. Whereas standard rules of Greek syllabification allow one vowel or diphthong per syllable, Wenham, *Elements*, 19, asserts that the initial iota of Ἰουδαῖος has a consonantal sound like "y" in "yes."

51 A practice followed by Esler in his earlier commentary on Galatians; see *Conflict and Identity*, 66.

52. Ibid., 67, 71–72. Esler discusses this passage in a dispute with Cohen over the proper meaning of γνήσιος. In his parallel account (*Ant.* 17.254), Josephus omits γνήσιος and instead opts simply for an intensive modifier (αὐτῶν τε Ἰουδαίων πλῆθος).

53. A point emphasized by Horsley, *Galilee*, 13. "Because of differing local and regional histories," he writes, "the Judean and Galilean and Samaritan peoples had somewhat different customs and practices while sharing a common Israelite history and cultural tradition" (*Jesus and Empire*, 10).

54. Malina and Pilch, *Book of Acts*, 29. The ESV approximates periphrasis with its consistent use of explanatory footnoting.

55. Von Wahlde, "'The Jews' in the Gospel of John," 49, recognizes both a "national" and a "regional" meaning to the term in the first century but argues for using "Judean" strictly for the latter in English translation. The problems are especially acute in Acts, where the term appears frequently for "Jews" of the Diaspora. Even here Luke's meaning is subject to nuance. Luke notes, for example, that Paul made converts from among the οἱ Ἰουδαῖοι in the synagogue at Thessalonica (Acts 17:1), yet a few verses later Luke can speak without equivocation of the οἱ Ἰουδαῖοι who obstructed Paul's message (17:5)! Green, *Theology of the Gospel of Luke*, 69, wisely cautions against construing "the

all, it is not as though modern Jews have nothing in common with their ancient counterparts.⁵⁶ In 1 Thess 2:14, English audiences must understand that Paul's condemnation is not upon all Jews irrespective of time and place but upon a certain segment of Judean society that played a culpable role in the death of Jesus. To lessen this perception by making all Jews into Judeans is like inserting a "fatal comma," which, as the Holocaust has shown, really can kill.⁵⁷

APPENDIX
Articular Attributive Participles in 1 Thessalonians

1 Thess 1:7—ὥστε γενέσθαι ὑμᾶς τύπον πᾶσιν <u>τοῖς πιστεύουσιν</u> ἐν τῇ Μακεδονίᾳ καὶ ἐν τῇ Ἀχαΐᾳ.

1 Thess 1:10—καὶ ἀναμένειν τὸν υἱὸν αὐτοῦ ἐκ τῶν οὐρανῶν, ὃν ἤγειρεν ἐκ [τῶν] νεκρῶν, Ἰησοῦν <u>τὸν ῥυόμενον</u> ἡμᾶς ἐκ τῆς ὀργῆς <u>τῆς ἐρχομένης</u>.

1 Thess 2:4—ἀλλὰ καθὼς δεδοκιμάσμεθα ὑπὸ τοῦ θεοῦ πιστευθῆναι τὸ εὐαγγέλιον, οὕτως λαλοῦμεν, οὐχ ὡς ἀνθρώποις ἀρέσκοντες ἀλλὰ θεῷ <u>τῷ δοκιμάζοντι</u> τὰς καρδίας ἡμῶν.

1 Thess 2:10—ὑμεῖς μάρτυρες καὶ ὁ θεός, ὡς ὁσίως καὶ δικαίως καὶ ἀμέμπτως ὑμῖν <u>τοῖς πιστεύουσιν</u> ἐγενήθημεν . . .

1 Thess 2:12—παρακαλοῦντες ὑμᾶς καὶ παραμυθούμενοι καὶ μαρτυρόμενοι εἰς τὸ περιπατεῖν ὑμᾶς ἀξίως τοῦ θεοῦ <u>τοῦ καλοῦντος</u> ὑμᾶς εἰς τὴν ἑαυτοῦ βασιλείαν καὶ δόξαν.

1 Thess 2:13—Καὶ διὰ τοῦτο καὶ ἡμεῖς εὐχαριστοῦμεν τῷ θεῷ ἀδιαλείπτως, ὅτι παραλαβόντες λόγον ἀκοῆς παρ' ἡμῶν τοῦ θεοῦ ἐδέξασθε οὐ λόγον

Jews" in Luke' writings as a monolithic group. The option of translating οἱ Ἰουδαῖοι with quotation marks in English ("the Jews") could be appropriate in certain antagonistic contexts in John (but see Sheridan, "Issues," 692).

56. Noted by Sheridan (ibid., 695), who reminds us that "modern Jewish religious identity is still conceived of in terms of peoplehood, Torah/halakah and covenant."

57. It was not without some degree of confirmation that I discovered after the completion of this paper a translation of 1 Thess 2:14–15 that respects both the geographical meaning of Ἰουδαῖος and the restrictive nature of the participle. In the Complete Jewish Bible (David Stern, 1998), the text reads: "For, brothers, you came to be imitators of God's congregations in Y'hudah that are united with the Messiah Yeshua—you suffered the same things from your countrymen as they did from the Judeans who both killed the Lord Yeshua and the prophets . . ." Perhaps it is telling (and unfortunate) that we find this translation only in a version particularly sensitive to Jewish-Christian relations.

ἀνθρώπων ἀλλὰ καθώς ἐστιν ἀληθῶς λόγον θεοῦ, ὃς καὶ ἐνεργεῖται ἐν ὑμῖν <u>τοῖς πιστεύουσιν</u>.

1 Thess 2:14–15—ὑμεῖς γὰρ μιμηταὶ ἐγενήθητε, ἀδελφοί, τῶν ἐκκλησιῶν τοῦ θεοῦ <u>τῶν οὐσῶν</u> ἐν τῇ Ἰουδαίᾳ ἐν Χριστῷ Ἰησοῦ, ὅτι τὰ αὐτὰ ἐπάθετε καὶ ὑμεῖς ὑπὸ τῶν ἰδίων συμφυλετῶν καθὼς καὶ αὐτοὶ ὑπὸ τῶν Ἰουδαίων <u>τῶν</u> καὶ τὸν κύριον <u>ἀποκτεινάντων</u> Ἰησοῦν καὶ τοὺς προφήτας καὶ ἡμᾶς <u>ἐκδιωξάντων</u> καὶ θεῷ <u>μὴ ἀρεσκόντων</u> καὶ πᾶσιν ἀνθρώποις ἐναντίων . . .

1 Thess 4:5—μὴ ἐν πάθει ἐπιθυμίας καθάπερ καὶ τὰ ἔθνη <u>τὰ μὴ εἰδότα</u> τὸν θεόν . . .

1 Thess 4:8—τοιγαροῦν ὁ ἀθετῶν οὐκ ἄνθρωπον ἀθετεῖ ἀλλὰ τὸν θεὸν <u>τὸν [καὶ] διδόντα</u> τὸ πνεῦμα αὐτοῦ τὸ ἅγιον εἰς ὑμᾶς.

1 Thess 4:13—Οὐ θέλομεν δὲ ὑμᾶς ἀγνοεῖν, ἀδελφοί, περὶ τῶν κοιμωμένων, ἵνα μὴ λυπῆσθε καθὼς καὶ οἱ λοιποὶ <u>οἱ μὴ ἔχοντες</u> ἐλπίδα.

1 Thess 4:15—Τοῦτο γὰρ ὑμῖν λέγομεν ἐν λόγῳ κυρίου, ὅτι ἡμεῖς <u>οἱ ζῶντες</u> <u>οἱ περιλειπόμενοι</u> εἰς τὴν παρουσίαν τοῦ κυρίου οὐ μὴ φθάσωμεν τοὺς κοιμηθέντας·

1 Thess 4:17—ἔπειτα ἡμεῖς <u>οἱ ζῶντες</u> <u>οἱ περιλειπόμενοι</u> ἅμα σὺν αὐτοῖς ἁρπαγησόμεθα ἐν νεφέλαις εἰς ἀπάντησιν τοῦ κυρίου εἰς ἀέρα· καὶ οὕτως πάντοτε σὺν κυρίῳ ἐσόμεθα.

1 Thess 5:9–10—ὅτι οὐκ ἔθετο ἡμᾶς ὁ θεὸς εἰς ὀργὴν ἀλλὰ εἰς περιποίησιν σωτηρίας διὰ τοῦ κυρίου ἡμῶν Ἰησοῦ Χριστοῦ <u>τοῦ ἀποθανόντος</u> ὑπὲρ ἡμῶν, ἵνα εἴτε γρηγορῶμεν εἴτε καθεύδωμεν ἅμα σὺν αὐτῷ ζήσωμεν.

Works Cited

Aland, Kurt, and Barbara Aland. *The Text of the New Testament.* Translated by Erroll F. Rhodes. Rev. ed. Grand Rapids: Eerdmans, 1989.

Barrett, C. K. *The First Epistle to the Corinthians.* Harper's New Testament Commentary. New York: Harper and Row, 1968.

Barth, Markus. *Ephesians 1–3.* AB 34. New York: Doubleday, 1974.

Bockmuehl, Markus. "1 Thessalonians 2:14–16 and the Church in Jerusalem." *Tyndale Bulletin* 52 (2001) 1–31.

Bruce, F. F. *Paul: Apostle of the Heart Set Free.* Grand Rapids: Eerdmans, 1977.

———. *1 and 2 Thessalonians.* WBC 45. Waco: Word, 1982.

Buell, Denise Kimber. *Why This New Race? Ethnic Reasoning in Early Christianity.* New York: Columbia University Press, 2005.

Cohen, Shaye J. D. *The Beginnings of Jewishness: Boundaries, Varieties, Uncertainties* Berkeley: University of California Press, 1999.

Dunn, James D. G. *Romans 1–8.* WBC 38A. Dallas: Word, 1988.

Efroymson, David P. "Let *Ioudaioi* Be *Ioudaioi*: When Less is Better." *Explorations* 11 (1997) 5.

Elliott, John H. "Jesus the Israelite Was Neither a 'Jew' nor a 'Christian': On Correcting Misleading Nomenclature." *JSHJ* 5 (2007) 119–55.

Esler, Philip F. *Conflict and Identity in Romans: The Social Setting of Paul's Letter.* Minneapolis: Fortress, 2003.

———. *Galatians.* New Testament Readings. New York: Routledge, 1998.

Fee, Gordon D. *The First and Second Letters to the Thessalonians.* New International Commentary on the New Testament. Grand Rapids: Eerdmans, 2009.

Frame, James E. *A Critical and Exegetical Commentary on the Epistles of St. Paul to the Thessalonians.* International Critical Commentary. Edinburgh: T. & T. Clark, 1912.

Gilliard, Frank D. "The Problem of the Antisemitic Comma between 1 Thessalonians 2:14 and 15." *NTS* 35 (1989) 481–502.

Green, Joel B. *The Theology of the Gospel of Luke.* New Testament Theology. Cambridge: Cambridge University Press, 1995.

Hagner, Donald A. "Paul's Quarrel with Judaism." In *Anti-Semitism and Early Christianity: Issues of Polemic and Faith*, edited by Craig A. Evans and Donald A. Hagner, 128–50. Minneapolis: Fortress, 1993.

Horsley, Richard A. *Galilee: History, Politics, People.* Valley Forge, PA: Trinity, 1995.

———. *Jesus and Empire: The Kingdom of God and the New World Disorder.* Minneapolis: Fortress, 2003.

Jensen, Morten Horning. *Herod Antipas in Galilee: The Literary and Archaeological Sources on the Reign of Herod Antipas and Its Socio-Economic Impact on Galilee.* 2nd ed. WUNT 2/215. Tübingen: Mohr/Siebeck, 2010.

Josephus. Translated by H. St. J. Thackeray et al. 13 vols. LCL. Cambridge: Harvard University Press, 1926–65.

Kostenberger, Andreas. *John.* Baker Exegetical Commentary on the New Testament. Grand Rapids: Baker Academic, 2004.

Lowe, Malcolm. "Who Were the Ἰουδαῖοι?" *NovT* 18 (1976) 101–30.

Malherbe, Abraham J. *The Letters to the Thessalonians.* AB 32B. New Haven: Yale University Press, 2000.

Malina, Bruce J., and John J. Pilch. *Social-Science Commentary on the Book of Acts.* Minneapolis: Fortress, 2008.

———. *Social-Science Commentary on the Book of Revelation.* Minneapolis: Fortress, 2000.

———. *Social-Science Commentary on the Letters of Paul.* Minneapolis: Fortress, 2006.

Malina, Bruce J., and Richard L. Rohrbaugh. *Social-Science Commentary on the Gospel of John.* Minneapolis: Fortress, 1998.

Martyn, J. Louis. *Galatians.* AB 33A. New York: Doubleday, 1998.

Meier, John P. *A Marginal Jew: Rethinking the Historical Jesus.* Vol. 3: *Companions and Competitors.* Anchor Bible Reference Library. New York: Doubleday, 2001.

Pearson, Birger A. "1 Thessalonians 2:13–16: A Deutero-Pauline Interpolation." *HTR* 64 (1971) 79–94.

Pilch, John J. "No Jews or Christians in the Bible." *Explorations* 12 (1998) 3.

Rhoads, David. "Social Criticism: Crossing Boundaries." In *Mark and Method: New Approaches in Biblical Studies,* edited by Janice Capel Anderson and Stephen D. Moore, 145–79. Rev. ed. Minneapolis: Fortress, 2008.

Richard, Earl J. *First and Second Thessalonians.* Sacra Pagina 11. Collegeville, MN: Glazier/Liturgical, 1995.

Ridderbos, Herman. *The Epistle of Paul to the Churches of Galatia.* New International Commentary. Grand Rapids: Eerdmans, 1953.

Schlueter, Carol J. *Filling Up the Measure: Polemical Hyperbole in 1 Thessalonians 2:14–16.* JSNTSup 98. Sheffield: JSOT Press, 1994.

Sheridan, Ruth. "Issues in the Translation of οἱ Ἰουδαῖοι in the Fourth Gospel." *JBL* 132 (2013) 671–95.

Sloyan, Gerard S. *John.* Interpretation. Atlanta: John Knox, 1988.

Verhoef, Eduard. "Die Bedeutung des Artikels τῶν in 1 Thess 2:15." *Biblische Notizen* 80 (1995) 41–46.

Wahlde, U. C. von. "'The Jews' in the Gospel of John: Fifteen Years of Research (1983–1998)." *Ephemerides Theologicae* 76 (2000) 30–55.

Weatherly, Jon A. "The Authenticity of 1 Thessalonians 2:13–16." *JSNT* 42 (1991) 79–98.

Wenham, J. W. *The Elements of New Testament Greek.* Cambridge: Cambridge University Press, 1965.

Wilson, Stephen G. "'Jew' and Related Terms in the Ancient World." *Studies in Religion/ Sciences Religieuses* 33 (2004) 157–71.

5

"For our Lord was pursued by the Jews . . ."
The (Ab)Use of the Motif of 'Jewish' Violence against Jesus on a Greek Amulet (P. Heid. 1101)[1]

Joseph Emanuel Sanzo

ON FEBRUARY 25, 2004, Mel Gibson's film, *The Passion of the Christ*, was released in theaters throughout the United States of America. Its violent images, anti-Semitic representation of the Jews, and historical infelicities and inaccuracies immediately aroused the ire of film critics, activists, and historians of the ancient world. One of the more astute essays written in response to Gibson's film was penned by the honoree of this volume, my Doktorvater and friend, S. Scott Bartchy.[2] Scott's article not only appropriately highlighted Gibson's disregard for history (e.g., the early dating of Isaiah 53 in the opening frame and the portrayal of Pilate as a pensive ruler) and for the writings of the New Testament (e.g., the lack of reference to Jesus' concern for the poor and the addi-

---

1. This essay was written with the support of the Center for the Study of Christianity at the Hebrew University of Jerusalem, Israel. I would especially like to thank the Center's Director, Prof. Brouria Bitton-Ashkelony, for her guidance during my postdoctoral fellowship in 2013–2015. I would also like to thank Ra'anan Boustan and Flavia Ruani for their helpful comments and suggestions on earlier drafts of this paper. Of course, I am responsible for any shortcomings in this paper. Abbreviations: *ACM* (=Meyer and Smith, eds., *Ancient Christian Magic*); *GMA* (=Kotansky, *Greek Magical Amulets*); *PGM* (=Preisendanz, ed., *Papyri Graecae Magicae*); *Suppl.Mag.* (=Daniel and Maltomini, eds., *Supplementum Magicum*).

2. Bartchy, "Where is the History?" 313–28.

tions to the passion story based on the meditations of Anne Catherine Emmerich [1774–1824]), but it also offered his readers a very personal critique of the *Passion*; his confession of feeling "emotionally abused" while watching Gibson's depiction of the crucifixion deftly captured the emotions felt by many of us who suffered through this film.[3] Moreover, Scott appropriately highlighted the social implications of disassociating Jesus from his Judean roots within the film's twenty-first century American context—not to mention its vivid depiction of the Jews as bloodthirsty villains.[4] But then again, it is not surprising that Scott would write an article that so beautifully melded critical scholarship with a heart-felt concern for the personal and social impacts of Gibson's *Passion*. Indeed, through his teaching and publications Scott has modeled for many of us how to unite the study of antiquity with concerns for social justice in our own time. Scott's life and work thus provide a point of contrast—and Mel Gibson's film, a point of complement!—to the artifact at the center of the following essay: an amulet from late antique Egypt inscribed with an accusation of Jewish violence.

Introduction

Scholarship on the role of boundary demarcation in the construction and maintenance of early "Christian" identities has blossomed in recent years. Much of this scholarly discourse has centered on the boundaries between "Christians" and "Jews" in their nascent interactions with one another. Contrary to earlier portraits of "Judaism" and "Christianity" as discrete religions after a definitive "parting of the ways,"[5] historians of religion now talk of a continued and messy negotiation of identity between members of the Jesus movement(s) and ethnic Jews, with points of unity and rupture throughout Late Antiquity.[6]

In response to the porous boundaries that imperfectly separated "Jews" and "Christians" in social reality, followers of Jesus deployed various themes in their writings to establish and maintain clear distinctions between "their" communities and "Jewish" communities.[7] Perhaps the most common

---

3. Ibid., 319.
4. Ibid., 318.
5. See especially Dunn, *Parting of the Ways*.
6. See especially the various essays in Becker and Reed, *Ways that Never Parted*, and Boyarin, *Border Lines*.
7. Boyarin, *Border Lines*, 1–33.

theme was that of the "Jewish violence" against Christ and his followers.[8] Foreshadowing Mel Gibson's *Passion*, many early Christian writers depicted the "Jews" as a violent lot—one that was especially preoccupied with seeking out the "true" followers of God.

This motif found its way into an unexpected venue, P. Heidelberg inv. G 1101 (hereafter P. Heid. 1101), a fifth- or sixth-century CE amulet that was discovered near ancient Egyptian Babylon.[9] The following formula is part of the amulet's complex ritual to heal eye migraine and eye discharge:

> For our Lord was pursued by the Jews (Ιουδέον), and he came to the Euphrates River and stuck in his staff, and the water stood still. Also you, discharge (ῥεῦμα), stand still in the name of our Lord, who was crucified, from head to toe-nails . . . [10]

8. The motif of Jewish violence against Christ was not only ubiquitous in early Christian discourses, but it also shaped how specific characteristics (e.g., blindness and pride) that Christians attributed to Jews were conceptualized. On this point, see Shaw, *Sacred Violence*, 287–88.

9. For the *editio princeps*, see Maltomini, "Cristo all'Eufrate," 149–170. For subsequent editions, see Rupprecht, *Sammelbuch griechischer Urkunden aus Ägypten*, no. 12719; Daniel and Maltomini, *Suppl.Mag.* 1: 90–96, no. 32.

10. The extant Greek text:....[..]....αντυω..ρ...[.]εγνια εἰς τῇ (read τί) ἂν θέλις (read θέλεις or θέλῃς)· ἅγιος ἅγιος ἅγιος.ηρ.... τόνδε εἴ τήνδε (mag. signs)[.].... ορθω.... ὃς ὁρκίζο (read ὁρκίζω) σε τὸν Τουμηηλ Ηλ, ὅς ὁρκίζο (read ὡς ὁρκίζω) σε, ῥεῦμα[ ] (magic signs).....ατ.... αλεντ..ου..υκκατα παχὺ ἤτε (read εἴτε) λεπτὸν ἤτε (read εἴτε) ἁρμυρὸ[ν] (read ἁλμυρόν) ἤτε (read εἴτε) δρυμύτατου (read δριμύτατον), ὁρκίζο (read ὁρκίζω) σε κατὰ τον λεγόντον (read τῶν λεγόντων)· ἅγιος ἅγιος ἅγιος [κ(ύριο)ς] Σαβαωθ ὁ θ(εό)ς, ὁ θ(εὸ)ς Ἀδοναει Αοθ, ἀποθεραπεύσατε ὀφθαλμοὺ[ς] ἀπὸ ἡμικράνου (read ἡμικρανίου) καὶ παντύου (read παντοίου) ῥεύματος αὐτον (read αὐτῶν) · ὁ γὰρ κύριος ἡμον ἐδ[ι]όκεντο (read ἡμῶν ἐδιώκετο) ἀπὸ τον Ἰουδέον (read τῶν Ἰουδαίων) καὶ ἔλθεν (read ἦλθεν) εἰς τὸν Εὐφράτιν (read Εὐφράτην) ποταμ[ὸ]ν καὶ ἔπιξεν τὶν (read ἔπηξεν τὴν) ῥάβδον αὐτοῦ καὶ ἔστη τὸ ὕδρο (read ὕδωρ)· καὶ σύ, ῥεῦμα, στῆ[θι] ὀν[ό]ματι{γ} κ(υρίο)υ ἡμον (read ἡμῶν) τοῦ σταυρεθέντος (read σταυρωθέντος) ἀπὸ κεφαλις (read κεφαλῆς) μέχρι ὀνύχον (read ὀνύχων)..[.].γεε Μιχαηλ, Γαβριηλ, Ουρηηλ (read Ουριηλ), Ραφαηλ, λῦε, λῦε πόνους, λῦε, ἤδ[η] ἤδη ταχὺ (mag. signs). English translation: "... for what you wish. Holy, holy, holy, protect (?) a certain man or a certain woman (mag. sign) . . . I adjure you by Toumêêl Êl, for I adjure you, discharge (mag. sign) . . . thick or thin or salty or very bitter, I adjure you by those who say 'Holy, holy, holy is the Lord Sabaôth the God, the God Adonai Aoth'; heal the eyes from migraine and every sort of discharge from them. For our Lord was pursued by the Jews, and he came to the Euphrates River and stuck in his staff, and the water stood still. Also you, discharge, stand still in the name of our Lord, who was crucified, from head to toe-nails . . . Michaêl, Gabriêl, Ourêêl, Raphaêl, undo, undo the pains, undo, now now, quickly (mag. signs)." Text and translation are based on Daniel and Maltomini, *Suppl.Mag.* 1: 92. It does not seem that P. Heid. 1101 was originally tailored to a particular individual (cf. "a certain man or a certain woman" [τόνδε εἴ τήνδε]); if it was not, it should be classified among those "master texts" that were subsequently used as applied amulets (e.g., Schmidt 1). Of course, it is also possible that this phrase was accidently copied from a

This passage is an example of what scholars of ancient magic call a *historiola* (i.e., a short narrative used for ritual power).[11] This particular *historiola* operated on the basis of a direct and explicit analogy between the stilling of the Euphrates River and the cessation of eye discharge. In other words, the ritual specialist has explicitly merged the realm of Jesus' miraculous act at the Euphrates River with the world of his or her (potential) client. Accordingly, this is a variation of a special sub-class of *historiolae*, known in scholarship as the *similia similibus* formula (i.e., "just as . . . so also . . .").[12]

Of particular significance for the concerns of this paper is the opening phrase of the ritual narrative, "for our Lord was pursued by the Jews." Why did the ritual specialist introduce Jesus' miraculous act at the Euphrates River with this accusation of attempted Jewish violence? In the discussion to follow, I will merge insights from recent scholarship on the theme of "Jewish" violence against Jesus and his followers with research on ancient amulets in order to determine the ritual function of the reference to attempted Jewish violence on P. Heid. 1101. With the help of this cross-disciplinary synthesis, I will argue—albeit tentatively—that this portrayal of the Jews was intended to establish the proper religious affiliation of the client.

"For our Lord was pursued by the Jews": Beyond Source Criticism

On account of the peculiar content of this *historiola*, the little scholarship that has been devoted to it has been almost exclusively confined to source-critical aims. For instance, the amulet's original editor, Franco Maltomini, found a source-critical solution to this *historiola* in the ninth-century CE *Jordansegen* tradition.[13] The ritual artifacts in this tradition share a basic *similia similibus* formula, usually to stop a hemorrhage: as the Jordan River stopped before Jesus, so may the hemorrhage stop. Maltomini conceded, however, that this solution cannot account for the references to the Euphrates River and to the Jewish pursuit of Jesus.[14]

---

formulary, as Daniel and Maltomini suggest (*Suppl.Mag.* 1: 92).

11. See especially Frankfurter, "Narrating Power," 457–76.

12. On the *similia similibus* formula, see Faraone, "Agonistic Context," 8–10. Daniel and Maltomini note that the analogical connection is established in P. Heid. 1101 by the phrase, "καὶ σύ" (*Suppl.Mag.* 1: 95; cf. Maltomini, "Cristo all'Eufrate," 165).

13. Ibid., 152–56. For texts representative of the *Jordansegen* tradition, see Ebermann, *Blut- und Wundsegen in ihrer Entwicklung*, 24–35; Daniel and Maltomini, *Suppl. Mag.*, 91 n. 2.

14. Maltomini, "Cristo all'Eufrate," 156.

Building on the work of Maltomini, Gianfranco Fiaccadori suggested that the Eusebian version of the correspondence between Abgar, king of Edessa, and Jesus could have been the source for the references to the Euphrates River and to the Jewish pursuit of Jesus.[15] Fiaccadori highlighted that, in this version of the correspondence, the boundary of Edessa is specifically marked off in reference to the Euphrates River. Moreover, Eusebius notes that the Jews were threatening Jesus.[16] Despite these similarities, however, in the Eusebian version of this correspondence Jesus declines Abgar's request to travel to Edessa and perform the healing; instead, it is the disciple Thaddeus who heals the Edessan king. Faced with this rather significant tension in the data, Fiaccadori entertained the novel possibility that P. Heid. 1101 preserves a version of this tradition in which Jesus actually makes the trip to Edessa.[17]

While the source-critical endeavors of Maltomini and Fiaccadori have offered interesting and creative solutions to the potential sources behind P. Heid. 1101, they have left an important issue insufficiently addressed: even if we concede that the practitioner utilized the Abgar/Jesus correspondence as a source, we have yet to explain why that practitioner isolated and selected the persecuting-Jew motif in particular for his or her ritual. Why was this motif chosen and what was its function?

Making the question of function even more pressing is the dislocated nature of the accusation of attempted Jewish violence within the overall formal structure of the *historiola*. The phrase, "for our Lord was pursued by the Jews," is technically not part of the *similia similibus* formula; it does not have a corresponding analogue in the second portion of the formula.[18] Thus, the identification of its function within the ritual is of paramount importance. Does the phrase merely establish the narrative setting for the ritual analogy or was it intended to accomplish something more?

Suggesting an additional function for this phrase in the ritual of P. Heid. 1101 is its likely activation of what John Miles Foley has called "traditional referentiality."[19] This term refers to the numerous associations within a given social context that are evoked through the performance of a well-known authoritative tradition. Foley argued that even a short or paraphrased reference to such a tradition calls to mind multiple associations

15. Fiaccadori, "Cristo all'Eufrate (P. Heid. G. 1101, 8 ss.)," 59–63.
16. Ibid., 61.
17. Ibid., 63.
18. According to Maltomini, Kurt Treu observed the dislocated nature of this phrase within the incantation, stating that it did not seem to serve a magical function ("Cristo all'Eufrate," 156).
19. Foley, *Immanent Art*, esp. 38–60.

with it.[20] Building on the work of Foley, H. S. Versnel has shown that this kind of metonymic transfer is frequently operative in "magical" contexts.[21]

Indeed, the theme of the Jewish persecution of Jesus and Christians was a well-established and authoritative tradition in Late Antiquity. Moreover, its usage typically served a specific social function. Thus, I believe we can gain insight into the primary ritual function of the Jewish pursuit of Jesus on P. Heid. 1101 by examining the use of this motif within the social world of Late Antiquity.

The Ritual Function of the Jewish Pursuit of Jesus on P. Heid. 1101

The decision to introduce this *historiola* with the Jewish pursuit of Jesus was not made in a vacuum; rather, the motif of the "violent Jews" played an important role in the early Jesus movement's attempt to create and maintain its distinctive identity. Whether taking the form of Jews persecuting "Christians," as in the so-called ἀποσυνάγωγος passages from the Gospel of John,[22] or of the Jewish responsibility for the death of Christ, as in the accusations of deicide by Melito of Sardis in Peri Pascha,[23] the theme of Jewish violence was frequently used to construct, preserve, and clarify religious difference.[24] The message was simple: we are fundamentally distinct from those people, who murdered our Lord and his followers.

There is compelling evidence that this social dimension of the persecuting-Jews motif made an impact on the ritual world of late antique Egypt. For example, the previously mentioned Abgar/Jesus correspondence, which highlights the Jewish persecution of Jesus, is the most widely attested "extra-canonical" tradition in this context.[25] In fact, to speak of it as

---

20. Foley, *Immanent Art*, 7.

21. Versnel, "The Poetics of the Magical Charm," 124. Derek Collins has been critical of the appropriateness of "traditional referentiality" for the "magical" use of Homeric traditions (*Magic in the Ancient Greek World*, 108).

22. John 9:22; 12:42; 16:2 (cf. Rev 2:9; 3:9; *Mart. Pol.* 12.2; 13.1; Tertullian, *Scorpiace* 10.9).

23. E.g., *Peri Pascha* 72, ll. 505–8; 73, ll. 520, 524; 96, ll. 711–16. For commentaries on these passages, see Lieu, *Image and Reality*, 199–240.

24. Fredriksen, "*What Parting of the Ways?*" 35–63; Frankfurter, "Violence and Religious Formation," 142–43.

25. On the importance of the Abgar tradition for apotropaic contexts, see Drioton, "Un apocryphe anti-arien," 306–26; Skemer, *Binding Words*, 96–105.

"extra-canonical" is misleading, as one Coptic amulet juxtaposes the *incipit* of Jesus' letter to Abgar with the *incipits* of the four Gospels.[26]

The Jewish hatred and persecution of Jesus is highlighted most forcefully in Abgar's letter. According to Eusebius, the Edessan king wrote, "I heard that the Jews are mocking you, and wish to ill-treat you."[27] An even more incendiary version of this statement can be found on P. Oxy. 4469, a fifth-century CE Greek amulet: "for I have heard that the Jews murmur against you and persecute you, desiring to kill you."[28] The prominence of this authoritative tradition within apotropaic contexts indicates that many practitioners were exposed to literature in which the theme of Jewish violence against Jesus was used to clarify religious boundaries.

Moreover, accusations of Jewish violence were incorporated into many other kinds of texts and contexts in late antique Egypt. For example, Athanasius of Alexandria offers the following advice to Marcellinus in a letter, "should you wish to censure the treachery of the Jews against the Savior, [recite] the second psalm."[29] In addition, this rhetorical tactic penetrates two pseudepigraphical dialogues between Egyptian "Christians" and "Jews": the *Dialogue of Athanasius and Zachaeus* (e.g., 35, 130) and the *Dialogue of Timothy and Aquilla* (e.g., 41.17).[30] Also, during the Easter season, congregants were likely to hear repeatedly of the Jewish responsibility for the death of Christ.[31]

Furthermore, much of the extant manuscript evidence for texts that utilize this invective from other regions of the ancient Mediterranean comes from the sands of the Egypt. In other words, although originally written elsewhere, these texts were active *in Egypt*. For instance, as several scholars

26. Brit. Lib. Or. 4919(2) (Sanzo, "Brit. Lib. Or. 4919[2]," 98–100).

27. "καὶ γὰρ ἤκουσα ὅτι καὶ Ἰουδαῖοι καταγογγύζουσί σου καὶ βούλονται κακῶσαί σε" (*Hist. eccl.* I. xiii. 8). Translation by Kirsopp Lake in Eusebius, *Ecclesiastical History*, 89.

28. "[κ]αὶ γὰρ ἤκ[ου]σα ὅτι Ἰαουδεοι κα[ταγο]γ γ ὑζουζίν σου κ[αὶ διώ]κουσίν σε βουλόμενοί σ[ε ἀπο]κτ[εῖναι]" (Maltomini, "4469. Letter of Abgar to Jesus [Amulet]," 122–29). Translation based on Maltomini, "4469. Letter of Abgar to Jesus [Amulet]," 126. It should be noted that P. Oxy. 4469's version of Abgar's letter has many affinities with the Syriac tradition of the same letter (Maltomini, "4469. Letter of Abgar to Jesus [Amulet]," 124).

29. *Ep. Marc.* 15.

30. Varner, *Ancient Jewish-Christian Dialogues*. In addition, an anti-Jewish dialogue is extant (in lacunose form) on a papyrus from Oxyrhynchus (Hunt, "2070. Anti-Jewish Dialogue," 9–14).

31. This can be seen in the sermons of Augustine in North Africa (e.g., *Serm.* 218–229 and *Tract. ep. Jo.* 1–10). For the connection between the North African liturgy and Egyptian Babylon, evident from a Latin amulet that was discovered with P. Heid. 1101 (P. Heid. L 5), see Daniel and Maltomini, "From the African Psalter and Liturgy," 253–65.

have noted, the theme of Jewish violence plays a particularly important role in the Gospel of John—one of the most popular Gospels in Egypt during Late Antiquity.³² Beyond the numerous manuscripts of John and the other canonical Gospels, the aforementioned *Peri Pascha* by Melito of Sardis is extant in at least three manuscripts from late antique Egypt.³³ In addition, the so-called *Gospel of Peter*, which has a particularly strong emphasis on the Jewish responsibility for the death of Jesus, is extant in multiple manuscripts from this region and period.³⁴

To be sure, the label "Jews" in these texts may not have always referred to ethnic Jews. For instance, a common tendency of early heresiologists was to associate "heretics" with "Jews"—whether juxtaposing "Jewish" and "heretical" characteristics or simply using the term "Jews" to identify a heretical body.³⁵ In Egypt, the label "Jews" was deployed metaphorically in various "inter-Christian" disputes, including those between so-called Nicene Christians and Arians³⁶ as well as between pro-Chalcedonians and anti-Chalcedonians.³⁷ It should be stressed, however, that this metaphorical usage of the "Jews" was also designed to establish or maintain religious difference.

Identifying the specific source(s) or reference(s) behind the *historiola* in P. Heid. 1101 is beyond the concerns of this essay. What interests me is that the practitioner was part of a religious and scribal culture that was immersed in the rhetorical construct of the "violent Jews" for defining its religious boundaries.³⁸ It seems likely, therefore, that this social function was *evoked* through "traditional referentiality" and *invoked* in some way when the practitioner included the Jewish pursuit of Jesus on the amulet.

32. E.g., Reinhartz, "'Jews' and Jews in the Fourth Gospel," 341–56; Freyne, "Vilifying the Other and Defining the Self," 117–43.

33. P. Chester Beatty XII (Bonner, *Homily on the Passion by Melito Bishop of Sardis*, 1–180; Hall, "Melito Papyri," 476–508); P. Bodmer XIII (Testuz, *Papyrus Bodmer XIII*; idem, "Un nouveau manuscrit de l'homélie 'Peri Pascha' de Méliton," 139–41); P. Oxy. XIII 1600 (Grenfell and Hunt, "1600. Treatise on the Passion," 19–21).

34. P. Cair. 10759 (Bouriant, *Fragments du texte grec du livre d'Énoch*, 137–42); P. Oxy. XLI 2949 (Coles, "2949. Fragments of an Apocryphal Gospel[?]," 15–16; cf. Lührmann, "POx 2949: EvPt 3–5 in einer Handschrift des 2./3. Jahrhunderts," 216–26); P. Oxy. LX 4009 (Lührmann and Parsons, "4009. Gospel of Peter?" 1–5). It is also possible that a fragment from the Fayûm (P. Vindob. G 2325) contains portions of the Gospel of Peter, but this is more unlikely (Ehrman and Pleše, *Apocryphal Gospels*, 375).

35. Cameron, "Jews and Heretics—A Category Error?" 345–60; Boyarin and Burrus, "Hybridity as Subversion of Orthodoxy?" 433–36.

36. Brakke, "Jewish Flesh and Christian Spirit," 453–81.

37. E.g., Stephen of Heracleopolis Magna (*Panegyric on Apollo* 9, trans. and ed. K. H. Kuhn, 14–16).

38. Wilson notes that Christians used the term "Jew" mostly as a marker of boundaries ("'Jew' and Related Terms," 157–71).

But the likely presence of this type of evocation raises an important question: what function would boundary demarcation and identity construction serve in a ritual healing context? In order to address this issue, it is important to observe a distinction that David Frankfurter has drawn between the "*historiola* proper," where the power comes by virtue of the narrative itself, and the "clausal *historiola*," where the narrative supports a directive utterance (e.g., a command).[39] As part of the "clausal *historiola*" category, a *similia similibus* formula thus operates in association with the contiguous command or directive utterance. Since such a command requires the speaker to make demands on the god or gods, its efficacy—at least in part—is dependent upon speaker's traditional status. As Frankfurter notes:

> In the case of the directive utterance, which includes prayer and magical command, the speaker's mind-set, preparation, traditional status, and purity are of paramount importance since the force of that utterance explicitly comes from that 'I' who says the words.[40]

It should be emphasized that, in addition to the imperative within the *similia similibus* formula, P. Heid. 1101 includes at least one—and probably two—other imperatives and three adjurations, which use the formula "I adjure you" (ὁρκίζο [read ὁρκίζω] σε). This reliance on appeals to the various divine representatives would have required the status of the speaker or client to be impeccable.

It is in this performative context that the primary ritual aim of the accusation of attempted Jewish violence should be situated: it showcased the "orthodoxy" or proper "Christian" status of the client through a rejection of any "Jewish" affiliation—whether the "Jews" in mind were ethnic Jews or metaphorical Jews. In other words, it was a strategy of differentiation. I maintain that by displaying the proper traditional status of the party involved, the practitioner believed he or she could better the chances that the transcendent entities would listen to the various appeals for healing.[41] This, in turn, would have increased the likelihood of the client receiving the desired result—the cessation of eye migraine and eye discharge and the accompanying pain.

---

39. Frankfurter, "Narrating Power," 469.

40. Ibid., 467. For the importance of proper traditional status as it relates to the failed exorcism in Acts 19:13–17, see Bates, "Why Do the Seven Sons of Sceva Fail?" 417–18.

41. The status of the client was also likely improved by the other traditional elements in the text (e.g., the proper angelic representatives and the Trisagion).

Conclusions

In this brief essay, I offered a new approach to the *historiola* in P. Heid. 1101, which synthesized insights from the fields of early Christian studies and ancient magical studies. The social function of the motif of Jewish violence against Jesus and his followers during Late Antiquity served as an interpretive lens for understanding the ritual function of the narrative's opening phrase ("for our Lord was pursued by the Jews"). I argued that the motif of attempted Jewish violence in P. Heid. 1101 was not used simply to establish the setting of the *historiola*, but it was also used to demonstrate the traditional purity of the client through a rejection of a "Jewish other."

Beyond merely explicating the ritual language of a particular *historiola*, this essay models the kinds of interpretive questions that can be raised when the contested nature of "Christianity" during Late Antiquity is placed at the forefront. I argue that an emphasis on the contested nature of "Christianity" will also lead scholars of ancient magic to challenge some of the governing taxonomies in the field. Indeed, scholarship on amulets has not adequately appreciated the complex ways practitioners constructed "orthodoxy"; rather, scholars have typically used ecclesiastical literature as the metric for organizing "Christian" and "Jewish" (and "Pagan") ritual practice.[42] Prototypes of "Christianity" based on other domains of Late Antiquity are thus imposed on amuletic language. As a result, scholars often divide the language on a single amulet into two or more discrete categories—"Christian" and "non-Christian" (sometimes divided into "Jewish" and "Pagan").[43] But are such divisions consistent with the ways practitioners expressed their ritual and religious identifications or "orthodoxies"?

P. Heid. 1101 demonstrates rather acutely the disjuncture between scholarly and ecclesiastical taxonomies, on the one hand, and the categories operative in applied ritual contexts, on the other hand. For instance, despite the practitioner's negative presentation of the "Jews" (i.e., as the pursuer of the protagonist Jesus Christ), he or she invokes positively various angels/entities (Adonaei, Sabaôth, Michaêl, Êl, Toumêêl, Gabriêl, Ourêêl, and Raphaêl), which are typically labeled "Jewish" by scholars of ancient magic.[44] Certainly these "good" characters were not understood as "Jewish" within the overall logic of the ritual; rather, contrary to their origins, the

---

42. On this tendency in scholarship, see Sanzo, *Scriptural Incipits on Amulets from Late Antique Egypt*, 10–14.

43. E.g., de Bruyn and Dijkstra, "Greek Amulets," 180–81; Shandruk, "Christian Use of Magic," 31–57.

44. E.g., LiDonnici, "'According to the Jews,'" 88; de Bruyn and Dijkstra, "Greek Amulets," 180–81; Hunt, "1152. Christian Amulet," 253.

angels/deities are clearly part of the same religious tradition as Jesus—what might be labeled "Christian" for convenience. Bifurcating the language of P. Heid. 1101 into "Jewish" and "Christian" domains thus fundamentally misrepresents—indeed, inverts!—the way the practitioner has constructed "orthodoxy" in the ritual.[45]

Taking seriously the manifold ways practitioners constructed and expressed their "orthodoxies" will lead us to construct anew the boundaries between "Christian," "Jewish," and "Pagan" ritual practices. Moreover, as I hope to have illustrated in this essay, attention to the negotiations of "orthodoxy" on amulets can also lead to new hermeneutical possibilities.

Works Cited

Bartchy, S. Scott. "Where is the History in Mel Gibson's *The Passion of the Christ*?" *Pastoral Psychology* 53 (2005) 313–28.

Bates, Matthew W. "Why Do the Seven Sons of Sceva Fail?: Exorcism, Magic, and Oath Enforcement in Acts 19,13–17." *Revue biblique* 118 (2011) 408–21.

Becker, Adam H., and Annette Yoshiko Reed, eds. *The Ways that Never Parted: Jews and Christians in Late Antiquity and the Early Middle Ages*. TSAJ 95. Tübingen: Mohr/Siebeck, 2003. Reprinted, Minneapolis: Fortress, 2007.

Bonner, C. *The Homily on the Passion by Melito Bishop of Sardis and Some Fragments of the Apocryphal Ezekiel*. London: Christophers, 1940.

Bouriant, U. *Fragments du texte grec du livre d'Énoch et de quelques écrits attribués à Saint Pierre*. Paris: Leroux, 1892.

Boyarin, Daniel. *Border Lines: The Partition of Judaeo-Christianity*. Philadelphia: University of Pennsylvania Press, 2004.

Boyarin, Daniel, and Virginia Burrus. "Hybridity as Subversion of Orthodoxy? Jews and Christians in Late Antiquity." *Social Compass* 52 (2005) 431–44.

Brakke, David. "Jewish Flesh and Christian Spirit in Athanasius of Alexandria." *JECS* 9 (2001) 453–81.

Cameron, Averil. "Jews and Heretics—A Category Error?" In *The Ways that Never Parted: Jews and Christians in Late Antiquity and the Early Middle Ages*, edited by Adam Becker and Annette Reed, 345–60. TSAJ 95. Tübingen: Mohr/Siebeck, 2003. Reprinted, Minneapolis: Fortress, 2007.

Coles, R. A. "2949. Fragments of an Apocryphal Gospel(?)." In *The Oxyrhynchus Papyri*. Vol. 41, edited by Gerald M. Browne, R. A. Coles, et al, 15–16. London: Egypt Exploration Society, 1972.

Collins, Derek. *Magic in the Ancient Greek World*. Malden, MA: Blackwell, 2008.

Daniel, Robert W. and Franco Maltomini, eds. *Supplementum Magicum*. 2 vols. Opladen: Westdeutscher Verlag, 1990–92.

———. "From the African Psalter and Liturgy." *ZPE* 74 (1988) 253–65.

de Bruyn, Theodore S. and Jitse H. F. Dijkstra. "Greek Amulets and Formularies from Egypt Containing Christian Elements: A Checklist of Papyri, Parchments,

---

45. For other amulets that challenge the boundaries between "Judaism," "Christianity," and "Paganism," see, for example, *GMA* 45, *GMA* 53, *PGM* P2, *PGM* P5a, *PGM* P6a, and *PGM* P7.

Ostraka, and Tablets." *Bulletin of the American Society of Papyrologists* 48 (2011) 163–216.

Drioton, E. "Un apocryphe anti-arien: La version copte de la correspondance d'Abgar, roi d'Édesse, avec Notre Seigneur." *Revue de l'Orient chrétien* 20 (1915–17) 306–26.

Dunn, James. *The Parting of the Ways: Between Christianity and Judaism and Their Significance for the Character of Christianity*. Philadelphia: Trinity, 1991.

Ebermann, Oskar. *Blut- und Wundsegen in ihrer Entwicklung*. Palaestra: Untersuchungen und Texte aus der deutschen und englischen Philologie 24. Berlin: Mayer & Müller, 1903.

Ehrman, Bart D., and Zlatko Pleše. *The Apocryphal Gospels: Texts and Translations*. Oxford: Oxford University Press, 2011.

Eusebius. *Ecclesiastical History*. Translated by Kirsopp Lake and J. E. L. Oulton. 2 vols. LCL. Cambridge: Harvard University Press, 1926, 1932.

Faraone, Christopher A. "The Agonistic Context of Early Greek Binding Spells." In *Magika Hiera: Ancient Greek Magic and Religion*, edited by Christopher A. Faraone and Dirk Obbink, 3–32. New York: Oxford University Press, 1991.

Fiaccadori, Gianfranco. "Cristo all'Eufrate (P. Heid. G. 1101, 8 ss.)." *La parola del passato* 41 (1986) 59–63.

Foley, John Miles. *Immanent Art: From Structure to Meaning in Traditional Oral Epic*. Bloomington: Indiana University Press, 1991.

Frankfurter, David. "Narrating Power: The Theory and Practice of the Magical *Historiola* in Ritual Spells." In *Ancient Magic and Ritual Power*, edited by Marvin Meyer and Paul Mirecki, 457–76. Boston: Brill Academic, 2001.

———. "Violence and Religious Formation: An Afterward." In *Violence in the New Testament*, edited by Shelly Matthews and E. Leigh Gibson, 140–52. New York: T. & T. Clark, 2005.

Fredriksen, Paula. "What Parting of the Ways? Jews and Gentiles in the Ancient Mediterranean City." In *The Ways that Never Parted: Jews and Christians in Late Antiquity and the Early Middle Ages*, edited by Adam Becker and Annette Reed, 35–63. TSAJ 95. Tübingen: Mohr/Siebeck, 2003. Reprinted, Minneapolis: Fortress, 2007.

Freyne, Sean. "Vilifying the Other and Defining the Self: Matthew's and John's Anti-Jewish Polemic in Focus." In *"To See Others as Others See Us": Christians, Jews, "Others" in Late Antiquity*, edited by Jacob Neusner and Ernest S. Frerichs, 117–43. Scholars Press Studies in the Humanities Series. Chico, CA: Scholars, 1985.

Grenfell, Bernard P. and Arthur S. Hunt. "1600. Treatise on the Passion." In *The Oxyrhynchus Papyri*. Vol. 13, edited by Bernard P. Grenfell and Arthur S. Hunt, 19–21. London: Egypt Exploration Society, 1919.

Hall, S. G. "The Melito Papyri." *Journal of Theological Studies* 19 (1968) 476–508.

Hunt, Arthur S. "1152. Christian Amulet." In *The Oxyrhynchus Papyri*. Vol. 8, edited by Arthur S. Hunt, 253. London: Egypt Exploration Society, 1911.

———. "2070. Anti-Jewish Dialogue." In *The Oxyrhynchus Papyri*. Vol. 17, edited by Arthur S. Hunt, 9–14. London: Egypt Exploration Society, 1927.

Kotansky, Roy. *Greek Magical Amulets: The Inscribed Gold, Silver, Copper, and Bronze Lamellae*. Pt. 1, *Published Texts of Known Provenance*. Opladen: Westdeutscher Verlag, 1994.

LiDonnici, Lynn. "'According to the Jews:' Identified (and Identifying) 'Jewish' Elements in the *Greek Magical Papyri*." In *Heavenly Tablets: Interpretation, Identity and Tradition in Ancient Judaism*, edited by Lynn LiDonnici and Andrea Lieber, 87–108. Journal for the Study of Judaism Supplements 119. Leiden: Brill, 2007.

Lieu, Judith. *Image and Reality: The Jews in the World of the Christians in the Second Century.* Edinburgh: T. & T. Clark, 1996.

Lührmann, Dieter. "POx 2949: EvPt 3–5 in einer Handschrift des 2./3. Jahrhunderts." *ZNW* 72 (1981) 216–26.

Lührmann, Dieter, and P. J. Parsons. "4009. Gospel of Peter?" In *The Oxyrhynchus Papyri.* Vol. 60, edited by R. A. Coles, M. W. Haslam, and P. J. Parsons, 1–5. London: Egypt Exploration Society, 1994.

Maltomini, Franco. "Cristo all'Eufrate P. Heid.G.1101: Amuleto cristiano." *ZPE* 48 (1982) 149–70.

———. "4469. Letter of Abgar to Jesus (Amulet)." In *The Oxyrhynchus Papyri.* Vol. 65, edited by M. W. Haslam, A. Jones, et. al, 122–29. London: Egypt Exploration Society, 1998.

Meyer, Marvin W., and Richard Smith, eds. *Ancient Christian Magic: Coptic Texts of Ritual Power.* San Francisco: HarperSanFrancisco, 1994. Reprinted, Boston: Brill Academic, 2001.

Preisendanz, Karl, ed. *Papyri Graecae Magicae: Die griechischen Zauberpapyri.* 2 vols. Re-edited by A. Henrichs. Stuttgart: Saur, 1973.

Reinhartz, Adele. "'Jews' and Jews in the Fourth Gospel." In *Anti-Judaism and the Fourth Gospel,* edited by R. Bieringer et al., 341–56. Louisville: Westminster John Knox, 2001.

Rupprecht, Hans-Albert. *Sammelbuch griechischer Urkunden aus Ägypten.* Vol. 16. Wiesbaden: Harrassowitz, 1985.

Sanzo, Joseph E. "Brit. Lib. Or. 4919(2): An Unpublished Coptic Amulet in the British Library." *ZPE* 183 (2012) 98–100.

———. *Scriptural Incipits on Amulets from Late Antique Egypt: Text, Typology, and Theory.* Studies and Texts in Antiquity and Christianity 84. Tübingen: Mohr/Siebeck, 2014.

Shandruk, Walter. "Christian Use of Magic in Late Antique Egypt." *JECS* 20 (2012) 31–57.

Shaw, Brent. *Sacred Violence: African Christians and Sectarian Hatred in the Age of Augustine.* Cambridge: Cambridge University Press, 2011.

Skemer, Don C. *Binding Words: Textual Amulets in the Middle Ages.* University Park: Pennsylvania State University Press, 2006.

Testuz, M. *Papyrus Bodmer XIII: Méliton de Sardes; Homélie sur la Pâque; Manuscrit du IIIe siècle.* Cologny-Genève: Bibliotheca Bodmeriana, 1960.

———. "Un nouveau manuscrit de l'homélie 'Peri Pascha' de Méliton." *Studia Patristica* 3 (1961) 139–41.

Varner, William. *Ancient Jewish-Christian Dialogues: Athanasius and Zacchaeus, Simon and Theophilus, Timothy and Aquilla: Introductions, Texts, and Translations.* Studies in the Bible and Early Christianity 58. Lewiston, NY: Mellen, 2004.

Versnel, H. S. "The Poetics of the Magical Charm: An Essay in the Power of Words." In *Magic and Ritual in the Ancient World,* edited by Paul Mirecki and Marvin Meyer, 105–58. Boston: Brill Academic, 2001.

Wilson, Stephen G. "'Jew' and Related Terms in the Ancient World." *Studies in Religion/Sciences Religieuses* 33 (2004) 157–71.

6

"One in Christ"
The View from Torah and Shoah

Zev Garber

S. SCOTT BARTCHY BROUGHT Christian Scriptures and early Christian history to UCLA and also founded the Center for the Study of Religion. I have fond memories of speaking at the Center on multiple occasions and found Scott to be a gracious host, perceptive commentator, and excellent coordinator of lecture presentations and Q & A with the audience. Noteworthy was his erudite written response to my remarks on Mel Gibson's *Passion* and his engagement with the comments I presented at the inaugural Faculty/Student Seminar Series sponsored by the UCLA Center for Jewish Studies (October 10, 2011). I spoke on the Synoptic Jesus in the context of history and tradition, seeking ways of understanding Jesus in the religious and cultural milieu of Second Temple Judaism and in the spirit of reconciliation, and encountering the Jewish Jesus in a dialogue between Jews and Christians. Predictably, Scott badgered me with terminology issues and for a second in Royce Hall 306 I looked at the cover of my *Jewish Jesus* volume displayed on a screen above my head and internally screamed, "Why, Lord, Why"?

Introduction

In an e-mail communication, Bartchy informed me that his deep interest in Jewish-Christian relations began in his teenage years when his father served (for 25 years) as the (Gentile) tenor cantor for the Jewish Temple in Canton, Ohio.[1] A comforting thought which underscores the intent and direction of my essay.

My reasoning for emphasizing the Jewishness of Jesus in Torah and Shoah is straightforward and transforming: dialogue celebrating uniqueness. As a practicing Jew who dialogues with Christians, I have learned to respect a primary belief ("One in Christ") that Christians understand to be the way of the scriptural Jesus on their confessional lives. Also, Jew and Christian in dialogical encounter with select biblical texts can foster mutual understanding and respect as well as personal change and growth within their faith affirmation. Moreover, the interfaith study of Scriptures respects differences and requires that the participants transcend the objectivity and data-driven detachment of standard academic approaches and encourages students at whatever level to enter into an encounter with Torah and Testament without paternalism, parochialism, and prejudice. In this vein, I offer a Jewish perception on "you are one in Christ Jesus" as expression of appreciation and friendship to a collegial friend who welcomes biting Jewish questions and reflections on sacred Christian texts. My essay embraces Torah thoughts, Jewish Jesus, and Shoah (Holocaust) theology.

Elsewhere I have written about the historical Jesus.[2] Here I attempt to make sense of the Christ of faith in the context of Jewish-Christian dialogue and informed by an admonition attributed to the Jewish Jesus, "The scribes and Pharisees sit on Moses' seat; therefore, do whatever they teach you and follow it."[3]

The Jesus of the classic Christian belief: Is he important to Israel, the people and the religion? Or fulfilled Torah? Is belief in the death and resurrection of Christ reflective of Mosaic monotheism or expressive of the

---

1. "Brother Zev" communication, July 1, 2014.

2. Garber, "Do Not Hurt Them," 49–56; Garber, "Partisan's Imagination," in *Mel Gibson's Passion*, 63–69, and reprinted with slight change in Garber, *Jewish Jesus*, 13–19. Also, in my forthcoming edited volume entitled, *Teaching the Historical Jesus*, I contribute a chapter on teaching Jesus in the classroom and content issues related to Jewish Studies.

3. Matt 23:2–3a. Bartchy's essay ("Jesus, the Pharisees, and Mediterranean Manliness") in *Teaching the Historical Jesus*, portrays Jesus as rejecting pharisaical behavior, dress, teaching, and outward male socialization. New Testament passages are taken either from the RSV or the NRSV translations and Hebrew Bible passages are JPS (1917 translation).

triune God of Christianity? Part of the problem stems from definition and intent. Some want to talk history, others theology. Some dance to Pan's lyre (Nicaea, Constantinople, Chalcedon) and others to David's harp (Bethlehem, Galilee, Jerusalem). Still others want to focus on text in the context of time and clime. Consider the word "Christ" and its corollary, vicarious atonement sacrifice, used so frequently in discussions and depictions of Second Testament theology.

As a Jew, I assess the Easter faith as derived from critical scholarship in search of the historic Jesus, not faith affirmations, however insightful. For me, Jesus did not teach the traditional negative teachings about the Jews derived from sentences in the Gospels and Pauline Christology, and Augustine, Aquinas, and Reformation theology, which have influenced acts of cruelty and persecution against them throughout the ages. Also, to say, "Jesus our Lord points the way to God" means that the God-man of the hypostatic union is metaphorical and not the ultimate force called God. Christian believers and educators can benefit from Jewish/Hebraic hermeneutics in teaching about Jesus' love and compassion.[4] That is to say, by focusing on Jesus as a Pharisee, the Christian believer properly recovers the oral traditions preceding and following from the Jesus way. More importantly, associating Jesus with proto-rabbinic (Pharisaic) thought places the moral and spiritual message of Jesus in a sound Jewish context, which underscores a salient message: demythologize the Jewish guilt in the death of Jesus and demystify dogmatic Christology. Anything less than this combined effort would be to assail, not advocate, Christ in a post-Shoah cross-cultural world.

A basic component of interfacing between Jews and Christians is to respect and understand the revelatory assertions of the other, but equality in dialogue does not mean ready acceptance of the other's religious doctrines and theology. Consider here the curious story of the Fig Tree. In Mark, it is written: "He was hungry; and seeing in the distance a fig tree in leaf, he went to see if he could find anything on it. When he came to it, he found nothing for it was not the season for figs. And he said to it, 'May no man ever eat fruit from you again' . . . and Peter . . . said unto him: 'Master, behold the fig tree which you cursed is withered away.'"[5]

Further in the text, the curse is explained to his followers as an admonition of faith in God. Set in the context of the Second Temple period, however, early church tradition addresses Jesus' caustic words to the Temple authorities, which, in the course of Church history, are extended to the

---

4. Cf. Mark 12:29 and Deut 6:4; Matt 22:37, Mark 12:30, Luke 10:27 and Deut 6:5; Matt 22:39, Mark 12:31, Luke 10:27b and Lev 19:18.

5. Mark 11:12–14, 21 and a shorter parallel in Matt 21:18–19.

whole Jewish nation in Jesus' name. Christian creedal faith affirms that Jesus the Christ and God the Father are united "unconfusedly, unchangeably, indivisibly, inseparably."[6] And this "teaching of contempt"[7] has contributed to the near total destruction of European Jews in Hitler's Europe. Add human disaster in the aftermath of natural disaster ("acts of God"), and I see a damning message in the curse of a blameless tree ("it was not the right time of year for the figs").[8]

There is no doubt that many Christians accept the proclamation of the Fig Tree as the Word of God as it is. I do not. I see in this enigmatic passage a deviation of "The Earth is the Lord's, and the fullness thereof" (Ps 24:1) and an aberration of the Lord's word to Adam and Eve's children not to destroy Earth but "to till and to keep it" (Gen 2:15). And I suspect that the Teacher from Galilee would agree.

Eternal Torah

There is a line of basic continuity between the beliefs and attitudes of Jesus and the Pharisees, between the reasons that led Jesus into conflict with the religious establishment of his day and those that led his followers into conflict with the Synagogue.

Two of the basic issues were the role of the Torah and the authority of Jesus. Rabbinic Judaism could never accept the Second Testament Christology since the God-man of the "hypostatic union" is foreign to the Torah's teaching on absolute monotheism. As the promised Messiah,[9] Jesus did not meet the conditions which the prophetic-rabbinic tradition associated with the coming of the Messiah. For example, there was no harmony, freedom, peace, and amity in Jerusalem, and enmity and struggle abounded elsewhere in the Land. This lack of peace denied the validity of the Christian claim that Jesus fulfilled the Torah and that in his Second Coming the tranquility of the Messianic Age will be realized. As Rabbi Jesus, he taught the divine authority of the Torah and the prophets (Matt 5: 17–20), and respect for its presenters and preservers,[10] but the Gospels claimed that his authority

---

6. Jesus, truly man and truly God at one and the same time, was proclaimed such at the Council of Chalcedon (451 CE).

7. Term is associated with Jules Isaac (1877–1963), French Jewish authority on antisemitism, who, in an audience with Pope John XXIII in 1960, persuaded the Holy Father to consider the errors of the Church's teachings on the Jews. Isaac's writings were influential in the declaration of *Nostra Aetate*, Vatican Council II (1965).

8. Mark 11:13.

9. See, among others, Matt 26:62–64; Mark 14:60–62; Luke 22:60–70.

10. Matt 23:1–3a. See footnote 2 above.

was equally divine and that it stood above the authority of the Torah. The disparity of the Jewish self and the Gentile other in the ancestral faith of Jesus is abolished in the new faith in Jesus: "There is neither Jew nor Greek, slave nor free, male and female, for you are all one in Christ Jesus."[11] I see this testimony as a major point of contention between the Jesus way and the way of rabbinic *halakha* ("the Path," a phrase embracing both Torah and Talmud law) that ultimately led to the severance of the Jesus party from the Synagogue. The disparity between them acquired new intensity after the passing of the Jewish Jesus and the success of Pauline Christianity. On the latter, take Paul's letter to the Galatians, for example. Noteworthy is his position, "a person is justified not by works of law but through faith in Jesus Christ" (2:16; see too 2:21; 3:2; 5:2), which is buttressed by Paul's argument that the Torah is mediated by angels and ensnared in sin and has never played a salvific role (3:19–22), and finalized by the charge that Israel of the flesh is neither the true seed of Abraham (3:16) nor of God (6:16).

The doctrine of the eternity of the Torah is implicit in biblical verses such as the following: "A perpetual statute throughout your generations in all your (lands of) dwellings" (Lev 3:17) and "throughout the ages as a covenant for all time" (Exod 3:16). Biblical (Proverbs, in which Torah equals wisdom), Apocryphal (the wisdom of Ben Sirah), and Aggadic (*Genesis Rabbah*) traditions speak of the pre-existence of Torah in Heaven. Though the Talmud acknowledges the pre-revelation existence of Torah in Heaven, which was later revealed to Moses at Sinai, it concentrates more on Torah's eternal values.

Jewish thinkers from the first century to the nineteenth century have proclaimed the Torah eternal, some in terms of metaphysics, others in terms of theology, and most in defense of Judaism against the political polemics of Christianity and Islam, both of which teach that aspects of Torah are temporal or have been superseded. In the first century, Philo Judaeus spoke metaphysically of the Torah as the word (*logos*) of God, the beginning of creation. In the tenth century, Saadia Gaon proclaimed that the Jews were unique only by virtue of Torah; if the Jewish nation will endure as long as the heaven and earth, then Torah must also be eternal. Maimonides extolled the perfection (eternity) of Torah, regarding which there is neither addition or deletion. After Maimonides, the issues of the eternity of the Torah became routine; the Torah's eternity became an undisputed article of belief. The schools of Kabbalah, however, declared that the pre-existent form of

---

11. Gal 3:28. Also, 1 Cor 12:13 and Col 3:11. A capsule note on Jewish and Greek parallels to this defining Christian formula is made by Cohen in Levine and Brettler, eds., *Jewish Annotated New Testament*. See "Letter of Paul to the Galatians," 339.

Torah is eternal but that the words and message of the Torah are recycled every 7,000 years.

In the nineteenth century, the *Wissenschaft des Judentums* (Scientific Study of Judaism) movement, inspired by the scholarship of biblical critics, presented a historical-critical approach to Torah study. As a result, the traditional concept of the eternity of the Torah became a non sequitur and the idea of the Torah as a human book prevailed. By the mid-twentieth century, however, responding to negative trends in higher biblical criticism, which reflected aspects of classical Christian bias and labeled "higher" anti-Semitism,[12] critical studies by Jewish loyalists helped to reaffirm the Jewishness of the Bible. To conclude, no matter how a Jew views the nature of Torah—as a kind of "mythicizing history," or a product of the people for the people, or written (inspired) by God—its inspirational, national, and religious legacy is eternal.

Paul Matters

Stern halakhic Jews question the sincerity about and applicability of Jewish-Christian interfaith dialogue. Their two-point concern: ultimate religious beliefs cannot be communicated or shared, and that dialogue diminishes parochial religious identity and belief. I fully understand this position but repairing not parting of the Way is the call I choose to follow. How and why is attempted in this unit on Paul related matters.

Paul, born in Tarsus in Asia Minor to a wealthy and identified Jewish family, traveled to Jerusalem to drink from the wellsprings of Pharisaic thought. His words and psychological drive, molded in the Greco-Roman Diaspora, clashed with core beliefs of the Jerusalem Jesus party, and led to bouts of anguish, depression, and discomfort.[13] Nonetheless, his conversion on the road to Damascus stilled his prolonged sense of guilt-by-persecution of malcontents to the Temple authority and endowed him to proclaim the "Son of God" triumphant among the Gentiles.

Christian Scriptures focus on Paul's discontent with other Jewish believers in the fledgling Christian movement regarding how to teach meaningfully God-in-Christ, his teaching *about* Jesus for the different Christian communities in the Mediterranean world, his emphasis on the centrality of Jesus' resurrection, and his ubiquitous teaching to Jew and Gentile alike

---

12. Term attributed to Solomon Schechter (1847–1915), chief architect of Conservative Judaism and Catholic (community) Israel, whose reputation began in his recovery of the Cairo *Geniza*.

13. My description of Paul of Tarsus is extracted from my review of Chilton.

that the title "Israel, the Chosen People" is not determined by kinship nor land nor sanctuary nor obedience to the Torah but defined by the faith-claim that the risen Jesus, the Christ, is the Son of God. On the latter, Paul severely departs from thousands of co-believers who attest to the divinity of Jesus while obeying the teaching of Moses and from the Apostles James and Peter, who affirmed respectively God's Spirit in the way of Torah and the centrality of the Temple worship and its purity laws and who baptized not pagans but God-fearers.

Paul's *modus operandi* was to teach biblical covenantal theology by way of the resurrection in order to proclaim that Jesus' sense of himself as the new Adam, whose death at Calvary has joined the people of the circumcision and the people of the uncircumcision "to God in one body through the cross" (Eph 2:11, 16). To enact his radical Christology and to challenge the Temple obsession of the mother church, Paul trekked to Jerusalem, the heart of the Jesus movement. There, he went to the Temple, the bosom of Judaism, to offer a sacrifice on behalf of Jewish Christians and by acknowledging that Gentiles live by an abbreviated Noachide tradition, uniting Gentile and Jewish believers in a single spiritual Israel (Acts 21:17–26). Alas, this was not to be. Paul with a large group of Nazirites in his entourage was met by a riotous mob in the Temple precincts. He was beaten by temple police, charged with profaning the holy place, and had to defend his honor before the Sanhedrin. In order to avoid a conspiracy that sought to kill him, for his safety he was handed over to Claudius Lysias, the Roman captain, and later to Felix, the governor in Caesarea. In 62 CE, the year that James was stoned to death by the order of the High Priest, Ananus—an act that broke the link to the centrality of the Temple—Paul was released and spent his last years unfettered in Rome. Contesting Rome's imperial ideology, he was executed under Nero in 64 CE.

New Testament Christianity sets for the Christian reader a difficult but commendable task: to proclaim core Christian dogma (Easter faith) and dicta (Jesus "the living bread that came down from heaven" [John 6:51] heralds a *eucharista*, "the Lord's death, until he comes" [1 Cor 11:26]) without a hint or utterance of anti-Semitism. However, the necessary faith in Jesus Christ has bred in Church history a minimalist teaching on the importance of Torah. "The word is near you on your lips and in your heart because if you confess with your lips that Jesus is the Lord and believe in your heart that God raised him from the dead, you will be saved" (Rom 10:8–9), suggesting that Christ, not Torah, is the centrifugal force in confession and belief. Nonetheless, Paul advocates that the circumcised and the uncircumcised share in the oneness of God through faith (Rom 3:27–31).

The Jewish reader should be aware of and sensitive to claims of Christian identity that are derived from the Hebrew Scriptures. For the most part, progressive New Testament scholarship penetrates the wall of separation and suspicion of "law and grace" and enables the believer in the Second Testament to appreciate the story of how Jesus was not only God's Son but the cosmic reality of divine nature itself fully in terms of Israelite religion, that is to say, in accordance with the teaching of Moses but not necessarily in the exegesis of the sages of Israel. Alongside—not in place of—the Jewish insights, the how and why of the Christian relationship to the Sinai covenant is presented in the Christian spirit of scriptural inspiration and tradition, a strong sign that centuries-old "teaching of contempt"[14] is not desirable nor doable for Christians in dialogue with Jews. Dialogue is where a shared biblical tradition is the surest sign that the stumbling blocks of religious intolerance can be overcome. Ideally, the goal of interfaith scriptural dialogue is that the Gentile Church appreciates its Jewish origins and that Jews understand the importance of the mystery of God's presence in the "body of Christ." Furthermore, interfaith dialoguers ought to respect the integration of Sinai revelation (Written Torah) with rabbinic activity (Oral Torah) and recognize that a Jew named Saul later known as Paul was destined to change Judaism's mental landscape forever.

Shoah Theology: Neither, Either, Both Jew and Gentile

Questioning God in the face of Evil is as old as the Bible, as the story of Job and the words of Jesus at the Crucifixion attest.[15] But the savagery of the Shoah places the Nazi brutality in a category by itself. For many survivors of the Kingdom of Night, the aching question, "Where was God when six million Jews, one and a half million of them children, and other ethnic (e.g., Sinti and Roma people) and religious groups (Confessing Church, Jehovah's Witnesses, etc.) perish in an indescribable catastrophic evil?" is answered by a deafening silence from Heaven and righteous anger born in frustration on Earth.

How may a Jewish traditionalist and Jewish modernist respond to painful questions of divine silence in the murder of millions in the heart of Christian Europe? The traditionalist may say that there are miracles recorded in biblical literature but there are also fundamental principles. The

---

14. See note 7.

15. The words of Jesus on the cross, "*Eli/Elohi, Eli/Elohi, lama sabachtani*" (Matt 27:46; Mark 15:34) exemplify the ubiquitous cry of the Jew, "Why, O Lord, do you remain silent?"

Torah is clear that the staff Moses used to split the Sea of Reeds lost its power soon after the battle against Amalek (Exodus 17). May this not be the Torah's way of saying that in the face of evil, heavenly intervention is not necessarily determined by Man's plight? There are catastrophic events in history that Man will have to conquer. The lachrymose history of the Jews in Christian Europe served as a preamble to Hitler's inferno. And the world in general and Christendom in particular did very little. Thus "where was God?" should be discussed fairly. Emotional retort ought not dismiss defense of God in the face of evil.[16]

The modernist rejects the idea that God is a super ally in the sky. In Judaism, every individual is created in God's image (Gen 1:26). In classical rabbinic theology, *imago Dei* is understood that Man and God are co-creators and co-responsible. However, the modernist substitutes "godliness" for God. Why? Because wherever God is used as noun He becomes a person, a thing, an object or a Son, and this for the modern rationalist becomes idolatry. Godliness has all the attributes that monotheists ascribed to God, and which Man is obligated to imitate. When humankind is callous, when it turns its back to the predators, when it allows homelessness and brutality to exist, it betrays the Godhood in all of us. Man has to behave in godliness. That God will intervene in times of agony and anguish is an illusion and therefore will end in disillusion. The question is, does the individual have an ethical and sophisticated conception of the God idea to make one understand what the world is and what the world ought to be? The point is that Man must never forget the evil that was committed before and during the Shoah, but we dare not forget the altruistic good done by individuals against all odds. The good is that spark of humanity.[17]

My position, however, is to view theodicy and history and "all in Christ" by "historiosophy,"[18] whose importance is demonstrated in biblical and rabbinical literature. The agonizing questions may be anchored in historical events, but the question's religio-historical understanding lies in the paradigmatic value of "faith knowledge." The position is that in responding

16. From an interview with Rabbi Marvin Hier, dean and founder of the Simon Wiesenthal Center in Los Angeles, *LA Times,* April 21, 2001.

17. From an interview with Rabbi Harold Schulweis, head Rabbi at Valley Beth Shalom, Encino, California, *LA Times,* April 21, 2001.

18. Seeing events of history as paradigms infused in interpretive explanations. See "The Ninety-Three Beit Ya`akov Martyrs," in Garber, *Shoah,* 97–104. The book's Foreword and Preface, respectfully written by two Christian pioneers of Holocaust Studies in America, Franklin Hamilton Littell (Protestant, Temple University) and Harry James Cargas (Roman Catholic, Webster University), endorse highly my application of historiosophy to dialogue with Torah, Midrashim, and Shoah. Also, see Moore, "A Little Historiosophy," 136–39.

to God and Shoah, one must move beyond historiography to historiosophy if the goal is to maintain a commitment to life and memory and not affixation on death and finality.

In the face of Evil, Godspeech is the language of silence. I believe that was the condition in Deut 30:11–20, which states that God brings life and death, curse and blessing. The divine instruction proclaims: choose life so that you and your offspring would live. Having said that, the very same passage says that the command is not in heaven, as the Torah is not in heaven. The text says that the command is very near to you. It is "in your mouth and in your heart, to observe it" (v. 14). That is where you begin with the response to the question of faith after the Shoah. If Judaism's understanding is a covenant with God, then God is restricted by choice of both Heaven and Earth. Man has free will. For man to have free will means that God is self-restricted when it comes down to Man's determination, one's fate, for better or worst. It is one way of suggesting that Judaism is a religion of accomplishment and achievement. The Jew has got to see this as a sign of seeking life under all circumstances, including the Shoah. It is not a question of where was/is God in travesty. The question is, where was/is Man?

In sum, it is acceptable to God-wrestle. That is basic Judaism, and its greatest strength. To ask "where was God?" in the Nazi inferno is permissible. *Both* Jew and Greek/Gentile bear witness to the slaughter of numberless innocents in the lands of Christendom. The response is intuitively conveyed in Exodus 24. Moses read from the Book of the Covenant before the people, and they respond, "All that the Lord has spoken, we will do (*na'aseh*), and we will hear (*nishma'*)" (v. 7). I profess ("in your mouth") therefore I act and by so doing I understand. Providentially, the image of God-as-*Na'aseh* is testified by acts of concentration camp inmates, whose caring, kindness, nurturing, sacrifice, and suffering are sacral acts of everyday *kedušša* (holiness) that places God's presence on the cremated body of Israel.

Mistaken is the teaching that God was absent in Auschwitz. Pitiful is the post-Shoah thinking that is unable or unwilling to reconcile human suffering with the existence of a good and loving God. Acknowledge that God dwells among Israel, in her travels and travails, even if the people cannot sense Him in exilic and genocidal acts. Counter the trope of divine hiddenness by finding Rudolf Otto's *mysterium tremendum et fascinas* in that which attracts and repels even to what is defiled. Sense that the rupture of the Sinai covenant is restored by everyday acts of humaneness. Think historiosophically that the covenantal love between God and Israel is sensed in God's suffering presence in the camps. Know that revelation and redemption were continually retrieved and sustained in the Event by genuine nurturance and close human relationships.

There is neither male and female but not at the expense of obliteration. Never forget the sanctified character of the valorous women of the Shoah. Their nobility, efficiency, nurturing, devotion, obedience, truthfulness, sacrifice, and unquestionable suffering, which reveal the female face of God while always respecting Her male component, is inspiring. From Abraham being acquiescent to offering his beloved son as a holocaust on Moriah to God's permitted crucifixion of his Beloved Son at Cavalry to the murder of His chosen children in Auschwitz, the *kol ishah* (woman's voice) has been traditionally neglected, distorted, or worse. For example, in the camps, the male covenantal relationship (circumcision mark, facial hair, fringes, phylacteries, prayer, responsa, Torah-Talmud study, etc.) are ubiquitously expressed and remembered even in death. But the woman is without overt and covert religious signs. Her naked body, analogous to the naked face of God, speaks volumes of indifference, silence, and forgetfulness in Judaism, the patriarchal religion. Yet her last earthly act, caressing a babe, before both are shot by the Nazi murderer, brought Heaven down to Hell. God's presence in the pit and in the fire with woman and child is a stark wake-up call that post-Shoah theology should not continue as usual. This way of correcting masculinist theology does not diminish the paradox of God and the Shoah, but serves to make the issue more significant and inclusive, and therefore also unveils God more completely.[19]

Auschwitz Binding: God-Wrestling in the Night

Heaven and earth (is called) to witness that whether it be Gentile or Israelite, man or woman, slave or handmaid, according to the deeds that one does, so will the Holy Spirit rest on him/her.[20]

Midrash, in the Rabbinic mind, is hermeneutics derived from biblical inquiry, an attempt to explain the text in as many ways as seems possible to the inquiring mind of the Jewish sage. In Jewish and Christian dialogue on sacred texts, the term also embraces doctrinal, ethical, religious, and social

---

19. Remarks inspired by Raphael, *Female Face*. See my review.

20. *Tanna DeVei Eliyahu*, a midrash consisting of two parts, whose final redaction took place at the end of the tenth century CE. The first part is called "Seder Eliyahu Rabbah" (thirty-one chapters); the second, "Seder Eliyahu Zuṭa" (fifteen chapters). A distinct reference to this midrash occurs in *b. Ket.* 106a: "Elijah used to come to R. Anan, upon which occasions the prophet recited the Seder Eliyahu to him." The Haggadah speaks of six periods of Jewish history divided into three eras: (1) the present world; (2) the messianic period; and (3) the future world. The theme of *derekh 'erets* (quality life) made possible by doing proper precepts is a binding thread in this collection of midrashic ethical thought. The cited maxim of divine retribution is illustrative.

concerns. The message of Auschwitz then for the Jew and Christian is not survival alone. There is something more important than physical survival, and that is preventing moral bankruptcy. When Auschwitz (survival at any price) contends with Sinai and Calvary (moral standards), Sinai and Calvary must prevail. Nazi Germany is an example of what can happen when Auschwitz prevails. On European anti-Semitism, Sigmund Freud argued that the practitioners were "badly christened," and were forced into Christianity by bloody compulsion. Their true essence, barbaric polytheists, subliminally rejected the triumphant Church militant. So "(T)he hatred for Judaism is at bottom hatred for Christianity, and it is not surprising that in the German National Socialist revolution this close connection of the two monotheistic religions finds clear expression in the hostile treatment of both."[21]

Holy Scriptures teach that God's enduring covenant is with the destiny of Israel. Moses professes that the Children of Israel are eternal and Paul confesses that the foundation of *Heilsgeschichte* is founded in their existence (Rom 9:1–6 and Rom 11), and both acknowledge that their fate testifies to the transcending power of God in history. In Exod 32, Moses defends Israel who is referenced as a stiffnecked people but in whom God's moral self in history is rooted. Moses argues that however just God's position is (e.g., the Golden Calf apostasy), His decision to destroy them would be *the sine qua non* factor for the Egyptians (that is to say, the nations of the world) not to expect any notion of heavenly justice. The Torah declares, *tsedek, tsedek tirdof* ("justice, justice shall you pursue," Deut 16:20), and Moses requests that God must be perceived as doing no less. Also at stake is God's covenantal promise to the Patriarchs that He will enable their "offspring (to be) as numerous as the stars of heaven . . . And the Lord relented and renounced the punishment He had planned to bring upon His people" (Exod 32:13–14).

So what to make of Auschwitz? In the fire of the crematoria, God's Child (Exod 4:23) was cremated. Was this ultimate crime for the sake of the covenant and for the glory of His Name? In Egyptian bondage of yore, God heard the cry of the people, and God remembered His covenant with the Patriarchs, and He redeemed. The thousands and thousands of Jews from the *shtetlakh* (Jewish villages) of Eastern Europe refused to abandon the yoke of the covenant. Their oath of survival, mixed with dirges of pain, hoped that God would stop the indescribable *churban*. But Heaven shed no tears. The position that the Shoah pairs Jewish history and the Jewish view

---

21. Freud, *Moses and Monotheism*, 117.

of God raises a frightening theological question. Are we to conclude that in the "Flicker of the Jews' last hour, Soon Jewish God, Your eclipse?"[22]

The question underscores the perpetual dilemma in covenant theology. Were the *Endlösung* to be fully enacted there would be no covenant, since on the altar of Auschwitz, the commitment to the Torah directive, "Choose life" (Deut 30:19), would go up in flames. Were the Jews treated as ordinary victims of Nazi incarceration, this would forsake the ultimate concern of covenantal belief. In Auschwitz, God is challenging Israel's commitment to the covenant. In actuality, the Jew is also challenging God's commitment to the covenant. In the context of covenant theology as played out in the death camps, mutual challenges are expected. Indeed, these challenges do not diminish the paradox of Auschwitz, but serve to make the issue more significant and more troubling, and therefore also more of hope. In the heat of the Nazi inferno, the unconditional commitment of both partners is tested and endures.

And what to say to the post-Shoah Jew and Christian? Respect the difference. To honor the memory of the brutally murdered, we must never forget nor forgive. For the Christian believer, may I suggest that "One in Christ" (Gal 3:28) mandates Christian attentiveness to the fate and faith of the murdered Jews of Europe under the symbol of the "Crooked Cross" (swastika) tragically nurtured by *Adversus Judeo*; and for the practicing Jew, the Torah commands that we restore flesh to bones, personality to numbers, and novelty to *novum*—a doable memorial to those who suffered in the consuming fire and, we believe, were sustained by the supernal light which does not consume nor diminish.

Works Cited

Bartchy, S. Scott. "Jesus, the Pharisees, and Mediterranean Manliness." In *Teaching the Historical Jesus: Issues and Exegesis*, edited by Zev Garber. London: Routledge, forthcoming.

Freud, Sigmund. *Moses and Monotheism*. Translated by Katherine Jones. 1939. Reprinted, New York: Vintage, 1967.

Garber, Zev. "Do Not Hurt Them." In *Holocaust Scholars Write to the Vatican*, edited by Harry James Cargas, 49–56. Contributions to the Study of Religion 58. Westport, CT: Greenwood, 1998.

———. "Jacob Glatstein." In *Reference Guide to Holocaust Literature*, edited by Thomas Riggs, 110–11 and 466–67. Farmington Hills, MI: St. James, 2002.

———. Review of Bruce Chilton. *Rabbi Paul: An Intellectual Bibliography*. Review of Biblical Literature (2005) http://www.bookreviews.org.

22. Jacob Glatstein. On Glatstein, the man and his poetry (Yiddish), see my entries in Riggs, *Reference Guide*, 110–11 and 466–67.

---, ed. *The Jewish Jesus: Revelation, Reflection, Reclamation.* Shofar Supplements in Jewish Studies. West Lafayette, IN: Purdue University Press, 2011.

---, ed. *Mel Gibson's Passion: The Film, The Controversy, and Its Implications.* Shofar Supplements in Jewish Studies. West Lafayette, IN: Purdue University Press, 2006.

---. "The Ninety-Three Beit Ya'akov Martyrs: Towards the Making of Historiosophy." In Zev Garber, *Shoah, The Paradigmatic Genocide: Essays in Exegesis and Eisegesis*, 97–104. Studies in the Shoah 8. Lanham, MD: University Press of America, 1994.

---, ed. *Teaching the Historical Jesus: Issues and Exegesis.* Routledge Studies in Religion. London: Routledge, forthcoming.

Levine, Amy-Jill, and Marc Zvi Brettler, eds. *The Jewish Annotated New Testament: New Revised Standard Version Bible Translation.* New York: Oxford University Press, 2010.

Moore, James F. "A Little Historiosophy: An Essay in Honor of Zev Garber." *Shofar* 28 (2009) 136–39.

Raphael, Melissa. *The Female Face of God at Auschwitz: A Jewish Feminist Theology of the Holocaust.* Religion and Gender. London: Routledge, 2003.

7

To Serve as Slave
Footwashing as Paradigmatic Status Reversal

Mark A. Matson

THE RECEPTION OF THE New Testament is often one of a culture-bound misreading. As typically economically comfortable western Christians, steeped in a sense of personal independence, we often (usually?) hear and absorb those texts that fit our cultural values and our predispositions. One of the teachers who challenged me to hear texts in a more intense way, to listen for cultural differences, and to question my own built-in predispositions was Scott Bartchy. His effort to be attentive to the social context and social challenge that the text offers us has been formative on how I approach gospel research. It is in honor of Scott's deep appreciation for cultural challenges that this paper is offered.

The footwashing in the Fourth Gospel (John 13:1–17) is one of those texts that is often read and then overlooked. After all, what do we do with John's striking and unique scene in which Jesus partially disrobes, stoops down, and washes the feet of his disciples? How are we to understand the significance of this? Moreover, what do we do with the fact that this displaces, in John, any notice of a meal that was to be repeated symbolically in the later church? Is Jesus' command to repeat his action of footwashing, perhaps offered in the place of, or related to, a symbolic final meal, meant to be taken literally by subsequent Christians?

It will be the thesis of this paper that the footwashing in John is fundamentally a story of status reversal, but a status reversal that was meant to have paradigmatic significance for his disciples and subsequent followers. The full impact of the status reversal depends, however, on some understanding of the place that footwashing held in ancient cultures and of the status of those who performed footwashing. Indications for these can be gleaned from ancient literature, but also from parallel "footwashing" examples in the gospels. Given its prominent place in the farewell discourse, and its explicit call for imitation, both the act and the meaning seem important parts of a new pattern (παράδειγμα/paradigm) for behavior in the community of believers.

The Footwashing in John 13

As is well known, the narrative of the Fourth Gospel varies significantly from the Synoptic portrayal. The passion narrative is no exception. While some major elements are common between John and the Synoptics (e.g., a "triumphal" entry, a final meal, trial before Pilate, crucifixion, burial, and resurrection), their arrangement varies, often significantly. For instance, Jesus does not "cleanse" the temple in the final Passion Week, nor does John relate a trial before the Jewish authorities.[1] Indeed, while the chronology relative to the Sabbath is remarkably similar, still it varies from the Jewish calendar related in the Synoptic Gospels so that, in John's Gospel, Jesus is crucified at approximately the time the Passover lambs are being sacrificed on Nisan 14, and therefore the final meal in John could not possibly be a Passover meal (contra the Synoptic presentation).[2] As a result, careful attention to John's own distinctive narrative logic is important.

In John, we find the Passion week beginning not with the triumphal entry (cf. Mark 11:1–11), though John does narrate a dramatic entry shortly afterwards, but rather it begins with a dinner held in Bethany at the home of Lazarus (John 12:1–8); this event explicitly initiates the final week, being introduced by the phrase "six days before the Passover" (NRSV is used throughout, unless noted). At this dinner, Jesus is served by Martha and, importantly, Mary anoints Jesus' feet with costly perfume and wipes the feet with her hair. The conflict over the use of such costly perfume leads Jesus to

---

1. The term "cleanse" is used here only nominally for the incident in the temple. This action is, as I have argued elsewhere, best considered a symbolic demonstration predicting the destruction of the temple. See Matson "Contribution to the Temple Cleansing," and Matson, "The Temple Incident."

2. Matson, "Historical Plausibility."

anticipate, albeit obliquely, his upcoming burial. But in John, the reader is already aware that the "Jews" plan to kill Jesus (11:45–53), so this reference only serves to continue the trajectory of the narrative—what awaits Jesus is death. This trajectory is given more emphatic form in a short soliloquy by Jesus about his upcoming death (12:27–33).

Jesus' final meal, then, begins the next major scene in John, introduced by another explicit time marker: "Now before the festival of the Passover ..." (John 13:1). It is in this context that Jesus knows that his "hour has come to depart from this world," and thus this scene at the final meal marks the beginning of the last moments of Jesus' life. This final meal is the setting for the long extended discourse in John that leads to his betrayal and arrest, the so-called Farewell Discourse that begins in chapter 13 and extends to chapter 17. As a result, the footwashing, which dominates the initial scene of this final meal, sets the tone for the entire Farewell Discourse.

The footwashing in John 13:1–20 occurs explicitly in the context of a meal, as the introductory phrase δείπνου γινομένου indicates. This phrase is best translated simply as "it being meal-time," rather than following common translations which interpret this to mean that Jesus' footwashing somehow interrupts the meal or follows it, as in the NRSV's "during supper." The phrase simply indicates that the setting for the various events all take place at a normal dinner setting.[3] Indeed, the dinner setting, while important for understanding the event, is almost eclipsed by the various notices of finality that surround it: Jesus knows the "hour" has come, he loves the world to the end, and the devil has already cast betrayal into the heart of Judas. Moreover, no real meal is narrated. We only know that it is meal time, but little or no emphasis is given to the meal itself; and this fits with it being a non-Passover meal setting—other meals in John's gospel are not given detailed attention.

The meal setting is important, though, for understanding why Jesus does what he does. John reports Jesus rising from the dinner table, setting aside his cloak (ἱμάτια), and then wrapping a linen cloth around him (διέζωσεν). By describing Jesus in this way, especially in his removing his clothing and girding himself round with only a linen cloth, the Fourth Gospel portrays the scene in such a way as to focus on a self-humiliating aspect

3. There has been substantial disagreement by commentators about whether the footwashing intrudes in the middle of the dinner scene or not. The dinner setting begins with the phrase δείπνου γινομένου, often translated "during dinner." While such participial phrases might refer to chronological time relative to the main sentence, it is noteworthy that this is likely a genitive absolute clause, and as a result distinct from the activity of the main sentence. The genitive, then, very likely is simply descriptive of the time, and thus better translated "it being supper time." See also Coloe, "Welcome to the Household of God," who also cites Bultmann for a similar reading.

to his actions. A dinner guest might expect a household servant or slave to wash his feet as a gesture of hospitality, or possibly one might anticipate a basin (either a νιπτῆρα or ποδανιπτήρ / ποδάνιπτρον) being provided. Certainly, banquets were one of the most frequent occasions for footwashing.[4] That the feet of his disciples were washed at a dinner was not what was striking, and little notice is paid to the footwashing per se in John 13. *Who* performed the service, however, and in *what manner*, was unusual. The footwashing engenders a striking dialogue between Jesus and Peter over the role of footwashing, which then subsequently gives rise to a typical Johannine teaching monologue (13:12–20).

When Jesus came to Peter, Peter first questions why Jesus would be washing his feet (13:7), and then emphatically rejects it: "You shall never wash my feet." The question and expostulation both seem to arise from the perceived reversal of social status: *Jesus* should not be washing his feet. When Jesus argues that if Peter refuses he would have no part in Jesus, Peter then overreacts with a request to be washed all over. The issue, Jesus suggests, is not cleanliness, but submission and service.

Jesus then focuses on the point of the footwashing. "So if I, your Lord and Teacher (ὁ κύριος καὶ ὁ διδάσκολος), have washed your feet, you also ought to wash one another's feet" (John 13:14). Lord and teacher both indicate one with high status, and as a result it is clear that Jesus understands that his footwashing is a breach of normal social boundaries. The action and the perception by Peter, and the response by Jesus, all undergird the social context of a footwashing. The footwashing as such fits perfectly well in the dinner setting, and this footwashing per se does not raise concerns. What became the focal point, though, was the fact that the host and leader performed the footwashing, assuming the role normally assigned to a servant or slave.

Cultural Understanding of Footwashing

Footwashing was a fairly common practice in antiquity and is attested in the Old Testament, in Greco-Roman literature, and in Hellenic and Hellenistic artifacts (e.g., decorated vases). The primary context of the footwashing is the household, especially the dinner setting. While there are examples of footwashing in cultic settings, the largest number of examples does come from domestic settings.[5] The dinner or banquet setting was apparently a very

---

4. Thomas, *Footwashing in John 13*, 46–50.

5. Ibid. Thomas offers extensive examples of footwashing in antiquity, including cultic and domestic settings in ancient Israel (27–31, 31–40) and in Greco-Roman society (42–44, 44–50).

common opportunity for footwashing to take place. As John Christopher Thomas notes, "By far the best documented and most frequent accounts of footwashing are to be found in contexts where the washing precedes a meal or banquet."[6]

A couple of examples might help underscore the way footwashing was seen, both in Jewish and Greco Roman contexts. The first is the offer of water for footwashing to Abram's guests at the oaks of Mamre in Genesis 18. There, Abram asks for water to be brought as a sign of hospitality while a meal is prepared. In the Masoretic Text of Gen 18:4, the text suggests that water should be brought and the messengers of God should wash their own feet (second person plural imperative). The Septuagint, however, offers a slightly different understanding, and instead renders the verb "to wash" using a third person plural imperative: "Let them wash your feet," suggesting that not only would water be provided, but the actual washing of the feet would also be provided by others, presumably by Abram's servants.[7] At any rate, both show the importance of footwashing as a sign of hospitality, especially linked to dining.

Plutarch describes a banquet associated with the Pan-Athenian games which was notably luxurious, so much so that the liquid offered for footwashing was spiced wine rather than simply water: "and particularly the foot-basins (ποδανιπτῆρα) of spiced wine that were brought to the guests as they entered . . ."[8] The reference to a foot-basin being offered seems to be natural at a banquet such as this, but in this case it is notable for its contents of wine. The rather unremarkable aspect of a foot-basin being offered is suggestive of more extensive cultural pattern of footwashing at dinner settings.

Footwashing as a sign of hospitality is very frequently depicted in the form of a servant washing the feet of the guests. Thomas offers a number of examples drawn from Homer, Petronious, and Plutarch. One notable example from Plutarch's *Life of Pompey* underscores the relationship between footwashing and the service of a slave:

> Now, when it was time for supper and the master of the ship had made such provision for them as he could, Favonius, seeing that Pompey, for lack of servants, was beginning to take off his own shoes, ran to him and took off his shoes for him, and helped him to anoint himself. And from that time on he continued to give Pompey such ministry and service as slaves give their masters,

---

6. Ibid., 47.
7. Ibid., 35.
8. Plutarch, *Phocion* 20.2.

even down to the washing of his feet and the preparation of his meals . . .[9]

Here toward the end of the *Life of Pompey*, we have a scene that clearly depicts washing feet (and seemingly so for dining, as the close link to preparation of meals might suggest) as the role of a servant or slave.

Perhaps an equally illustrative example of the subordinate role that washing feet involves can be found in the Hellenistic Jewish romance, *Joseph and Aseneth*. This religious romance seeks to explain in an entertaining way how the Jewish Joseph, a mighty prince in Egypt, came to marry Aseneth, a daughter of a pagan priest. Early in the narrative, Joseph arrives at Pentephres' house and "they washed his feet" (ἔνιψαν)—clearly an act of hospitality.[10] Although it is not clear who performed the washing, the same people set a table for him, so ostensibly it would be servants or slaves. When Aseneth later is moved to prayer and confession as part of a conversion to God (and as part of her romantic response to Joseph), she prays to God that she might become "his maidservant and slave (παιδίσκην καὶ δούλην) . . . And I will make his bed, and wash his feet (νίψω τοὺς πόδας αὐτοῦ), and wait on him (διακονήσω), and be a slave (δουλεύσω) for him and serve him forever and ever."[11] In Aseneth's prayer, she, a noblewoman, is expressing the degree of her love and her willingness to give up prerogatives in order to have this new relationship. Taking on the role of a "slave"—which is specifically linked to footwashing—underscores her radical role reversal. This vow to place herself in a subservient status relative to Joseph, expressed in the prayer in *Jos. Asen.* 13, is subsequently fulfilled when they are first married:

> And she brought him water to wash his feet. And Joseph said, "Let one of the virgins come and wash my feet." And Aseneth said, "No, my Lord, because you are my lord from now on and I (am) your maidservant (παιδίσκη). And why do you say this (that) another virgin (is) to wash your feet? For your feet are my feet and your hands are my hands, and your soul my soul, and your feet another woman will never wash."[12]

This romance, which comes from approximately the same time period as the Fourth Gospel, certainly highlights the importance of footwashing as a sign of hospitality, but it also underscores the Jewish and Greco-Roman perspective on the status of those who perform footwashing: they are low

---

9. Plutarch, *Pompey* 73.6–7.
10. *Jos. Asen.* 7.1.
11. *Jos. Asen.* 13.15.
12. *Jos. Asen.* 20.2–5.

status, maidservants and slaves, who also serve (διακονέω). Aseneth's conversion also highlights the possible valorization of role reversal for religiously-linked reasons. Notably, Aseneth takes on the role now of servant and slave, and part of that role is to wash Joseph's feet. And this role reversal seems to arise from both domestic and religious motivations.

John's representation of Jesus washing the feet of his disciples certainly fits with other ancient perspectives on this act of hospitality. Footwashing was a normal part of dining hospitality, but normally would consist of water being offered for guests or, if an act of washing was offered, it would be expected to be by a servant or slave. Jesus' action of washing feet, especially the feet of his disciples, would be as running counter to cultural expectations. Jesus taking the role normally reserved for servants or slaves would certainly have been seen as a role reversal, as indeed is expressed in both the reaction by Peter (John 13:8) and by Jesus' explicit teaching (John 13:12–16). The dialogue confirms what we would expect from the larger cultural pattern.

Other Footwashings in John and Luke

The footwashing by Jesus in John 13 is not, however, the only example of footwashing in the New Testament.[13] A look at the other examples can helpfully inform us on how to interpret Jesus' washing of the disciples' feet. The two other examples are John 12:1–8 and Luke 7:36–50, although both are more commonly associated with "anointing" than footwashing.

John 12:1–8

Most commentators on the opening story in John 12 refer to it as an "anointing" of Jesus by Mary.[14] But is it what we would normally call an "anointing?" John does use the word ἀλείφειν, which certainly does mean to smear with oil. It is a word often used for "anointing" the dead—that is, smearing the body with fragrant oils and spices. But it should be noted that John does not use the term often connected with symbolic anointing, χρίειν, the word

---

13. Thomas makes this observation as well, also referring to John 12:1–8 and Luke 7:36–50 as footwashing episodes. Perhaps even more intriguing for me was the way Kitzberger read all three of these texts as indicating footwashing ("Love and Footwashing"). So also, Wainwright, "Anointing/Washing Feet."

14. See, for instance, Brown, *Gospel according to* John, 1:447; Schnackenburg, *Gospel according to St. John*, 365; Moloney, *Signs and* Shadows, 180; Keener, *Gospel of John*, 2:862.

commonly used to translate מָשַׁח.[15] But perhaps the anointing designation comes in part because John's story bears some strong familiarity with Mark's and Matthew's version of Jesus being "anointed" on his head: it is a dinner setting, the ointment is νάρδου πιστικῆς, and the dispute over the use of such valuable ointment results in Jesus' admonition that the ointment has some meaning in reference to his burial, a one-time situation, while the poor will always be there.

But John's story has such notable differences that even any faint echo of "anointing" heard from Mark's gospel seems to be lost, if ever there was one.[16] Mary's ointment is a very large quantity—a λίτραν (pound?)—most of which seems to be saved for Jesus' later burial as noted in John 12:7, "let her keep it for the day of my burial" (RSV), which is quite different than the reference in Mark where the "anointing" is an actual proleptic burial anointing. But most notably, the action of smearing with oil (ἤλειψεν) is inextricably linked with wiping it up (ἐξέμαξεν). And the object of both these actions is the feet, not the head. So Mary smears with ointment and then wipes it up using her hair as a wiping cloth. That this act of washing/smearing the feet and wiping it up again is the central focus is confirmed by an earlier reference to this act in the gospel at John 11:2. There, in the narrator's introduction of Mary and Martha, Mary's later action is anticipated, and the language there also highlights the smearing of oil and the wiping of the feet with hair.

But a more extensive examination of John's description of Mary's action suggests that John has attached quite a bit of narrative significance to her action. The setting is a dinner at Lazarus' house. Mary and Martha have prepared the dinner, and Martha served (διακόνειν). We might be tempted to see Mary and Martha as hosts, and yet that function seems to be reserved (or at least implied) for Lazarus: he reclined at the table with the dinner guests. We do not hear of Mary or Martha joining the guests at the dinner table.[17] Martha at least is explicitly described in a servant role. As a result, having her counterpart, Mary, assume a similar serving role of "washing the feet" fits well in the situation. As noted previously, footwashing was often connected with

---

15. Cf. Hearon, who examines the terminology of anointing (John and Luke) in "Story," 109–11.

16. By faint echo in Mark, I suggest that anointing is by no means an obvious interpretation there either. The language used in Mark is μυρίζω, to smear, not χρίω. And while Jesus is "smeared" on the head, there is no explicit connection to Peter's previous acclamation of him as the Christ, the anointed one.

17. Nor probably should we expect to see Mary or Martha in that situation; women did not usually join in public meals in antiquity. See Corley, *Private Women, Public Meals*, 26.

hospitality, as with a dinner setting, and the menial role of washing feet would have been reserved for a lower-status individual. The repeated emphasis on Mary wiping up the ointment with her hair suggests that this is indeed meant to be understood as a form of footwashing. Rather than using water, Mary has washed Jesus' feet with expensive ointment, and she has wiped them up not with a towel, but with her own hair. John's depiction of this footwashing is one in which a common act of hospitality has been transformed by extravagant means (expensive ointment, hair) into both a footwashing *and* personal service of devotion. And the extravagance and more personal action of Mary lead the reader to connect this also with the personal interaction between Jesus and Mary that was previously related before Lazarus was raised (John 11:28-37). The dinner scene in John 12 is closely linked (prospectively and retrospectively) with the Lazarus episode in John 11.

It is notable that, while the social setting of the dinner scene depicted in John 12 is not atypical, the story seems to focus its attention especially on this act so as to suggest that it was particularly important. Narratively, we are led to focus, approvingly, on Mary's actions. First, the act of smearing the feet with oil and then wiping them with her hair is anticipated at the beginning of the Lazarus story (11:1-2). This introduction to the Lazarus episode marks Mary and Martha as particularly noteworthy (a proleptic anticipation), and in addition Mary is then given special notice even beyond Martha. Secondly, in the "footwashing/anointing" episode of 12:1-8, the main attention is given to Mary and her action. While Lazarus is identified as the reason Jesus comes to Bethany, and so the likely householder, and while Martha is identified as "serving," the focus quickly shifts to Mary's striking gesture of hospitality. The reference to the fragrance of the ointment or perfume "filling the house" even seems to indicate that the action crowds out other actions and other conversation. Her gesture even results in criticism by Judas (who has already been identified as the betrayer, John 6:71), which, with Jesus' approving rejoinder to that criticism, underscores its importance and positive evaluation.

Taken together, then, Mary's action seems to be one of hospitality, but perhaps hospitality of a special sort. While Mary's social role as providing hospitality for guests allows the "footwashing/anointing" to fit within social bounds, it also strains them a bit. Would Mary and Martha naturally assume a servant/slave role? If the washing/anointing of Jesus' feet is within social bounds, drying the feet with her hair begins to seem more personal than normal.[18] Indeed, this issue of using her hair to dry off his feet often

---

18. See my draft paper, "Curious Case." Of special note also see Cosgrove, "Unbound Hair."

draws questions of propriety; the meaning of using unbound hair to dry feet will be addressed more extensively below in the discussion of the woman in Luke 7. Since it seems to be more "washing" than anointing, does this act of service by Mary anticipate Jesus' action? In other words, is Mary's action here proleptic also, leaning forward toward Jesus' own radical act of hospitality and service? It would seem so.

Luke 7:36–50

But Mary's footwashing is not the only one in the gospels. In Luke's gospel we find a striking counterpart to Mary's actions. Indeed, we have here one of the striking similarities between the Gospels of Luke and John.[19]

In Luke's narrative of Jesus' early ministry, he is shown eating a dinner at the house of Simon the Pharisee. A "sinner" woman comes into the dinner area and, standing behind him, wets his feet with her tears, wipes up the excess wetness with her hair, and then anoints his feet with oil. This action causes a violent reaction from Simon, who criticizes Jesus for allowing this activity from someone he should have known was a sinner. In response to this criticism, Jesus challenges Simon on the point of hospitality, since he had not provided water for Jesus to wash his feet, or a welcoming kiss on entering the house, or oil to anoint him. These are all, Jesus suggests, common forms of providing hospitality. But, Jesus notes, the woman in her act of contrition, has performed all of these acts of hospitality: she washed Jesus feet, kissed them, and anointed them, thus satisfying all three of these acts of hospitality (Luke 7:44–46).

What many scholars have noted, of course, are the strong points of similarity in particulars between Luke's "sinful woman" scene, and Mary's "anointing" in John. Perhaps it would be well to review these. First, in both cases the oil is smeared (ἤλειφεν in both cases) on Jesus' feet, not his head. In both cases the feet are wiped (ἐκμάσσω) with the woman's hair. These striking details certainly suggest some kind of linkage, either of tradition or literary relationship. And this striking similarity has often pointed scholars toward some element of textual knowledge or a literary relationship; given the normal dating of John being late, this has usually meant seeing John reliant on Luke.[20]

What is particularly interesting about the Lukan story is the explicit connection to hospitality. The wetting of the feet is compared to water

---

19. See Matson, *In Dialogue with Another Gospel?* 91–164.

20. One study that has strongly argued for John's reliance on Luke here is Bailey, *Traditions*.

provided for footwashing: the tears are the water for washing, and the hair then serves as the towel for the expected drying/wiping of the feet. Moreover, the smearing of ointment on the feet is also linked to an act of hospitality, though compared to a more normal act of anointing one's head upon entering. All of these actions are contextualized within the normal framework of ancient dining situations, including it would seem, the potential act of anointing one's head as an act of hospitality. Indeed, the central conflict issue of the story interprets the actions of the woman as appropriate because they are contrasted with what Simon *should have done* in such a dining setting: he *should have* provided water for feet, oil for his head, and a kiss of hospitality (Luke 7:44-46). Her actions, as such, are not problematic, because they are cited approvingly within the dining context. The problem with the woman's actions is not *what* she did, but *who* she is. It is her status as a sinner that raises the criticism by Simon the Pharisee, and Jesus returns to that at the end when he forgives her sin. On the other hand, the example of her footwashing/drying action is used instead as supportive material in a comparative argument offered by Jesus: what she did was more honorable than what Simon did (not) do. Had her actions, even the use of let-down hair, been of great concern one would expect that to arise in the story.[21] It does not.

But perhaps more can be gleaned from this story as well. First, we might notice the physical actions: the woman enters the dining hall and is able to move relatively easily to a place where she can wet, wipe, and anoint Jesus' feet. She stands over Jesus' feet to do this. All of this suggests a dining situation like a *triclinium*, where the diner is reclining with feet directed away from the center of the room where food would be brought. While women would not normally participate in such a meal as a diner, such a proscription would not necessarily apply to slave or servant women who would serve food.[22] So while women's presence "at table" would be unusual, some women's presence at a meal was certainly not unknown. The woman's entrance might have happened, then, quite normally until she was recognized. But in this case her position behind Jesus, in the area of his feet at the periphery of the dining hall, certainly places her in a low-status position. And that is what we have come to expect. Footwashing, when offered, was provided by slaves or low-status servants. The entire scene fits with the social structure of ancient dining situations.

21. As with the Mary episode discussed above on the issue of unbound hair, see Cosgrove, "Unbound Hair." Cosgrove argues that letting hair down in public is not inherently sexual in nature. He offers a number of examples that suggest it was common as a sign of grieving, or of religious devotion, both of which would fit a scene where footwashing with tears leads to the forgiveness of sins.

22. Corley, *Private Women, Public Meals*, 15, 24-34.

Much has been made of Luke's identification of the woman as a "sinner" (ἁμαρτωλός). Often the actions of wiping Jesus' feet with her hair are linked to the identification of her as a "sinner": sexual motives or overtones are implied from her action. The woman is then often identified as a prostitute. There is, however, no indication in this scene that there are any sexual overtones, or that the woman is a prostitute. In fact there is no direct linkage between her being a sinner and her actions; Jesus is indicted by Simon for his lack of *prophetic* knowledge of her status as sinner, not for allowing a ribald or suggestive action to take place, or even for failing to know her "sinful" status on the basis of the actions themselves. As Charles H. Cosgrove has noted, the letting down of hair, even of wiping feet, can be seen in antiquity as actions of penitence and/or grief.[23] And this, indeed, is how Luke interprets things—her actions were due either to her devotion or penitence (not her "profession"), but in any case they are motivated by faith ("Your faith has saved you," Luke 7:50).

Footwashing in John as Status Reversal

How, then, should we read John's account of the footwashing? What indications in the text should alert us to the importance of the role it plays in the Gospel of John? And, as my attention to other "footwashings" in the Gospels suggests, how might these other accounts inform a reading of John 13?

It is important to attend first to the logic of John 13 itself. In even a casual reading of this scene in John, the reader is aware of the uncomfortable element of role reversal. Jesus' actions, taking a basin and towel and washing his disciples' feet, are by any account a surprise and prompt discomfort. The scene is introduced with words from the narrator that Jesus has "loved his own," and is about to die; but even more than that, Jesus knows "that the Father had given all things into his hands, and that he had come from God, and was going to God" (John 13:3). In other words, the narrative begins with a strong reminder of the high status of Jesus, a status confirmed by God himself. Jesus, then, by stripping down and washing feet is introducing a radical role reversal.

This role reversal is heightened, as we already discussed, by the exchange between Jesus and Peter. Because Jesus, by taking the low status role of foot-washer, makes Peter uncomfortable, Peter protests. But Jesus connects accepting the footwashing with embracing or rejecting a connection with himself (ἐὰν μὴ νίψω σε οὐκ ἔχεις μέρος μετ' ἐμοῦ). To be a "part of" Jesus requires accepting his radical redefinition of status. This discomfort

---

23. See Cosgrove, "Unbound Hair."

over the status reversal lies at the center of the footwashing scene, and the source of that discomfort clearly lies in the disjuncture between what Jesus does and the cultural norms for this act of hospitality: such actions were performed by servants or slaves.

The discomfort associated with the role reversal that is acted out between Jesus and Peter is subsequently articulated even more clearly in the speech that follows. Jesus affirms here his high status in relationship to the disciples (he is Lord and Teacher), which indeed serves as the basis for the significance of his footwashing. One might be tempted to see here even a divine status being implied, given the definite article on ὁ κύριος. This is certainly possible, given the shadow which the prologue casts over the entire narrative. Such a linkage, however, is not necessary to underscore the importance of the inherent social discomfort already present with a teacher washing his disciples' feet. Jesus affirms, however, that a central element of the nature of his relationship with them, and therefore their relationship with one another, is to be found in this very act of role reversal. It is precisely because he has stooped to wash their feet that they also should wash one another's feet. Role reversal is, then, a part of Jesus' fundamental mission. And he reaffirms this by saying that he has given them an example (ὑπόδειγμα) that is to serve as a pattern for their own future behavior.[24]

Moreover, given the discomfort over status reversal that Jesus' actions have created, how should the reader understand the aphorism in v. 16, "a slave is not greater than his master, nor is one who is sent greater than the one who sent him" (my translation)? Is this meant simply to support the authority of Jesus in mandating that the disciples ought to wash one another's feet? In other words, does it suggest: "You should do this [that is, wash one another's feet] because I am your master and I say so?" If so, this would seem to undermine the shocking nature of the status reversal. In fact it would almost negate the whole concept of status reversal. Or does it, instead, suggest that Jesus sees himself in the role of slave compared to God, the one who sent him, and thus the disciples should emulate even more his servant/slave action as part of a greater testimony to God's plan? It would seem that the logic of the discourse falls on the latter meaning, that Jesus takes a slave role toward his disciples as a reflection of his own relationship with God, and that as a result the disciples should be prepared to take that same role with respect to one another as a reflection of their own inclusion "in Christ."

It was noted earlier that the John 13 footwashing comes as the culmination of a narrative build-up that anticipates this role reversal. When Jesus

---

24. According to Neyrey, the disciples (Peter in particular) undergo a ritual (an action that changes status). But this ritual then prompts the subsequent suggestion that this should/has become a ceremony ("Footwashing in John 13:6-11").

washes the disciples' feet in John 13, the reader certainly would recall that Jesus' own feet were washed (or at least anointed) by Mary not many days previously. As a result we should probably also see that, rhetorically, the movement from the first footwashing in John (Mary washing Jesus' feet) to the second footwashing (Jesus washing the disciples' feet) carries with it an implicit comparison that moves from lesser to greater. The first footwashing is indeed an act of devotion or commitment. The second, then, must be even more so. But if so, what kind of devotion or commitment is it?

In John 12, of course, we see an act of devotion that fits well within the social construction of the time: it is a dinner scene, and Mary anoints/washes Jesus' feet with an expensive ointment in her own home. The act itself is not surprising in and of itself, or at least the narrative gives no hint of that. Mary's act of anointing/washing Jesus feet, even to the extent of using her let-down hair as a drying towel, seems to provoke no response from others at the dinner party. The only reaction that arises is to the cost of the ointment, not the washing of his feet or the use of her hair. And perhaps one reason for this is that Mary is a woman, and therefore her actions cohere with a role that is more or less acceptable for women (as the story of Aseneth also seems to imply).

Narratively, Mary's "anointing/washing" in John 12 serves as a crucial foreshadowing of the later footwashing in John; Jesus' footwashing, then experiences a rhetorical boost because it has been anticipated in Mary's actions. That Mary's "anointing/washing" functions in this rhetorical manner is suggested by the fact that it also has been anticipated in the story—that is, by means of the introduction of Mary in the beginning of the Lazarus episode. At the beginning of the narratively important Lazarus-raising miracle (which itself explicitly points toward the resurrection), the narrator introduces Mary and Martha by way of focusing on Mary's role in anointing Jesus' feet and wiping them with her hair. This act of "anointing/washing" is apparently seen as noteworthy by John; from this point on we are looking for her to anoint Jesus' feet and wipe them with her hair. And so this notation in John 11:2 is the first sign-post pointing toward Jesus' own footwashing act. The actual narrative of Mary's actions at the dinner party in John 12 is a second sign-post, still pointing forward. And here again, as in the raising of Lazarus, we see a link to the future resurrection, when Jesus defends her actions: "so she might keep it for the day of my burial . . ." This two-step narrative foreshadowing, then, serves to highlight Jesus' action at the meal as particularly significant.

But, as Ingrid Rosa Kitzberger notes, it is difficult to read Mary's anointing/washing without also reading Luke's anointing/washing in Luke

7:36–50 alongside it.²⁵ A narrative reading of John that focuses simply on the internal structure of John would not normally turn to the Luke passage. For many readers, however, the Lukan passage is connected at least within the matrix of social/cultural perspectives which can help shed light on John's footwashing. Moreover, it is at least possible that Luke's "footwashing" represents an interpretation of John's various footwashings.²⁶

There is yet another passage in Luke that provides an additional "echo" of the footwashing narrative in John, though not dealing with the footwashing motif directly. We will recall that in John's Gospel, the footwashing and the teaching that follows takes place during the last supper which Jesus shares with his disciples; the dinner setting has already been noted. Jesus interprets his actions by concluding with these words, "If then I, your Lord and Teacher, have washed your feet, you also ought to wash one another's feet . . . Amen, amen, I tell you, servants (δοῦλος) are not greater than their master, nor are messengers greater than the one who sent them. If you know these things, you are blessed if you do them" (John 13:14, 16–17). In a very similar way, in Luke's Gospel, we find Jesus speaking directly about status reversal in a teaching unit just following the final supper (which in Luke is a Passover). In Luke 22:24–26, the question of status is in dispute among the disciples, and Jesus uses this dispute to offer his dominical teaching.

In Luke's discussion of status reversal, Jesus notes a pattern of behavior among the Gentiles: they desire to "exercise lordship" (κυριεύουσιν) over others. It is important to note that what likely is in view is the patron-client relationship that was common in the Greco-Roman world; indeed Jesus seems to point to this situation by referring to the status that derives from being in such a relationship is to be known as a "benefactor" (Luke 22:25). But for the followers of Jesus things are to be different: the leader is the one who serves. While benefaction, offering meals and services to clients, could be seen as a form of service, the larger reason for it is to accrue status and honor. Jesus seems to suggest something more radical than offering occasional meals or gifts. In this passage, Luke is probably using as a source Mark 10:42–45 (|| Matt 20:25–28). Luke, however, varies from the other synoptic accounts by, first, placing it after the final supper, and then also by relating this directly to Jesus' own activity or example at the table: "For who is greater, the one who sits at the table or one who serves? Is it not the one at the table? But I am among you as one who serves" (Luke 22:27). This strong echo of John's saying at the footwashing in Luke emphasizes the

---

25. Kitzberger, "Love and Footwashing."

26. Assuming the possibility, or even likelihood, that Luke relied on John as a source, as I have suggested especially in *In Dialogue with Another Gospel?*

paradigmatic element of Jesus' own service, which in John is made explicit: "For I have set you an example, that you also should do as I have done to you" (John 13:15).²⁷ Does Luke imagine Jesus actively serving at the table? Or is this simply an echo of John's more explicit example of Jesus serving his disciples?

We can, of course, add the ubiquity of slavery as one more part of the social landscape which John seeks to reflect in his Gospel, if only perhaps to modify it by portraying Jesus' own counter-cultural actions.²⁸ It was not uncommon for slaves to serve as household servants, though freedmen could also function in the role. But the ubiquity of slavery did allow terms such as "serve" (διακονέω) and "serve as slave" (δουλεύω) to function at times almost as synonyms, and carry many of the same implications.²⁹ And within this lexical relationship, John's comment that a slave is not greater than a master (John 13:16) sounds strikingly similar to Luke's implied comment that the one who "sits at table" is greater than the one who serves. And in both cases Jesus is said to have taken the lower status position.

What we have, then, is a complex of passages that involve footwashing or footwashing/anointing (in both John and Luke) that highlight the value of status reversal. And the footwashing account in John is linked further to teachings in both Luke and John that follow the final dinner scene which explicitly refer to status reversal as a core part of Jesus' ministry. Moreover, this teaching on status reversal is not just taught didactically, but is enacted in the presence of his disciples.

John's Footwashing as a Central Act of Hospitality and Love

If the foregoing discussion suggests anything, it is that John 13 has a particularly important role, theologically and pedagogically, in both the Fourth Gospel and the Gospels as a unit. In the Fourth Gospel, the narrative buildup of Mary as the one who "anointed Jesus' feet" gives it a special place in that Gospel. It serves as a proleptic anticipation of Jesus' own washing activity, but also then allows for a buildup—a move from lesser to greater—from her footwashing to his. Mary anoints/washes Jesus as a woman who takes a servant role; but Jesus washes his disciples' feet as a slave might wash on behalf

---

27. Matson, *In Dialogue with Another Gospel?*, 274–79.

28. On the ubiquity of slavery in the NT world, of course, see Bartchy, *ΜΑΛΛΟΝ ΧΡΗΣΑΙ*, 37–62 and Bartchy, "Slavery (Greco-Roman)."

29. See, for instance, the comment of Rendstorff that in the LXX the verb δουλεύω word group even crowded out synonyms such as διακονέω (*TDNT* 2:265).

of a host. In both cases, Mary and Jesus offer hospitality to their guests. And if we listen to Luke 7:36–50, we hear Jesus himself bless such intrusive hospitality. While Mary's action is perhaps unusual, it is not culturally shocking; she can easily be seen doing this as a woman—offering hospitality on behalf of the host, Lazarus. But for Jesus to do this is an indication of a major reversal; it is shocking.

Because it is such a strong act of status reversal and is shocking, we might well wish to identify its primary function in John. Is this footwashing primarily meant to point to Jesus' actions as an example of sacrificial love?[30] That is, is the focus on Jesus' actions as perhaps a proleptic activity pointing to his own crucifixion, an even greater act of service? Or is the focus of this meant to be the establishment of a "sacramental ceremony"?

The thrust of the narrative in which Mary's actions anticipate Jesus' footwashing would point to the importance of Jesus' sacrificial activity. That Mary's "footwashing" already begins to anticipate the crucifixion only lends weight to this. If, then, we only had Jesus' footwashing activity following Mary's earlier footwashing, we might be led to focus on Jesus' act of service as a kind of proleptic sacrificial act.[31]

But Jesus' footwashing does not end with v. 11. Rather, John transitions from the actual footwashing to a teaching unit that focuses almost entirely on the need for the disciples' subsequent activity. "I have set you an example that you should also do as I have done to you" (13:15). The *ritual* activity of washing the disciples' feet, even to the point of a dispute with Peter, serves to draw the disciples into Jesus' coming glorification as an incorporating act.[32] It is as if he is already anticipating his teaching in John 15:3–4, "You have already been cleansed by the word that I have spoken to you. Abide in me as I abide in you." The ritual activity, then, serves to bind them together ("If I don't wash you, you have no part in me"). But the focus on the disciples' subsequent activity suggests a *ceremony*. That ceremony—a footwashing ceremony to be continued—is meant to remind the disciples

---

30. Here I single out a few of the possible meanings of Jesus' action as suggested in Clark-Soles, "John 13: Of Footwashing and History." She especially considers as likely or highly possible meanings for the historical Jesus: purity, honor, friendship, and sacrificial love. Clark-Soles's focus is less on John's narratively constructed meaning and more on the historical likelihood of the various actions of Jesus.

31. In Clark-Soles's discussion, anticipation of the burial is distinct from sacrificial love, and far less likely.

32. Coloe, 414–15, suggests something like what I call here an "incorporating act," called by her a "welcome into the Father's household." But Coloe's reading sees only the incorporation, without the central focus of status reversal. Coloe sees this more focused on Christ's glorification, while I see the concern focused more on the believers' need to emulate such status reversal.

of the need to engage in ongoing status reversal.[33] They are to serve, not be served. After all, the connection between Jesus's example and subsequent activity of willingly offering himself on the cross, which is certainly status reversal, is at the heart of Jesus' one commandment in John: " . . . love one another. Just as I have loved you, you also should love one another" (13:34).

Works Cited

Bailey, John Amedee. *The Traditions Common to the Gospels of Luke and John*. NovTSup 7. Leiden: Brill, 1963.

Bartchy, S. Scott. *ΜΑΛΛΟΝ ΧΡΗΣΑΙ: First-Century Slavery and the Interpretation of 1 Corinthians 7:2*. SBLDS 11. Missoula: Scholars, 1973. Reprinted, Eugene, OR: Wipf & Stock, 2003.

———. "Slavery (Greco-Roman)." In *ABD*, 6:65–73.

Brown, Raymond E. *The Gospel according to John*. 2 vols. AB 29, 29A. Garden City, NY: Doubleday, 1966.

Clark-Soles, Jaime. "John 13: Of Footwashing and History." In *John, Jesus and History*, Vol. 2, edited by Paul Anderson et al., 255–69. SBL Symposium Series 44. Atlanta: Society of Biblical Literature, 2009.

Coloe, Mary L. "Welcome to the Household of God: The Footwashing of John 13." *Catholic Biblical Quarterly* 66 (2004) 400–415.

Corley, Kathleen E. *Private Women, Public Meals: Social Conflict In The Synoptic Tradition*. Peabody, MA: Hendrickson, 1993.

Cosgrove, Charles H. "A Woman's Unbound Hair in the Greco-Roman World, with Special Reference to the Story of the 'Sinful Woman in Luke 7:36–50." *JBL* 124 (2005) 675–92.

Hearon, Holly E. "The Story of 'the Woman Who Anointed Jesus' Feet as Social Memory: A Methodological Proposal for the Study of Tradition as Memory." In *Memory, Tradition and Text: Uses of the Past in Early Christianity*, edited by Alan Kirk, 99–118. Semeia Studies 52. Atlanta: Society of Biblical Literature, 2005.

Joseph and Aseneth. Translated by C. Burchard. In *Old Testament Pseudepigrapha*. Edited by James Charlesworth. Garden City, NY: Doubleday, 1985.

Keener, Craig S. *The Gospel of John*. 2 vols. Peabody, MA: Hendrickson, 2003.

Kitzberger, Ingrid Rosa. "Love and Footwashing: John 13:1–20 and Luke 7:36–50 Read Intertextually." *Biblical Interpretation* 2 (1994) 190–206.

Matson, Mark A. *In Dialogue with Another Gospel? The Influence of the Fourth Gospel on the Passion Narrative of the Gospel of Luke*. SBLDS 178. Atlanta: Society of Biblical Literature, 2001.

———. "The Historical Plausibility of John's Passion Dating." In *John, Jesus and History*, Vol. 2, edited by Paul Anderson, Felix Just, and Tom Thatcher, 291–312. Atlanta: Society of Biblical Literature, 2009.

---

33. Interestingly, Clark-Soles considers status reversal as less likely for a meaning for Jesus. She certainly acknowledges that this is the intent of the narrative in John. For her, though, this is not as likely a meaning for the (historical) Jesus. Given the connection with Luke, and the variety of teachings on status reversal in the Gospels, I argue otherwise.

———. "The Contribution to the Temple Cleansing by the Fourth Gospel." In *1992 SBL Seminar Papers*, edited by Eugene H. Lovering, Jr., 489–506. Atlanta: Scholars, 1992.

———. "The Temple Incident: An Integral Element in the Fourth Gospel's Narrative." In *Jesus in Johannine Tradition*, edited by Robert Fortna and Tom Thatcher, 145–53. Louisville: Westminster John Knox, 2001.

———. "The Curious Case of Luke's and John's 'Anointing' Stories." Unpublished SBL paper delivered at joint session of Synoptic Gospels and John, Jesus and History sections, 2013. https://www.academia.edu/6398711/The_Curious_Case_of_Lukes_and_Johns_Anointing_Story.

Moloney, Francis. *Signs and Shadows: Reading John 5–12*. Minneapolis: Fortress, 1996.

Neyrey, Jerome H., SJ. "Footwashing in John 13:6–11: Transformation Ritual or Ceremony?" In *The Social World of the First Christians: Essays in Honor of Wayne A. Meeks*, edited by L. Michael White and O. Larry Yarbrough, 198–213. Minneapolis: Fortress, 1995.

Plutarch. *Life of Phocion*. Translated by B. Perrin. LCL. Cambridge: Harvard University Press, 1969.

———. *Life of Pompey*. Translated by B. Perrin. LCL. Cambridge: Harvard University Press, 1968.

Kittel, Gerhard, and Gerhard Friedrich, eds. *Theological Dictionary of the New Testament*. Translated by Geoffrey W. Bromiley. 10 vols. Grand Rapids: Eerdmans, 1964–76.

Schnackenburg, Rudolf. *The Gospel according to St. John*. Translated by Kevin Smyth. New York: Herder & Herder, 1980.

Thomas, John Christopher. *Footwashing in John 13 and the Johannine Community*. JSNTSup 61. Sheffield: JSOT Press, 1991.

Wainwright, Elaine. "Anointing/Washing Feet: John 12:1–8 and Its Intertexts." In *I Sowed Fruits Into Hearts (Odes Sol. 17:13) : Festschrift for Professor Michael Lattke*, edited by Pauline Allen et al., 203–20. Early Christian Studies 12. Strathfield, NSW: St. Paul's, 2007.

8

Trouble in the Hood
A Multidimensional Contextualization of Romans 13:1–7

Rick F. Talbott

SCOTT BARTCHY HAS A reputation for lecturing with passionate perspicuity and masterfully translating complex theoretical issues into helpful heuristic paradigms. His university courses and publications are exemplary in this regard. Using social-scientific analysis, Scott has elevated our understanding of how ancient systems of slavery, gender, and honor/shame shaped the early Jesus movements. Scott introduced me to the social-scientific analysis of the New Testament while I was in graduate school at UCLA. Gaining new insights from his lectures and publications has been like watching the performance of a familiar play from the vantage point of having a back-stage pass. His influence continues to stimulate and inform my work on the New Testament. This chapter is a case in point.

Scott's insistence that interpreters always align texts with their socio-historical contexts remains an invaluable paradigm for uncovering, describing, and explaining the New Testament as inextricably connected to its ancient Mediterranean world. Doing so produces a *contextualized text*—a scholarly construct carefully assembled with various theoretical models and the use of one's scientific imagination.[1] Contextualization of the New

---

1. I use "contextualized text" in a similar fashion to Elisabeth Schüssler Fiorenza's "rhetorical situation" and John Elliott's "rhetorical strategy" both of which suggest the

Testament serves as a heuristic lens for better understanding the social, political, and economic dynamics behind the text's theological language. Contextualizing the New Testament should not isolate the text's social context from its theological or religious content. Such bifurcation tends to blur the important symbiotic relationship between the social or religious dimensions of the New Testament.

I apply a multidimensional, contextualized approach to a problematic and controversial text—Rom 13:1–7—in order to imagine the possible scenario(s) Paul of Tarsus addressed. This approach is based on recent information taken from a variety of archeological and textual sources about local neighborhoods (*vici*) in first-century CE Rome. Rome's neighborhood organization, administration, economics, religion, and social make-up necessitate careful reconsideration of the complex socio-historical context behind this passage. Recent works on ancient Rome also undermine certain assumptions about the role of the emperor and his imperial authorities in the affairs of these local neighborhoods where Christ communities resided. I argue that placing Rom 13:1–7 in the multifarious context of Rome's local neighborhoods suggests that Paul was exclusively addressing local issues directly impacting one or more Christ communities. Therefore, Rom 13:1–7 represents part of Paul's directives to help Christ communities resolve conflict with their neighbors and the neighborhood authorities. This analysis makes it highly unlikely that Paul was encouraging submission to the emperor or any imperial authority.

Social-scientific analysis of this passage is especially important because of this text's lingering potential for abuse in Paul's name. How did Paul expect Christ communities in Rome to relate to sanctioned authorities who could exercise power against them and other subalterns in the city? Also problematic is the fact that Rom 13:1–7 continues to elude modern interpreters' attempts to adequately explain why an "anti-imperial Paul" would seemingly require submission to "governing authorities." One can easily understand how the conundrum surrounding this passage has caused significant disagreement among scholars and Christians. But complacency and ignorance about how Rom 13:1–7 has been used to justify atrocious abuses of power against vulnerable people is startling and unacceptable.

Neil Elliott provides several painful examples of how Pauline texts in general and Rom 13:1–7 in particular have been used to justify atrocities

---

text's possible historical, social, and cultural situation and setting (Schüssler Fiorenza, "Rhetorical Situation," 286–403; Schüssler Fiorenza, *Rhetoric and Ethic*, 105–28; J. H. Elliott, *What Is Social-Scientific Criticism?*, 69). I also contend that biblical texts examined through social categories can bring greater clarity to the specific historical and social situations that shaped the texts.

by governing authorities.² In a chapter called, "Paul In Service to Death," Elliott draws attention to various religious and political juggernauts in our nation's early history who notoriously leaned on Pauline texts to subordinate, oppress, and—at times—violently punish women and slaves.³ He also cites specific examples where Rom 13:1–7 helped quell Christian resistance to the Nazi regime. Elliott's reminders include accounts of how our government found support from right-wing evangelists for the "freedom fighters" in Nicaragua and Angola.⁴ Under the guise of opposing liberation theology, mainline churches tolerated violent policies associated with the "New World Order" by authoritatively quoting this passage from U.S. pulpits and insisting that "the Bible says we must obey the President."⁵ In this same chapter, Elliott goes on to suggest that such misuses of Paul's letters—and Romans 13 specifically—stem from de-politicizing and domesticating Paul of Tarsus (something I first heard from Scott). Elliott concludes this chapter with an ironic twist. He claims that liberating Paul's "authentic voice" would enable his ancient writings to actually help liberate modern victims of oppressive power.

With approximately 2.1 billion Christians today either directly or indirectly influenced by Paul's letters, what possible impact could Rom 13:1–7 have? For example, Pentecostal Christianity continues to grow rapidly in Asia and especially in China;⁶ and the continent of Africa, facing great economic, political, and religious-based conflict, now has more Christians than North America. In the U.S., both conservative and liberal Christians remain ambivalent over foreign policies, gay marriage, and immigration—all of which relate to the notion of submission to secular authority. So much could be at stake when Christian communities seeking direction for their relationship to state authorities turn to Romans 13. With Scott Bartchy, I also believe that Paul's writings—including Rom 13:1–7—can be used to negotiate and transform oppressive uses of power in human relationships and institutions.⁷

But just how does one "liberate Paul" when his rhetoric of submission to "governing authorities" in Rom 13:1–7 sounds so straightforward, clear, and absolute to some? Other misinterpretations of Paul opt to silence what is perceived as a type of colonizing and imperialistic rhetoric.

---

2. N. Elliott, *Liberating Paul*, 3–24; 214–30.
3. Ibid., chapter 1.
4. Ibid., 15–16.
5. Ibid., 14.
6. Barker, "Engendering Charismatic Economies," 2, 8.
7. Bartchy, "Undermining Ancient Patriarchy"; Bartchy, "Who Should Be Called Father?"

Such misappropriated machinations to identify Paul's voice as part of the re-inscription of abusive power thrive among some New Testament scholars.[8] But others suggest that even Rom 13:1–7 itself does not necessarily demand blind obedience to Roman "ruling authorities."[9] Perhaps v. 4 could be understood to militate against pernicious "governing authorities" if they did not rule as Paul says, "for your good." In this case Christ communities in Rome could have had the option to determine when it was appropriate not to submit to governing authorities. But Paul did not provide an escape clause for malevolent authorities. Still others insist that—in reality—the governing authorities "established by God" determine the rules of their political system to which Christ communities must submit "for a divinely ordered society."[10] Elliott refers to Paul's apocalyptic mindset to suggest that any submission to the governing authorities would have been accepted as a temporary condition and thus tolerated knowing one day such authorities would be accountable to God.[11] This approach sounds similar to those who insist one must hold Romans 13 in mitigating tension with Revelation 13 (Rom 13:11; 14:11; 1 Cor 15:27–28; Phil 2:9–11; 3:20).[12] And if Tacitus's comments about public unrest in Rome around 58 CE and Suetonius's reference to "tumults" under Claudius could be connected with Rom 13:1–7—as a few hypothesize—then some additional light may be shed on this passage.[13] These suggestions remain speculative for lack of sufficient evidence. James Kallas has proposed that Rom 13:1–7 could not have been written by Paul in spite of the fact that we have no solid evidence of textual corruption.[14] Expanding on Käsemann, Elliott says that Paul's rhetoric of submission could be seen as rather routine advice given the plight of Diaspora Jews under fire from "vicious anti-Jewish propaganda."[15] Therefore Elliott thinks Paul's reference to "the authorities as servants of God" is a rhetorical device "to keep members of the *ekklēsia* from making trouble in the streets."[16] But why does Elliott think members of the Christ communities in Rome would have resorted to making "trouble in the streets?" Were they actually "re-

---

8. See Castelli, *Imitating Paul*; Kittredge, "Corinthian Women Prophets"; Marchal, *Politics of Heaven*.

9. Käsemann, *Romans*, 357.

10. Dunn, *Romans*, 756.

11. N. Elliott, "Romans 13:1–7," 192; N. Elliott, "Letter to the Romans," 211.

12. Käsemann, *Romans*, 218.

13. Friedrich, Pöhlmann, and Stuhlmacher, "Zur historischen Situation," 131–66.

14. Kallas, "Romans XIII:1–7," 369.

15. N. Elliott, "Romans 13:1–7," 188; N. Elliott, "Letter to the Romans," 198.

16. N. Elliott, "Romans 13:1–7," 223.

sisting the authority"? How, and for what reason? Something seems to be missing here.

With the exception of seeing Rom 13:1–7 as an interpolation, all of the above suggestions need further contextualization to better understand this mercurial passage. But these explanations still leave the impression that Paul required some type of *carte blanche* submission to imperial authorities in obedience to God. Elliott suggests that Paul intended to mock imperial authorities by using some type of veiled rhetorical sarcasm.[17] Although I find Elliott's treatments of Rom 13:1–7 some of the most insightful and thorough, his analysis lacks specific information about the local situation in Rome.[18] For example, in *The Arrogance of Nations*, Elliott establishes his treatment of Romans and 13:1–7 in particular based on historical acts of anti-Semitism in Rome and "the nations'" arrogance towards "Judeans" as a conquered and barbaric people.[19] According to Elliott, "If Romans 13:1–7 really belongs to this letter, we should read these verses as part of an argument addressed to a church in which the Gentile Christian's inclination to dispossess the Jew, politically as well as theologically, has provoked the apostle's concern."[20]

A major component for Elliott's reconstruction of the historical situation behind Romans can be understood as Paul's own response to Roman imperial rhetoric. Borrowing from the works of the political scientist James Scott, Elliott claims Paul's anti-imperial rhetoric served as a type of "hidden transcript" intimating the opposition between Christ's rule and the emperor's claim to rule the nations of the earth.[21] Elliott believes Rom 13:1–7 addressed "specific historical circumstances in Rome" to which Paul added his more general and essential task to encourage "an ethos of mutual accommodation and harmony within the *ekklēsia* (12:3–13) and an ethic of non-retaliation towards enemies without (12:14–21)."[22]

I find it problematic that Elliott does not elaborate on these "enemies without" or offer any specific information to help identify the possible reference to "the governing authorities." He provides no suggestion as to the "specific historical circumstances in Rome" that would help us imagine Paul's directives in Rom 13:1–7. The documented hostility and disdain

17. N. Elliott, "Letter to the Romans," 210.

18. N. Elliott, "Romans 13:1–7"; N. Elliott, *Liberating Paul*; N. Elliott, *Arrogance of Nations*.

19. N. Elliott prefers "nations" and "Judeans" rather than "Gentiles" and "Jews" (*Arrogance of Nations*, 13–16, 44–50).

20. N. Elliott, *Liberating Paul*, 221.

21. N. Elliott, *Arrogance of Nations*, chap 1; Rom 1:4–6.

22. N. Elliott, *Liberating Paul*, 224.

towards Jews as "conquered people" must have begun to impact the Christ communities and their neighborhoods after the Jews returned to Rome under Nero. But was Paul simply using this occasion to encourage "an ethos of mutual accommodation and harmony *within* the *ekklēsia*"?[23] What might that occasion have been, more specifically? And what light would a further contextualized reading of Rom 13:1–7 shed on the specific situation involving the Christ communities at Rome? Elliott's rhetorical analysis actually departs from suggesting a more specific situation behind the text leading him to further generalizations. Elliott suggests that Paul's rhetorical strategy was to "focus the audiences' attention on the discernment of 'the good.'"[24]

The literary context of Rom 13:1–7 certainly seems to support Elliott's contention that Gentiles and Jews were at odds with each other in the congregations. Members of the Christ communities are exhorted "not to think more highly of oneself than one ought" (12:3)—a possible reference to Gentile arrogance.[25] Writing metaphorically, Paul suggests that—although diverse—each Christ community member actually belongs to one another and no member should consider themselves more valuable than other seemingly less honorable members (12:5).[26] Rather, Christ community members are to outdo one another in showing honor (12:11). Paul also exhorted them to serve and love one another with sibling-affection while meeting each other's needs and practicing hospitality (12:6–13).

But was Paul's appeal for "mutual accommodation and harmony" restricted to in-group members of the Christ communities? The verses just preceding 13:1–7 seem directed at non-Christ community members in their immediate neighborhood (12:14–21). Here he told Christ community members to "endure afflictions" (12:12), bless "the ones persecuting you" (12:14), "to live in peace with everyone as much as it is possible" (12:16, 18), "not to retaliate" (12:17, 19), and to provide food and drink "to one's enemies" thereby "overcoming evil by doing good" (12:20–21). The pericope just after 13:1–7—vv. 8 through 10—following Paul's admonition to "owe nothing to anyone" and "pay taxes" advocates "loving one's neighbor." Is the reference to "neighbor" directed towards Christ community members or outsiders—again—people in their immediate neighborhood? To whom do these verses refer? Who are the non-Christ community members that

23. Ibid., my emphasis.

24. N. Elliott, "Romans 13:1–7," 188.

25. See also 2:1–16, and N. Elliott's reference to the "pretentious person" as the Gentile, *Arrogance of Nations*, chap. 2.

26. N. Elliott maintains that Paul does not intend to blur, let alone remove, ethnic distinctions between Gentiles and Jews in Romans unlike Dunn and others who advocate the "New Perspective on Paul" (*Liberating Paul*, 69–71).

appear to be causing some sort of disruption and trouble (*thlīpsis*) for the Christ community members in Rome? What is the nature of this hostility between the church and its neighbors? And, who are the "governing authorities" in the midst of it all this conflict? Romans 12:9—13:10 seems to indicate four groups—the first two are Gentiles and Jews in the Christ communities. A third group was made up of local neighbors whom Paul exhorted the Christ communities to love and not retaliate against. The fourth group was the "governing authorities" who somehow got involved in this local conflict. So the specific occasion for Rom 13:1–7 looks much more complex than just rivalry between Christ community members over Gentile arrogance towards Jews.

Elliott rightly states that "there is no 'theology of the state' here," no demand for "unqualified obedience to the authorities."[27] He contends that Rom 13:1–7 "focuses the ethic of non-retaliation on a potentially volatile situation" by "cooperating with the authorities." Elliott stipulates further that the Christ communities had the "full assurance of Paul's apocalyptic affirmation that God disposes the rise and fall of empires."[28] But as much as Elliott and others have done to advance the discourse on Rom 13:1–7, we are still left with the lingering questions raised above. One wonders about the specifics behind what may have been causing the "potentially volatile situation" for the Christ communities in Rome that involved the "governing authorities." Why assume that Paul's reference to "governing authorities" were imperial authorities administering and policing the city's neighborhoods as if under the direct control of the emperor? Have Empire Studies and Postcolonial Biblical Criticism contributed to this assumption in Rom 13:1–7?

The value of Empire Studies and Postcolonial Biblical Criticism is that these methodologies sharpen the focus of New Testament studies.[29] Postcolonial scholars help us realize that neither Jesus of Nazareth nor Paul of Tarsus can be adequately understood apart from placing them against the backdrop of Roman imperial rhetoric, ideologies, and policies of colonization. For example, C. Davina Lopez's postcolonial approach rightly identifies Paul with the "colonized others"—himself a victim of imperial policies.[30] And Jeremy Punt observes how Paul's rhetoric both subverted and re-inscribed the Roman Empire.[31] But contextualizing Rom 13:1–7

27. N. Elliott, *Liberating Paul*, 224–25.
28. Ibid., 224.
29. See Horsley, "Introduction"; Schüssler Fiorenza, "Rhetorical Situation"; Stanley, *Colonized Apostle*.
30. Lopez, "Visualizing Significant Otherness," 80.
31. Punt, "Pauline Agency," 60.

with imperial authorities and the emperor in mind has also contributed to inaccurate generalizations about the role of imperial authorities in the daily life of local neighborhoods in first-century Rome. What justifies extrapolating imperial authorities and emperor as Paul's primary referents in Rom 13:1–7?[32] What justifies seeing an imperial subtext or hidden transcript behind Rom 13:1–7 as Gordon Zerbe does?

> Whereas Rom 12:19–20 presented God as having the sole prerogative for executing justice ("wrath"), here in Romans 13 the Roman *imperium* is portrayed as "God's minister" for the maintenance of order and justice. And whereas elsewhere Paul parodies the Roman *imperium* and predicts its doom, here its legitimacy is apparently certified using the commonplaces of Jewish and Hellenistic political rhetoric.[33]

Zerbe's assumption that Paul's use of *exousia* in 13:2 refers to the "Roman *imperium*" exhibits a tendency among some scholars using Postcolonial Criticism and Empire Studies to over-generalize and therefore misunderstand the role of imperial authorities in Rome.

Others have recently levied similar caveats regarding Empire Studies.[34] Karl Galinski rejects "the construction of early Christianity as a single-minded anti-imperial movement" and says Rom 13:1–7 shows that "Paul had contingencies."[35] Galinski criticizes the use of the word "anti-imperial" as "too heavy-handed and imprecise."[36] Gregory H. Snyder also asks if the "anti-imperial" rhetoric in the New Testament happened by design or incidentally.[37] I do not cite Galinski and Synder here to undermine the importance of situating the New Testament in its imperial context, but rather as a reminder that the text's specific context should serve as an indicator to determine the degree of involvement or influence imperial authorities or policies may have had. Such a nuanced approach to Postcolonial Criticism and Empire Studies would mitigate against unwarranted assumptions and over-generalizations, especially surrounding Rom 13:1–7. Paul's anti-imperial rhetoric elsewhere need not be superimposed on passages like Rom 13:1–7, especially when both the literary and historical contexts suggest something more specific and local.

32. N. Elliott, *Liberating Paul*, 196–99.
33. Zerbe, "Politics of Paul," 71.
34. Brodd and Reed, *Rome and Religion*.
35. Galinsky, "Cult of the Roman Emperor," 217.
36. Ibid., 222.
37. Synder, "Response to Karl Galinsky," 223.

The situation in Rome appears more complex according to recent works dealing with the city's neighborhood social and cultural demographics. Such information can be used to further contextualize Rom 13:1–7 in ancient Roman neighborhoods during the middle of the first century CE. These analyses also consider certain imperial policies instituted under Augustus that remained in place until the fourth century—a reminder that my caveat about Postcolonial Criticism and Empire Studies does not amount to abrogation but nuanced application of these approaches. Further contextualization of Rom 13:1–7 stems from analyzing three social dimensions that help us better imagine the local issues Paul addressed. First, I offer a brief description of Rome's economic system of trading, selling, and distributing grain—one that impacted every inhabitant from the poorest neighborhoods to the Emperor's palace. Second, I situate Christ communities comprised of Gentiles and Jews living in very crowded and poor neighborhoods in Rome prone to disorder over taxes, rents, foreign cults, food shortages, and a perennial hostility towards the "foreigner" (*peregrinus*). Roman ideology propagated by imperial rhetoric contributed to the Roman disdain for Jews as foreigners especially when grain was in short supply.[38] Jews' religious practices were also viewed with suspicion and were thought to have despised humanity—or as Tacitus put it—"They regard the rest of mankind with all the hatred of enemies."[39] Last, I describe and explain the political division and administration of first-century Roman neighborhoods reorganized under Augustus in 7 BCE. This analysis will reveal that Augustus' reorganization was designed for the specific purpose of preserving local order and fighting neighborhood fires—both of which could spread throughout Rome if not dealt with at the local level. Imperial policies shaped and were shaped by these three dimensions of social life in Rome. These social dynamics are indispensable for contextualizing Rom 13:1–7.

Rome's Grain Market

Based on current economic models of administrating and adjudicating Rome's market system, one can easily understand why the imperial government needed help from the private and local sectors to administrate the grain trade.[40] Rome's grain trade alone required a complex infrastructure that eventually reached the various neighborhoods through selling and distributing grain to the city's million inhabitants. Rome consumed ap-

38. Noy, *Foreigners at Rome*, 36, 38–39, 41.
39. Tacitus, *Hist.*5.5.1.
40. Temin, "Economy of the Early Roman Empire," 97–113.

proximately 200,000 metric tons of grain per-year in the early empire.[41] According to Keith Hopkins, "The volume of goods being traded was too large ... and the government was too small to have administered it directly."[42] So Rome's merchants functioned in a type of free market where the government intervened only occasionally.[43]

The entire economic enterprise in Rome depended more on the mechanism of honor, especially among guild members, than government jurisdiction.[44] It was not imperial authorities but a substantial force of public administrators and jurists that dealt with both private and public cases involving the grain trade alone. Even here, the Roman government and its courts did not intercede directly in the grain market unless it felt the need to control prices or adjudicate overt cases of fraud, broken contracts, and other forms of cheating.[45] "Moral hazards" presented a great challenge to Rome's market economy, so Rome created a variety of legal categories to adjudicate contract disputes.[46] Considering the above, it is hard to imagine Rome's government and courts having the administrative resources to oversee the everyday local issues and affairs of local neighborhoods.[47] Historically, imperial forces only intervened directly if a local incident threatened to unravel into a large-scale disturbance.[48]

Neighborhood Demographics in First-Century CE Rome

Social demographics reveal a very high population density in ancient Rome, whether one accepts a population of one million or three-quarter million residents.[49] The majority of the city's inhabitants was made up of the poor who lived in insulae—four-to-five story apartment buildings with significant

    41. Cascio, "Early Roman Empire," 639.

    42. Hopkins, "Taxes and Trade," 121.

    43. Temin, *Roman Market Economy*, 101.

    44. Ibid., 111.

    45. "Roman law famously lacked the law of agency" (ibid., 104).

    46. Ibid., 104.

    47. Augustus did once take over the administration of the city's food supply but only to bring an end to major disturbances (Lott, *Neighborhoods*, 119).

    48. "The Prefect of the *annona* had the power to issue contracts for the provision of state grain ... and his office was surrounded by the offices of private merchants. The Prefect appears to have engaged only a small staff, suggesting that his main tasks were to gather information about the grain trade and to coordinate with important merchants rather than to organize the entire market" (Sirks, *Food for Rome*, 14).

    49. For various population estimates, see Noy, *Foreigners at Rome*, 17.

threats of fire and crime for the residents. Peter Lampe's landmark work that investigated the possible locations of Christians living in Rome during the first and second centuries helps one imagine the crowded living conditions of the Christ communities.[50] Lampe identified four regions of ancient Rome where these communities most likely lived based on Roman writers, funeral inscriptions, later Christian traditions, and the regions known where Jews resided. Lampe selects a region known as Trastevere that Jews occupied in the first century BCE. It had a harbor with ship and brickyard workers of mixed ethnicities. Trastevere formed one of the poorest and most densely populated areas of Rome. A region called the Appian Way—just outside Rome's Porta Capena—was another likely place early Christ communities in Rome resided. This region also consisted of poor workers including Jews and various other ethnicities. Lampe mentions two additional regions where early Christ communities may also have lived and worshipped. The region known as Aventine reveals aristocratic housing mixed with poorer insulae. The other area called Mars Field also reveals wealthier domus, or houses.

If one extrapolates from Lampe's characterization of cramped, ethnically mixed, poor neighborhoods and rightly assumes with Robert Jewett that Christ communities most likely met in crowded *insulae* or apartment buildings, then Paul's appeal for harmony in Romans 12 and 13 can be seen as local conflict resolution rather than a vague universal mandate requiring obedience to governments. Anti-Jewish sentiment coupled with Roman pride against Jewish Christ community members would have come from people in the immediate neighborhood. Such neighbors would have pressured and ostracized or "labeled" their fellow Gentiles for their association with the "conquered Judeans." David Noy says, "The Jews were clearly regarded by outsiders as a separate and distinctive section of Roman society."[51] Competition for jobs also contributed to the resentment against Jews after they returned to Rome. Poor free citizens already had to compete with slaves for jobs.[52] Jews coming back into the labor market would have been viewed unfavorably by their Gentile neighbors just as immigrants in the history of the United States suffered persecution over competition for jobs. No doubt these social factors created tension against the Christ communities who accepted poor Jews returning to Rome under Nero. External pressure appears to have eventually begun to disrupt the sibling relationships Gentiles and Jews once enjoyed as "brothers and sisters" in Christ communities (Romans

---

50. Lampe, *From Paul to Valentinus*.
51. Noy, *Foreigners at Rome*, 36.
52. Temin, *Roman Market Economy*, 116–17; Jongman, "Early Roman Empire," 617.

9–15).⁵³ Ethnic hostility—exacerbated by competition for jobs and limited food supplies—undermined the Christ communities' unity (Rom 15:7–13).

I also suggest another possible contributing factor to the hostility against the Christ communities in Rome's neighborhoods. Archeological evidence reveals that every neighborhood in Rome had a common shrine or small monument called the *lares augusti* at its crossroad (*compitum*) where locals paid tribute to their neighborhood's protective spirits (*lares*), which also served to honor the emperor.⁵⁴ It is important to clarify that although Augustus supported the religious rites of the *lares augusti* as a means to bolster his neighborhood policies, we have no evidence that any neighborhood "ever erected a statue of the emperor at all."⁵⁵ Neighborhoods honoring the empire's policies of civil order and fire prevention cannot be construed as "promoting the emperor's [political] career," let alone worshipping him.⁵⁶ These policies amounted to keeping order, fighting and preventing fires, light-duty policing, and distributing water and food (see below). According to Bert J. Lott, honoring the emperor's policies became competitive between neighborhood authorities charged with keeping order in their respective local neighborhoods.⁵⁷ Rewards and re-appointment motivated the local authorities to maintain the *lares augusti* and keep order in the "hood." The emperor's policies also benefited these local authorities as well as the poor eking out a living in these crowded and volatile neighborhoods.

But what would happen if Christ communities chose not to participate in their neighborhood *lares augusti*? One can imagine that some sort of reprimand or reprisals may have been initiated by the local authorities as well as from the Christ community's neighbors who depended on the goodwill and fair administration of the local authorities. The Christ communities honored a rival deity—one in fact that they referred to as "lord" (Rom 1:4b)—and may have refused to participate and support the local *lares*. This fact, coupled with their refusal to participate in the *lares augusti*, would not have gone unnoticed, bringing suspicion on the entire Christ community. Seen as competing with the local cult and simultaneously challenging the

---

53. I suggest that Lee's assertion that local elites would have promoted differences among ethnic groups "in order to sow seeds of disunity, diffuse solidarity, and fortify their hegemonic superiority" would have destabilized local neighborhoods in Rome and does not represent the typical practice of Rome's local elite ("Paul, Nation, and Nationalism," 229–30).

54. This place also served for an important state holiday called *Compitalia*; see Lott, *Neighborhoods*, 3, 14, 148.

55. Ibid., 127.

56. Ibid.

57. Ibid., 169.

honor of local authorities, the Christ communities would have provoked a disruptive and contentious situation in their local neighborhoods. The Christ communities may have also threatened to stop or actually stopped paying taxes because of this situation—especially if part of the "taxes" went to support the *lares augusti* and support the neighborhood patrols (*vigeles*). This would have meant trouble if—as J. Christopher Fuhrmann thinks—the local authorities also collected local taxes![58] These possible scenarios make sense of Paul's conciliatory directives in Rom 13:1–7.

Could Paul have expected Christ community members to participate in the local *lares augusti* as a part of their civic duty to "give honor to those it is due"? Paul practiced and even advised Christ community members to participate in cultural activities that were seen as offensive—such as eating meet offered to idols—in order to maintain unity (1 Cor 10:25–31). After all, the *lares augusti* did not amount to "an official state cult" but functioned more as an expression of neighborhood identity and compliance to civic order under the auspices of Augustus' policies.[59] It seems likely that Paul would have encouraged the beleaguered Christ communities to continue to pay local taxes they benefited from as a show of honor to the local authorities. He also charged them to go the extra mile by extending charity and making peace with hostile neighbors. Paul asked the Christ community members not to retaliate in any manner but to even feed their enemies—which may have amounted to inviting them to their meal in Jesus's name!

Local Administration of Rome's Neighborhoods

Connected to this neighborhood imbroglio and complicating it further was the involvement or intervention of the "ruling authorities" provoking Paul's directives in Rom 13:1–7. But this scenario requires some background knowledge of local authorities in ancient Rome's neighborhoods. According to Fuhrmann, the Roman ideal had always been to resolve civic problems "without recourse to state institutions."[60] One such method to maintain order was making the head of the household or paterfamilias the most basic locus of power as *patria potestas*.[61] Throughout the ancient Mediterranean world—as in Rome—fathers were expected to keep their households in order, thus contributing to the security of their local communities. Local elites

---

58. Fuhrmann, *Policing*, 58.
59. Lott, *Neighborhoods*, 110–11.
60. Fuhrmann, *Policing*, 5.
61. See Fuhrmann, *Policing*, 50; Nippel, *Public Order*, 32; Bartchy, "Who Should Be Called Father?"

in Rome were likewise expected to help supervise community self-regulation and adjudicate problems in their respective neighborhoods. According to Fuhrmann, this "self-help" ideal proved to be "vital in every era of Roman civilization and was evident in every phase of Rome's legal history."[62] But the disorder of the late Republic and a major fire in 7 BCE motivated Augustus to reorganize the city of Rome into 14 regions further divided into 265 *vici* or neighborhoods.[63] Augustus later established a hybrid police-fire brigade in 6 CE—a night-watch force called *vigiles* or "watchmen." *Vigiles* were placed under the supervision of neighborhood authorities (*vicomagistri*) in each neighborhood (*vicus*).[64] Lott says each neighborhood originally had four *vicomagistri* usually from the class of freedmen but not from the Roman aristocracy—thus highlighting the vast social distance between the vicomagistri and the emperor himself.[65] The *vigiles* were comprised of ex-slaves and were generally expected to protect against fires, burglars, and maintain order in the neighborhoods they patrolled. It was this civilian policing and not the Roman military—let alone Praetorian soldiers—that patrolled local neighborhoods.

It is important to recognize that these civilian militias (*vigiles*) and the local authorities (*vicomagistri*) who governed them were not "under the direct command of Roman authorities (the emperor and officials working for him, such as governors or procurators)."[66] Neighborhood authorities (*vicomagistri*) responsible for public order would become "suspicious of any organization" not submitting to their control, making the magistrates feel "vulnerable to conspiracies and a distrust of organization."[67] As mentioned above, the Christ communities in Rome may have been under such suspicion exacerbated by neighborhood hostility towards Gentiles and Jews associating as fictive kin. The Christ communities may have also decided they could not support their neighborhood *lares augusti*. Not paying taxes to the *vicomagistri* and other local tolls would have almost certainly caused the type of trouble Paul addressed in Rom 12:9—13:7.

Given the above contextualization of first-century Rome, I suggest that Paul's reference to the "ruling authorities" actually referred to Rome's *vicomagistri*—local authorities overseeing squads of *vigiles* and appointed

---

62. Fuhrmann, *Policing*, 49.

63. Note, Rome's local neighborhoods existed prior to Augustus' organization of the *vici*.

64. Fuhrmann, *Policing*, 116.

65. Lott, *Neighborhoods*, 27.

66. Fuhrmann, *Policing*, 9.

67. Nippel, *Public Order*, 27.

to maintain order in their specific neighborhoods. *Vicomagistri* relied on local participation in the *lares augutsti* for this order and not the emperor or government officials. Paul appears to have addressed a specific instance of ethnic rivalry between neighborhood rivals—possibly residing in the same *insula* as Christ community members. This local agitation had begun to impact one or more Christ community meeting in crowded *insulae* in one or more of the neighborhoods in Trastervi or the Appian Way. I cannot rule out such a scenario for a house church in one of the more affluent regions of either Aventine or Mars Field. (This may be where Pricilla and Aquila had a Christ community meeting in their home [Rom 16:2–3].) But I do not think that Paul had the emperor or imperial authorities specifically in mind when writing Rom 13:1–7. *Vicomagistri* were not keen on running to their superiors since they were held accountable for maintaining order in their respective neighborhood.

Conclusion

This deep and localized contextualizing of Paul helps to "liberate" his rhetoric in Rom 13:1–7. A social-scientific approach to this passage limits its scope to matters involving Christ community members and their neighborhood authorities (*vicomagistri*). I have suggested that Rom 13:1–7 in its immediate literary and social context not only reflects tension in local neighborhoods between Gentile and Jewish Christ community members (N. Elliott) but also with their Gentile neighbors. The inclusion of Jews as "foreigners" (*peregrinus*) by Gentile Christ community members and the possible refusal of either the Jewish Christ Community members or the entire Christ community to support the local cult (*lares augusti*) would have led to conflict in the neighborhood. If supporting the *lares augusti* also involved financial support, this may explain Paul's references to "taxes" in 13:7. Such local "taxes" would have been used to finance the local patrols (*vigiles*). Participation in such cults functioned to stabilize neighborhood solidarity while honoring the emperor's policies—not worshiping the emperor. Although the emperor established the neighborhood authorities to oversee his local policies, these policies simply amounted to keeping order, preventing and fighting fires, as well as discouraging petty crimes. Non-military, civilian patrols (*vigiles*) acting under the direction of the neighborhood authorities actually carried out these policies.[68] Recent information about the immense amount of grain imported to Rome and the complexity of administering its sale and distribution primarily through private markets also makes it

68. See Lott, *Neighborhoods*, and Fuhrmann, *Policing*, for more information.

difficult to imagine that imperial authorities routinely got involved in the affairs of local neighborhoods.[69] For these reasons I have maintained that Rom 13:1–7 represents Paul's directives to resolve local conflict between and by Christ community members and their neighborhoods that fell under the jurisdiction of the neighborhood authorities. This passage should not be construed as either an example of Paul's inconsistent rhetoric towards imperial authorities or his admonition for unwavering obedience to all ruling authorities.

Paul was trying to facilitate cohesion of the mixed Christ communities who had become fictive kin through Israel's Messiah rather than requiring unfettered obedience to any and all ruling authorities. Paul's exhortations to Christ community members were directed at keeping the local situation from boiling over into further retribution from local agitators and local authorities. The city also required the emperor to rely heavily on local neighborhoods to govern and sustain the city's everyday needs and functions. Neither the forces of imperial rhetoric nor the Roman military kept civic order or administered daily life in Rome without local neighborhoods' ruling elites and their aids. I hope this chapter helps to continue the discourse on Paul of Tarsus and Rom 13:1–7 while paying tribute to one who has contributed significantly to our understanding of Paul and his writings.

Works Cited

Barker, Isabelle V. "Engendering Charismatic Economies: Pentecostalism, Global Political Economy, and the Crisis of Social Reproduction." Paper presented at the annual meeting of the American Political Science Association. Washington, D.C., September 1, 2005.

Bartchy, S. Scott. "Undermining Ancient Patriarchy: The Apostle Paul's Vision of a Society of Siblings." *BTB* 29 (1999) 68–78.

———. "Who Should Be Called Father? Paul of Tarsus between the Jesus Tradition and *Patria Potestas*." *BTB* 33 (2003) 135–47.

Brodd, Jeffrey and Jonathan L. Reed, eds. *Rome and Religion: A Cross-Disciplinary Dialogue on the Imperial Cult*. Society of Biblical Literature Writings from the Greco-Roman World Supplement Series 5. Atlanta: Society of Biblical Literature, 2011.

Cascio, Elio Lo. "The Early Roman Empire: The State and the Economy." In *The Cambridge Economic History of the Greco-Roman World*, edited by Walter Scheidel, Ian Morris, and Richard P. Saller, 619–47. New York: Cambridge University Press, 2013.

Castelli, Elizabeth A. *Imitating Paul: A Discourse of Power*. Literary Currents in Biblical Interpretation. Louisville: Westminster John Knox, 1991.

---

69. See Temin, *Roman Market Economy*.

Duling, Dennis C. "Paul's Aegean Network: The Strength of Strong Ties." *BTB* 43 (2013) 135–54.

Dunn, James D. G. *Romans 9–16*. WBC 38B. Dallas: Word, 1988.

Elliott, John H. *What Is Social-Scientific Criticism?* Guides to Biblical Scholarship. Minneapolis: Fortress, 1993.

Elliott, Neil. *The Arrogance of Nations: Reading Romans in the Shadow of Empire.* PCritCon. Minneapolis, Fortress, 2008.

———. "The Letter to the Romans." In *A Postcolonial Commentary on the New Testament Writings*, edited by Fernando F. Segovia and R. S. Sugirtharajah, 194–219. Bible and Postcolonialism 13. New York: T. & T. Clark, 2009.

———. *Liberating Paul: The Justice of God and the Politics of the Apostle.* 1994. Reprinted, Minneapolis: Fortress, 2006.

———. "Romans 13:1–7 in the Context of Imperial Propaganda." In *Paul and Empire: Religion and Power in Roman Imperial Society*, edited by Richard A. Horsley, 184–204. Harrisburg, PA: Trinity, 1997.

Friedrich, Johannes, Wolfgang Pöhlmann, and Peter Stuhlmacher. "Zur historischen Situation und Intention von Rom 13:1–7." *Zeitschrift für Theologie und Kirche* 73 (1976) 131–66.

Fuhrmann, J. Christopher. *Policing the Roman Empire: Soldiers, Administration, and Public Order.* New York: Oxford University Press, 2012.

Galinsky, Karl. *Augustus: Introduction to the Life of an Emperor.* New York: Cambridge University Press, 2012.

———. "The Cult of the Roman Emperor: Uniter or Divider?" In *Rome and Religion: A Cross-Disciplinary Dialogue on the Imperial Cult*, edited by Jeffrey Brodd and Jonathan L. Reed, 1–22. SBL Writings from the Greco-Roman World Supplement Series 5. Atlanta: Society of Biblical Literature, 2011.

———. "In the Shadow (or not) of the Imperial Cult: A Cooperative Agenda. In *Rome and Religion: A Cross-Disciplinary Dialogue on the Imperial Cult*, edited by Jeffrey Brodd and Jonathan L. Reed, 215–26. SBL Writings from the Greco-Roman World Supplement Series 5. Atlanta: Society of Biblical Litera-ture, 2011.

Hopkins, Keith. "Taxes and Trade in the Roman Empire (200 B.C.—A.D. 400)." *Journal of Roman Studies* 70 (1980) 101–25.

Horowitz, Donald L. *Ethnic Groups in Conflict.* Berkeley: University of California Press, 1985.

Horsley, Richard A. "Introduction: Gospel of Imperial Salvation." In *Paul and Empire: Religion and Power in Roman Imperial Society*, edited by Richard A. Horsley, 10–24. Harrisburg, PA: Trinity, 1997.

Jewett, Robert. *Romans: A Commentary.* Hermeneia. Minneapolis: Fortress, 2007.

Jongman, Willem M. "The Early Roman Empire: Consumption." In *The Cambridge Economic History of the Greco-Roman World*, edited by Walter Scheidel, Ian Morris and Richard P. Saller, 592–618. New York: Cambridge University Press, 2013.

Kallas, James. "Romans XIII: 1–7: An Interpolation." *NTS* 11 (1964–65) 365–74.

Käsemann, Ernst. *Commentary on Romans.* Translated by Geoffrey W. Bromiley. Grand Rapids: Eerdmans, 1980.

Kittredge, Cynthia Briggs. "Corinthian Women Prophets and Paul's Argumentation in 1 Corinthians." In *Paul and Politics: Ekklesia, Israel, Imperium, Interpretation: Essays in Honor of Krister Stendahl*, edited by Richard A. Horsley, 103–109. Harrisburg, PA: Trinity, 2000.

Lampe, Peter. *From Paul to Valentinus: Christians at Rome in the First Two Centuries*. Translated by Michael Steinhauser. Edited by Marshall Johnson. Minneapolis: Fortress, 2003.

Lee, Jae Won. "Paul, Nation, and Nationalism: A Korean Postcolonial Perspective." In *The Colonized Apostle: Paul through Postcolonial Eyes*, edited by Christopher D. Stanley, 223–35. Minneapolis: Fortress, 2011.

Lopez, Davina C. "Visualizing Significant Otherness: Reimagining Paul(ine) Studies) through Hybrid Lenses." In *The Colonized Apostle: Paul through Postcolonial Eyes*, edited by Christopher D. Stanley, 74–92. Minneapolis: Fortress, 2011.

Lott, J. Bert. *The Neighborhoods of Augustan Rome*. Cambridge: Cambridge University Press, 2004.

Marchal, Joseph A. *The Politics of Heaven: Women, Gender, and Empire in the Study of Paul*. PCritCon. Minneapolis: Fortress, 2008.

Noy, David. *Foreigners at Rome: Citizens and Strangers*. Wiltshire, UK: Classical Press of Wales, 2002.

Punt, Jeremy. "Pauline Agency in Postcolonial Perspective: Subverter of or Agent of Empire." In *The Colonized Apostle: Paul through Postcolonial Eyes*, edited by Christopher D. Stanley, 53–61. PCritCon. Minneapolis: Fortress, 2011.

Nippel, Wilfred. *Public Order in Ancient Rome*. Key Themes in Ancient History. Cambridge: Cambridge University Press, 1995.

Robinson, O. F. *The Criminal Law of Ancient Rome*. Baltimore: Johns Hopkins University Press, 1995.

Schüssler Fiorenza, Elisabeth. *Rhetoric and Ethic: The Politics of Biblical Studies*. Minneapolis: Fortress, 1999.

———. "Rhetorical Situation in I Corinthians." *NTS* 33 (1987) 386–403.

Sirks, Biudewijn. *Food for Rome: The Legal Structure of the Transportation and Processing of Supplies for the Imperial Distributions in Rome and Constantinople*. Studia Amstelodamensia ad epigraphicam, ius antiquum et papyrologicam pertinentia 31. Amsterdam: Gieben, 1991.

Snyder, Gregory H. "Response to Karl Galinsky, 'In the Shadow (or not) of the Imperial Cult: A Cooperative Agenda.'" In *Rome and Religion: A Cross-Disciplinary Dialogue on the Imperial Cult*, edited by Jeffrey Brodd and Jonathan L. Reed, 227–34. Society of Biblical Literature Writings from the Greco-Roman World Supplement Series 5. Atlanta: Society of Biblical Literature, 2011.

Stanley, Christopher D., ed. *The Colonized Paul: Paul through Postcolonial Eyes*. PCritCon. Minneapolis: Fortress, 2011.

Temin, Peter. "The Economy of the Early Roman Empire." *Journal of Economic Perspectives* 20 (2006) 133–51.

———. *The Roman Market Economy*. Princeton Economic History of the Western World. Princeton: Princeton University Press, 2013.

Zerbe, Gordon. "The Politics of Paul: His Supposed Social Conservatism and the Impact of Postcolonial Readings." In *The Colonized Apostle: Paul through Postcolonial Eyes*, edited by Christopher D. Stanley, 62–73. PCritCon. Minneapolis: Fortress, 2011.

9

1 Corinthians 7:17–24
Considering Stoic Argumentation and the Ἀδιάφορα of Slavery and Freedom

Rollin A. Ramsaran

NOT ONLY DID SCOTT Bartchy pique my interest in 1 Corinthians, but he also modeled how to teach, write, and relate well to others. It is a pleasure to follow his strong work in 1 Corinthians 7 with my own attempt to push the conversation forward—despite its shortcomings, I hope Scott treats this piece with the gentleness of love shown to my first critiqued paper in the Good Earth Restaurant in Westwood, California, now some 35 years ago!

A complex individual, the Apostle Paul may be properly described as eclectic in his use of persuasive methods. Four prominent perspectives have been investigated by New Testament scholarship: Paul as letter-writer, rhetorician, Jewish apocalyptist, and Hellenistic moralist. Paul can move from one perspective to another and often combines perspectives together as needed. In this essay, I examine Paul's role as a Hellenistic moralist, bringing alongside his rhetorical expression and his foundational stance as a Jewish apocalyptist. The topics of slavery and freedom were common among Greco-Roman moralists, and ἀδιάφορα ("indifferent matters") formed a central reasoning strategy among the Stoics. Using this background, I investigate Paul's discussion of slaves in 1 Cor 7:21–23 more closely, within the context of 1 Cor 7:17–24.

Stoic Argumentation as Background for Paul's Persuasion

The Hellenistic period brought a movement toward individualism and with it a shift in the focus of philosophy. Rather than focusing on the city-state structure, Hellenistic philosophy asked how the inner guidance of the individual (i.e., the development of morals) produced proper actions. Teachers of philosophy in the Hellenistic period are called moralists.¹ According to Malherbe, moralists at the time of the New Testament practiced a "koine" (common) or eclectic philosophy. Teachers such as Plutarch, or Philo, or even the Apostle Paul were aware of teachings from a variety of schools: Stoic, Epicurean, Cynic, and Middle Platonic. Moralists combined various teachings from multiple schools into a multifaceted whole—though one school tradition might be the primary base from which the teachings of other schools were supplemented.²

Roman Stoicism was the most prominent moralist tradition during the Greco-Roman period.³ Hence, it is not surprising that the Apostle Paul would know of its teachings and is willing to use its argumentation to contextualize his gospel among Gentile audiences who presumably relate to these ideas as well. The relationship of the Apostle Paul to Stoicism has a long history of inquiry. More recently, it has been pointedly advocated by Troels Engberg-Pedersen in *Paul and the Stoics* and *Cosmology and Self in the Apostle Paul*.⁴ Besides ἀδιάφορα, other patterns of Stoic argumentation in Paul have been investigated: οἰκείωσις/"appropriation" (Engberg-Petersen); *meditatio*/"meditation" (Ramsaran); τὸ σύμφορον/"common advantage" (Chang); Cynic/Stoic marriage debates (Deming).⁵

My interest in the concept of ἀδιάφορα in 1 Corinthians 7 appeared in my 1996 work on Paul's rhetorical maxims in 1 Corinthians 1–10.⁶ Continued work investigated Paul's ἀδιάφορα maxims, of which 1 Cor 7:19 was one of three (2003).⁷ Simultaneously and independently, Deming was working on the concept of Paul's use of indifferent things, with specific discussion of

---

1. Meeks, *Moral World*, 19–42.
2. Malherbe, *Moral Exhortation*, 12–13.
3. Stowers, "Paul and Self-Mastery," 527.
4. Engberg-Pedersen, *Paul and the Stoics*, provides an excellent review of literature in 306–7, n. 10.
5. Ibid.; Ramsaran, "Steps of the Moralists," 284–300; Chang, *Community, the Individual, and the Common Good*; Deming, *Paul on Marriage and Celibacy*, respectively.
6. Ramsaran, *Liberating Words*, 42–43.
7. Ramsaran, "Paul and Maxims," 429–56.

1 Cor 7:25–38 and 7:20–23.[8] Earlier J. Paul Sampley (2002) also examined the use of ἀδιάφορα in 1 Corinthians 7.[9] Commentary writing since 2002, however, has not taken much note of the Stoic background of ἀδιάφορα.

Was Paul a Stoic?

Paul's basic orientation is that of a Jewish apocalyptist, and it is thereby different from that of the Stoic moralist.[10] Paul does share a moral reasoning pattern similar to the moralists of his time. He holds to a pattern of moral progress that seeks to identify and do the "good" in a consistent fashion, in order to reach the "goal" of "human flourishing."[11] The foundation of Stoic thought was a providential divine reason that led human beings along a path to the "best life possible." Despite outside circumstances, every individual was capable of choosing the "good." The Stoics identified the "good" as that which was internal to them (within their control) as opposed to that which was external (not within their control).[12] The chief virtue was "self-mastery"—the ability to choose the good with consistency by right reason, thereby achieving human flourishing.[13]

The foundation of Paul's thought, on the other hand, is belief that the creator God has altered the cosmic structure through the death and resurrection of Jesus, such that human beings are led along a new and empowered path toward the "triumph of God."[14] In Paul's Judean apocalyptic pattern, the shape of that story is: (1) critique of rulers, (2) restoration of the people of God, and (3) full inclusion of faithful believers through resurrection.[15] Believers have the ability to identify the "good" as that which is present in the "new creation" that moves toward full restoration at Christ's coming.

---

8. Deming, "Paul and Indifferent Things," 390–97. Deming shows no knowledge of my previous work in note # 6 above; he spoke in a general way about Stoic indifference in *Paul on Marriage and Celibacy*, 155–56 (based on his 1991 dissertation).

9. Sampley, "First Letter to the Corinthians," 880–82.

10. For Paul's orientation within an apocalyptic framework, see Beker, *Paul the Apostle*, 135–81.

11. Malherbe, *Moral Exhortation*, 12–13, for the pattern among the moralists. For an application of the pattern by Paul, see Phil 3:8–14, albeit Paul's understanding of "human flourishing" is faithful movement toward God in the present, leading to transformation and full life at Christ's coming.

12. Lesses, "Virtue and the Goods of Fortune," 98–101.

13. Stowers, "Paul and Self-Mastery," 524–29.

14. Beker, *Paul the Apostle*, 176–81.

15. For this pattern applied directly to 1 Cor, see Ramsaran, "Resisting Imperial Domination," 89–101.

The chief virtue is a "Spirit-mastery"—the ability of the human self to join together with the empowering Spirit of God, producing a variety of gifts that lead to the flourishing of the individual within community.[16]

In considering 1 Cor 7:17-24, we note that Paul is not a Stoic, but he is capable of making use of Stoic argumentation to help community members identify and make right moral choices in the time before God's coming triumph. The form of Stoic argumentation we encounter is that of ἀδιάφορα or "indifferent matters."

"Paul's Moral Reasoning and the Good in 1 Corinthians"

Moralists taught about how to act in the world in a way that was consistent with nature—and for the Stoics, particularly what is appropriate to one's true human nature. Stoics, like other moralists, made distinctions between the good and the vices. The good was what was "good in itself," not being dependent on anything else. Hence, the good and those actions that come forth from what is good in itself are the basis for virtue (consistently practiced goods) and "human flourishing."[17] The opposite of the good and what comes forth from it are the vices.

In the larger context of 1 Corinthians, we see that Paul perceives the chief good and appropriate goal of the human being to be a proper relationship to the living God through Christ (3:21-23). Hence, Paul addresses community members as "saints" or "those set apart [for God]" (1:2).[18] What comes forth from this good is properly ordered social actions in conformity to Christ's cruciform pattern, leading to proper discernment of God's will and right choices.[19] Believers are oriented and set apart to God in order to form and, then, start other faithful communities within the world.

For Paul, too, the opposite of the good and what comes forth from an antithetical stance toward God is an improper disposition and its resulting vices. In 1 Corinthians 1-4, Paul examines the inner disposition of boasting and its resulting divisive behaviors (1:11-13; 3:3-4; 4:6-8). In 1 Corinthians

---

16. Paul's confidence in Roman "self-mastery," found in Rom 1-2, shows a disdain for its ability to make life right with God, while his discussion of the Spirit's work with and on behalf of believers in Romans 5-8 is transformative (with the gifted structure of the community apparent in Romans 12). On "self-mastery" and its relationship to the argument in Romans, see Stowers, *A Rereading of Romans,* 42-82; 324-25.

17. Lesses, "Virtue and the Goods of Fortune," 99-100.

18. All translations are my own, unless otherwise noted.

19. Gorman, *Cruciformity,* 75-94, esp. 92-94.

5–6, Paul more pointedly demonstrates the unacceptable consequences of a boasting and unrestrained "personal freedom"[20] that stands apart from the holy community/temple that God is erecting (6:19–20; cf. 3:16–17). Using two vice lists (5:9–12; 6:9–10), Paul establishes appropriate boundaries against unholy and worldly structures (sexual immorality, 5:1–13; unjust law courts, 6:1–11). Vices are antithetical to the good and moral life.

First Corinthians 6:12–20 prepares for Paul's argumentation in 1 Corinthians 7. Paul shifts the moral perspective from the Corinthians' own unrestrained maxim—"All things are permissible to me!"—to the perspective of what is or is not *advantageous* for social obligations within the community of believers—"All things are permissible, *but not all things are helpful*" (6:12). First Corinthians 7:1 opens up the chapter with the same structure: Paul quotes a Corinthian maxim ("It is well for a man not to touch a woman") and, then, argues what is not advantageous, what is advantageous, and what is more advantageous with respect to male and female relationships in the community of believers.[21]

"How Do You Act if You Don't Know What Will Happen?"

First Corinthians 7 considers the appropriateness of women and men to abandon marriage obligations for either alternative spiritual arrangements or separation (7:1–16). Additionally, Paul considers the suitability of single persons to marry in a traditional or spiritual manner or remain single as a religious vocation (7:25–40).[22]

First Corinthians 7:17–24 has been labeled a digression;[23] it is, however, very well connected to chapter 7. Crucial for our purpose is the opening verse: "Therefore, unless peace is at stake, each person should seek to live properly,[24] in accordance to the context assigned by the Lord, in accordance with God's call to be set apart. And this is a directive I give in all my churches" (7:17). The translation "Therefore, unless peace is at stake" gives

---

20. "All things are permissible to me!" (1 Cor 6:12).

21. Ramsaran, *Liberating Words*, 40–43, for a full discussion of Paul's strategy.

22. This paragraph follows closely the wording in my previous work: Ramsaran, "Paul and Maxims," 446.

23. So Sampley, "First Letter to the Corinthians," 879, who acknowledges that a digression properly integrates with the surrounding material on both sides.

24. Περιπατέω ("to walk") has the strong metaphorical sense of "to conduct one's life." See BAGD, 649. The translation "seek to live properly" is justified by the deliberative nature of the chapter (cf. 7:1, 8, 10, 12, 25–26, 35, 40) and the inclusive nature of the directive for all Paul's churches (v. 17c).

true recognition to Εἰ μὴ ("nevertheless") as a continuative connector of exception.[25] Following closely on the contingencies of life posed at the closing of the previous section (7:16),[26] Paul raises the question moving forward, "How do you act/walk if you do not know what will happen?" Paul's answer is: (1) maintain the internal good, (2) start from where you find yourself, and (3) make proper judgments with respect to ἀδιάφορα.

Paul, as with the Stoics, thinks of the good as that which is internal, that which is good in itself, *and the outcomes that flow from the good*. For Paul, the believer's relationship to God, through the death of Jesus Christ, in the power of the Spirit, and subject to the covenantal outcomes of God's expectation, marks the supreme good. This is the main reference point, clearly marked by the "call" language in our text (7:17, 20, 24). When Paul centers on the good in contrast to ἀδιάφορα (indifferent matters) or even vice, *he speaks primarily in outcomes*. In our text, what truly matters is "peace" (1 Cor 7:17 as translated above) and "doing the commandments of God" (7:19). By analogy with the ἀδιάφορα maxim of 7:19, we can add "faith working itself out in love" (Gal 5:6) and "a new creation" (Gal 6:15).[27] In contrast to vice, consider the importance given to the fruit of the Spirit: "love, joy, peace, patience, kindness, goodness, faithfulness, gentleness, and self-control" (Gal 5:22).

Paul's "predestination" language surely has roots in his own heritage from the scriptures of Israel.[28] When he speaks of "seek to live properly in the context *assigned by the Lord*," his language at least mirrors the Stoic idea of the world reason that ultimately controls all things to a final destiny.[29] Within that framework, the human mind dealt with contingencies through proper choices. Such language is dangerous for an apocalyptist,[30] but here

---

25. "Since this usage 'excepts' a preceding negative, it almost certainly goes back to vs. 15b: 'The brother or sister is not bound in such cases . . . Nevertheless . . .'" Fee, *1 Corinthians*, 309.

26. First Corinthians 7:16: "Wife, how do you know whether you will save your husband? Husband, how do you know whether you will save your wife?"

27. For an analysis of the three ἀδιάφορα maxims together and how they point to what truly matters for Paul, see Ramsaran, "Paul and Maxims," 437–48.

28. Romans 9:6–18 is indicative of both Paul's perspective and use of the scriptures of Israel.

29. Meeks, *Moral World*, 48–49.

30. Apocalyptic recognizes the loss of control by God and the presence of evil in human history for a time, but it also acknowledges the re-establishment of control through the coming victory of God. Paul's predestination language seems to reflect a strong movement toward the latter perspective. Certainly then, as well as today, it is troublesome to credit God with 'assigning" some human beings to places of deep-seated oppression and not others.

Paul desires to emphasize God's control in the world. He is realistic that most folks have little opportunity to change their social circumstances or location, but he must still recognize the open possibilities and expectations set in motion by the Christ-event and required by "God's call." After Paul's own calling, he did not remain an enemy of God, nor did he continue to persecute the churches, nor ostensibly did he maintain Pharisaic connections and standing, but he chose to renounce his own position of status (Phil 3:4–11). As commentators note, 1 Corinthians 7 is marked by guidance that allows "exceptions" in light of new conditions and ongoing contingencies of life.[31] Where each person is met by the call of God is adequate and even a God-given place.[32] The believer's ongoing circumstances are, however, always in tension, even subject to variation or change by God's call to be set apart.[33]

The early Cynics identified virtues, vices, and "indifferent matters" as components of articulating the moral life. It was the Stoic tradition following Zeno, however, which extensively elaborated on the function and place of ἀδιάφορα. Between the good that led to virtues and the vice that was antithetical to it was a broad range of options and situations that neither contributed to the good or the bad—they were properly called "indifferent matters."[34] The Stoic chief virtue was "self-mastery" or the ability to obtain to the good in itself and to properly navigate the ἀδιάφορα in support of the practice of the good. This was accomplished by the human mind (νοῦς) aligning itself with the world reason (λόγος) and making proper judgments about (1) the good (that which is internal) and (2) *the use of* ἀδιάφορα (things, properly, external/outside to oneself and one's control).[35]

Stoic ἀδιάφορα are usually expressed in pairs of options: life, death; health, disease; pleasure, pain; strength, weakness; wealth, poverty; reputation, low repute, etc.[36] Paul follows suit in places such as Phil 1:20–24 (life, death), Phil 4:11–13 (wealth, poverty), 1 Cor 8:8 (idol meat), Gal 2:6 (reputation, low repute), and the ἀδιάφορα maxims (1 Cor 7:19; Gal 5:6;

---

31. Horsley, *1 Corinthians*, 96.

32. Sampley, "First Letter to the Corinthians," 880–81.

33. Hence, my translation above, "This is a directive I give in all my churches." Paul does not give a "rule" (RSV, NRSV) but directions on how to make good decisions and walk accordingly. Διατάσσω ("make arrangements," LSJ, 414; cf. "order, direct, command," BAGD, 189) is a word Paul uses when ordering proper community life (see 1 Cor 11:34).

34. Meeks, *Moral World*, 48–50.

35. Ibid., 47–49. "All 'external things,' that is, everything but the choices we make about the mental impressions which alone we control, are morally 'indifferent' (*adiaphora*)" (49). Lesses, "Virtue and the Goods of Fortune," 102–11.

36. See Jaquette, *Discerning What Counts*, 45–46.

6:15).³⁷ Indifferent matters are not simply categorizations. They are external states from which a moral agent may or may not have the ability to move. When choice is in play, however, Stoics advocated that indifferent matters be reckoned according to advantage ("preferred indifferent") or disadvantage ("non-preferred indifferent") in relationship to obtaining the good and its outcomes.

Paul believes and affirms God's will to bring the cosmos to its directed and right destiny. But he also knows of the contingencies of life in the present order that marked the Hellenistic age.³⁸ "How do you act/walk if you do not know what will happen?" Paul's answer is: (1) maintain the internal good, (2) start from where you find yourself, and (3) make proper judgments with respect to ἀδιάφορα.

1 Corinthians 7:17–24

Chapter 7 appears to reflect Paul's teaching in Gal 3:23,³⁹ male/female relationships, and, then, the pairing of Jew/Gentile and slave/free in 7:17–24. Again, we are reminded of the "external" nature of ἀδιάφορα. This concept helps to protect the legitimacy of an "internal pursuit" of the good from those things that remain external/out of one's control: the restraints of marriage, ethnicity, and household roles. Ἀδιάφορα are expressed in terms of the external and the physical body, the good in terms of the internal and the human reasoning process. Below, with slavery, we see the physical state used metaphorically to describe the internal state.

Keeping in mind Paul's anthropology will guide us in considering the argument in 1 Cor 7:17–24, particularly as we encounter the discussion of slaves and slavery in vv. 20–23. Paul believes that, without relinquishing one's own will, each human being is always under the control of some outside power. For Paul, the question of human existence is centered on a lordship issue: What power will one be under? This is the language of the household, and part of the household is the master and slave relationship. In Rom 6, Paul indicates that human beings have two possibilities for

---

37. Jaquette, *Discerning What Counts*, 100–96.

38. As reflected in Phil 4:12: "I know how to be abased, and I know how to abound; in any and all circumstances I have learned the secret of facing plenty and hunger, abundance and want." The Stoics, too, "seek to place the responsibility for securing *eudaimonia* [human flourishing/happiness] firmly within the individual moral agent's power and to remove the vagaries of Tyche [Luck]" (Jaquette, *Discerning What Counts*, 39).

39. A seminal observation brought to the discussion of this text by Bartchy, *ΜΑΛΛΟΝ ΧΡΗΣΑΙ*, 162–65 . See, Sampley, "First Corinthians," 882; Deming, *Paul on Marriage and Celibacy*, 154.

lordship: slavery/obedience to sin's power or slavery/obedience to Christ's pattern of righteousness (6:6–11, 16–18). Christ's death breaks the bonds of the apocalyptic power of slavery to sin's power (6:10) and transfers lordship/obedience to God and the apocalyptic power of righteousness (6:13, 17–18; and elaborated in Romans 8 as being enabled by the power of the Spirit). First Corinthians 7:23 resonates with the same message: "You were bought with a price [i.e., Christ's death]: do not become slaves of human beings [i.e., sinful human standards and values]." Already in 1 Corinthians 5–6, Paul had pointed out sinful human conventions and values (impropriety in family sexual mores, taking believers to court to defraud, cult immorality) and pronounced, "You are not your own; you were bought with a price. So glorify God in your body" (6:19b–20; cf. 3:23—"and you are Christ's, and Christ is God's").

The following outline will draw together some points and present a structure from which to examine 1 Cor 7:17–24:[40]

A   Directive: Live appropriate to one's place and call—v. 17

    B   Illustration: Circumcision/uncircumcision mark ethnic indifferences; *neither is a "preferred"*—v. 18

        C   *How to Walk*: Maxim = "Circumcision is nothing and uncircumcision is nothing, but what is something is *doing the commandments of God*"—v. 19

A′   Repetition of directive, focused on maintaining one's call—v. 20

    B′   Illustration: Being set apart to God makes social status an ἀδιάφορον; however, social movement from slavery to freedom *is a "preferred"*; mutual equality among community members is through a common internal disposition—vv. 21–22

        C′   *How to Walk*: Exhortation = "You were bought with a price; *do not become slaves of human beings*"—v. 23

A″   Repetition of directive focused on remaining with God *in whatever situation*—v. 24

First Corinthians 7:17–24 emphasizes the internal good as the call of God into faithful relationship and the various situations that community members find themselves in as external indifferent matters. Paul's strategy is to encourage community members to maintain the internal good (their call) and the outcomes proper to it and to relativize the externals.

---

40. This outline has been reproduced with changes from Ramsaran, "Paul and Maxims," 446.

1 Corinthians 7:17

Verse 17 guides Paul's discussion in this section. The emphasis is how one "walks" or lives in light of two poles: (1) navigating the Lord's assigned position, and (2) navigating the call to be set apart to God in a context of peace. Paul's syntax lays the two poles alongside each other and then places the imperative in emphatic position at the end (thus walk!).[41] What is the relationship between the assigned place one finds oneself in and the call of God? In the context of ἀδιάφορα, the assigned place is external (an indifferent matter) and the call is internal (that which is "good in itself"). The external is variable and open to moral discernment; the internal is primary and one needs to align with it and its proper outcomes (= live/walk). This is Paul's "directive" in all the churches.[42]

While the primacy of "God's call" is evident by the repeated forms of "call/calling" used in this section (7:17, 18, 20, 21, 22, 24) and by the distinct structure of the directive in 7:17, reinforced by repetition at 7:20 and 7:24 (see outline), this emphasis has often subtly shifted or been lost to an overemphasis of "the assigned place."[43] From the standpoint of Paul's use of Stoic argumentation, this is not helpful. The internal good, God's call, and its outcome of peace, is properly and in every case of most importance, but the externals are taken for their advantage, pushed aside in cases of disadvantage, and remain in place and are of no concern when they are neutral.

1 Corinthians 7:18–19

Paul presents the first of two illustrations that reinforce living in proper relationship to God. In a world in which differences between Jews and non-Jews were well known, Paul highlights ethnic differences as ἀδιάφορα. Paul's words are balanced and well-paced with each question followed by an answer: Circumcision? Do not seek to remove; Uncircumcision? Do not seek circumcision. Paul provides a maxim highlighting what is of most importance: "doing the commandments of God." Various interpretations of "doing the commandments of God" have been given.[44] Stoic argumentation regarding ἀδιάφορα suggests an outcome from a proper disposition

---

41. Ἑκάστῳ ὡς ἐμέρισεν ὁ κύριος, ἕκαστον ὡς κέκληκεν ὁ θεός, οὕτως περιπατείτω. ("To each as the Lord assigned, each as God has called, thus walk!")

42. See note 33 above.

43. One striking example is the NIV (1984), "Nevertheless, each one should retain the place in life that the Lord assigned him and to which God has called him."

44. See Thiselton, *First Epistle to the Corinthians*, 551–52.

centered on the good. Hence, Paul is indicating behavior that is the outcome of one's being set apart (holiness)—or put another way, responding to God's call as the chief good. It is plausible that Paul has the context of his teaching in the whole letter in mind, not limited to, but possibly inclusive of Jewish Torah and the words of Jesus.[45] As ἀδιάφορα, neither circumcision nor uncircumcision is preferred—or non-preferred. Leave them as they are and continue to follow the will of God.

The Corinthians do not have issues with "circumcision" or "law." Thus Paul can confidently illustrate his point with these neutral indifferent matters. Paul's ἀδιάφορα, however, must be assessed according to their relationship to the good and this can vary under different circumstances. In Galatians, Paul, while indicating that circumcision and uncircumcision are indifferents (Gal 5:6; 6:15), by no means thinks circumcision is "neutral" for Gentile believers—at best it is "non-preferred."[46] Wrong thinking regarding ἀδιάφορα threatens to undo the good, God's grace, and one's call. By Paul's writing of Romans, a strong connection between circumcision and the good is made in support of common ground for a mixed audience of Jews and Gentiles. Thus Paul internalizes the concept—"real circumcision is a matter of the heart, spiritual and not literal" (Rom 2:28).[47] The marker of being set apart to God and within God's people is written on the heart.

1 Corinthians 7:20

Verse 20 is a shorter repetition of v. 17—"Each in the calling in which (you) were called, in this remain." Again, the "calling" is primary by word repetition and emphatic first position. The place one is encountered by God (an indifferent matter) is to the background of the calling itself, and the social roles and obligations connected with this place must be inferred by the interpreter from the context.[48] This aligns with Stoic argumentation regarding ἀδιάφορα.

---

45. Along these lines, see Ramsaran, "Paul and Maxims," 447.

46. "Now I, Paul, say to you that if you receive circumcision, Christ will be of no advantage to you" (Gal 5:2, RSV).

47. Paul uses this technique below when dealing with the slave/free ἀδιάφορα.

48. Bartchy, ΜΑΛΛΟΝ ΧΡΗΣΑΙ, 132–59, provides a discussion of "The Theology of Calling" that remains seminal in identifying structural features and connections within the full context of 1 Corinthians.

1 Corinthians 7:21-23

Verse 21 opens with a question, marking a parallel structure to Paul's first illustration in verse 18. From there, things are much different. First, Paul switches from general address (τις—"anyone"; ἕκαστος—"each") to second person singular specific address ("Were you a slave when called?"). This indicates an ongoing concern among slaves in the community.[49] Second, Paul's practical advice is not to move out of slavery—as there is little chance of that—but to "not worry about it." Paul's advice matches the Stoic tradition about external ἀδιάφορα outside of one's control. Paul does not balance the pair of ἀδιάφορα using a second question as he did with circumcision/uncircumcision. Rather he states that the movement to "freedom," when available, is a "preferred" indifferent—"But if you are able to become free, then rather use [the freedom]."[50]

Paul's next move is to show that all community members stand in a transformed relationship to God—a called relationship. Allowing "legal slavery" and "legal freedom" to stand as ἀδιάφορα, Paul now (in a Stoic manner) internalizes freedom[51] *and slavery* as "right thinking" regarding the good. Each community member presumably has a legal status of either slave or free, but each community member has been called into a relationship that operates with *both* freedom and slavery. Slavery represents a disposition of obedience to God through lordship to Christ with the outcome of life patterned on Jesus' self-giving love for others. Freedom represents the power of the Spirit to open up new possibilities and giftedness in a community of equal participation. Paul writes to help the Corinthians balance the two perspectives: "freedom constrained by love."[52] Hence, Paul, once again, emphasizes the area the Corinthians struggle with—alignment with those who advocate human standards and conventions of the world, rather than proper holiness before God: "You were bought with a price;[53] do not become slaves of human beings!" Walk according to your call and proper freedom, not according to the world's ways.

---

49. Sampley, "First Letter to the Corinthians," 880.

50. For the variety of options to translate μᾶλλον χρῆσαι, see Thiselton, *First Epistle to the Corinthians*, 553–59. Thiselton is appreciative of Bartchy's perspectives regarding 7:21 in its larger context, but stops short of accepting the specific syntactical argument for "(as a freedman) live according to [*God's calling*]" in 7:21b (italics mine).

51. Jaquette, *Discerning What Counts*, 91–96, for the Stoics and internalization of freedom.

52. Ramsaran, *Liberating Words*, 66–73.

53. And, therefore, have a new lord. The image is from the slave market.

1 Corinthians 7:24

This final directive of the section has been broadened from 7:20 with the addition after ἐν of a relative pronoun, ἐν ᾧ: "in what[ever] [situation]."[54] Also, the "call" is reinforced with the addition of παρὰ θεῷ ("before God") in emphatic final position:[55] "Each in whatever situation God called you, in this [calling] remain before God!" For Paul, "maintaining a single-minded, proper stance before God negates connection with other idolatrous spiritual and human influences. Fidelity to God provides a springboard to a number of issues that lie ahead in 1 Corinthians (7:23, 35; 10:20-22; 11:27-30; 12:2-3; 15:24-28; 16:13, 22)."[56]

Conclusion

With regard to Paul's views on slavery, we need to ask how and in what ways "free status" might function as a "preferred" in helping one along to the full power of God's good news and its outcomes: maintaining the integrity of one's call; peace; doing the commandments of God; faith working through love; new creation. In addition, however, we must be critical enough to question Paul's use of ἀδιάφορα. Does it help justify slavery by looking the other way with regard to real human hurt and oppression in light of an apocalyptic imminence (1 Cor 7:26; "the present distress")? Does internalization of freedom have the potential (as it did for the Stoics) to prioritize the mind over the full range of bodily existence? Orlando Patterson reminds us that every slavery is a social death—"permanent, violent, and personal domination of natally alienated and generally dishonored persons."[57] Jennifer A. Glancy shows strongly that even household slaves had no true control over their bodies and were subject to abuse—both corporeal and sexual.[58] Peter Oakes and Moyer V. Hubbard have helpfully and imaginatively written slaves' lives into the narrative of early Pauline communities, asking how Paul's ethical norms and demands might be outside a slave's control and,

---

54. See discussion in Fee, *1 Corinthians*, 320-22.
55. Fee, *1 Corinthians*, 320-22.
56. Ramsaran, "Paul and Maxims," 447.
57. Patterson, *Freedom*, 9-10, 21-22.
58. Glancy, *Slavery in Early Christianity*, 9-29.

thereby, causing much unease.[59] In such situations, ἀδιάφορα and the separation of the body and the inner life may have been comforting for a slave.[60]

Will Deming has taken the bold step of suggesting that Paul considered "slavery" to be a "non-preferred" *adiaphoron*.[61] While I do not see this explicitly in the text of 7:20-23, implicitly the historical context and the hard questions to be asked—by Paul, his community members, and now the modern interpreter—no doubt present challenges to slavery *as a neutral indifferent matter*. With his own Israelite background steeped in the story of God's deliverance of a people from slavery, his hope in apocalyptic deliverance from the Roman Empire's death machine, and his certain knowledge of the abusive and bodily reality of Roman slavery in his own time, Paul may have struggled to discern consistent counsel for his community members. As Brad Ronnell Braxton reminds us, Paul himself may not have found resolution to the problem of slavery in his time.[62] Paul's counsel does, however, provide us with a present and powerful trajectory of recognizing and encountering the slaveries of our own time and constructing theologies that attend to creating communities that extend in concrete ways the self-giving love of Christ—with even greater awareness and less blinders to the full range of human experience and exploitation.

Works Cited

Bartchy, S. Scott. *ΜΑΛΛΟΝ ΧΡΗΣΑΙ: First-Century Slavery and 1 Corinthians 7:21*. SBLDS 11. Missoula, MT: Society of Biblical Literature, 1973. Reprinted, Eugene, OR: Wipf & Stock, 2003.

Beker, J. Christian. *Paul the Apostle: The Triumph of God in Life and Thought*. Philadelphia: Fortress, 1980.

Braxton, Brad Ronnell. *The Tyranny of Resolution: 1 Corinthians 7:17-24*. SBLDS 181. Atlanta: Society of Biblical Literature, 2000.

Chang, Kei Eun. *The Community, the Individual and the Common Good: 'to Idion' and 'to Sympheron' in the Greco-Roman World and Paul*. LNTS 480. London: Bloomsbury, 2013.

Deming, Will. "Paul and Indifferent Things." In *Paul in the Greco-Roman World*, edited by. J. Paul Sampley, 384-403. Harrisburg, PA: Trinity, 2003.

---

59. Oakes, *Reading Romans in Pompeii*, 143-49, on "Iris [the bar slave] and the redemption of the body." Speaking of the household slave girl Zoe's relationship to her Roman master, Speratus, at Corinth, Hubbard writes, "Memories of that evening's dinner party . . . the obligatory submission to Gaius Conelius's [Speratus's] advances . . . (*Christianity in the Greco-Roman World*, 13). Later that day, noting Zoe's coming into womanhood, former slave, Claudia asks, "and Speratus, is he . . . treating you well?" "'As well as can be expected,' answered Zoe, *looking away*" (16, emphasis added).

60. Or *may not* (!)—I raise the possibility above with great hesitation.

61. Deming, *Paul and Indifferent Things*, 393. He uses the term "rejected indifference."

62. Braxton, *Tyranny of Resolution*, 264-74.

―――. *Paul on Marriage and Celibacy: The Hellenistic Background of 1 Corinthians 7*. 2nd ed. Grand Rapids: Eerdmans, 2004.

Engberg-Pedersen, Troels. *Cosmology and Self in the Apostle Paul*. New York: Oxford University Press, 2010.

―――. *Paul and the Stoics*. Louisville: Westminster John Knox, 2000.

Fee, Gordon D. *1 Corinthians*. New International Commentary on the New Testament. Grand Rapids: Eerdmans, 1987.

Glancy, Jennifer A. *Slavery in Early Christianity*. 2002. Reprinted, Minneapolis: Fortress, 2006.

Gorman, Michael J. *Cruciformity: Paul's Narrative Spirituality of the Cross*. Grand Rapids: Eerdmans, 2001.

Horsley, Richard A. *1 Corinthians*. Abingdon New Testament Commentaries. Nashville: Abingdon, 1999.

Hubbard, Moyer V. *Christianity in the Greco-Roman World: A Narrative Introduction*. Peabody, MA: Hendrickson, 2010.

Jaquette, James L. *Discerning What Counts: The Function of the Adiaphora Topos in Paul's Letters*. SBLDS 146. Atlanta: Scholars, 1995.

Lesses, Glenn. "Virtue and the Goods of Fortune in Stoic Moral Theory." In *Oxford Studies in Ancient Philosophy*. Vol 7. Edited by Julia Annas, 95–127. Oxford: Clarendon, 1989.

Malherbe, Abraham J. *Moral Exhortation: A Greco-Roman Sourcebook*. Library of Early Christianity 4. Philadelphia: Westminster, 1986.

Meeks, Wayne A. *The Moral World of the First Christians*. Library of Early Christianity 6. Philadelphia: Westminster, 1986.

Oakes, Peter. *Reading Romans in Pompeii: Paul's Letter at Ground Level*. Minneapolis: Fortress, 2009.

Patterson, Orlando. *Freedom in the Making of Western Culture*. Vol. 1. New York: HarperCollins, 1991.

Ramsaran, Rollin A. "In the Steps of the Moralists: Paul's Rhetorical Argumentation in Philippians 4." In *Rhetoric, Ethic, and Moral Persuasion in Biblical Discourse: Essays from the 2002 Heidelberg Conference*, edited by Tom H. Olbricht and Anders Eriksson, 284–300. Emory Studies in Early Christianity 11. New York: T. & T. Clark, 2005.

―――. *Liberating Words: Paul's Use of Rhetorical Maxims in 1 Corinthians 1–10*. Valley Forge, PA: Trinity, 1996.

―――. "Paul and Maxims." In *Paul in the Greco-Roman World*, edited by J. Paul Sampley, 429–456. Harrisburg, PA: Trinity, 2003.

―――. "Resisting Imperial Domination and Influence: Paul's Apocalyptic Rhetoric in 1 Corinthians." In *Paul and the Roman Imperial Order*, edited by Richard A. Horsley, 89–101. Harrisburg, PA: Trinity, 2004.

Sampley, J. Paul. "The First Letter to the Corinthians." In *The New Interpreter's Bible*, Volume 10: *Acts, Introduction to Epistolary Literature, Romans, and 1 Corinthians*, 771–1003. Nashville: Abingdon, 2002.

Stowers, Stanley K. *A Rereading of Romans: Justice, Jews, and Gentiles*. New Haven: Yale University Press, 1994.

―――. "Paul and Self-Mastery." In *Paul in the Greco-Roman World: A Handbook*, edited by J. Paul Sampley, 524–50. Harrisburg, PA: Trinity, 2003.

Thiselton, Anthony C. *The First Epistle to the Corinthians*. New International Greek Testament Commentary. Grand Rapids: Eerdmans, 2000.

10

Do Not Exploit a Brother or Sister
Slavery and Sexual Ethics in 1 Thessalonians 4:1–8

K. C. Richardson

I HAD THE WONDERFUL privilege of studying with Scott Bartchy in the history of religion doctoral program at UCLA. Professor Bartchy ignited my interest in the social history of the early Christians: their ideas, their cultural values, their social relations, their economic condition, and the way in which their new status "in Christ Jesus" informed their engagement with the world around them. As I studied the documents of the New Testament and other early Christian writings, Professor Bartchy helped me to see that these texts offer something very rare in ancient literature—a window into the lives of common people. Most ancient texts reflect the worldview of their elite authors, but the early Christian writings provide something different: the perspective of those occupying the lower social strata of Greco-Roman society. Professor Bartchy not only stimulated my interest in these people but also helped me to formulate questions and guided me to methods for understanding them better. But as I quickly discovered, Professor Bartchy's academic interest in the social history of the early Christians represents not simply a distinguished scholar's field of expertise but also an expression of the personal values of one who sincerely cares about equal rights, economic justice, and human dignity for those who are often overlooked and forgotten. Scott Bartchy practices what he teaches. It is therefore a great privilege to contribute to this volume in honor of a mentor who is not only an excellent scholar but a fine person as well.

In this essay, I examine the intersection of two issues, slavery and sexuality, which have been at the center of Bartchy's academic interests. I do so by following up on his suggestion regarding 1 Thess 4:1-8, namely, that Paul was addressing the problem of slave owners sexually exploiting household slaves in the recently-founded Thessalonian Christian community.[1] In this essay, I argue that the sexual use of slaves provides the most likely scenario for understanding Paul's discussion of πορνεία in this passage. Compared with other instances in which Paul addresses issues pertaining to sexual morality, Paul does not clearly indicate the specific problem he is confronting in 1 Thessalonians 4.[2] Paul's ambiguity in this text, I argue, results from his effort to tread carefully when dealing with a very sensitive topic. His use of πορνεία to describe sexual intercourse with household slaves was a surprising challenge to conventional cultural assumptions; thus, Paul needed to persuade, not command, his audience to understand their sexual habits in a new light. The textual evidence is not conclusive, of course, so any effort to interpret this passage remains provisional. But in my view, this interpretation provides the most plausible scenario for understanding Paul's moral exhortation and helps to clarify several exegetical difficulties in this highly contested text.

The Sexual Exploitation of Household Slaves in Greco-Roman Society

The sexual exploitation of household slaves was a regular component of the master-slave relationship in Greco-Roman antiquity. Giving significant attention to the Roman world in his sociological analysis of slavery, Orlando Patterson claims to "know of no slave-holding society in which a master, when so inclined, could not exact sexual services from his female slaves."[3] Similarly, Moses I. Finley observes that the slave's "unrestricted availability in

---

1. Bartchy, "Slavery (Greco-Roman)," 69. Fee, *Letters to the Thessalonians*, 151, has also suggested this possibility but does not develop an argument in support of this view as I will attempt to do here.

2. First Corinthians provides several examples of this point. In 1 Cor 5:1-13, Paul specifies an instance of πορνεία as a man having sexual intercourse with his father's wife. Likewise, in 1 Corinthians 6, Paul discusses sexual intercourse with a prostitute as another instance of πορνεία. In 1 Corinthians 7, Paul clearly and explicitly discusses the sexual behavior of various categories of individuals in the Corinthian community. In light of this, the ambiguity of Paul's discussion in 1 Thessalonians 4 seems unusual.

3. Patterson, *Slavery and Social Death*, 173.

sexual relations" is a "commonplace in Graeco-Roman literature from Homer on."[4] The theme appears not only in literary sources, but also in Roman legal texts which refer frequently "to slaveholders' advances on their male and female domestic servants, to the purchase of slaves for sexual relations, and to the alteration of a male slave's physical appearance (long hair) and body (castration) for sexual purposes."[5] Jennifer A. Glancy sums up the situation in the first-century Greco-Roman world well when she states, "Sexual access to slave bodies was a pervasive dimension of ancient systems of slavery. Both female and male slaves were available for their owners' pleasure."[6]

Most ancient people considered this practice to be morally acceptable behavior. In its sexual ethics, Greco-Roman society was concerned primarily with adultery (μοιχεία) due to its significant legal ramifications for inheritance and civic membership. Kyle Harper observes that "Greek men were fixated on the issue of legitimacy, and they found the solution to their concerns in the strict regulation of the sexuality of honorable women."[7] In this social context, μοιχεία should be understood narrowly, as the violation of an honorable woman by a man who was not her husband, an adulterer (μοιχός). Technically, a woman did not commit adultery; rather, she was a victim, along with her husband, of wrongdoing which violated the integrity of the household. According to Harper, "The respectable woman was expected to maintain her virginity until marriage and her chastity within marriage. Respectable women were ἐλεύθεραι, literally 'free women.' Ἐλεύθεραι were wives, daughters, widows—women whose sexual honor was a concern to a citizen male, her κύριος."[8] Within this framework, a man who had sexual intercourse with a slave, whether a prostitute or household slave, was not committing adultery because the slave had no legal status to protect and no other male's rights were violated in the encounter. While a wife might object on a personal level to her husband's extramarital sexual affairs with prostitutes and household slaves,[9] this was not considered to be "adultery."[10] In fact, prostitution "was accepted, even valorized in Greek and later Roman culture" because it "was considered a social necessity, an alternative to the violation of respectable women, in the Roman Empire no

---

4. Finley, *Ancient Slavery and Modern Ideology*, 95.
5. Joshel, *Slavery in the Roman World*, 40.
6. Glancy, *Slavery in Early Christianity*, 21.
7. Harper, "Porneia," 366–67.
8. Ibid., 367.
9. Glancy, *Slavery in Early Christianity*, 23.
10. Harper, "Porneia," 367.

less than in classical Greece."[11] Sexual intercourse with household slaves was likewise both commonplace and morally acceptable, serving as an approved outlet for avoiding the potential problems of adultery, again because of the slave's lack of social status.[12]

In addition to being a socially acceptable outlet for sexual gratification, the sexual use of household slaves also reinforced the cultural and social ideology of the Roman slave system and gained further legitimacy in the public consciousness as a result. In a society obsessed with male honor, owning slaves provided a means by which even low-status free citizens could display their social superiority. According to Keith Bradley, "the right to enslave and to keep enslaved was taken as axiomatic in Roman society, and in a milieu in which civic freedom was not looked upon as naturally available to all, slave-owning served constantly to validate and enhance the status of those who were free."[13] For this reason, a slave owner needed to observe no boundaries when it came to the bodies of his slaves. Sexual exploitation therefore dramatically illustrated the slave owner's unlimited freedom in contrast to the slave's complete vulnerability. As Bradley states, "the rightlessness and degradation of the slave were made manifest in countless ways, but particularly through sexual exploitation and physical abuse."[14]

Paul's converts undoubtedly shared these views. Most were probably careful to avoid adultery, but visiting prostitutes and sexual intercourse with their household slaves would have been routine and acceptable behavior. Paul's sexual ethics, derived from contemporary Judaism, employed an expanded conception of πορνεία that viewed such behavior as morally unacceptable.[15] Yet, Paul's first-century pagan converts would have found his views surprising and counterintuitive. After all, these common sexual practices were precisely the means by which his converts *did* honor the institution of marriage, in that such behaviors provided culturally approved options for avoiding adultery, a form of sexual misconduct with far more significant implications in the Greco-Roman city. A modern reader of Paul's first letter to the Thessalonians should not be surprised, then, that not only did Paul have to repeat himself on this topic,[16] but also needed to tread lightly when doing so. It is noteworthy that when Paul discusses πορνεία in

---

11. Ibid., 368.
12. Glancy, *Slavery in Early Christianity*, 50–53.
13. Bradley, *Slavery and Society at Rome*, 29.
14. Ibid., 28.
15. Harper, "*Porneia*," 376–79.
16. 1 Thess 4:1–2 suggests that Paul is revisiting a topic that he had previously discussed with them.

his letters—aside from instances in which the term and its cognates appear in vice-lists—he typically does so by means of extended theological reflection on the issue.[17] In other words, Paul does not simply condemn πορνεία, he explains why it is unacceptable for those who are "in Christ." The one exception to this is 1 Cor 5:1–13, in which Paul rebukes the Corinthians for giving approval to the man who "was living with his father's wife" (1 Cor 5:1).[18] While Paul does reflect theologically on the practice of removing the leaven in preparation for the Passover feast in order to make the point that the Corinthian Christians should have expelled the offender from the assembly (1 Cor 5:6–8), he does not feel the need to reflect theologically on the offense itself, precisely because even pagans knew better![19] When Paul challenges popularly sanctioned sexual morality, however, he explains his understanding theologically and seeks to persuade, not command, his audience to act accordingly. Paul follows a similar procedure in 1 Thess 4:1–8. Again, while Paul does not specify the issue at hand, the textual evidence in my view points toward the sexual exploitation of household slaves as the background for Paul's moral exhortation here. In the paragraphs that follow, I examine this evidence and make a case for seeing Paul's words here as a prohibition of improper sexual relations with household slaves within the Thessalonian Christian community.

First Thessalonians 4:1–8: A Corrective to the Sexual Exploitation of Slaves in the Thessalonian Christian Assembly

Paul introduces this section as a reminder to the Thessalonians of ethical instructions given previously about how to conduct themselves in a manner pleasing to God (1 Thess 4:1). Paul acknowledges that they have already made good progress toward this goal but also indicates that further work may be necessary.[20] These introductory verses suggest that Paul is going to be addressing a situation in which old habits die hard. Perhaps many of the members of the Christian assembly had embraced Paul's earlier instructions

---

17. In 1 Cor 6:12–20, for example, Paul reflects theologically on the implications for human sexuality of the resurrection as well as the idea of the body as a temple of the Holy Spirit. In 1 Cor 10:1–13 Paul reflects on the scriptural precedent of the Israelites' sin in the desert as a warning to the Corinthians to avoid idolatry and sexual immorality.

18. Unless otherwise noted, biblical citations are from the NRSV.

19. τοιαύτη πορνεία ἥτις οὐδὲ ἐν τοῖς ἔθνεσιν (1 Cor 5:1).

20. καθὼς καὶ περιπατεῖτε, ἵνα περισσεύητε μᾶλλον (1 Thess 4:1).

about their sexual practices while some had not. Another possibility is that while the entire church had adopted Paul's teaching, some individuals had fallen back into previous patterns of behavior. One can easily imagine that some Thessalonian Christians, though well-intentioned, may have found it difficult to follow through with their earlier commitment to abstain from sexual encounters with their household slaves. Here Paul reminds them of their commitment but also seems to concede that following through on it may not come easily for them. Nevertheless, Paul expects them to attend to these moral exhortations with the utmost seriousness, not as his own personal advice but as instructions from the Lord Jesus.[21]

In verse 3, Paul comes to his main point in this section when he writes, "for this is the will of God, your sanctification (ἁγιασμὸς)." Abraham J. Malherbe notes that the term ἁγιασμὸς "is a noun describing action . . . not a state or condition."[22] This is consistent with Paul's suggestion in verse 1 that moral behavior is always a work-in-progress. More importantly, Paul's use of this term draws his discussion of sexual morality into the realm of cultic purity. Paul understood sexual conduct to be a religious matter, something about which God is concerned. This would have been a new concept for the recently-converted Thessalonian Christians. Greco-Roman people certainly knew a tradition of moral instruction, but in the context of philosophy, not religion.[23] The Hellenistic moral philosophers were concerned with the effect of sexuality upon the individual, exhorting their followers to achieve happiness through personal moderation and self-control. By locating sexual morality in the realm of cultic purity, however, Paul raises the stakes dramatically. The connection between cultic purity and moral behavior was a Jewish and early Christian concept, derived from the divine pronouncement in Lev 19:2, "Be holy, because I the Lord your God, am holy."[24] Paul assumes this basic orientation in 1 Thessalonians by placing moral behavior in the context of religion and eschatology; moral behavior is the way one serves God (δουλεύειν θεῷ) and awaits his son from heaven (ἀναμένειν τὸν υἱὸν αὐτοῦ ἐκ τῶν οὐρανῶν) (1 Thess 1:9-10).[25] Paul's repeated use of the term

---

21. ἐρωτῶμεν ὑμᾶς καὶ παρακαλοῦμεν ἐν κυρίῳ Ἰησοῦ (4:1); οἴδατε γὰρ τίνας παραγγελίας ἐδώκαμεν ὑμῖν διὰ τοῦ κυρίου Ἰησοῦ (4:2).

22. Malherbe, *Letters to the Thessalonians*, 225.

23. Malherbe, "Ethics in Context," 1-10.

24. Fee, *Letters to the Thessalonians*, 144-45. It is noteworthy that the statement in Lev 19:2 introduces a series of laws in which cultic and moral concerns seem to be haphazardly mixed. In other words, the Torah does not really distinguish (in terms of importance or priority) between laws governing the cult and those governing social relations.

25. Malherbe, "Ethics in Context," 6.

ἁγιασμῷ, "sanctification," throughout this passage (vv. 3, 4, and 7), clearly emphasizes this connection between religious purity and moral behavior. For Paul and his converts, sexual behavior is no longer simply a matter of one's own attempt to live rationally and find happiness through self-control; rather, sexuality affects one's relationship with God.

What follows in 1 Thess 4:3-6 is the continuation of a lengthy sentence in which Paul places a series of infinitive clauses in apposition to one another, the result of which is a further explanation of what he means by "the will of God, your sanctification" (1 Thess 4:3a). The first of these clauses is that "you abstain from fornication" (1 Thess 4:3b). The translation of πορνεία as "fornication" is misleading here in that it suggests all forms of extramarital sexual activity.[26] Like μοιχεία ("adultery"), πορνεία has a more limited range of meaning in this context. In the Greco-Roman world, πορνεία was a relatively rare word and referred specifically to the activity of a prostitute, a πόρνη or πόρνος, not to the activity of the one soliciting his or her services.[27] In late Second Temple Judaism, however, πορνεία became an ilicit form of sexual behavior, not only for the provider but also for the male customer.[28] Thus, the term had a somewhat broader meaning in Paul's Jewish context. Nevertheless, Paul did not use the term as a general reference to illicit (from a Jewish perspective) sexual behavior. Paul was not referring to adultery; he had a term for that, μοιχεία. Likewise, Paul probably did not have in mind what we would call "premarital sex." In a society of arranged marriages in which there were significant age differences between men and women at the time of marriage and in which young women remained under the authority of their fathers prior to marriage, neither casual sexual encounters between consenting adults nor "premarital" sex between engaged young lovers would have been common. When Paul referred to πορνεία he meant sexual intercourse with prostitutes and slaves.

The NRSV translates the second infinitive clause as "that each of you know how to control your own body in holiness and honor" (4:4). This verse has been the subject of extensive debate. At issue is the meaning of the phrase τὸ ἑαυτοῦ σκεῦος κτᾶσθαι. The RSV reflects the traditional interpretation when it translates this as, "to take a wife for himself," with σκεῦος having the meaning of "wife." In an extensive treatment of the question,

---

26. See Malina, "Does *Porneia* Mean Fornication?" and Jensen, "Does *Porneia* Mean Fornication?" for a rebuttal of Malina's position. More recently, see the discussion in Harper, "*Porneia*," who understands the Pauline use of πορνεία as an example of the contemporary Jewish response to the sexual practices approved by Greco-Roman society to avoid adultery, namely prostitution and intercourse with slaves.

27. Harper, "*Porneia*," 369.

28. Ibid., 371.

Jay E. Smith argues against this view, citing not only the rarity of this usage for σκεῦος, but also Paul's preference for the term γυνή when referring to "wife," along with the difficulty of interpreting "not with lustful passion" (4:5) in the context of a marriage relationship.[29] Smith instead offers the translation, "that each one of you know how to control your own member in a holy and honorable way" and states that "'member' could be understood simply as 'body' but strongly hints at the meaning 'sexual organ.'"[30] In my estimation, this view is most likely. Thus, Paul is urging the Thessalonian Christians to gain mastery over their sexual desires and the improper use of their bodies. Much like the Corinthians who euphemistically claimed that "food is meant for the stomach and the stomach for food" (1 Cor 6:13), the Thessalonian Christians may also have assumed that the satisfaction of the sexual appetite is simply a natural part of the human experience and as such incurs no moral judgment. Yet, just as Paul says to the Corinthians, "The body is meant not for fornication but for the Lord, and the Lord for the body" (1 Cor 6:14), he makes a similar point to the Thessalonians. He reiterates here the theme of "holiness," reminding the church once again that sexual behavior is indeed a matter of concern to God.

But Paul goes one step further by claiming that Thessalonian sexual behavior is not only a matter of "holiness" but also of "honor," τιμῇ (4:4b). Social scientific analysis over the last three decades has fruitfully drawn attention to the significance of the Mediterranean cultural value of male honor for New Testament interpretation.[31] Honor was perhaps the most valued possession of a first-century Mediterranean male. Protecting one's honor required constant vigilance because every social interaction was a potential honor-contest in which much could be gained or everything lost. Every male sought opportunities to dominate others while at the same time avoiding any sort of loss of his own honor. In this context, the Thessalonians would have found Paul's exhortation highly puzzling. To dominate someone sexually was an expression of male honor. Abusing slaves, in particular, re-

---

29. Smith, "1 Thessalonians 4:4," 78.

30. Ibid., 105. Many recent commentators concur on reading σκεῦος as either "body" or more specifically, "sexual organ," and κτᾶσθαι as "gaining mastery" over it. See for example, Bruce, *1 and 2 Thessalonians*, 83; Fee, *Letters to the Thessalonians*, 146–49; Richard, *First and Second Thessalonians*, 198; Trozzo "Thessalonian Women," 39–52 (Trozzo understands σκεῦος as a reference to the bodies of both men and women; thus Paul was addressing both sexes his in moral exhortation here); and Yarborough, "Sexual Gratification," 217–21.

31. For an early example see Malina, *New Testament World*, 25–50 [3rd ed., 27–57]. Much of Bartchy's own work has addressed this subject. See for example, Bartchy, "Undermining Ancient Patriarchy," 68–78; and Bartchy, "Who Should be Called Father?" 135–147.

inforced in the Roman household the hierarchical values of Roman society. Yet Paul claims here that sexual *restraint* is an expression of male honor. In other words, *not* dominating another sexually or using her (or him) as an object for one's own personal gratification represented honorable self-mastery in the Christian community. It is important to note here that Paul did not discard the contemporary cultural values of cultic purity and male honor; modern readers should not consider Paul to be "counter-cultural" in this regard. Paul maintained the familiar categories but challenged popular assumptions concerning them. Consistent with his inherited Jewish morality, Paul *expanded* the concept of cultic purity for his Gentile Christian communities to include a concern for proper sexual behavior. Perhaps more novel and surprising to his audience, Paul *redefined* male honor as sexual restraint rather than dominance and exploitation.

The next verse serves as an illustrative antithesis to the previous instruction. Paul exhorts the Thessalonians to "control your own body in holiness and honor, not with lustful passion, like the Gentiles who do not know God" (4:5). One interesting point to note here is Paul's attempt to re-socialize the Thessalonian Christians into a fundamentally Jewish framework. These recently converted pagans are no longer "Gentiles," in Paul's estimation, but are now God's people, having turned from idols to serve him (1:9). Though Paul writes this letter perhaps no more than just a few months after his initial contact with the Thessalonian converts, he describes Gentile behaviors as something completely foreign to them. God's people, Paul insists, use their bodies in purity and honor; those who do not know God use their bodies for πάθει ἐπιθυμίας, "lustful passion." But what does this phrase mean? As noted above, understanding σκεῦος to mean "wife" complicates the interpretation of πάθει ἐπιθυμίας.[32] If Paul is condemning "acquiring a wife with lustful passion," this would imply that he held a negative view of sexual intimacy within marriage.[33] Influenced by contemporary Hellenistic moral philosophy, Paul could have regarded sexual pleasure as something to avoid, even in marriage, because this was a failure of "reason" to bridle one's "passions,"[34] but in my view this view seems unlikely. If, on the other

32. Smith, "1 Thessalonians 4:4," 78.

33. Depending on one's interpretation of Paul's discussion of issues of marriage and celibacy in 1 Corinthians 7, it is entirely possible that he had a negative view of sexual intercourse even within marriage. Many interpret Paul's argument in that chapter to be that sexual intercourse within marriage was merely a concession for those who might otherwise succumb to sexual immorality. Virginity, abstinence within marriage, and celibacy were preferable for those who had the "gift" (1 Cor 7:7). For this interpretation of Paul see for example, Roetzel, *Paul*, 135–151; and Brown, *Body and Society*, 44–57.

34. Malherbe, *Letters to the Thessalonians*, 229–31; Fredricksen, "Passionless Sex," 23–30.

hand, "lustful passion" refers to the use of one's own body then Paul's point was not specifically that sexual pleasure in marriage is wrong, but rather more generally that sexual behavior should be characterized by appropriate restraint. If Paul is referring here to sexual intercourse with prostitutes and household slaves, his point would be that in contrast to those who saw this sort of sexual behavior as a morally neutral gratification of normal, physical needs, those who are "in Christ" should practice restraint because they recognize that sexual pleasure should not be one's primary pursuit. In short, Paul raises the stakes of human sexuality by linking sexual behavior to the two greatest concerns of ancient Mediterranean society: ritual purity and male honor. In doing so, Paul makes the common and morally acceptable practice of sex with slaves and prostitutes an act that negatively affects both one's relationship with a holy God and one's identity as an honorable male.

Up to this point, Paul's exhortation about abstaining from πορνεία could be interpreted equally well as addressing both sexual intercourse with public prostitutes and with one's household slaves. Presumably both types of sexual activity had been common practice for the Thessalonian Christians prior to their conversions, and apparently continued to be for at least some of them when Paul writes this letter. Two items in v. 6, however, strongly suggest that Paul specifically has in mind the problem of intercourse with household slaves and that this is the primary matter he is addressing in this passage.

The first part of v. 6 is another in the series of infinitive clauses that further explains and specifies what Paul means at the beginning of the section when he writes, "this is the will of God, your sanctification" (4:3). Paul continues the thought with, "that no one wrong or exploit a brother or sister in this matter" (4:6a). The term ὑπερβαίνειν is a New Testament *hapax legomenon*, but in other contemporary literature conveys the notion of "going beyond," "overstepping," or "transgressing a boundary."[35] The term πλεονεκτεῖν generally has to do with "taking advantage of" or "outwitting" someone.[36] One could interpret πλεονεκτεῖν to mean that Paul is referring to some sort of fraud in a business transaction, particularly in light of the fact that he uses the term in relation to πράγματι. For this reason, some commentators think that Paul shifts in v. 6 to a new topic: holiness as ethical behavior in business dealings.[37] I concur with the majority of recent com-

---

35. BAGD, 840.
36. Ibid., 667.
37. For example, see Richard, *First and Second Thessalonians*, 188–89, 200–202. Richard argues that Paul's use of an articular infinitive to introduce the clause in v. 6 indicates a change of subject and that Paul's use of the related noun forms of πλεονεκτεῖν normally occurs in the context of "cheating" and "greed" in financial matters (1 Thess 2:5; 1 Cor 5:10–11; 6:10; 2 Cor 9:5; and Rom 1:29). Other Pauline uses of the verb form,

mentators, however, who see this verse as a continuation of Paul's discussion of sexual holiness.[38] Among those who take this view, some interpret the phrase, "to wrong or exploit a brother," to be a reference to adultery, in the sense that the offending party "oversteps" the boundaries and "defrauds" his Christian brother by violating his wife.[39] Again, a problem with this view is that Paul had no reason to speak about μοιχεία in such a roundabout way. Pagan as well as Jewish audiences recognized the impropriety of such behavior and would hardly have needed an explanation. In other contexts, for example, Paul speaks frankly about μοιχεία and sees no need to explain his rationale for condemning it.[40] Paul's sibling language here also rules out sexual intercourse with prostitutes, since he seems to be referring to the sexual violation of someone within the Christian fellowship.

If "defrauding a brother or sister" is neither adultery nor consorting with prostitutes, sexual intercourse with household slaves emerges as an attractive interpretive option. Pauline Christian assemblies included slaves and frequently also their owners.[41] Paul's favorite term for referring to members of the Christian community was ἀδελφοί, "brothers and sisters,"[42] and it appears that Paul included slaves in this kinship terminology. In Gal 3:28, for example, Paul identifies slaves as those whose status "in Christ" neutralizes any sort of handicap within the church that they would have normally experienced in the larger society due to their social status. In Phlm 15–16, Paul expresses his hope that Philemon will welcome back his slave, Onesimus, "no longer as a slave but more than a slave, a beloved brother—especially to me but how much more to you, both in the flesh and in the Lord." Though it seems likely in this case that Paul hoped Philemon would manumit

---

however, while perhaps including a financial component, seem to indicate a broader, relational meaning for "take advantage of" (2 Cor 7:2; 2 Cor 12:17–18). See also Malherbe, *Letters to the Thessalonians*, 231–33, for a survey of the interpretive options.

38. For example, see Furnish, *1 Thessalonians*, 91; Fee, *Letters to the Thessalonians*, 150–51; Beale, *1-2 Thessalonians*, 115–23; Malherbe, *Letters to the Thessalonians*, 231–32; Wanamaker, *Epistles to the Thessalonians*, 154–55; Best, *Epistles to the Thessalonians*, 165–66; Bruce, *1 and 2 Thessalonians*, 84–85.

39. Malherbe, *Letters to the Thessalonians*, 232–33; Williams, *1 and 2 Thessalonians*, 75.

40. The terminology for "adultery," "adulterer," and "to commit adultery" is rare in the Pauline letters (Rom 2:22; 13:9; and 1 Cor 6:9), but where it occurs the meaning is unambiguous. Instructive is Paul's use of μοιχοί in 1 Cor 6:9 which he distinguishes from πόρνοι in this list of vices.

41. Bartchy, *ΜΑΛΛΟΝ ΧΡΗΣΑΙ*, 58–62; Glancy, *Slavery*, 46–49.

42. Bartchy, "Undermining Ancient Patriarchy," 68–78; Hellerman, *Ancient Church as Family*, 92–126.

Onesimus,⁴³ we cannot be sure that Paul expected Christian slave owners to free their slaves in every situation. The larger point seems clear, however, that Paul wanted slaves and masters to relate to each other as "brothers and sisters." In the context of Paul's discussion of πορνεία in 1 Thess 4:3-8, "to wrong or exploit a brother or sister" seems to refer to "crossing a boundary" by engaging in sexual behavior that would be inappropriate for Christian brothers and sisters. Previously when the relationship involved an owner and his piece of property, there would have been no basis, as we have seen, for any moral judgment against such behavior. But now that the "possessed body" had become a "sibling," the situation has changed.

So far, Paul has presented the positive side of the argument for avoiding πορνεία by framing the issue in relational terms—it is a violation of a brother or sister—and by relating sexual behavior to fundamentally important cultural values—purity and honor. In the second part of v. 6, Paul warns of a negative deterrent for this behavior: "the Lord is an avenger in all these things." This statement provides another clue that Paul's focus in this passage is the sexual use of slaves. In this word of warning, Paul draws upon a prominent theme in the Hebrew Bible, namely, that God reserves his violent anger for the strong and powerful who harm the weak and vulnerable.⁴⁴ For example, Psalm 94, which in the LXX uses the same phrase that Paul uses here, ἔκδικος κύριος ("the Lord is an avenger"), is a call to Yahweh to punish the arrogant oppressors of his people:

> O LORD, you God of vengeance,
> > you God of vengeance, shine forth!
> Rise up, O judge of the earth;
> > give to the proud what they deserve!
> O LORD, how long shall the wicked,
> > how long shall the wicked exult?
>
> They pour out their arrogant words;
> > all the evildoers boast.
> They crush your people, O LORD,
> > and afflict your heritage.
> They kill the widow and the stranger,
> > They murder the orphan,
> and they say, "The LORD does not see;
> > the God of Jacob does not perceive. (Ps 94:1–7)

---

43. Bartchy, "Philemon, Epistle to," 309.

44. As is so often the case in Paul's writings, his Trinitarian assumptions make it difficult to determine if he is referring here to Yahweh or to the Lord Jesus Christ at the Parousia.

The motif of God's violent anger against injustice appears also in the Hebrew legal tradition in laws governing social relations within Israel. An apodictic law (representing the direct words of God) in the Covenant Code states, "You shall not abuse any widow or orphan. If you do abuse them, when they cry out to me, I will surely heed their cry; my wrath will burn, and I will kill you with the sword, and your wives shall become widows and your children orphans" (Exod 22:22–24). The God of Israel takes up the cause of the weak and vulnerable and promises to exact vengeance on those who oppress and exploit them.

Of all participants in the Pauline Christian assemblies, household slaves most needed to be reassured of the promise of God's special protection of the weak and vulnerable. Without slave owners experiencing a "transform[ation] by the renewal of [their] minds" (Rom 12:1)—which I argue Paul is trying to effect here in this passage—slaves remained vulnerable to their abuse, including their exploitative sexual advances. For this reason, Paul recognized that the Thessalonian Christian slave owners also needed a grave reminder to shock them out of their complacent maintenance of the status quo: God will seek vengeance on those who take advantage of the powerless. As we have seen, Paul employs a multi-dimensional strategy for persuading the Thessalonian Christians to understand previously acceptable sexual behavior in a new light. He first appeals to their positive aspirations by arguing that sexual restraint toward household slaves not only preserves cultic purity but also serves to advance one's honor. Now in verse 6, Paul motivates by fear, warning of divine retribution for the mistreatment of the most vulnerable ones in their midst.

Paul began this piece of moral instruction with a general statement that God's will was for the sanctification of the Thessalonian Christians. After a lengthy sentence which spelled out the nature of this sanctification (vv. 3–6), Paul begins to sum up this passage with a new sentence in which he returns to the general theme of Thessalonian sanctification: "For God did not call us to impurity but in holiness" (v. 7). The aorist form of the verb καλέω refers back to the Thessalonians' conversion when God "called" them through Paul's proclamation of the gospel, and they responded positively by "turning to God from idols, to serve a living and true God" (1:9). The moral exhortation of vv. 3–6 delineates some of the continuing implications of that past event. Yet Paul can also speak of God's call in the present tense when he refers to "God who calls (καλοῦντος) you into his own kingdom and glory" (1 Thess 2:12). It seems that Paul recognized a definitive moment when the Thessalonian Christians had come to be "in Christ" but that their sanctification was a work-in-progress that required their own intentional efforts, supported by his continued reminders and encouragement. In this passage,

Paul addresses the sexual use of household slaves as a vestige of their previous way of life that stood in the way of continued growth in holiness.

Interpreters comment upon the significance of Paul's use of prepositions in this sentence (ἐπὶ ἀκαθαρσίᾳ ... εν ἁγιασμῷ).[45] Fee interprets both prepositions as indicating purpose, which seems most likely in this context; thus, "God's purpose in calling them did not have sexual sin as its goal. Rather ... [God's call] was for the purpose of their living 'in holiness,' meaning that 'holiness' was to be the context that framed all of life both within and outside the community of faith."[46] The strong adversative ἀλλὰ separates the two prepositional phrases and indicates that there are two clear and mutually exclusive options before the Thessalonian Christians: to live according to God's will and purpose in the pursuit of holiness or to continue in impurity, a condition incompatible with God's intention for his people.

Paul concludes the passage with one final sentence in which he impresses upon the Thessalonian Christians God's authority in this matter while also assuring them of God's gracious support of their own faltering steps toward sanctification. In the first part of the sentence, Paul writes, "Therefore, whoever rejects this [Paul's preceding moral exhortation] rejects not human authority but God" (1 Thess 4:8). In other places, Paul distinguishes between clear instructions from the Lord and his own pastorally motivated spiritual guidance. For example, in 1 Cor 7:10, Paul issues a command to Christian married couples against divorce, emphasizing that this injunction comes not from him but from "the Lord." Paul most likely has in mind the strong position taken by Jesus against divorce remembered in the Jesus tradition.[47] A few verses later, however, in 1 Cor 7:12-16, Paul advises that a Christian husband or wife should remain married to his or her unbelieving spouse but acknowledges that he is the source of this instruction, "not the Lord" (7:12). In that case, Paul was making a moral inference for a new situation that had not been encountered by the historical Jesus, based on a clear principle from the Jesus tradition. In 1 Thess 4:8, Paul says that to reject his moral reasoning is to reject the authority of God (θεὸν). When Paul uses the term κύριος, the referent is ambiguous; Paul uses the term interchangeably for the God of Israel and the Lord Jesus Christ. By using the term θεός here, Paul seems to be referring to the clear commands of the God of Israel, articulated in the Jewish scriptures. To what could he be referring? As I observed previously, Paul's language in v. 6 regarding God as an avenger of the weak and powerless is common in the Old Testament.

---

45. See Malherbe, *Letters to the Thessalonians*, 234, for options.
46. Fee, *Letters to the Thessalonians*, 152.
47. Mark 10:2-11//Matt 19:3-9//Luke 16:18; Matt 5:31-32.

Most likely, therefore, Paul's statement in verse 8 reinforces the warning in v. 6 against doing harm to the weak and vulnerable in the community of God's people.

The overarching theme of 1 Thess 4:3–8 is the sanctification of the Thessalonian Christians. Paul has used the term ἁγιασμὸς three times in the short span of six verses (vv. 3, 4, and 7). He is concerned about Thessalonian sanctification generally throughout the letter but here specifically addresses their sexual behavior, drawing a clear contrast between their present impurity and God's desire for their advancement in holiness. Up to this point, Paul has focused his attention on the Thessalonians' behavior, what they should and should not do in order to be honorable and holy. Now in the last part of the sentence, Paul reminds them that they are not alone or powerless in their quest for sanctification. Rather, God has given them his Holy Spirit (8:b). Fee observes that "holy" is not simply part of the identifying title of the third person of the Trinity in this verse, but rather a description of the Spirit given by God to empower and support Thessalonian sanctification.[48] On the one hand, God's gift of the Holy Spirit leaves the Thessalonians without excuse; God has provided the spiritual resources they need to change their ways and live in a manner pleasing to him. But Paul's words also reassure them that in spite of their own frail efforts, God will continue to work in and with them to achieve the results he desires. Sanctification for Paul involves a divine-human partnership.

Conclusion

In this essay, I have argued that the sexual exploitation of household slaves within the Thessalonian Christian community provides the most likely background for Paul's moral exhortation in 1 Thess 4:3–8. Several clues point to this interpretation. Paul's use of the term πορνεία narrows his focus to sexual intercourse with prostitutes and household slaves; adultery and what we would refer to as "premarital sex" would have been covered under the term μοιχεία, an act the Thessalonians already regarded as improper and generally would have avoided without the need for Paul's moral exhortation here. Instead, Paul senses the need in this passage to persuade his audience of a position that would have been strange and counterintuitive for them. He does so by recasting shared cultural values, insisting that the sexual use of household slaves both defiles the sacred space of the Christian fellowship and dishonors those who engage in the act. Paul's reference to exploiting a "brother or sister" and his reminder that "the Lord is an avenger" (v. 6)

---

48. Fee, *Letters to the Thessalonians*, 153–55.

points to God's special concern for the weak and vulnerable with the Christian community: the sexually exploited male and female household slaves.

As modern readers, we would prefer that Paul had more explicitly condemned the sexual use of household slaves if that were indeed the issue he was addressing in 1 Thess 4:3-8. He does not indulge us on this point, however. In fact, Paul seems to be reticent about the institution of slavery in general. Certainly there are indications in his letters of his own personal views, but nowhere do we see a sustained critique of the institution itself. Some have interpreted this supposed silence on slavery as Paul's tacit approval of the status quo within his Christian assemblies. Glancy, for example, argues that Paul's strong language about purity would have effectively excluded slaves from participation in the Pauline house-church movement; thus, for Glancy, when Paul states in 1 Thess 4:4 that the Thessalonian Christian should "control his own vessel" he is *recommending* that the Christian slaveholder make use of his slave, his σκεῦος, sexually, in order to avoid πορνεία, which Glancy confines strictly to visiting prostitutes.[49] In Glancy's view, rather than condemning the sexual use of slaves, Paul actually commends the practice. In a rather extreme expression of a similar viewpoint, Joseph A. Marchal argues that in the letter to Philemon, Paul's play on words in describing Onesimus as "useful" suggests not only that he is encouraging Philemon to use his slave sexually, but also that Paul himself had made use of Onesimus in the same way.[50] For these interpreters, rather than simply turning a blind eye to the practice, Paul was an active participant himself.

Admittedly, Paul is not as explicit in affirming the dignity and value of slaves as our modern age would like him to have been. If he were truly against the abuse of slaves, specifically in this case their sexual abuse, why would he have not spoken more clearly on the subject in 1 Thess 4:3-8? Part of the answer, I think, is that Paul's first audience already knew the specific circumstances surrounding the topic under discussion. In this letter Paul is now simply reminding them of his earlier instructions about matters that continued to be problematic in their fellowship. More importantly, however, I think that Paul writes with some ambiguity (to us), not just here but in all of his discourse concerning slavery, because he was trying to persuade, rather than force, his audience to adopt a radically new worldview and way of life. Paul realized that incremental steps to improve relations between slaveholders and slaves within the Christian fellowship were more realistic for his

---

49. See Glancy, *Slavery in Early Christianity*, 39-70 (particularly p. 70 for the culmination of her argument) for her analysis of slavery in the Pauline churches. See Osiek, "Female Slaves," 255-74, for similarly pessimistic conclusions about the likelihood of slave participation in the Pauline assemblies.

50. Marchal, "The Usefulness of Onesimus," 249-70.

house church assemblies than a full-scale assault on the institution of slavery for which there would have been little hope of success.

This model of realism with respect to slavery, rather than idealism, continued in the Deutero-Pauline letters. Margaret Y. MacDonald argues that even though the household code of Col 3:18—4:1 reflects the perspective of the Roman *paterfamilias*, when read alongside other elements of the letter—for example, exhortations to sexual morality (3:5) and the honor bestowed on slaves (2:14-15 [implicitly] and 3:11)—one sees a more balanced concern for the well-being of slaves.[51] MacDonald states, "the house church community reflected in Colossians did not abolish slavery, but created a vision where slave and free were presented as living harmoniously while living by the same moral standards."[52] Colossians reflects a tone of realism regarding owner-slave relations. The author promotes incremental improvements in the relations between owners and slaves in the Christian assembly rather than a general call for the dismantling of the slave system. According to MacDonald, "the link between sexual immorality and the sexual use of slaves is not treated explicitly because the author of Colossians was *walking on eggshells*."[53] I would argue that Paul faced a similar situation in Thessalonica.

Modern historians should not interpret Paul's apparent ambiguity on slavery as tacit support for the status quo but rather as the response of one facing the significant intellectual, social, and cultural constraints of his historical context. As Patterson observes, "Paul neither defended nor condemned the system of slavery for the simple reason that in the first-century Roman imperial world in which he lived the abolition of slavery was intellectually inconceivable, and socially, politically and economically impossible."[54] Though Paul could not have plausibly challenged the institution of slavery itself, all the evidence suggests that on a personal level he "was a humane caring soul in regard to slaves and their plight" and that he "clearly considered the condition of slavery a great misfortune and personal tragedy."[55] Had Paul been able to foresee the way in which later interpreters would misuse his words to legitimate slavery and oppression, his personal sympathy toward slaves suggests that he would have expressed his opposition to their abuse more explicitly. Paul's words in 1 Thess 4:1-8, though not as clear and definitive as we would like, indicate that Paul was indeed concerned about the

---

51. MacDonald, "Slavery, Sexuality, and House Churches," 94-113.
52. Ibid., 113.
53. Ibid., 105, emphasis added.
54. Patterson, "Paul, Slavery, and Freedom," 266.
55. Ibid., 269.

well-being of slaves in his house-church assemblies. In the Christian community, the sexual use of slaves could no longer be defended as a morally neutral and socially beneficial practice as it was in the society at large. Paul's words certainly fall short of a magisterial pronouncement, but do instead reflect the realistic, incremental steps of one who was slowly trying to guide his churches into the new reality of being "in Christ Jesus."

Works Cited

Bartchy, S. Scott. *ΜΑΛΛΟΝ ΧΡΗΣΑΙ: First-Century Slavery and 1 Corinthians 7:21*. SBLDS 11. Missoula, MT: Society of Biblical Literature, 1973. Reprinted, Eugene, OR: Wipf & Stock, 2003.
———. "Philemon, Epistle to." In *ABD*, 5:305–310.
———. "Slavery (Greco-Roman)." In *ABD*, 6:65–73.
———. "Undermining Ancient Patriarchy: The Apostle Paul's Vision of a Society of Siblings." *BTB* 29 (1999) 68–78.
———. "Who Should Be Called Father? Paul of Tarsus between the Jesus Tradition and *Patria Potestas*." *BTB* 33 (2003) 135–47.
Beale, G. K. *1–2 Thessalonians*. IVP New Testament Commentary. Downers Grove, IL: InterVarsity, 2003.
Best, Ernest. *The First and Second Epistles to the Thessalonians*. Black's New Testament Commentary. Peabody, MA: Hendrickson, 1986.
Bradley, Keith R. *Slaves and Masters in the Roman Empire: A Study in Social Control*. New York: Oxford University Press, 1984.
———. *Slavery and Society at Rome*. Key Themes in Ancient History. New York: Cambridge University Press, 1994.
Brown, Peter L. *The Body and Society*. New York: Columbia University Press, 1988.
Bruce, F. F. *1 and 2 Thessalonians*. WBC 45. Nashville: Nelson, 1982.
Fee, Gordon D. *The First and Second Letters to the Thessalonians*. New International Commentary on the New Testament. Grand Rapids: Eerdmans, 2009.
Finley, M. I. *Ancient Slavery and Modern Ideology*. London: Chatto & Windus, 1980.
Fredrickson, David. "Passionless Sex in 1 Thessalonians 4:4–5." *Word & World* 23 (2003) 23–30.
Furnish, Victor Paul. *1 Thessalonians, 2 Thessalonians*. Abingdon New Testament Commentaries. Nashville: Abingdon, 2007.
Glancy, Jennifer A. *Slavery in Early Christianity*. Minneapolis: Fortress, 2006.
Harper, Kyle. "*Porneia*: The Making of a Christian Sexual Norm." *JBL* 131 (2011) 363–83.
Hellerman, Joseph H. *The Ancient Church as Family*. Minneapolis: Fortress, 2001.
Jensen, Joseph. "Does *Porneia* Mean Fornication? A Critique of Bruce Malina." *NovT* 20 (1978) 161–84.
Joshel, Sandra R. *Slavery in the Roman World*. Cambridge Introduction to Roman Civilization. New York: Cambridge University Press, 2010.
MacDonald, Margaret Y. "Slavery, Sexuality, and House Churches: A Reassessment of Colossians 3.18—4.1 in Light of New Research on the Roman Family." *NTS* 53 (2007) 94–113.

Malherbe, Abraham J. *The Letters to the Thessalonians.* AB 32B. New Haven: Yale University Press, 2000.

———. "Ethics in Context: The Thessalonians and Their Neighbours." *Hervormde Teologiese Studies* 68 (2012) 1–10.

Malina, Bruce J. "Does *Porneia* Mean Fornication?" *NovT* 14 (1972) 10–17.

———. *The New Testament World: Insights from Cultural Anthropology.* Atlanta: John Knox, 1981. [3rd ed., 2001.]

Marchal, Joseph A. "The Usefulness of an Onesimus: The Sexual Use of Slaves and Paul's Letter to Philemon." *JBL* 130 (2011) 749–70.

Osiek, Carolyn. "Female Slaves, Porneia, and the Limits of Obedience." In *Early Christian Families in Context: An Interdisciplinary Dialogue*, edited by David L. Balch and Carolyn Osiek, 255–274. Grand Rapids: Eerdmans, 2003.

Patterson, Orlando. "Paul, Slavery, and Freedom: Personal and Socio-Historical Reflections." *Semeia* 83–84 (1998) 263–79.

———. *Slavery and Social Death: A Comparative Study.* Cambridge: Harvard University Press, 1982.

Richard, Earl J. *First and Second Thessalonians.* Sacra Pagina 11. Reprint with updated bibliography. Collegeville, MN: Glazier/Liturgical, 2007.

Roetzel, Calvin J. *Paul: The Man and the Myth.* Personalities of the New Testament. Minneapolis: Fortress, 1999.

Smith, Jay E. "1 Thessalonians 4:4: Breaking the Impasse." *Bulletin for Biblical Research* 11 (2001) 65–105.

Trozzo, Lindsey M. "Thessalonian Women: The Key to the 4:4 Conundrum." *Perspectives in Religious Studies* 39 (2012) 39–52.

Wanamaker, Charles A. *The Epistles to the Thessalonians.* New International Greek Testament Commentary. Grand Rapids: Eerdmans, 1990.

Williams, David J. *1 and 2 Thessalonians.* New International Biblical Commentary. Peabody, MA: Hendrickson, 1992.

Yarbrough, Robert W. "Sexual Gratification in 1 Thess 4:1–8." *Trinity Journal* 20 (1999) 215–32.

11

Galatians 3:28 and the African Story
J. Ayodeji Adewuya

" . . . the people's reading of the Bible is framed by their history and culture."[1]

WRITING THIS ESSAY, I am reminded of Chimamanda Ngozi Adichie's video on "*The Destructive Power of the Single Story*."[2] In the video, Adichie, of Nigerian descent as I am myself, warns against telling a story from just a single perspective in as much as doing so results in stereotypes that may have no basis in fact. As I watched the video, I cannot but think of my dear friend Scott Bartchy in whose honor I am writing. He has been an exception in telling stories both as a historian and biblical scholar.[3]

My purpose in this essay is to offer a reflection on the African story in light of Gal 3:28. I do so by looking at some aspects of the African story to

---

1. Mosala, *Biblical Hermeneutics*, 3.

2. http://friendsofjustice.wordpress.com/2013/11/07/the-destructive-power-of-the-single-story.

3. I first met Professor Bartchy ("Scott" as I fondly call him) in 1996 when I paid him a visit at UCLA to have a conversation with him on 1 Cor. 7:12–16. He introduced me to the Society of Biblical Literature and we have been dialogue partners ever since, always passionately discussing issues of social justice and racial equality. When we meet every year at the SBL, I have always enjoyed listening to him as he retells (with much disdain) the story of Constantine's "conversion" and adoption of Christianity as the state religion, something which by and large has been considered to be something great for the cause of Christianity for so many years.

see how, on the one hand, the story affects the understanding of the text and, on the other hand, the latter becomes a liberating text as Paul might have intended it to be. This essay contends that although Paul does not advocate the obliteration of social distinctions or identities, such distinctions and identities do not confer any advantage upon any particular group. They are also irrelevant in terms of the relationships among the people of God. All are now equal "in Christ."

In order to advance the thesis just stated, the essay will proceed first, by looking briefly at the social cultural milieu in which Paul wrote. Second the essay will examine the inequalities that Africans have experienced (and continue to experience) as a result of colonization and a missionary enterprise that failed to take seriously Paul's words in Gal 3:28. Finally, the essay will focus on Gal 3:28 and see how an African who reads what Paul says could feel the sense of liberation that he opined.

In various ways Paul's complex socio-religious world in which Scripture was read and appropriated is not much similar to the world today. As Aliou Niang argues, Paul's hermeneutical discourse counters colonial discourses by creating new typologies that better describe members of his communities (Gal 2:11–5; 3:27–29).[4]

My point of departure in this essay is the African story, a story that has always been told as a "single" story. In so doing I take seriously Fernando Segovia's suggestion of the reader taking his or her ethnicity and cultural identity seriously in the process of interpretation, something that he describes as "the hermeneutics of otherness and engagement, whose fundamental purpose is to read the biblical text as an other—not to be overwhelmed or overridden, but acknowledged, respected and engaged in its very otherness."[5] A distortion of the history of Africa as well as the wrong perception about Africans is not new. As Achile Mbembe notes,

> the African human experience constantly appears in the discourse of our times as an experience that can only be understood through a negative interpretation. Africa is never seen as possessing things and attributes properly part of "human nature." Or, when it is, its things and attributes are generally of lesser value, little importance, and poor quality. It is this elementariness and primitiveness that makes Africa the world par excellence of all that is incomplete, mutilated, and unfinished,

---

4. Cf. Niang, *Faith and Freedom*, 13. I have greatly benefitted from Niang's work both in terms of historiography and the hermeneutical method.

5. Segovia, "Toward a Hermeneutics of the Diaspora," 58.

its history reduced to a series of setbacks of nature in its quest for humankind.[6]

Africa: Colonization, Ethnicity, and Gender

The story of Africa will remain incomplete without paying attention to colonization, something that profoundly affected, and continues to affect, the image of Africa. The imposition of colonialism on Africa altered its history forever. African modes of thought, patterns of cultural development, and ways of life were forever impacted by the change in political structure brought about by colonialism. Colonization of Africa by European countries was a monumental milestone in the development of Africa. Colonialism did not only influence the economic and political development of Africa but also the African people's perception of themselves. Europe justified its colonization of Africa on grounds that it was its moral duty to "uplift" Africans from their primitive state. Ample evidence suggests that all European powers did not think much of Africans or African culture and history. Writings by Europeans who visited Africa before the actual colonization show views of individuals determined to look at Africa through their cultural prisms and conclude that Africans were backward and uncivilized. Preoccupation with skin color and other physical traits as measures of "civilization" was strong and consistent. Europeans, therefore, felt that colonization was right and that they had a mission "to civilize" Africans.

In most of the British colonies, the indigenous people and the British were segregated. Social institutions were maintained for different racial groups. In Kenya, where significant Asian, Arabic (Islamic), and European communities settled, there were separate facilities for each of those groups, the best facilities, of course, being reserved for Europeans. The separate schools were often racially designated, as were hospitals and bathrooms in public buildings. Residences were segregated, with Africans in the cities confined in "African locations" with conspicuously crowded and inferior housing. It can be conceded that in a very general sort of way, the British tried to convert Africans into British ladies and gentlemen.

Similarly, the French looked down on the Africans and on African culture. They had a social policy to buttress their colonial rule in Africa, known as "the assimilation policy." This policy was based on the very laudable revolutionary ideal of human equality, but only under French suzerainty.

---

6. Mbembe, *On the Postcolony*, 1.

> Thus the French, when confronted with people they considered barbarians, believed it their mission to convert them into Frenchmen. This implied a fundamental acceptance of their potential human equality, but a total dismissal of African culture as of any value. Africans were considered to be a people without any history, without any civilization worthy of the name, constantly at war with one another and fortunate to have been put in touch with the fruits of French civilization.[7]

The relationship between the colonial governments and the missions in Africa was truly a symbiotic one—missionaries and the colonial authorities forged a very close working relationship. Although schools were run and staffed by missionaries they were subsidized in varying degrees by colonial governments whose interest in missionary education was simply to ensure that enough Africans were educated to meet the limited need for semiskilled workers in colonial bureaucracies. The missionaries had total control over the religious curriculum. Mission schools taught that the European presence in Africa was to benefit the African people and to uplift them from a state of barbarism. African customs were discouraged. African languages were banned in mission schools. African heritage was ridiculed and suppressed. The goal was to give Africans a new identity by requiring them to use new, Christian names, failure of which resulted in ridicule and insults. Humiliation and suffering, such as were being endured by Africans during colonialism, were thought to be ennobling and spiritually cleansing. In a similar manner that the Gentile Christians of Paul's time were regarded as "second class" believers, Africans were in many cases treated by their colonizers and missionaries as subhuman. D. J. East, a missionary to West Africa, states that "Africa is a moral wilderness, and her inhabitants, as they have been too correctly described, are wolves to each other."[8]

The foregoing description of Africans mirrors the treatment of the "others" in Paul's Greco-Roman milieu. Gentiles, women and slaves were simply "others." With regards to slaves, A.-J. Festugiere observes,

> Many an inscription lists slaves in the plural as *somata*, after the cattle *ktemata*. Such neuter plurals express a category of objects, a property that one possesses. In Rome the slave is a *res:* something bought and sold . . . For the peasant Cato, a slave out of service is worth less than an old cow: one can at least eat the cow. Seneca's beautiful preaching never brought about such changes. Having carefully penned his Letter XLVII to Lucilius, Seneca

---

7. Crowder, *Senegal*, 2.
8. East, *Western Africa*, 5–6.

would never have dined with his own slaves. There would have been at least two separate tables set up.⁹

Georg W. F. Hegel derogatorily describes sub-Saharan Africans to his European audience as a calcified sample waiting to be unearthed by Europe. In his view "Africa proper, as far as History goes back, has remained for all purposes of connection with the rest of the world shut up; it is the Gold-land of childhood, which lying beyond the day of self-conscious history, is enveloped in the dark mantle of Night."¹⁰ He describes the Senegalese as "hordes" and thinks their behavior reflected "the most reckless inhumanity and disgusting barbarism . . ."¹¹ Charles de Secondat Baron de Montesquieu similarly reduces Africans living on the Atlantic shore to the status of "savages and barbarians."¹² That negative depictions of Africans are based on travelers', explorers', and missionaries' accounts is also well documented.¹³ In his reconstruction of European self-understanding and depictions of Africans, T. Carlos Jacques sees an epistemological process in which classical typologies that reduced Africans to savage barbarians are re-framed into a yet more dehumanizing label: Primitive. He posits that the concept "primitive" is a category of thought that is born of an epistemological shift at the end of the eighteenth century. This shift was not the result of any superior knowledge that Europe suddenly acquired of "Others." It was rather the product of a new way in which Europe understood itself, a self-understanding that was manifested in many different ways.¹⁴ Philip Curtin is certainly correct that "today as in the eighteenth century, many people are subject to a variety of xenophobic feelings about people who are racially different from themselves."¹⁵

9. Festugiere, *L'Enfant d'Agrigente*, 104–5.

10. Hegel, *Philosophy of History*, 92.

11. Ibid., 93, 91–93. Interestingly, Hegel cites missionary accounts to bolster his descriptions of Africans.

12. Montesquieu, *Spirit of Laws*, 212.

13. Curtin, *Image of Africa*, v–ix, 11–27, notes how these reports led to the construction of "separate species of man." Perhaps one of the worst caricatures of Africa and its people is to be found in Conrad's *Heart of Darkness*, 251–61. Mbiti, *African Religions and Philosophy*, 8–12. Mbiti rightly complains about distorted accounts of African cultures and religions.

14. Baum, *Shrines*, 9, agreeably states that Europeans "saw themselves as bringing Africa into history and into the light of religious faith. To reinforce this sense of otherness, Africa was labeled as pagan, animist, fetishist, polytheist, primitive, or oral . . . All these labels proclaim the absolute difference between European and African: the former possessed a dynamic culture and a long history, while the latter was frozen in primordial time."

15. Curtin, *Image of Africa*, 30.

Underlying Paul's assertion in Gal 3:28 is the issue of identity. Who constitutes the new people of God? Here we shall briefly examine the problem of ethnicity within the African context and how Gal 3:28 could function as a liberating text for various African communities, with particular reference to intermarriage among Christians of different ethnicities. Ethnicity has been variously defined. In its basic sense, an ethnic group is a group of people whose members identify with each other through a common heritage, often consisting of a common language, culture, religion, ideology or geographical area. Ethnicity is an identity.[16] As a result, it inevitably occupies a great space within the political arena and also it is the easiest and most natural way for people to mobilize around basic human needs such as security, food, shelter, economic well being, inequality, land distribution, autonomy, and recognition.[17] It is common knowledge that people are organized in their traditional milieu by their ethnicity. Thus, in Africa and indeed, in other parts of the world, ethnic groupings give identity to people within the context of nationalism.

As Bruce J. Berman notes, "In the precolonial world the most striking features of African identities and communities was their fluidity, heterogeneity and hybridity; a social world of multiple, overlapping and alternate identities with significant movement of peoples, intermingling of communities and cultural and linguistic borrowing. The boundaries of communities were frequently ambiguous and identities contextually variable."[18] In other words, one could argue for ethnicity in the African context as a dynamic discourse that negotiated between the poles of fixity and fluidity, something that appears similar to Paul's vision in Gal 3:28, where Paul's communal vision of the church seems to be defined, not strictly in terms of ethnicity, but rather against it. Berman notes that "The Africa encountered by European colonizers in the 19th century was multi-ethnic with different forms of self-governing. Unfortunately the dynamism of the African discourse of ethnicity was destroyed by colonization. The colonizers created ethnic tension between the many diverse groups throughout Africa. The colonizers defined, classified, numbered and mapped African ethnic groups to create

---

16. The term ethnicity refers to a group of people with a common socio/cultural identity such as language, common worldview, religion and common cultural traits. It is used interchangeably with the term Tribe. Unfortunately, the early European writers used the term "tribe" to refer to a group of uncivilized people, as if it had a different meaning from the term "ethnic group." A European writer will refer to ethnic Albanians because they are Europeans and refer to the Igbo or Yoruba as "tribe," a word that has derogatory connotations.

17. Kelman, "*Social-Psychological Dimensions of International Conflict*," 64–65.

18. Berman, "*Ethnicity and Democracy in Africa*," 6–10.

administrative units to facilitate better political and institutional control. Colonization also created inequalities between ethnic communities based on the manner and degree of involvement in the colonial political economy. The impact of these policies was a new cleavage of class, exacerbating existing internal differences of gender, generation, and clienthood. Power was given to some at the expense of others creating frustration and competition only serving the colonial power.

Nigeria is a case in point. In 1947 the country was divided into three political regions including the three main ethnic groups: the North with the Hausa-Fulani, the West with the Yoruba, and finally the East with the Igbos. As the nation marched towards independence, the issue was reduced to the quest for ethnic dominance with minority groups rebelling and fighting for ethnic dominance. At this time, ethnic and sub-ethnic loyalties threatened the survival of both East and West, while the North was religiously divided between Christianity and Islam. It was a period of politicized ethnicity and competition for resources which worsened the relationships between ethnic groups.

As mentioned earlier, there is not an aspect of African life and history that has not been impacted by colonization and Western missionary outreaches. However, the extent of the impact of colonization and missionary activity on gender relations in Africa remains a subject of debate among African scholars. How do Africans view women? There are three predominant views. The first, of which the female scholar Zulu Sofola is representative, argues that African culture was favorable to women in contrast to the European culture which was seen as not only foreign but also destructive to the African female psychic, suggesting that "unfortunately their alien culture descended upon us with their male-defined, male-centred and entirely male cosmology and dislodged the female component of African social order."[19] In contrast to this position is that which views the African culture as oppressive to women. In support of this view Mercy Amba Oduyoye states that "matriliny may give the impression of the structural dominance of women in certain parts of Africa, but (even where the marriage is not virilocal) no real power resides in the hands of the woman. As to political power, even the matrilineal, matrilocal Asante are not matriarchal."[20] J. A. Omoyajowo takes a mediating position. On the one hand he admits the oppressive nature of some aspects of African culture with regards to women and, on the other hand, suggests that other aspects ascribe status to women and

---

19. As cited by Bateye, "Forging Identities," 3.
20. Oduyoye, *Hearing and Knowing*, 123

enhance a collective self-esteem of women.²¹ Thus, he maintains that there is something positive in African culture with respect to women.

Regardless of the oppressive traditional values, attitudes, and structures imposed on women in the Yoruba traditional society, there are accounts of Yoruba women's exploits that can raise their collective self-esteem. Omoyajowo goes as far as to attest that "The traditional Yoruba society with all its prejudices against women, religion, more than any factor plays a major role in ascribing status to women."²² The issue of gender, particularly the place of women in society, is a controversial one among the Yoruba. The culture of the early mission-oriented churches was European. Understandably, European culture to the early African converts was synonymous with the practices of the church and hence had a "divine mandate" as it was supposedly Bible-based. This situation had definite implications for women particularly as it relates to the African practice of polygamy. Because European culture does not permit polygamy, the oppression of women as directly attributable to polygamy was not present. In this way the church was considered to be liberating in some aspects to women. However, the European culture of that time was that of the Victorian era that upheld the attitude and accepted the idea that man was a superior being meant by God and nature to dominate the world, while women were meant to obey and serve. Olubunmi Smith observes that "the promulgation of Western patrilineal and patriarchal ideologies by missionaries, as well as the introduction of colonial education, concretized the subordination of women by imposing replicated western patterns of sexisms."²³ Thus there was a kind of ambivalence on the part of African women converts towards European culture. They had the attitude that European culture in some instances was more liberating than oppressive for the African woman and that the demands of the European missionary church culture on them were much less rigorous than that of African culture. Nevertheless, European missionaries still perpetuated female servitude to the male.²⁴

The Message of Galatians 3:28

The interpretation of Gal 3:28 has suffered some misconceptions that need to be addressed if one is to make sense of what Paul is trying to articulate. First, it has been wrongly assumed by many interpreters that the verse has

21. Omoyajowo, "The Role of Women in African Traditional Religions," 3.
22. Ibid.
23. Smith, "Feminism in Cross-Cultural Perspective," 13.
24. Bateye, "Forging Identities," 2.

no present social implications. The meaning is only spiritual. In other words the passage is simply to be viewed as a "pie in the sky," eschatological ideal, that is, a laudable and ideal goal that will find its fulfillment at Christ's return. Without doubt and as commonly agreed, Paul's theology is often driven by eschatology. As Brad R. Braxton notes, "Undoubtedly eschatological hope—the assurance that Christ will return and assist in the establishment of God's sovereignty—plays an integral role in Paul's overall theology."[25] However, an interpretation that limits the passage to a future realization is, at the very least, questionable on both rhetorical and grammatical grounds. Cognizant of the linguistic significance of Gal 3:28, Wayne A. Meeks proffers that Gal 3:28 has the "power to assist in shaping the symbolic universe by which" the Galatian Christians would be distinguished "from the ordinary 'world' of the larger society." He suggests that it might be called a "performative language."[26] In other words, the Galatians Christians had the opportunity of shaping the worldview of the larger society if their "lives together" in the community were based on being "in Christ" rather than on social ethnic distinctions that shaped the behaviors of the world around them. Hans Dieter Betz suggests that the expression "'neither male nor female' is probably a variation of the well-known Hellenistic political slogan 'Greeks and barbarians.'"[27] He asserts that the slogan powerfully "promises or proclaims the unity of mankind through the abolition of the cultural barriers separating Greeks and non-Greeks," and the Jews adopted it, "correctly assuming that they themselves belong to the barbarians."[28] In doing so, and by turning the order of the phrase around, Betz suggests, the Jews "claimed that they were realizing the old political ideal."[29] He further asserts that,

> There can be no doubt that Paul's statements have social and political implications of even a revolutionary dimension . . . These ideals include the abolition of the religious and social distinctions between Jews and Greeks, slaves and freemen, men and women. These social changes are claimed as part of redemption and as the result of the ecstatic experiences which the Galatians as well as other Christians have had. Being rescued from the

---

25. Braxton, *No Longer Slaves*, 93.

26. Meeks, "Image of the Androgyne," 182.

27. Betz, *Galatians*, 191. Rare in biblical interpretation is the general consensus reached by key Pauline scholars who regard Gal 3:26–29 as a baptismal formula. See Burton, *A Critical and Exegetical Commentary on the Epistle to the Galatians*, 203–10.

28. Betz, *Galatians*, 192.

29. Ibid.

present evil aeon (Gal 1:4) and being changed to a "new creation" implies these radical social and political changes.[30]

It is certainly true that for Paul, the family of faith takes priority over human kinship. One must ask what the exigency was that Paul was addressing. How urgent was the rhetorical situation that Paul was addressing?

An essential component of a letter's rhetorical situation is its controlling exigency—"an imperfection marked by urgency; it is a defect, an obstacle, something wanting to be done, a thing which is other than it should be."[31] The exigency functions as the organizing principle: "It specifies the audience to be addressed and the change to be effected."[32] So, what then is the rhetorical situation in Galatians? It is evident that the crisis that engulfed the Galatian churches was more urgent than Christ's return. Paul's pressing concern in Galatians 3 was about the possibility of defection of his converts and, as such, was about *present* harmony among his converts. As Braxton succinctly puts it, "From his (Paul) perspective, without a present remedy to this crisis there very well could be no future for his converts."[33] Grammatically, the prevalence of the present tense in verse 28 suggests a present reality. In Jewish society the Jew, the freedman, and the male were all superior, while the Gentile, the slave, and the female were all inferior.

Second, Gal 3:28 is sometimes understood to imply an obliteration of social distinctions. As such, the unity in the Church is understood to be achieved through the abolition of social distinctions—replaced with an amalgamated, undifferentiated Christian identity. However, one must say that if indeed the thrust of Gal 3:28 is the obliteration of social distinctions, then the basis of Paul's own missionary activity and evangelistic mission is undermined.[34] Paul's proclamation of the gospel to the Gentiles was aimed at bringing them into the church with their distinct identity as Gentiles who are not to be saddled with obedience to the law as a means of their inclusion in the people of God. The issue in Gal 3:28 is that of dominance or power which was being exerted by one over the other because of those differences. Anthony C. Thiselton rightly notes, "To *remain* Jewish or non-Jewish does not spring from general indifference, but from its *salvific* irrelevance. As in

---

30. Betz, *Galatians*, 190. Against Betz, in Gal 3:28 Paul is emphasizing equality between male and female before God. This applies to other identities as well. See Esler, *Conflict and Identity in Romans*, 10–13. See also Scroggs, "Paul and the Eschatological Woman," 283–303.

31. Bitzer, "Rhetorical Situation," 252.

32. Ibid.

33. Braxton, *No Longer Slaves*, 93.

34. Ibid.

the case of gender, such distinctions are not abrogated wholesale . . . The new creation *transforms* and *relativizes* such distinctions, but they have a place."[35] As William S. Campbell also asserts, "So whilst, eschatologically, there is no longer Jew or Greek, this does not mean that these are not abiding realities in ethical matters in everyday life of the churches."[36] Unity in Christ does not lend itself to an undifferentiated identity. It comes as a result of each person's and each Christian community's relationship with Christ— relationships that not only ensure that we treat each other with respect, but also ensure that we relate with one another with equality and mutuality despite our "otherness" and many differences. Raphael Lowe's remarks are poignant: "The sociological basis on which Christianity rests is not ties of kinship, as in the case of Judaism, but that of fellowship—fellowship in Christ . . . Such fellowship may acknowledge kinship as a potential ally, it may regard it indifferently, as consisting of an unequivocal force; or repudiate it, as being a distracting encumbrance. Whichever position it holds, the ties of kinship are, for Christianity, in the last resort expendable."[37]

Conclusions and Implications

In concluding this essay, the following conclusions could be made. First, the present-day society, particularly in the Western world, continues to struggle with a system where circumstances of birth, education, ethnicity, social status, and education continue to define how people are treated. Even in matters of justice, one could hardly speak of equality. Christians cannot retreat into their citadel of spiritual unity and ignore their responsibilities as members of the society. The inferential truth in this passage is that, as people of equal value in the eyes of God, none, whether believers in Christ or not, should be discriminated against by those who profess to be followers of Christ.

Second, as David L. Balch avers, "the early baptismal confession— 'there is no longer Jew or Greek' (Gal 3:28a)—is an assertion from below: '[we] Jews [Asians, non-Europeans] are not inferior!'"[38] Paul was a counter-colonist whose message decolonizes by freeing the colonized to be conscious of their divine status as children of the promise (Gal 4:23, 28, 31), regardless of their cultural contexts, ethnicity, gender, and social status (Gal 3:28).[39]

---

35. Thiselton, *The First Epistle to the Corinthians*, 550–51.
36. Campbell, *Paul and the Christian Identity*, 92.
37. Lowe, *Position of Women in Judaism*, 52–53.
38. Balch, "ΜΕΤΑΒΟΛΗ ΠΟΛΙΤΕΙΩΝ," 153.
39. Niang, *Faith and Freedom*, 138.

Thus the African can shout, "Hallelujah!" Christ has freed the African/African-American to say yes to "blackness or African-ness," and the woman to say yes to her "female-ness." Galatians 3:28 does not promote a "race-less" or "gender-less" society but one in which each person could embrace and celebrate not only oneself but also the "other."

Third, the Christian community must continue to maintain and manifest the unity of all believers in Christ and affirm radical equality despite differences of status, sexuality or ethnic origin. Within the community, equality must pave the way for each member assuming responsibility according to his/her gifts. Stereotypical and traditional roles must lose their force and the ideas and leadership that develop community life must become everyone's responsibility. Racial distinctions are irrelevant in the church and racial discrimination in the church is sinful. Paul's message in Gal 3:28 must be brought to bear on the day-to-day life of the people of God. Paul's hermeneutic powerfully shapes and frees enslaved people with a view to creating new postcolonial communities in Christ. As the language of Gal 3:28 shows, the principle forms of social domination that prevailed in Roman imperial society were supposedly transcended in the new alternative society. Presumably this formula expressed at least the ideal social relations in the new movement, the ἐκκλησία, for Paul in his own mission. Paul was adamant that there be "no longer Jew or Greek" in the assemblies he helped organize among the peoples of Asia Minor and Greece. That is, in contrast to the ideology of the Roman imperial order, for Paul history had run toward its fulfillment not through Rome but through Israel.[40]

Fourth, we must be careful that in striving to articulate an account of identity and social dynamics in opposition to that which characterized the Greco-Roman milieu of Paul we do not obliterate the difference. As Nancy Fraser writes of those involved in identity politics:

> Stressing the need to elaborate and display an authentic, self-affirming and self-generated collective identity, it [identity politics] puts moral pressure on individual members to conform to a given group culture. Cultural dissidence and experimentation are accordingly discouraged, when they are not simply equated with disloyalty. So, too, is cultural criticism including efforts to explore intragroup divisions, such as those of gender, sexuality and class. Thus, far from welcoming scrutiny of, for example, the patriarchal strands within subordinated culture, the tendency of the identity model is to brand such critique as "inauthentic." The overall effect is to impose a single, drastically simplified

---

40. Horsley, "Paul and Slavery," 177.

group-identity which denies the complexity of people's lives, the multiplicity of their identifications and the cross-pulls of their various affiliations.[41]

Finally, I would like to conclude the essay with the story about the hymn, "In Christ There Is No East or West," written in 1908 by the noted English writer, John Oxenham. The song was part of a script for a pageant at a giant missionary event sponsored by the London Missionary Society's exhibition, "The Orient in London." An interesting account of the impact of this hymn relates an incident during the closing days of World War II when two ships were anchored together, one containing Japanese aliens, and the other American soldiers, all waiting to be repatriated. For an entire day they lined the rails, glaring at one another. Suddenly someone began to sing "In Christ There Is No East Or West." Then another on the opposite ship joined in. Soon there was an extraordinary chorus of former enemies united praising God with these words:

> In Christ there is no East or West,
> in him no South or North,
> but one great fellowship of love
> thoughout the whole wide earth.
>
> In him shall true hearts everywhere
> their high communion find,
> his service is the golden cord
> close-binding all mankind.
>
> Join hands, disciples of the faith,
> whate'er your race may be!
> Who serves my Father as a son
> is surely kin to me.
>
> In Christ now meet both East and West,
> in him meet South and North,
> all Christly souls are one in him,
> throughout the whole wide earth.[42]

---

41. Fraser, "Rethinking Recognition," 112.
42. Osbeck, *Amazing Grace*, 34.

Works Cited

Bach, David L. "ΜΕΤΑΒΟΛΗ ΠΟΛΙΤΕΙΩΝ: Jesus as Founder of the Church in Luke-Acts: Form and Function." In *Contextualing Acts: Luke's Narrative and Graeco-Roman Discourse*, edited by Todd Penner and Caroline Vander Stichele, 139–88. Society of Biblical Literature Symposium Series 20. Atlanta: Society of Biblical Literature, 2003.

Bateye, Bolaji Olukemi. "Forging Identities: Women as Participants and Leaders in the Church among the Yoruba." *Studies in World Christianity* 13 (2007) 1–12.

Baum, Robert Martin. *Shrines of the Slave Trade: Diola Religion and Society in Precolonial Senegambia*. New York: Oxford University Press, 1999.

Berman, Bruce J. *"Ethnicity and Democracy in Africa."* JICA Research Institute, No. 22 (November 2010) 6–10.

Betz, Hans Dieter. *Galatians*. Hermeneia. Philadelphia: Fortress, 1979.

Bitzer, Lloyd F. "The Rhetorical Situation." In *Rhetoric: A Tradition in Transition*, edited by Walter R. Fisher, 1–14. East Lansing: Michigan State University, 1974.

Braxton, Brad R. *No Longer Slaves: Galatians and African American Experience*. Collegeville, MN: Glazier/Liturgical, 2002.

Burton, Ernest de Witt. *A Critical and Exegetical Commentary on the Epistle to the Galatians*. International Critical Commentary. Edinburgh: T. & T. Clark, 1980.

Campbell, William S. *Paul and the Christian Identity*. London: T. &T. Clark, 2008.

Champion, Craige. "Romans as BAPBAPOI: Three Polybian Speeches and the Politics of Cultural Indeterminacy." *Classical Philology* 95 (2000) 425–44.

Conrad, Joseph. *Heart of Darkness: An Authoritative Text, Background and Sources Criticism*. 3rd ed. Edited by Robert Kimbrough. London: Norton, 1988.

Crowder, Michael. *Senegal: A Study in French Assimilation Policy*. New York: Oxford University Press, 1962.

Curtin, Philip. *The Image of Africa: British Ideas and Actions 1780–1850*. Madison: University of Wisconsin Press, 1964.

East, D. J. *Western Africa: Its Condition, and Christianity the Means of Its Recovery*. London: Houlston & Stoneman, 1844.

Esler, Philip F. *Conflict and Identity in Romans: The Social Setting of Paul's Letter*. Minneapolis: Fortress, 2003.

Festugiere, A.-J. *L'Enfant d'Agrigente*. Chrétienté 6. Paris: Cerf, 1941.

Fraser, Nancy. "Rethinking Recognition." *New Left Review* 3 (2000) 107–20.

Hegel, Georg W. F. *Philosophy of History*. Translated by J. Sibree. New York: Prometheus, 1991.

Horsley, Richard A. "Paul and Slavery: A Critical Alternative to Recent Readings." *Semeia* 83/84 (1998) 19–65.

Jacques, T. Carlos. "From Savages and Barbarians to Primitives: Africa, Social Typologies and History in Eighteenth Century Philosophy." *History and Theology* 36 (1997) 190–215.

Kelman, Herbert. "Social-Psychological Dimensions of International Conflict." In *Peacemaking in International Conflict: Methods and Techniques*, edited by I. William Zartman, 61–110. Washington, D.C.: United States Institute of Peace Press, 2007.

Lowe, Raphael. *The Position of Women in Judaism*. London: SPCK, 1966.

Mbembe, Achille. *On the Postcolony*. Berkeley: University of California Press, 2001.

Meeks, Wayne A. "The Image of the Androgyne: Some Uses of a Symbol in Early Christianity." *History of Religions* 13 (1974) 165–208.

Montesquieu, Charles de Secondat Baron. *The Spirit of Laws*. Translated by Hon. Frederic R. Couldert. New York: Colonial, 1899.

Mosala, Jerry Itumeleng. *Biblical Hermeneutics and Black Theology in South Africa*. Grand Rapids: Eerdmans, 1989.

Niang, A. C. *Faith and Freedom in Galatia and Senegal: The Apostle Paul, Colonists and Sending Gods*. BibIntSer 97. Leiden: Brill, 2009.

Oduyoye, Mercy Amba. *Hearing and Knowing: Theological Reflections on Christianity in Africa*. Maryknoll, NY: Orbis, 1986.

Olajubu, Oyeronke. "Seeing through a Woman's Eyes: Yoruba Religious Tradition and Gender Relations." *Journal of Femininist Studies in Religion* 20 (2004) 41–60.

Omoyajowo, J. A. "The Role of Women in African Traditional Religions and among the Yoruba." In *African Traditional Religion in Contemporary Society*, edited by J. K. O. Olupona, 73–80. New York: Paragon, 1991.

Osbeck, Kenneth W. *Amazing Grace: 366 Inspiring Hymn Stories for Daily Devotions*. Grand Rapids: Kregel, 1996.

Scroggs, Robin. "Paul and the Eschatological Woman." *Journal of the American Academy of Religion* 40 (1972) 283–303.

Segovia, Fernando F. "Toward a Hermeneutics of the Diaspora: A Hermeneutics of Otherness and Engagement." In *Reading from This Place*. I. *Social Location and Biblical Interpretation in the United States*, edited by Fernando F. Segovia and Mary Ann Tolbert, 55–68. Minneapolis: Fortress, 1995.

Smith, P. O. "Feminism in Cross-Cultural Perspective: Women in Africa." *Transformation: An International Dialogue of Evangelical Social Ethics* 6 (1989) 11–17.

Snowden, Frank M. *Before Color Prejudice: The Ancient View of Blacks*. Cambridge: Harvard University Press, 1983.

Thiselton, A. C. *The First Epistle to the Corinthians*. New International Greek Testament Commentary. Grand Rapids: Eerdmans, 2000.

12

Preaching Δοῦλος
Hard Saying or Stumbling Block?

Bruce E. Shields

Scott Bartchy and I have been friends since college days. Our mutual interests in biblical studies, preaching, and music have helped us weather many storms. My copy of his published dissertation is a gift from him inscribed "with gratitude..." That dissertation was prepared for publication while he and I worked together in Tübingen, Germany. His encouragement of me in my own dissertation research is beyond measure.

My work on this chapter brought back to me a Bartchy memory of a session at an SBL meeting when his presentation on slavery in the first century Roman Empire was treated harshly by a respondent who was an African-American woman. She attacked his description of that slavery as being too mild. She was clearly unable to hear his objective description of the state of some (not all) slaves in that era, since she was filtering the term *slave* through her own cultural memory of American slavery. Scott had the good sense not to argue with her. I was proud of him for that.

Of course, that womanist scholar was not alone in her critique of New Testament scholars who, in her opinion, painted too rosy a picture of slavery in the first-century Roman Empire. The double volume of *Semeia* 83–84 in 1998 was dedicated to correcting this earlier reading. The essays by Richard

A. Horsley[1] and Orlando Patterson[2] are especially important to the ongoing debate.

And in the twenty-first century we are still faced with the quandary of how to preach New Testament texts that clearly call followers of Jesus δοῦλοι Χριστοῦ. A *Christian Century* news article dated March 1, 2011, by Adelle Banks, indicates resistance among scholars and preachers in the African-American community to this Greek phrase's translation as "slaves of Christ." A few admit that the harshness of the slavery terminology is an important part of its original intent, but many still cannot bring themselves to use the term in a positive way.

My hope is that this chapter will help somewhat with this issue by encouraging scholars and preachers alike to see the importance of radical obedience for the Christian life. I know of no human culture that does not resist what Jesus meant by taking up one's cross[3] and following him. Therefore, we shall look closely at some representative texts in Galatians and Romans that use slavery as a metaphor for following and serving Jesus; and then we'll consider whether or how such texts should be preached.

To begin, we recognize that the word δοῦλος and its cognates would have elicited a very negative reaction in both Greek and Roman people of the first century. There are also a number of other related terms that would have elicited similar reactions.[4] Slavery was common, but non-slaves did not see being a slave as desirable in any way. At the same time, as Bartchy discovered, there were slaves who were trusted and respected members of Roman and Greek households. Therefore, as Dale A. Martin has shown,[5] to adopt slave terminology to describe one's relationship with a deity was not unheard of in the ancient world; however, it would still have likely shocked most educated Roman and Greek citizens.

On the other hand, the people of Israel are often referred to as slaves of the Lord in the Hebrew Bible. The Septuagint translators often used the Greek term δοῦλος in such texts to translate the Hebrew עבד.[6] Thus Paul

---

1. Horsley, Callahan, and Smith, "Introduction," 1–15; Horsley, "Slave Systems," 19–66; Horsley, "Paul and Slavery," 153–200.

2. Patterson, "Paul, Slavery and Freedom," 263–79.

3. Cross-bearing appears not to have the heavy connotation that slavery carries, since direct knowledge of crucifixion is not registered in our collective memory banks, as slavery is.

4. The words οἰκονόμος and παῖς are just two of these.

5. Martin, *Slavery as Salvation*, 60–68. Even though Martin brings together some interesting information and exegesis, I am convinced that he overreaches his evidence when he deals with slavery as a primary soteriological term for Paul.

6. Whether or not these terms referred to chattel slavery, they certainly describe

and other writers of early Christian documents had a precedent in this usage from their Jewish background, although in the Hebrew Bible slave terminology in reference to God is usually plural, i.e. it is the people as a whole who are slaves of Yahweh, and so the emphasis is not on individuals.[7] In addition to the Hebrew Bible usages, the early Christians also had the parables of Jesus, many of which used slave-master relationships to illustrate something about the reign of God.[8] Perhaps most surprising is Jesus' statement in Matt 20:27, "and whoever wishes to be first among you must be your slave."[9] This use of δοῦλος works to upend the whole status fabric of the first century Mediterranean world.[10]

Δοῦλος in Galatians

Paul's epistle to the Galatians is one of his earliest letters, and its primary concern appears to be to convince the Galatian believers that a return to Torah observance would be equivalent to choosing slavery over freedom. However, Paul labels himself early on as a slave of Christ (Χριστοῦ δοῦλος, Gal 1:10), seeking God's approval instead of human approval. This works in much the same way as do his opening words identifying himself as "an apostle—sent neither by human commission nor from human authorities, but through Jesus Christ and God the Father who raised him from the dead . . ." If being an apostle commissioned by Christ and God is equivalent to being a slave of Christ, then this slavery is not a status downgrade but rather a sign of authority—authority belonging to God, not to Paul, since he, like a slave, acts on behalf of the master.

However, when Paul gets into the heart of his argument against their turning back to the imprisonment (3:23) of the law, he quickly points out that as a result of their baptism into Christ, "There is no longer Jew or Greek, there is no longer slave or free, there is no longer male and female; for all of you are one in Christ Jesus" (3:28). Then he returns to the metaphor of slavery, this time in contrast to adoption as God's children. In 4:1–11 we

---

a status of people who were under the control, either by ownership or livelihood, of another. See Callender, "Servants of God," 67–82, and Wright, "*Ebed/Doulos*," 67–111.

7. See Rengsdorf, "δοῦλος, σύδουλος, κτλ.," 266–269.

8. See especially Matt 18:23–35; Matt 21:33–41/Mark 12:1–11/Luke 20:9–19; Matt 24:45–51; Matt 25:14–30/Luke 19:12–27.

9. English translations throughout this essay are from the New Revised Standard Version.

10. There are several other terms one could investigate, and the term δοῦλος could be studied in other New Testament texts (e.g., Jas 1:1 and 2 Pet 1:1), but I am limiting myself to δοῦλος in Galatians and Romans.

find Paul maintaining that heirs are no better than slaves until they come to the age of authority. In his words of application, "while we were minors, we were enslaved [δεδουλωμένοι] to the elemental spirits of the world" (4:3). He then argues that God sent his Son "to redeem [ἐξαγοράσῃ] those who were under the law, so that we might receive adoption as children."[11] The result is, then, "So you are no longer a slave but a child, and if a child then also an heir through God" (4:7). The realization of adoption then leads to Paul's exhortation that they not turn back to slavery "to the weak and beggarly elemental spirits."[12]

Chapter 4 closes with Paul's allegory of Hagar, the slave woman, and Sarah, the free woman, along with their sons. Although he does not use a form of δοῦλος in describing Hagar, he does use δουλείαν in verse 24 to describe what her child was born into—slavery. His closing exhortation here is, "So then, friends, we are children, not of the slave but of the free woman" (4:31).

Once Paul has established the negative references to slavery in this part of his argument against a law-centered approach to salvation, he can turn to slavery again as a positive metaphor. In 5:13 he encourages the Galatian believers "through love [to] become slaves to one another." What the NRSV translates here as "become slaves" is the imperative verb δουλεύετε. He is not so much looking at the status of slavery as its practice. In other words, the love of believers for one another should lead to loving service for the good of the other. The slave's primary goal as a slave was to please the master, so each believer should act in such a way as to please his/her brother/sister in the Lord.

Galatians closes with one more hint at Paul's self-identification as a slave, when in 6:17 he writes, "From now on, let no one make trouble for me; for I carry the marks of Jesus branded on my body." Martin argues persuasively that Paul's use of στίγματα here must refer to the tattoo or brand mark put on a slave to designate who his/her master was.[13] It is, of course, likely that Paul had actual marks on his person "earned" in his mission work, having encountered resistance and outright persecution as early as his first journey. In any case, these various uses of slave terms in Galatians indicate that Paul could use the metaphor either negatively or positively in reference both to becoming a Christ-follower and to living out his will in life.

---

11. It is important to point out that what is translated here in the NRSV as "children" is actually "sons," which in Paul's culture would be connected to inheritance, another favorite term in this passage.

12. This is not the place to deal with Paul's use of στοιχεῖα, but it appears to refer to at least unhelpful cosmic realities somehow connected in Paul's mind with dependence on the law.

13. Martin, *Slavery as Salvation*, 59-60.

Δοῦλος in Romans

Paul begins his letter to the believers in Rome by identifying himself as Παῦλος δοῦλος Χριστοῦ Ἰησοῦ. This is usually read as his attempt not to claim special authority over the Roman church, since he apparently had nothing to do with its founding and had not yet visited it. There is good reason to understand it that way, but as often happens with Paul there is likely more to it than simple humility. As we shall see, he comes back to the slavery metaphor several times in the epistle; but first we'll look briefly at other metaphors Paul uses in Romans to help us understand what he means by justification.

Paul begins his summary of salvation in both 3:21–26 and 5:1–11[14] with a statement about righteousness/justification, both of which are translations of δικαιοσύνη. This word and its cognates come from the semantic domain of courts and legal procedures[15] and appear to be Paul's favorite terms for describing what we are likely to call salvation as the act of God as universal judge declaring a human being to be righteous and thus making (creating) him or her righteous. In this paragraph of Romans 3, Paul points to the universality of sin and the justification by grace as an act of redemption (ἀπολυτρώσεως). This second soteriological term comes from the context of slavery, alluding to the practice of purchasing a slave to free him/her from the previous owner.[16] Paul goes on to say that this redemption in Christ Jesus was effected by God's offering of Christ as a ἱλαστήριον. This word comes from the Jerusalem temple, since it is used in the LXX to talk about the mercy seat over the ark of the covenant in the holy of holies. So this is religious terminology connected to atonement of the sins of God's people. The paragraph is brought to a neat ending with δικαιοῦντα as an *inclusio*.

Then in 5:1–11 Paul comes back to this description, using yet other words as metaphors for salvation. He begins again with our being "justified by faith," which leads him to point out that we now have "peace with God through our Lord Jesus Christ." So peace (*shalom*) with God is a result of justification. The next member of Paul's soteriological glossary is access (προσαγωγὴν) to grace, which gives us hope (ἐλπίδι) of the glory (δόξης) of God, since in 3:23 he has said a result of sin is our lack of that glory. He then shows the stream of suffering, endurance, and character that brings us to hope. In 5:6–9, Paul deals with the death of Christ for us because of God's

---

14. See my fuller exposition in *Preaching Romans*, 102–8.

15. Louw and Nida, *Semantic Domains*, 1:557. They also list this family of words under moral and ethical qualities and related behavior and other similar domains.

16. Ibid., 1:488, define ἀπολυτρώσεως as "to release or set free, with the implied analogy to the process of freeing a slave."

love, bringing him to the terminology of salvation: "Much more surely then, now that we have been justified by his blood, will we be saved through him from the wrath of God" (v.9). To be saved (σωθησόμεθα) is future oriented and specifically here refers to deliverance from God's wrath, which Paul has mentioned in 1:18. In verse 10 Paul goes to another semantic domain, with the use of the terms "enemies" and "reconciled" (κατηλλάγημεν). Here he doubles both reconciliation and salvation in verses 10b and 11. This shows that Paul's glossary of soteriological metaphors is broad and deep, drawing as they do from many different life experiences. The family of slavery metaphors is one of these, and he makes good use of it in succeeding chapters.

Paul returns to the slavery metaphor in Rom 6:12–23. He has used the opposites of death and life in 6:1–11, and now he turns to slavery and freedom. He begins by talking about dominion (βασιλευέτω), as he exhorts the Roman believers not to present their members to sin, since that gives sin authority, but to present those members to God, thus coming under the dominion of God. The rest of the chapter is punctuated with slavery terms. Since the life of a slave is one of continual obedience of the master, Paul uses forms of δοῦλος and ὑπακούω appropriately in his exposition here:

> Do you not know that if you present yourselves to anyone as obedient slaves, you are slaves of the one whom you obey, either of sin, which leads to death, or of obedience, which leads to righteousness? But thanks be to God that you, having once been slaves of sin, have become obedient from the heart to the form of teaching to which you were entrusted, and that you, having been set free from sin, have become slaves of righteousness. I am speaking in human terms because of your natural limitations. For just as you once presented your members as slaves to impurity and to greater and greater iniquity, so now present your members as slaves to righteousness for sanctification. When you were slaves of sin, you were free in regard to righteousness. So what advantage did you then get from the things of which you now are ashamed? The end of those things is death. But now that you have been freed from sin and enslaved to God, the advantage you get is sanctification. The end is eternal life. For the wages of sin is death, but the free gift of God is eternal life in Christ Jesus our Lord.

In this exposition, the choice is not between slavery and freedom, but rather between slavery to sin and slavery to righteousness or to God. Of course, since in Paul's background becoming a slave of God happens when one is freed from slavery to humans, as in the exodus from Egypt,[17] we can understand him to say that true freedom comes only with our giving God the dominion in our lives. This freedom/slavery leads, he says, to sanctification and eternal life.

In chapter 8 Paul emphasizes freedom in the Spirit, which of course has slavery or bondage in its background. In vv. 14-17 Paul contrasts life according to the flesh and its slavery with life as children of God and its freedom from fear. Then in lofty words of eschatological hope he promises that "the creation itself will be set free from its bondage [δουλείας] to decay and will obtain the freedom of the glory of the children of God" (v. 21).

There is one other section of Romans that I find interesting in this regard. In 14:1—15:13 Paul exhorts the Roman believers to maintain their unity in Christ by seeing one another not according to their differences of opinion and practice, but according to their mutual relationship with God in Christ. Apparently the church in Rome was having difficulties incorporating differences over foods and special days, and perhaps other issues, possibly connected to the return of Jewish believers banned from the city under Claudius. Allusions to the slave-master relationship appear throughout the passage. Romans 14:4 reads, "Who are you to pass judgment on servants [οἰκέτην] of another? It is before their own lord [κυρίῳ] that they stand or fall." He proceeds to emphasize this relationship which fellow believers should honor. Then he insists in verse 18, "The one who thus serves [δουλεύων] Christ is acceptable to God and has human approval." Chapter 15 begins with the instruction that believers should try to please their neighbors, not themselves. One hears the echo of slavery here, since the slave is expected to do everything to please the master. Paul uses Christ as the ultimate example, for his work was to do the will of God. In v. 8 Paul even describes Christ as having "become a servant [διάκονον] of the circumcised on behalf of the truth of God . . ." Thus following Christ should determine their attitude toward themselves and one another. Except for his mentions of households in chapter 16, this is his last use of this metaphor in Romans.

In our look at slavery terms in Romans we have seen a grand panoply of terms used metaphorically in Paul's discussion of what it means to be a Christ-follower. Slavery is one of those metaphors, and because some family trees include slaves this metaphor touches emotions in scholars and believers in general. I shall conclude this chapter with a look at how preachers might approach these terms and texts.

---

17. Lev 25:55: "For to me the people of God are servants whom I brought out from the land of Egypt: I am the LORD your God."

Δοῦλος in Preaching

Metaphors are tricky linguistic forms. A talented and thoughtful communicator can make good use of them. Metaphors can help the hearer/reader visualize an otherwise abstract concept. They can also help the hearer/reader see how an exhortation can assume flesh and blood and be lived out in real life. However, since they sometimes have a real referent and at other times they refer to something in another semantic domain, they present a challenge to the person using them. The challenge is to know how the hearer/reader will receive the metaphor.

The complication increases when we find a metaphor in one setting and try to use it in another. In our case, of course, we are trying to take a metaphor that worked in an ancient culture and use it in a culture of the 21st century. Some of Paul's metaphors, ἱλαστήριον (mercy seat) for instance, must be explained to a contemporary audience, since most of us are not familiar with the accoutrements of Herod's temple or the rituals of the Day of Atonement. As a result, recent translations interpret it in different ways. The term καταλλαγή (reconciliation), on the other hand, is easily understood and applied, since it deals with familiar human relational issues. However, slavery terminology presents us with a real conundrum. The history of slavery is long and complicated. In scholarship we can refer to that history and to the many works of research into the nature of slavery. In preaching we would put people to sleep with such erudition. Here we touch a most important question for the preacher: How do the people hear?

In my study of the works of the apostle Paul I often ask myself that same question in a historical form: How did Paul's intended audience hear and respond to this or that statement? What was it in their experience that would enable them to grasp Paul's intent? A cursory reading of 2 Thessalonians and 2 Corinthians shows that he was not always understood as he meant to be; and yet we read him as a great communicator. A helpful interpretive question in this regard is: What was Paul aiming at? What was his ultimate goal in this writing? It is often difficult even in our own writing or speaking to distinguish between the goal of our rhetoric and the strategies we use to attain the goal, but it is important that we ask this question. For this reason I have tried in my treatment of texts in Galatians and Romans to put them into their larger contexts by discussing what Paul must have been trying to accomplish in the lives of believers in Galatia and Rome. But even those local aims should be seen in the more radical aim of Paul's mission to his whole world. As Horsley puts it, "Paul cannot be understood to be helping legitimate the Roman institutional order, intentionally or unintentionally . . . Paul himself expected the dominant order to be terminated soon with the imminent *parousia* of his

Lord. Insofar as Paul knew the symbolic universe of Roman imperial society, he appears to have been using it in order to subvert and replace the institutions it legitimated."[18] Thus we need to see Paul's writings as calls to radical changes in both worldview and behavior.

The same question should be put to our own works of communication. What is it we are trying to accomplish in the minds, hearts, and lives of the receivers of this communication?

When we have a clear aim in mind we should be able to make the complex decisions about the use of metaphors as a strategy to accomplishing the aim. So the preacher's aim and the hearer's communication register are closely related issues in the rhetorical choices of preparing to preach. Instead of contemplating what we as preachers need to say or not say, we should first think about what our hearers need to hear in order to accomplish our aim (or better, God's aim) for them.

In regard to slavery terms, the preacher should recognize that they are metaphors and that there are many other metaphors used by the biblical speakers and writers to help their people understand and visualize their relationship with God. We should also realize that it might be more important to do what those writers did than to say what they said. They found life experiences that they could use as metaphors; and those pictures, parables, similes, and analogies helped their audiences to become believers and maintain their faith. This should not necessitate inventing totally new ways of stating the gospel and speaking about the faith and life of the believer, but it should free preachers to find 21st century ways of describing "the old, old story of Jesus and his love."

I do not have ultimate answers to questions about using or not using slavery terms in contemporary sermons. What I try in my own preaching and what I teach in my seminary homiletics classes is to know the audience as well as possible. The most important criterion for evaluating preaching is what the audience hears—really hears. When Paul said, "Faith comes from what is heard, and what is heard comes through the word of Christ" (Rom 10:17), he was leaning on centuries of prophetic examples going back to the basic confession of monotheistic faith, "Hear, O Israel: The LORD is our God, the Lord alone" (Deut 6:4). That *shema* kind of hearing leads to total obedience to the will of God. Ancient people saw such obedience—such hearing—as the basis of the slave-master relationship. However, if our hearers are distracted by slave terms and so do not hear what the biblical writers aimed at by using them, we who preach would do well to search our own imaginations to find more familiar terms that will help our hearers to dedicate themselves

---

18. Horsley, "Paul and Slavery," 164.

to radical trust in God. The parent-child relationship works with some, but there are people who have had such an abusive relationship with one or more parents that it might also be problematic. The military metaphors about unquestioned obedience could work well in some communities and not so well in others. The teacher/mentor-student relationship is another possibility, but again its effectiveness depends on the hearers. Even athletic metaphors can be effective. All of these appear in our scriptures, and they all are limited to the way they are heard in specific situations.

As I said earlier, metaphors are tricky. However, a preacher who knows her/his audience well should be able to make good judgments about what will work well and what will not. Preachers should do their very best to help people hear well, but preachers should also be aware that such hearing, as Paul put it, is by means of the word, or, as I like to put it, the utterance, of Christ (ῥῆμα Χριστοῦ, Rom 10:17b).

Works Cited

Bartchy, S. Scott. *ΜΑΛΛΟΝ ΧΡΗΣΑΙ: First-Century Slavery and the Interpretation of 1 Corinthians 7:21*. SBLDS 11. Missoula, MT: Society of Biblical Literature, 1973. Reprinted, Eugene, OR: Wipf & Stock, 2003.

———. "Slavery (Greco-Roman): New Testament." In *ABD*, 6:65–73.

Callender, Dexter E., Jr. "Servants of God(s) and Servants of Kings in Israel and the Ancient Near East." *Semeia* 83–84 (1998) 67–82.

Harrill, J. Albert. "Paul and the Slave Self." In *Religion and the Self in Antiquity*, edited by David Brakke, Michael L. Satlow, and Steven Weitzman, 51–69. Bloomington: Indiana University Press, 2005.

Horsley, Richard A. "Paul and Slavery: A Critical Alternative to Recent Readings." *Semeia* 83–84 (1998) 153–200.

———. "The Slave Systems of Classical Antiquity and their reluctant Recognition by Modern Scholars." *Semeia* 83–84 (1998) 19–66.

Horsley, Richard A., Allen Dwight Callahan, and Abraham Smith. "Introduction: The Slavery of New Testament Studies." *Semeia* 83–84 (1998) 1–15.

Kittel, Gerhard, and Gerhard Friedrich, eds. *Theological Dictionary of the New Testament*. Translated by Geoffrey W. Bromiley. 10 vols. Grand Rapids: Eerdmans, 1964–1976.

Louw, Johannes P., and Eugene A. Nida, eds. *Greek-English Lexicon of the New Testament Based on Semantic Domains*. 2nd ed. New York: United Bible Societies, 1989.

Martin, Dale A. *Slavery as Salvation: The Metaphor of Slavery in Pauline Christianity*. New Haven: Yale University Press, 1990.

Patterson, Orlando. "Paul, Slavery and Freedom: Personal and Socio-Historical Reflections." *Semeia* 83–84 (1998) 263–79.

Shields, Bruce E. *Preaching Romans*. St. Louis: Chalice, 2004.

Wright, Benjamin G., III. "*Ebed/Doulos*: Terms and Social Status in the Meeting of Hebrew Biblical and Hellenistic Roman Culture." *Semeia* 83–84 (1998) 83–111.

13

Constructing Euodia and Syntyche
Philippians 4:2–3 and the Informed Imagination

Robert F. Hull Jr.

SCOTT BARTCHY WAS MY immediate predecessor in the faculty position to which I was invited at Emmanuel School of Religion (now Emmanuel Christian Seminary) in 1977. He has been a constant source of encouragement to me through the years, both by means of personal comments at professional meetings and his sending along early drafts of essays and offprints of his published articles. It was he who first began to raise my consciousness with regard to the social and theological issues with which this *Festschrift* is concerned. It is a pleasure to dedicate this contribution to Scott and to congratulate him on his retirement from the UCLA Department of History.

Of Provocation and Frustration

> Εὐωδίαν παρακαλῶ καὶ Συντύχην παρακαλῶ τὸ αὐτὸ φρονεῖν ἐν κυρίῳ. ναὶ ἐρωτῶ καὶ σέ, γνήσιε σύζυγε, συλλαμβάνου αὐταῖς, αἵτινες ἐν τῷ εὐαγγελίῳ συνήθλησάν μοι μετὰ καὶ Κλήμεντος καὶ τῶν λοιπῶν συνεργῶν μου, ὧν τὰ ὀνόματα ἐν βίβλῳ ζωῆς. (Phil 4:2–3)

This essay was provoked by a sermon I heard more than 25 years ago. The preacher was a better-than-average homiletician with his Master of Divinity from a quality seminary. In dealing with the theme of unity and discord within the church, he took as an example, Euodia and Syntyche, "or," he said, "as I prefer to call them, 'You're-Odious' and 'Sure-Touchy.'" I thought it a pretty creative laugh line, whether the preacher invented the names or not. At the same time, I found it troubling. It is the only comment I remember from the sermon, probably because I had by that time encountered many exemplary women students struggling to be taken seriously both by their male counterparts in seminary and the churches they hoped to serve. Even a cursory reading of the Letter to the Philippians had made it clear to me that, whatever the nub of the problem was between these two co-workers of Paul, it should not be trivialized into a "cat fight" or a "hen fight" between a couple of prickly women.[1] There had to have been more at stake than personal issues.

At the same time, it is enormously difficult to say exactly what was at stake and why Paul found it necessary in such a short letter to "call out" two women before the whole congregation. Everything we know about them and their situation is divulged in only 38 words. The history of the exegesis of these 38 words is a record of both the ingenuity and the desperation of interpreters of the text. In the brief survey that follows, my goal is to sift out from the efforts of this train of interpreters what I regard as the most probable construction of Euodia and Syntyche of Philippi. I use the word "construction" rather than "reconstruction" advisedly, with an appreciative nod to Dale Allison and his book *Constructing Jesus: Memory, Imagination, and History*. Influenced by modern memory studies, Allison avers that, with the best will in the world and the most sophisticated analysis of the data available, we can never *re*construct the past; rather, we select, arrange, and interpret the information we have such that we construct, not only the past, but even our memories of our own past.[2] If this is true even of characters about whom we have dozens of stories and documents, how much more is it the case with figures we know only by means of a few lines in an ancient letter.

At the same time, because women get comparatively so little attention in the literature of earliest Christianity, it is critically important to attend to texts in which they are mentioned as active in the mission and expansion of the church. When we begin to notice such texts, we can never read the New Testament in the same way. For example, as Mark Goodacre points out, we can read the Gospel of Mark almost to the end without realizing that there

---

1. Brooten, "Women and the Churches," 53.
2. Allison, *Constructing Jesus*, 1–13.

were women accompanying Jesus and his male disciples; finally we come to Mark 15:40–41, where we find at the cross "women looking on from afar, among whom were Mary Magdalene, and Mary the mother of James the younger and of Joses, and Salome, who, when he was in Galilee, followed him and ministered to him" (RSV). Once we have read this detail, we would be wise to imagine women among the disciples in every Markan scene in Galilee.[3] The efforts of scholars, especially feminists, to give a voice to the silent partners of Paul and to tell their stories is important; but we have to remember that we, not these silent women, are the writers of the stories we tell, and it is our voices, not theirs, that we use in the telling. This requires the use of imagination, yes, but a disciplined and well-informed imagination.[4]

Euodias and Syntyches?

Some ways of interpreting Phil 4:2–3 either minimize the importance of Euodia and Syntyche in the congregation or write them out of the story altogether. William Tyndale (1534) rendered both terms as masculine ("Euodias" and "Sintiches"). The Authorized Version (KJV) follows Tyndale for "Euodias," but not for Syntyche, perhaps supposing the two were a married couple. One could be excused for suspecting a masculine bias on the part of the translators. A masculine form of each of the names is known from the inscriptions, Greek sources yielding the spelling Εὔωδος[5] and one Latin inscription attesting to Sintichus.[6] One would not expect the transliterations used in Tyndale and the AV, however, for either of these forms; moreover, the two are then referred to by the feminine pronoun αὐταῖς and the feminine relative ἅιτινες (v. 3). The matter is not so simple, however, because Tyndale construes verse 2 as standing alone, such that "Euodias and Sintiches" do not serve as the antecedent of αὐταῖς and the relative ἅιτινες. He translates "I praye Evodias, and besiche Sintiches that they may be of one accorde in the lorde. Yee and I besiche the faythfull Yockfelowe, helpe the women who labored with me in the gospel." Thus he has in mind, on the one hand, two quarreling men, and on the other hand, some women who labored with Paul in the gospel. Similarly, the AV understands "Euodias" and Syntyche

---

3. See podacre.blogspot.com, NT Pod 65, Thurs., Mar. 28, 2013.

4. In the following, I do not deal with the question of the literary integrity of the letter. I am persuaded by the arguments in favor of integrity (Garland, 141–73 and Reed), but the debate has little bearing on one's interpretation of 4:2–3.

5. Moulton-Milligan, 263; one inscription has Εὐώδιος; see Zahn, *Introduction* I, 533.

6. Moulton-Milligan, 615, citing only *CIL* XII, 4703.

to be referred to only in v. 2, with some unidentified "women who laboured with me in the Gospel" as the referents in v. 3. It is, of course, possible that Tyndale and the translators of the AV were influenced by a masculine bias that inclined them to think that, if two persons were important enough in the church for Paul to address them by name, at least one of them must certainly be male. Although neither translation is troubled by the reality that some women labored with Paul in the Gospel, the circumstance that these women are not identified with the two named persons marginalizes the latter as just two persons who had a disagreement. And the grammatical construal that underwrites their translations seems quite unnatural.[7]

There is also a minor textual variant that could have the effect of demoting Euodia and Syntyche from the rank of σύνεργοι: At 4:3 Codex Sinaiticus and P16 (POxy 2009) read "Clement and my co-workers and the rest" (Κλήμεντος καὶ τῶν συνεργῶν μου καὶ τῶν λοιπῶν), rather than "Clement and the rest of my co-workers." In my judgment this is almost certainly an inadvertent scribal error,[8] not an "antifeminist" alteration.

It's All about Euodia and Syntyche

At the other extreme, rather than limiting the place of Euodia and Syntyche, some scholars magnify their importance so far as to find in their disagreement the main purpose of the letter. On the basis of a literary study of Philippians, David E. Garland judges that the Philippian church was crippled by internal disputes and conflicts. He writes, "It is my contention that Paul carefully and covertly wove his argument to lead up to the impassioned summons in 4:2. He wrote primarily to defuse the dispute between these two women that was having disastrous repercussions for the unity of the church."[9] Nils Dahl attaches a similar importance to the disagreement between the two women,[10] as does Boyd Luter.[11] The most thoroughgoing analysis of the letter as a response to conflict is the 1992 Aberdeen dissertation of Davorin Peterlin. Peterlin discerns allusions to disagreements about theodicy, prompted by Paul's sufferings (1:12–26) and pagan social pressure against the church (1:27–30). He conjectures a "pro-Paul party" and

---

7. It is noteworthy, however, that both translations read "Junia" at Rom 16:7, which argues against a masculine bias.

8. This is a "subsingular" reading; i.e., the scribes of the two MSS in question independently made the same error.

9. Garland, "Composition and Unity," 173.

10. Dahl, "Euodia and Syntyche."

11. Luter, "Partnership in the Gospel," 411–20.

an "anti-Paul party," led, respectively, by Euodia and Syntyche, arguing that the question of Paul's financial support was a source of controversy between these two putative "parties."[12]

The value of these studies has been to draw attention to recurring emphases on unity, humility, and selflessness in the letter, such that Paul's entreaty to the two women may be coherently related to a central theme, rather than based on a personal "feud" between the two. Against those who doubt the literary unity and integrity of the letter,[13] the above studies focus on the unifying elements. Nevertheless, I do not believe those readings of the letter that identify community discord as *the* precipitating purpose can bear the weight imposed upon them. To be sure, the situation addressed by Paul in Philippians may be more difficult to pin down than in any other of the letters attributed to him. A reasonable case can be made that the hiatus in the church's financial support (4:10-11) had been caused, in part, by disagreement among the believers about how much to send and perhaps even whether such support should be continued (4:14-17). It may be that Paul's strong emphasis on being united in the same love and purpose (2:2-3; 4:2) alludes to serious divisions within the community (1:15, 17; 2:14). Even so, the letter, on the whole, is suffused with such fervent expressions of love and joy (1:7-8, 25; 2:17-18; 4:1, 4, 10) as to justify the conclusion that Greek and Roman rhetoric of friendship dominates the letter.[14] To insist that the disagreement between Euodia and Syntyche is *the* precipitating cause of the letter depends on a mirror-reading of all of this friendship language as a corrective to the divisions in the church.

The Acts Connection

Many scholars have turned to the account of the birth of the Philippian church in Acts 16:13-14 to help construct the identity of Euodia and/or Syntyche. As is well known, the first convert in that city was the woman Lydia, a seemingly-independent head-of-household who was a dealer in purple dye. As early as 1908 Theodor Zahn suggested the possibility that "Lydia" was an ethnic nickname, meaning "the Lydian woman," since she was from Thyatira in the province of Lydia.[15] Some years later, his colleague Paul Ewald mooted the suggestion that either Euodia or Syntyche might

12. Peterlin, *Paul's Letter to the Philippians*, 217-28.
13. For a summary of partition theories, see Reed, *Discourse Analysis*, 124-52.
14. See Johnson, *Writings of the New Testament*, 328-29.
15. Zahn, *Introduction*, 522. There is inscriptional evidence for "Lydia" as an ethnic cognomen.

have been "the Lydian woman," but conceded that this must remain only "an attractive possibility."[16] Gerald F. Hawthorne still sees "a certain credibility" in this conjecture.[17] Other scholars turn to the Acts account to suggest that, since Acts 17:4, 12 mention women of high social standing as converts at Berea and Thessalonica, the female converts at Philippi, including Euodia and Syntyche, were likely socially prominent: "At Philippi, at Thessalonica, at Beroea, the women—in some cases certainly, in all probably, ladies of birth and rank—take an active part with the Apostle."[18]

Although it is, in the strictest sense, impossible to construct an adequate account of Paul's chronology and ministry without the help of Acts, it is methodologically questionable simply to turn to Acts to construct the identity of persons mentioned in Philippians, but not in the narrative of Acts itself.[19]

The Macedonian Connection

By far the area of research most frequently exploited for its potential to help in constructing the identities of Euodia and Syntyche has to do with the social status and religious participation of women in Macedonia. Among contemporary commentaries, the typical point of entry is a two-page summary found in Tarn and Griffith's *Hellenistic Civilization*, beginning with this choice comment: "If Macedonia produced perhaps the most competent group of men the world had yet seen, the women were in all respects the men's counterparts . . ."[20] The authors go on to mention Macedonian women who were prominent in government, military affairs, civic patronage, and religious cults, adding: "From the Macedonian courts, (relative) freedom broadened down to the Greek home; and those women who desired emancipation—probably a minority—were able to obtain it in considerable measure."[21] One finds references to these pages in commentary after commentary.[22]

---

16. Ewald, *Philipper*, 212. He notes also (216) the possibility that the Clement of verse 3 might be the name of the jailer of Acts 16:27–34.

17. Hawthorne, *Phlippians*, 179.

18. Lightfoot, *Philippians*, 56.

19. Sampley points to the related practice of interpreting one of Paul's letters in a way that makes certain there is no disagreement with what Paul says on a related issue in another of his letters, a process Sampley calls "corpus harmonization"(*Pauline Partnership*, 54).

20. Tarn and Griffith, *Hellenistic Civilization*, 98.

21. Ibid., 98–99.

22. To mention only three, see Fee, *Philippians*, 391; Martin, *Philippians*, 8; and

Thirty years before Tarn and Griffith, J. B. Lightfoot had already called attention in his commentary to a number of funerary and monumental inscriptions from Macedonia in which women appear to be prominent, remarking, "The extant Macedonian inscriptions seem to assign to the sex a higher social influence than is common among civilised nations of antiquity."[23] A few years later William M. Ramsay expressed a similar opinion, including Asia Minor along with Macedonia as favorable to the advancement of women.[24] Scholars of today who take the trouble to cite primary sources seldom, if ever, go beyond these same nine inscriptions culled by Lightfoot from the *Corpus Inscriptionum Graecorum*.[25]

The most focused and extensive effort to relate the Philippian letter to the women of Macedonia, and specifically Philippi, is the doctoral dissertation of Lilian Portefaix, published under the title, *Sisters Rejoice: Paul's Letter to the Philippians and Luke-Acts as Received by First-Century Philippian Women*. She surveys archaeological, epigraphic, and literary sources in order to reconstruct the socio-cultural and religious backgrounds of women in Philippi at the time when the letter would have been received. She holds that these sources attest to a high visibility of religious cults holding special attraction for women. These findings undergird her reading of Philippians, which is based on "reception theory," as set forth in the work of Wolfgang Iser and Hans Robert Jauss. She interprets the letter according to the "horizon of expectations" (*Erwartungshorizont*) of the first two generations of women who became members of the Philippian church. Because Philippian women already had a keen interest in religious matters (as shown by the sources she has surveyed), they would have responded positively to Paul's portrayal of the church as a "celestial citizenship" (Phil 3:20; cf. 1:27) where women stood on equal ground with men. That Philippian women were ready to make sacrifices for religion also inclined them favorably to Paul's designation of himself and Timothy as "slaves" of Jesus Christ (1:1) and to the portrayal of Jesus himself as one who "took the form of a slave" (2:7).[26] She writes, "The picture Paul gives of Syntyche and Euodia as struggling in the cause of the gospel (Phil 4:3) accords with the one we already have of Philippian women's interest in religious matters."[27]

Thurston, *Philppians and Philemon*, 19. Each of these scholars quotes at least a portion of the "choice comment" mentioned above from Tarn and Griffith, *Hellenistic Civilization*, 98.

23. Lightfoot, *Philippians*, 56.
24. Ramsay, *St. Paul the Traveler*, 227.
25. See Lightfoot, 56, for references; cf. Witherington, *Women*, 98.
26. Portefaix, *Sisters Rejoice*, 136.
27. Ibid., 138.

A broader concentration on the religious interests and practices of the women of Philippi is Valerie A. Abrahamsen's *Women and Worship at Philippi: Diana/Artemis and other Cults in the Early Christian Era*. A self-described feminist study, the book offers a detailed analysis of the archaeological evidence for religious cults at or near Philippi up through the Byzantine era, focusing on their possible or probable connection with women. Her general conclusion is this: "The combined influence of Isis, Diana, the Horsemen and Dionysos vis-à-vis female cult officials—the *assumption* that women were to be among the leaders of any religious organization—was felt by the Christian community, and some female leaders of the dying pagan cults probably transferred their loyalty to Jesus the Christ (and his Holy Mother, the counterpart of Isis), became leaders in the new group and brought followers with them."[28] Among these Christian leaders were Euodia and Syntyche. Citing the work of other feminist scholars (Elisabeth Schlüssler Fiorenza and Mary Rose D'Angelo), Abrahamsen suggests that Euodia and Syntyche were a "missionary couple," possibly living together in a union parallel to that of husband and wife missionary couples.[29]

There are problems in highlighting the social and religious position of Macedonian women as helping to explain the place of Euodia and Syntyche (and Lydia) in the Philippian church. Beginning with the famous quotation from Tarn and Griffith, the examples of powerful women are all from the elite class, mostly from the Hellenistic era. After referring also to educated Greek women philosophers, magistrates, poets, and founders of clubs during the Roman era, Tarn and Griffith go on to write: "But most of these things clearly relate only to a minority."[30] High-status women (by birth, rank, or social order) anywhere in the Mediterranean world were always more visible and more influential than lower-status women. We should not assume that Euodia and Syntyche were high-status converts. Even the report in Acts that some of the "leading women" of Thessalonica (17:4) or "women of high standing" of Berea (17:12) became converts cannot be turned around to mean all the women converts in these cities were socially powerful. Moreover, we have no reason to believe that any of the named women converts in Acts were of high social status: Tabitha (9:36–42) and Prisca (18:2–3) were artisans; Lydia, although frequently assumed to have been wealthy and socially influential, was a merchant whose background and social status cannot be determined from the account in Acts.[31] To be sure, anyone who owned a

---

28. Abrahamsen, *Women and Worship*, 91, author's emphasis.
29. Ibid., 83, cf. 195.
30. Tarn and Griffith, *Hellenistic Civilization*, 99–100.
31. Many commentaries mistakenly suppose that Lydia must have been connected

house would have attained some measure of social respectability, but this alone would not have given that person elite status.

L. Michael White cautions against using raw archaeological data to construct a social description of the world of a text.[32] Drawing on two phases of excavation that occurred after the time of Lightfoot and Ramsay, White surveys 202 inscriptions from Philippi, noting that "general areas of participation by women at Philippi do not seem to stand out as appreciably higher than the proportion of inscriptions by prominent women from other regions of the empire . . ."[33] He readily acknowledges the evidence for the popularity in and around Philippi of religious cults traditionally associated with women, particularly the cult of Diana, but is skeptical of efforts to account for the conversion of women to Christianity in Macedonia on the basis of this evidence.

But do we really need the "Macedonian connection" to help us account for the place of Euodia and Syntyche in the church at Philippi? I don't think so. Throughout Paul's network of churches, one finds female co-workers.[34] Phoebe of Cenchreae, the eastern port of Corinth, is commended as both a διάκονος ("minister"? "deacon"?) and a patron (προστάτις) of many, including Paul (Rom 16:1-2). Prisca (Priscilla) was, along with her husband, a noted teacher and leader of house churches in Corinth (Acts 18:1-3), Ephesus (Acts 19:24-26), and Rome (Rom 16:3-5); the two had "risked their necks" for Paul. Junia and her husband (or brother?) were called "noteworthy apostles" (Rom 16:7)[35]; they were kinfolk of Paul and converts even before him. Nympha was leader of a house church in Colossae (Col 4:15).[36] If a socio-cultural explanation of the leadership of women in the Pauline churches is needed, we are on firmer ground simply pointing to a general "loosening up" during the late Republican and early Imperial period of many of the social strictures on women throughout the Roman world.[37]

---

with the expensive purple dye extracted from a shellfish and controlled by Imperial monopoly. There were two other, less expensive, types of purple dye, the most common derived from the madder root. We have no basis for determining which kind Lydia was involved in as a dealer. See G.H.R. Horsley, *New Documents*, 3, 53–54.

32. White, "Visualizing."
33. White, "Visualizing," 258, n. 71.
34. Bartchy, "Domestication."
35. I regard the old debate about whether to read "Junia" (female) or "Junias" (male) as now settled. See Epp, *Junia*.
36. Bartchy, "Can You Imagine?"
37. See Winter, *Roman Wives*.

What Can We Say About Euodia and Syntyche?

What is the picture we can draw of them by means of a disciplined imagination? They were surely Greeks, the Greek name "Euodia," meaning "Good Journey,"[38] "Syntyche," meaning "Good Luck." Even Paul's address to each of the women separately—"I encourage Euodia and I encourage Syntyche"—seems to accord them, or at least their disagreement, special status. It is fair to surmise that they were leading figures in the congregation at Philippi, having "struggled in the gospel" (συνήθλησαν) with Paul (4:3).

That they are included "with Clement and the rest" of Paul's "co-workers" (σύνεργοι, v. 3) underscores their status as missioners, with the same standing as Paul's male associates. Paul uses the term σύνεργος in his letters to refer to twenty different persons who carried out what we would today call "ministry" or "mission," whether itinerant or local. Included are such notables as Apollos (1 Cor 3:9), Prisca and Aquila (Rom 16:3–4), Silas (1 Thess 3:2), Timothy (Rom 16:21), and Titus (2 Cor 8:23). He never uses the term of "believers in general."[39] In 2:25–29, where Paul commends the ministry of Epaphroditus, his "co-worker and fellow-soldier," he says the readers should "hold in esteem all such ones," presumably including Euodia and Syntyche.[40] We need not infer that Euodia and Syntyche did their work "in the gospel" in the marketplace or on the street corner, since ordinary Greek women, even in Macedonia, had quite limited opportunities to operate freely in a public setting, particularly if they engaged in teaching;[41] but the power and influence of women within the home—including house churches—would have been considerable.[42]

It is certainly possible that they were leaders of two house churches, but nothing in the letter actually suggests this.[43] It is also possible, as many scholars have noted, that the two were among the διάκονοι addressed in Phil 1:1.[44] Indeed, Peterlin concludes, following a quite sophisticated argument,

---

38. A few manuscripts read Εὐώδια, meaning "sweet-smelling," or "fragrant."

39. Ellis, "Paul and His Coworkers," 440.

40. Luter, "Partnership," 415.

41. Winter, *Roman Wives*, 115–116.

42. For the opinion of Celsus and other cultured pagans about how the workshop-home promoted the work of evangelism by women see MacDonald, *Early Christian Women*. That such pagan portrayals may reflect an idealized notion of the social invisibility of women in the wider world is suggested by Osiek and MacDonald, *Woman's Place*, esp. ch. 10.

43. Osiek, *Philippians*, 111–12, opines that the two were *episkopoi* (1:1), not in the later technical sense of officeholders, but as "heads of local house churches."

44. See Lightfoot, *Philippians*, 158, and many other commentators.

that they *were* deacons (i.e., having a local church ministry similar to that of Phoebe in Corinth [Rom 16:1-2]).[45] In my judgment, his construction of the status and function of διάκονοι in the Pauline churches is more detailed and specific than warranted by the textual references.

As to the cause(s) of their disagreement, I do not believe we have enough evidence to identify precisely what it was they were quarreling about, although I believe it is reasonable to conclude that it was related to wider tensions within the whole church, as I have noted above.[46]

The injunction in 4:2 for Euodia and Syntyche "to think the same" (τὸ αὐτὸ φρονεῖν) points back to the similar injunction to the whole community in 2:2 "that you (pl.) think the same" (ἵνα τὸ αὐτὸ φρονῆτε), a plea that is reinforced by the following participial phrase "being of one mind" (τὸ ἕν φρονοῦντες). References to forms of φρονεῖν in both positive (2:5, 3:15) and negative senses (3:15, 19) draw the reader's attention to disagreements within the church, but do not allow us to pinpoint the problems.

Finally, I think it is important to emphasize the function of these women as both positive and negative examples in the letter. Rhetorically, the letter offers contrasting models of behavior by those who are friends of the gospel (Paul [1:12-26], Timothy [2:19-24], Epaphroditus [2:25-30]) and those who are enemies of the gospel (those who preach "from envy and rivalry" [1:15]; "opponents" of the Philippians [1:28]; "dogs, evil workers" [3:1-2]; "enemies of the cross of Christ" [3:18-19]).[47] Euodia and Syntyche cannot neatly be slotted into either list. They are negative examples, because they do not "think the same in the Lord" (4:2). At the same time, they are positive examples because they have "struggled together with [Paul] in the gospel" (4:3), which is precisely what Paul indicated in 1:27 as his hope for all the Philippians ("with one soul struggling together for the faith of the gospel," μιᾷ ψυχῇ συναθλοῦντες τῇ πίστει τοῦ εὐαγγελίου). But note that Paul ends on a positive note, aligning the two "with Clement and the rest of my co-workers whose names are in the book of life" (4:3).

This little exercise has uncovered no striking new evidence, framed no new theory about the place of Euodia and Syntyche in the Philippian church and in Paul's ministry. If my imagination is more restrained than that of some of the scholars whose work I have reviewed, it is because I long ago

---

45. Peterlin, *Paul's Letter to the Philippians*, 106-111, 123. Using Phoebe as a model for what the ministry of Euodia and Syntyche must have been is explaining one unknown by another, for, *pace* Peterlin, we cannot say precisely what is implied in Paul's commendation of her as "διάκονος of the church in Cenchrea" (Rom 16:1); but see Miller, "What Can We Say?"

46. See 3-4.

47. See Stowers, "Friends and Enemies."

took as a guiding premise Jacob Neusner's dictum: "What we cannot show, we do not know."[48] But I hope I have shown that, on any reading, these two women have earned a place of honor in the roster of Paul's companions in ministry and in the life of the church at Philippi.

Works Cited

Abrahamsen, Valerie A. *Women and Worship at Philippi: Diana/Artemis and other Cults in theEarly Christian Era*. Portland, ME: Astarte Shell Press, 1995.

Allison, Dale C. *Constructing Jesus*. Grand Rapids: Baker Academic, 2010.

Bartchy, S. Scott. "Can You Imagine Paul Telling Priscilla *Not* to Teach?" *Leaven* 4 (1996) 19–23.

———. "The Domestication of a Radical Jew: Paul of Tarsus." In *Maven in Blue Jeans: A Festschrift in Honor of Zev Garber*, edited by Steven Leonard Jacobs, 7–16. West Lafayette, IN: Purdue University, 2009.

Brooten, Bernadette J. "Women and the Churches in Early Christianity." *Ecumenical Trends* 14 (1985) 51–54.

Corpus Inscriptionum Graecorum. Edited by August Boeckh. Vol. 2. Berlin: Akademie der Wissenschaften, 1843.

Dahl, Nils A. "Euodia and Syntyche and Paul's Letter to the Philippians." In *The Social World of The First Christians: Essays in Honor of Wayne A. Meeks*, edited by L. Michael Whiteand O. Larry Yarbrough, 3–15. Minneapolis: Fortress, 1995.

Ellis, E. Earle. "Paul and His Co-Workers." *NTS* 17 (1971) 437–52.

Epp, Eldon Jay. *Junia: The First Woman Apostle*. Minneapolis: Fortress, 2005.

Ewald, Paul. *Der Brief des Paulus an die Philipper*. 3rd ed. Edited by Gustav Wohlenberg. Kommentar zum Neuen Testament 11. Leipzig: Deichert, 1917.

Fee, Gordon D. *Paul's Letter to the Philippians*. New International Commentary on the New Testament. Grand Rapids: Eerdmans, 1995.

Garland, David E. "The Composition and Unity of Philippians: Some Neglected Literary Factors." *NovT* 27 (1985) 141–73.

Hawthorne, Gerald F. *Philippians*. Word Biblical Commentary. Waco: Word, 1983.

Johnson, Luke Timothy. *The Writings of the New Testament*. 3rd ed. Minneapolis: Fortress, 2010.

Lightfoot, J. B. *St. Paul's Epistle to the Philippians*. London: Macmillan, 1868.

Luter, Boyd. "Partnership in the Gospel: The Role of Women in the Church at Philippi." *Journal of the Evangelical Theological Society* 39 (1996) 411–20.

MacDonald, Margaret Y. *Early Christian Women and Pagan Opinion*. Cambridge: Cambridge University Press, 1996.

Martin, Ralph P. *Philippians*. London: Marshall, Morgan & Scott, 1976.

Miller, J. David. "What Can We Say about Phoebe?" *Priscilla Papers* 25 (2011) 16–21.

Moulton, James Hope, and George Milligan. *The Vocabulary of the Greek New Testament Illustrated from the Papyri and Other Non-Literary Sources*. Grand Rapids: Eerdmans, 1963.

Neusner, Jacob. *What We Cannot Show, We Do Not Know: Rabbinic Literature and the New Testament*. Philadelphia: Trinity, 1994.

---

48. See Neusner, *What We Cannot Show, We Do Not Know*.

New Documents Illustrating Early Christianity. Sydney, Australia: Ancient History Documentary Research Center, Macquarie University, 1977-.
Osiek, Carolyn. *Philippians, Philemon*. Abingdon New Testament Commentaries. Nashville: Abingdon, 2000.
Osiek, Carolyn, and Margaret Y. MacDonald. *A Woman's Place: House Churches in Earliest Christianity*. Minneapolis: Fortress, 2006.
Peterlin, Davorin. *Paul's Letter to the Philippians in the Light of Disunity in the Church*. NovTSup 79. Leiden: Brill, 1995.
Portefaix, Lilian. *Sisters Rejoice: Paul's Letter to the Philippians and Luke-Acts as Received by First-Century Philippian Women*. Coniectanea biblica: New Testament Series 20. Uppsala: Almqvist, 1988.
Ramsay, William Mitchell. *St. Paul the Traveller and the Roman Citizen*. London: Hodder & Stoughton, 1896.
Reed, Jeffrey T. *A Discourse Analysis of Philippians: Method and Rhetoric in the Debate over Literary Integrity*. JSNTSup 136. Sheffield: Sheffield Academic, 1997.
Sampley, J. Paul. *Pauline Partnership in Christ: Christian Community and Commitment in Light of Roman Law*. Philadelphia: Fortress, 1980.
Stowers, Stanley K. "Friends and Enemies in the Politics of Heaven." Pages 105-121 in *Pauline Theology*, Vol. 1: *Thessalonians, Philippians, Galatians, Philemon*. Edited by Jouette Bassler. Minneapolis: Fortress, 1991.
Tarn, W. W., and G. T. Griffith. *Hellenistic Civilization*. 3rd ed. New York: Meridian, 1961.
Thurston, Bonnie B., and Judith M. Ryan. *Philippians and Philemon*. Sacra Pagina. Collegeville, MN: Michael Glazier/Liturgical, 2005.
White, L. Michael. "Visualizing the 'Real' World of Acts 16: Toward Construction of a Social Index." In *The Social World of the First Christians: Essays in Honor of Wayne A. Meeks*, edited by L. Michael White and O. Larry Yarbrough, 234-61. Minneapolis: Fortress, 1995.
Winter, Bruce W. *Roman Wives, Roman Widows: The Appearance of New Women and the Pauline Communities*. Grand Rapids: Eerdmans, 2003.
Witherington, Ben. *Women in the Earliest Churches*. Society for New Testament Studies Monograph Series 59. Cambridge: Cambridge University Press, 1988.
Zahn, Theodor. *Introduction to the New Testament*. Translated from the 3rd German edition by John Moore Trout et al. 1909. Reprinted, Grand Rapids: Kregel, 1953.

14

Galatians 3:28

An Aspect of Eschatological Asceticism in Paul

Robert James Mason

MY CONNECTION WITH S. Scott Bartchy began as a student of the now defunct Westwood Christian Foundation located beside the UCLA campus, the vision of another great Christian scholar, Robert O. Fife. At that time the Foundation was seeking a world-class scholar of Christian origins who would be able to negotiate between churches of the Restoration Movement, the American Christian scene, and the critical/creative environment across the street at UCLA. So when Dr. Bartchy accepted and began his distinguished career at UCLA, I was fortunate enough to profit from his mentorship. This is a relationship that has evolved beyond mentor/student; rather it is one that I look upon as foundational in setting my goals for critical studies in religion and in obtaining the tools that allow me to aggressively pursue those goals. But perhaps more importantly than his academic publications, he has always put his students first (and I for one am fundamentally grateful).

I want to also thank the editors of this volume for selecting topics of engagement hovering around Gal 3:27–28 that have been important issues that have consumed so much of Scott's scholarship. His dissertation focused on 1 Cor 7:21 and the concept of calling and freedom and hence his detailed study of slavery in the early Roman Empire. This has led to numerous articles related to issues of slavery along with publications on several of the key letters in the New Testament that touch on the institutional forms of the Roman slave system—what we today call 1 Corinthians and the letter of Philemon.

So, from my perspective, the text selection for this volume, Gal 3:27–28, accords well with Dr. Bartchy's initial and continuing fascination with the apostle Paul and the communities that he collaborated with over the course of his ministry. From the beginning of his tenure at UCLA and throughout his academic career he has sought to engage all in his discussions and articles: academics, churches, those who admire Paul and those who are not so impressed. As with all discussions on important topics, not all will agree, particularly when they involve complex issues, deep-seated values, or hesitancy to see both sides, but these deep-seated disagreements are further exacerbated when not all the voices are heard as I feel is the case with some of Dr. Bartchy's discussion points. From where I stand today I tend to place Bartchy's target audience somewhere in the middle of the spectrum of hermeneutical approaches to biblical texts, those readers and groups that still feel some tug and ownership in Christian Scriptures. Consequently his dialogue partners who embrace the postmodern critical perspectives criticize his lack of engagement with power relations, structures, and theory. Those critics, on the other hand, who hold the Christian Scriptures as more unique and special criticize his methodology as not taking into account the meta-authorial perspective that gives the texts their authority and normativity. Yet it is these last dialogue partners who could benefit most from a serious engagement with his viewpoint.

Galatians 3:27–28 has been part of a growing battle ground where under-examined views of power dynamics (between Paul and his churches as well as between different groups within his churches) have come under increasing scrutiny since the rise of post-modern criticisms of the New Testament in the 1960s. Beginning with questions concerning the extent and use of Paul's authority by feminist scholars and others, the questions have broadened into the way Paul's writings have been used by groups to influence different communities[1] and Bartchy has contributed several articles to this dialogue over power relations among the members of the early Christian communities—accessibility of divine power as well as the relations of power and freedom. All these studies have contributed to a greater understanding of the dynamics involved in community relations in terms of the way Paul and the groups he established addressed patriarchy, fictive kinship relations, and relations to broader societal structures. There is also a

---

1. Marchal, *Politics of Heaven*, offers a bibliography that highlights feminist and post-colonial scholars, especially those that have an interest in Pauline studies.

diversity of opinion in assessing the significance of Paul's approach to power that is connected to the gospel that he preached. How does Paul's message of freedom affect relations to the Roman government? How does Paul's gospel of reconciliation affect ethnic-identity? How does Paul's preaching of equality affect gender equality?

Many of the current Pauline studies that address Paul and power continue to misconstrue Paul's understanding of power because of an underappreciation of his ascetical outlook and its concomitant radical reappraisal and relativizing of all power relationships. This ascetic outlook, in turn, is based on a perception of asceticism that has limited its purview to Christian monasticism during the third through fifth centuries CE and current studies remain relatively uninformed of the recent reassessment of asceticism over the last 25 years. As will be discussed more fully below, asceticism is "a phenomenon recognized across cultural, and disciplinary boundaries" that uses "a specific mode of bodily resistance as an analytical wedge for describing alternative or countercultural activity."[2] The ascetic consciously decides to live and operate outside of the conventions of society. Traditional practices of self-denial and withdrawal reflect aspects of resistance to "discourses of power framed in opposition to conventional discourse."[3] The practices of the early Christian groups that we know about from Paul's letters fashioned alternative ways of socializing along with different ways of viewing their world. Utilizing this more expansive conceptualization of asceticism invites a broader database for analysis including the early Christian communities that Paul founded. Utilizing this ascetic lens not only opens fresh avenues onto Paul's interactions with his converts, but particularly in his letter to the Galatians, it uncovers connections concerning the relation between an ascetic outlook and Paul's understanding of a new identity in Christ that assists in getting past the "hopeless morass of conflicting categories attempting to explain the relationship of law to faith and Jew to Christian to Jewish-Christian."[4] The precedence of the "new creation" (6:15) over other dominant classifications/identities suggests that Paul is operating from an ascetic outlook, which will be explored more fully below.

As an early participant and respondent to these questions Paul Jewett called Gal 3:27–28 the "magna carta of humanity" in *Man as Male and Female* (1975), which only highlights the constructedness of hermeneutical approaches especially within more conservative groups since his response challenges the hermeneutical methodology of traditional evangelical

---

2. Vaage and Wimbush, "Introduction," 4.
3. Kloppenborg, "Making Sense of Difference," 154.
4. Valantasis, "Competing Ascetic Subjectivities," 214.

methodology. Rather than begin with texts such as 1 Timothy 2 or 1 Corinthians 11 as ways to establish the problematics of female leadership as in some sense 'definitive', Jewett shifts the beginning point of the debate from a local problem to an aspiration or goal. Elisabeth Schüssler Fiorenza published what has become a classic theological reassessment of Christian origins and theology from a feminist perspective, *In Memory of Her: A Feminist Theological Reconstruction of Christian Origins* (1983), which offered a thorough and erudite reconstruction of the role of women and the origins of Christianity. In addition, the tradition of publishing commentaries on biblical texts such as Paul's letter to the Galatians continued during this period, but with increased attention to 3:28 and its importance in the debate of women's roles in the church. Of the many that could be discussed, I highlight F. F. Bruce's *Commentary on Galatians* (1982), because of his reliance upon Bartchy's dissertation in his hermeneutical remarks concerning 3:28, which is part of Bartchy's critique of the traditional exegesis of Gal 3:28. In addition, there is the classic study on Galatians, Hans Dieter Betz's better recognized commentary on Galatians (1979) that, in an extended footnote, questions how the commentaries could so quickly pass over Paul's words in v. 28 and dismiss the political implications when he can describe the social and political ramifications as revolutionary.[5]

Over the course of the last 50 years, the analysis of this text has continued with application of a wide and increasing variety of hermeneutical tools. Yet at the same time more and more interpreters follow well-worn paths of analysis. One path focuses on comparison—how do Paul's words compare with other pericopes dealing with interpersonal relationships in his other letters such as 1 Corinthians 7 and 11? Or comparisons of Pauline texts with the letters ascribed to Paul such as Col 3:11 and 1 Timothy 2? Another path focuses not primarily on the text from Paul's perspective but from the perspective of the early Jesus communities to whom Paul is writing. In Gal 3:28 are we reading words that Paul created or that he adapted from another source, perhaps sayings from the Jesus tradition or from traditions that were being created within and by other early Jesus communities? In other words are we reading words that Paul formulated from his own theological perspective or are we reading phrases that were created within one of the Pauline communities that Paul incorporates into his correspondence perhaps in an adapted format? A further path follows the hermeneutical trajectory from Gal 3:28 through the late first and second-century churches and beyond, further adapting and adopting Paul's words as they developed reading strategies that used texts to interpret different texts. What were the different contexts

5. Betz, *Galatians*, 189.

in which Gal 3:28 was read in the light of other texts such as Matt 19:12 or Gen 1:27 and to what effect? Another path looks at the agitators that had begun to influence some of the members of the Galatian churches toward incorporating circumcision as a part of perfecting their religious experience. The literature covering these paths is quite extensive so that any further pursuit, it can be argued, will produce diminishing returns. So this study focuses on a construction of a comparative category that I will call "eschatological asceticism" as a heuristic tool to analyze aspects of the cultural identity that influenced Paul and the Jesus groups under his influence.

State of Pauline Eschatological Research

Comparative studies that focus on different aspects of Christianity and aspects of Pauline communities in particular are neither unique nor new. Yet justification for this present study revolves around the use of recent research and theorizing regarding asceticism and the re-evaluation of Paul's eschatological perspective in his letter to the Galatians to raise questions regarding the inconsistent approach of the traditional view that understands Paul's preaching and ethics from a "realized" eschatological perspective.[6] This realized eschatological perspective has contributed to re-imaging and domesticating Paul's mission and message. Many readers of Paul's letters have noticed from an early period that, at least initially, Paul anticipated an imminent return of the Lord (1 Thess 4:13—5:11), yet it is also noted that over the course of Paul's career, his perspective evolves to encompass a present perspective.[7] How quickly Paul's views begin to evolve and how Paul combines his future hope and present experience (commonly identified as some type of realized eschatology) have been contested ground for quite some time. Rather than seeing the structure of eschatological thought as a "realized" or even as an "already and not yet" configuration, Paul maintains his future eschatological outlook as in such passages as Gal 5:5, 21 and 6:7–9.

This combination of research areas provides a basis for the present comparative endeavor—using the lens of "eschatological asceticism" to view

---

6. Similar criticisms can be leveled at other eschatological perspectives (i.e. Proleptic and Inaugurated Eschatologies) that propose various ways of accommodating an (early) Christian self-identity (their "standing" before God) based on the effects Christ's death in the present.

7. Significantly (from an evangelical perspective) Longenecker, after a brief history of Pauline development theories and their critical assessment, acknowledges there are "three shifts in Paul's thought about the resurrection of believers [that] do seem to be evident in his letters" in Longenecker, "Is There Development in Paul's Resurrection Thought?" 200.

Paul's words in Gal 3:28. The recent reassessments in terms of Paul's future eschatological concerns and his relativizing of cultural/religious categorical constructions raise many questions, such as why and how did Paul and the communities he influenced construct their group identities? Did community membership alter the way slaves and masters interacted? Were female community members accorded equal respect and access as male members? How close could relationships develop between Jews and non-Jews or in members of the opposite sex? Using asceticism as a wedge (especially recent scholarly focus on asceticism) offers a fruitful line of investigation into how Paul could envision communities that were neither slave nor free, male and female, Jew nor Gentile. Recent studies of asceticism that problematize traditional understandings of the ascetic seem to open up a different perspective.[8] For instance, asceticism viewed as an endeavor to create a new subjectivity (self-understanding) in response to dominant cultural codes creates an explicit construction of power that opposes those dominant expectations. As Paul can affirm, "For neither circumcision counts for anything, nor uncircumcision, but a new creation" (6:15, NRSV). *Contemptus mundi* is a complex and multi-faceted worldview that is much broader than the fourth-century monastic movement. Paul's continued focus on future hope from a sociological or corporate viewpoint as well as on an individual level both corroborates and complicates Paul's ascetical perspective that remained with him throughout his apostolic career. This appears especially to be the case in regards to his approach to inter-relational practices. To what extent did an eschatological ascetic worldview inform the praxis of Paul? Was Paul an innovator in this regard? To what extent did such a worldview contribute to a formation of the group identities of the Jesus followers that comprised the Pauline communities as they engaged first-century Mediterranean cultural issues?

Traditional Pauline studies have focused on his life (conversion, journeys, mission, and psychological make-up) and his letters to the communities he sought to influence (theological and ethical elaboration). Yet Paul is adamant that both his self-identity and his mission in life are intimately connected and that connection he designates his "calling" (Gal 1:11–17). His words describing his "call" have generated much tangential discussion, but it is an important hermeneutical strategy that Paul's own understanding and further reflection about his experience must remain in focus.[9] He interpreted his vision/call as a "revelation" (1:15–16) for the purpose of establishing a

---

8. This would comprise the scholars associated with the Asceticism Group facilitated by Wimbush, Vaage and Valantasis, as well as others.

9. Ashton, *Religion of Paul*, 29.

vocation of preaching the "good news" to the *ethne*, or nations (2:7). So his calling was set within the context of Second Temple Jewish eschatological discourse, a framework that intimately connected the destiny of the Jewish people and their relationship with the nations.[10] Hence, these two foci become determinative as Paul constructs his self-identity and career.

The bibliography alone that addresses the events revolving around Paul's calling is vast and the amount of secondary literature itself demonstrates the difficulty of uncovering what precisely happened on the "Damascus road."[11] But more clarity can be attained in terms of how Paul himself interpreted the event. Paul describes it as a prophetic turning point that changes his vocational direction (1 Cor 15:8). His apostolic career focused on preaching to the non-Jewish nations of the good news of Jesus Christ, yet this preaching also included a demonstration of signs, wonders, and powers. Paul uses the term "charismata" to describe this display of unusual abilities, but it is significant that Paul connects these manifestations of "spiritual power" with the good news that he preaches.[12]

The current construction of categories (soteriology, eschatology, Christology, etc.) used to analyze Paul's religious understanding functions as an interpretive tool that assists readers to process data by emphasizing certain data and delimiting other data. Traditional theological categories that have developed over the course of Pauline studies, while helping modern readers digest Paul's importance as an apostle and foundational thinker, have also resulted in anachronistic perceptions of his thought and misperceptions of his practices. In many ways Paul's image has been softened and domesticated (i.e. Paul as a systematic theologian) and some of his more bizarre behavior, from our perspective, that he demonstrated among the Jesus-communities he established (i.e. his personal use of heavenly languages, miraculous healings, visions, etc.) have been downplayed so that his message is taken seriously (1 Cor 2:4–5; 14:18). Paul combines these outward spectacles and his self-identity together as the results of his calling that he further links with the rather ambiguous concept of apostleship. Apostleship functioned for Paul as a comparative category that he uses to link his career and identity with the twelve apostles (1 Cor 15:4–11). Apostles had seen Jesus, been commissioned by him, and been given authority to preach, which invested them with a right to high esteem among the members of the communities. But while this served Paul as a connection with the original

---

10. Fredriksen, "Judaizing the Nations," 232–52.

11. The term Damascus Road is used as a shorthand for Paul's call/conversion encounter with Christ.

12. 1 Thess 1:5; 5:19–21; Gal 3:1,4, 5; 1 Cor 1:6–7; 2:4–5, 12; 4:20; 14:18; 15:32; 2 Cor 12:2–5, 12–13.

leaders of the Jesus movement, further comparative modelling, using the ascetic category, will assist modern readers more adequately to understand the counter-cultural aspects of Paul's gospel.

Current Theories about Asceticism

While Christianity spawned many ascetic groups and developed rich ascetic practices and traditions, it has not been until relatively recently that scholars have developed theoretical models of asceticism that can be used as tools of inquiry into constructions of world-views that inform the earliest Jesus communities of which Paul was a part. Beginning in the 1980's scholars from different fields began development on theoretical models of asceticism for use in comparative research on variegated cultural phenomena, including early Christian experience based on the good news of Jesus Christ. Since this scholarly focus produced much fruitful theorizing, I will only highlight two key representatives and their models.

Geoffrey G. Harpham theorizes a "loose" sense of asceticism that posits asceticism as a universal phenomenon found in all time periods of human history and in all societies including modernity.[13] Asceticism is usually associated with practices and forms of renunciation. While the term asceticism can "plausibly cover many aspects of early Christianity, the concept exceeds the ideological limitation of that culture and hence it may be beneficial to consider the phenomenon as 'sub-ideological' or common to all culture."[14] In other words, in this expansive sense, asceticism is the cultural way of describing the common feature that permits communication or understanding between cultures—"a kind of MS-DOS of cultures or the fundamental ground onto which the particular culture is overlaid."[15] While this expansive view of asceticism is universal in scope, it is more than an "idea." The enduring quality of asceticism, its transcultural character, follows from its ability to establish and maintain oppositions—resistance-within-tension. For instance, even though early Christian rhetoric emphasized single-mindedness, asceticism never completely condemned or condoned culture. There has always been a Christian ambivalence toward the surrounding culture—what Paul refers to as the "world." In this expansive view, asceticism encompasses any act of self-denial that purposively results in empowerment or gratification. Self-denial itself is only one aspect of resistance that is fundamental to asceticism. Readers of Paul are familiar

13. Harpham, *Ascetic Imperative*, xiii.
14. Ibid., xiii.
15. Ibid., xi.

with the way he discusses challenges in terms of oppositions—flesh and spirit, law and grace, law and gospel, works of the law and faith in Christ. Yet even these oppositions only touch the surface of what I am calling Paul's ascetic outlook. Paul's ambivalent self-understanding is quite complex also. He describes his gospel as "not man's gospel" (1:11, RSV), explaining that he did not "receive it from man, nor was [he] taught it, but it came through a revelation . . ." (1:12, RSV). On the other hand, he feels compelled to get permission to preach his gospel from James, Cephas, and John (1:6–10). In addition, even at the level of the construction of his calling and gospel Paul's framework is perceived in ascetic categories of oppositions-in-tension.

Building on some of Harpham's innovative insights, Richard Valantasis defines asceticism as "performances designed to inaugurate an alternative culture, to enable different social relations, and to create a new identity."[16] Asceticism from this perspective executes a social function that ultimately results in retraining the "ascetic self" to exist in the new culture that is being constructed.[17] In this sense, Paul's "imitation" language that some scholars have interpreted as the rhetorical strategy by which Paul seeks to distribute unequal power relations over his converts could be contextualized as navigating a refashioned self amid a group counterculture rather than constructing power relations based on a model/copy metaphor.[18]

Past investigations that have explored the relationship that might have existed between asceticism and Christian origins, whether with Jesus, Paul, or the earliest Jesus communities have been skeptical of any solid connection.[19] But almost all of these studies have used what Harpham calls a "tight sense" of the term, seeing asceticism as an historical ideology, "a product of early Christian ethics and spirituality."[20] Yet an expansive conceptualization from such scholars as Harpham and Valantasis opens up analysis of

---

16. Valantasis, "Social Function," 548. Valantasis's main criticism of Harpham is the binary structuralist categories that Harpham uses. As Valantasis' definition shows, he focuses on the integration of a person or group into a certain culture. The focus is the individual self and how the self creates practices and navigates behaviors that allow new constructions of the self and *perceptions* of the culture that the self is negotiating.

17. Valantasis describes this result in terms of four major social functions (550–51).

18 Some standard works that address Pauline issues for the perspective of power include Castelli, *Imitating Paul*; Marchal, *Politics of Heaven*; Kittredge, *Community and Authority*; Polaski, *Paul and the Discourse of Power* among many others.

19. It has been common to seek connections between Christian origins and asceticism through the community at Qumram as they incorporated ascetic practices and were in the area during that time. But many studies find no connection to Jesus and few connections to Paul. Fitzmyer, *Dead Sea Scrolls*; Murphy-O'Connor, *Paul and* Qumran; Ziesler, *Christian Asceticism*; LaSor, *Dead Sea Scrolls*.

20. Harpham, *Ascetic Imperative*, xiii

Paul's communications with his churches through ascetical categories, such as opposition-in-resistance. For instance, the ascetic ideal does not seek the denial or negation of any type of human impulse of self-fulfillment (i.e. as in desire), but rather it is the enactment of opposition through resistance to that opposition. In a passage, arguably Paul's earliest correspondence, 1 Thess 4:9, he describes the group's experience of acquiring knowledge using a *hapax legomenon*, "God-taught" (θεοδίδακτοι). Paul maintains the ambiguity of the dynamic between direct and indirect revelation as he can still "exhort you, brethren, to do so more and more" (10). It is also interesting that this term "God-taught" has a trajectory that surfaces periodically within ascetic texts later on (i.e., *The Life of Antony*). This ascetic category impacted every aspect of Paul's ethics and practice. Paul discusses his self-identity as an upstanding member of the people of Israel (Phil 3:5-6; Gal 2:15; Rom 11:2), but he also understands that his experience of knowing Christ relativizes his national/religious identity (Phil 3:7-8; 1 Cor 9:19-23). In his letter to the Galatians, Paul refers to the Galatians' common experience of receiving the gospel—"did you receive the Spirit by works of the law or hearing with faith?" (Gal 3:2). This question is the beginning of an extended discussion concerning the nature of his gospel to the "uncircumcised"—the relation that Jews and non-Jews have before God now that Christ has come. His gospel includes experiences involved in receiving the Spirit, but at the same time he maintains a positive view of the law as of divine origin and of faith as belief in Christ Jesus. This ambiguity or tension is also an aspect of his eschatological asceticism. Paul's gospel involves "receiving" the Spirit (and witnessing powerful signs), but also faith in Christ Jesus. Paul's negotiation of these two aspects in the midst of forming ethnically heterogeneous communities takes up major portions of most of his letters. What place does the law (works of the law) play either as an entrance requirement or status maintenance? This is not a simple answer for Paul; it is tied up with the divine purpose of the law and place of non-Jews in God's ongoing relationship with his people. This leads us to the second focus that is a critical foreground to understand Paul's words in Gal 3:28.

Paul's eschatological perspective in Galatians

Over the history of studying Paul's letters, scholars have developed different perspectives from which to interpret Paul's views of eschatology, yet these various views can be catalogued into three basic viewpoints. First, at the end of the nineteenth century two scholars, Johannes Weiss and Albert Schweitzer, formulated what David E. Aune calls "The Consistent Eschatology

Model."[21] This model closely connects ethics and eschatology in a framework of apocalyptic discourse with a near-future timetable culminating with the Lord establishing his presence and rule over all his creation. Schweitzer's particular spin on this perspective proposed that Jesus' prophetic announcement of this coming kingdom failed to come to pass, and the subsequent history of Christianity was based on a failed realization of the Parousia and the abandonment of an eschatological focus as time progressed. Second, in the early twentieth-century, C. H. Dodd, in reaction to this eschatological view, proposed a view of the parables of Jesus that recognized a future orientation, but also recognized that there were many other passages that were oriented toward the present experience of the kingdom of God. A third view developed in the later twentieth-century as an alternative to these previous views, which Aune calls "The Proleptic Eschatology Model."[22] This model proposed an eschatological perspective popularly described as "already and not yet" where the kingdom of God is experienced as both a present reality and a future expectation.[23] The important effect Paul's eschatological viewpoint has on the way he corresponds with the groups under his influence has subsequently been the subject of many publications. In Paul's letters that explicitly address eschatological themes (1 Thessalonians, 1 Corinthians, and Romans) most readers notice a development of his eschatological viewpoint from his earlier, while other letters (Galatians, Philemon, and Philippians) have encouraged an assumed future eschatological perspective. This assumed development of his eschatological outlook becomes extremely significant because Paul's eschatological viewpoint is used to corroborate many other important issues within the Galatian context—his "indicative-imperative" structure toward ethics, the relationship between Paul's theological discourse in chapters 3–4 and his ethical discourse in chapters 5–6, the complexity of the moral problem affecting the Galatian members, the composition of his opposition in the community, and most significantly for the present discussion, the meaning of "neither Jew nor Greek . . . slave nor free . . . male and female" (3:28). So what is Paul's eschatological viewpoint in Galatians?

In a recent study of Paul's eschatological perspective in Galatians, Yon-Gyong Kwon challenges the current consensus that interprets Paul's thought using the proleptic eschatological model. Following Paul's own perspective of the crisis in Galatia, Kwon summarizes three aspects of the Galatians' disposition that according to Paul are a part of the problem: their apostatizing

---

21. Aune, "Eschatology (Early Christian)," 2:599.
22. Ibid., 2:600.
23. Ibid., 2:599.

behavior, Paul's negative view of the Galatian converts' standing before God, and Paul's assessment that the Galatians' deviation in behavior is "jeopardizing their future hope."[24] If the crisis is as dire as Paul perceives it, does it make sense to assume the "already and not yet" perspective adequately explains Paul's injunctions? The consensus viewpoint answers affirmatively based on Paul's discussion of justification by faith (Gal 2:15-21; 3:6-29), which itself is based on readings from Romans.

In Gal 2:15-21 Paul presents his initial discussion of justification by faith in the context of the "Antioch Incident." In verse 16 he summarizes his argument invoking the verb δικαιόω three times, using a present passive, an aorist subjunctive, and a future indicative. The aorist subjunctive does not have a temporal sense, and the future indicative is part of a quotation from Psalms (LXX) 142:2. In verse 16a Paul's use of the present indicative is not as clearly an indicator of time as the consensus view would have us believe. The lack of specific time indicators along with the use of the generic term ἄνθρωπος strongly suggests that δικαιοῦται has a gnomic sense that is brought out well by the NEB: "But we know that no man is ever justified by doing what the law demands." In verse 16a the participle "knowing" establishes the ground for the rest of the pericope; so since there is no other indicator of time, it is best to interpret Paul's statement as a general theological claim about how justification is implemented—in a gnomic sense.[25] This specific text points away from viewing Paul's discussion of justification in temporal terms but to the "how" or means of justification—not "by works of the law," but "through faith in Jesus Christ." So if the purpose of Paul's elaboration of justification fails to provide definitive temporal signposts, are we left without any hints as to Paul's self-understanding regarding his position or status "in Christ"? Fortunately, there are several passages where Paul iterates his expectations and future hope.

When Paul does discuss temporal perspectives as in Gal 5:5, 21 and 6:7-9, it is interesting that it is with a future orientation. In 5:5 what is noteworthy is that the verb "eagerly waiting for" is used almost exclusively for eschatological anticipation.[26] It appears that when Paul moves from the means of justification to discuss temporal issues, he views justification as a future hope to be awaited. So coupled with Paul's statements regarding the present status of the Galatians, Paul's perspective is that the eschaton is still in the future. Over the course of Paul's career, his views would evolve and develop, including his eschatological perspective, in response to pasto-

---

24. Kwon, *Eschatology in Galatians*, 56.
25. Ibid.
26. Rom 8:19, 23, 25; 1 Cor 1:7; Phil 3:20.

ral issues and challenges. But at least from the perspective of his Galatian correspondence, he still looked forward to an imminent future hope of salvation. Coupling this with the close chronological relationship between 1 Thessalonians and Galatians, one could postulate that Paul maintains a consistent eschatological perspective, a hope that the eschaton, which includes the hope of righteousness, would be inaugurated in the imminent future (1 Thess 4:13–18).[27]

Galatians 3:28 from an Eschatologically Ascetical Perspective

Before Krister Stendhal's epic treatise published in 1958,[28] the consensus view interpreted the equality proposed in Gal 3:28 to be limited to the spiritual or ideological domain with no regard to social conditions. But Stendhal claimed Gal 3:28 proposed a rationale for equality of the sexes such that the subordination of women, as it had been traditionally conceived, was called into question. This programmatic treatise opened up a flood of studies that explored different aspects or ways that the early Jesus communities associated with Paul implemented this equality.[29] This torrent of scholarly activity also brought into stark contrast the disparate ways that Paul addresses issues relating to women's roles in the churches. For instance, he can proclaim "there is neither male and female" (3:28) to the Galatians. Later to the Corinthians, in response to apparent inappropriate attire in their assemblies, he can use a foundational sacred text (Genesis 1–3) to establish the social subordination of women. Alluding to her inferiority he writes, "For a man was not made from woman, but woman from man. Neither was man created for woman, but woman for man" (1 Cor 11:8).

Dennis R. MacDonald posits three ways that scholars have sought to deal with this apparent disagreement. One, Gal 3:28 advocates a radical and revolutionary social program, but then later Paul is unable to maintain this radicalism. Two, in Gal 3:28 Paul is not calling for social change, but simply acknowledging that both men and women have equal access to God's grace. Three, that Gal 3:28 is not Paul's own creation, but a quotation that

27. Since the consensus view of Pauline chronology places 1 Thessalonians as Paul's first letter written in the late 40s and Galatians as the second written around 49 or 50, a lack of difference regarding eschatological perspective between the two letters is appropriate. Betz, *Galatians*, 9–12, summarizing the different views relating to the date of the letter along with other bibliographical data gives a possible chronological range between the years 50–55.

28. Stendahl, *Role of Women*.

29. Hogan, *No Longer Male and Female*, 7–8.

he adapted and used from a baptismal liturgy that originated in the earliest Jesus communities. Consequently, the differences between Gal 3:28 and other texts that are less egalitarian stem from the differences between more liberating early Jesus communities and Paul himself.[30]

Galatians 3:28 is one of several pericopes within the Pauline corpus that may have roots in traditional pre-Pauline baptismal sayings (the others include 1 Cor 12:13 and Col 3:10-11). MacDonald summarizes the contrary opinion that views Gal 3:28 as the most original based on grammatical and contextual reasons—second person plural used in a third plural context, the fuller formula when only the Jew/Greek pair is directly germane.[31] He also notes the clear reworking of the formula by Paul for use in the Galatians context. Again he summarizes consensus reasoning that proposes a form-critical analysis that results in a proposed pre-Pauline baptismal formula as follows:

> ... you have put on Christ.
> There is no Jew or Greek.
> There is no slave or free.
> There is no male and female.[32]

If Paul did adapt and use a traditional text in 3:28, it raises several further questions: From what communities did it originate? Why did he use the formula in his argument? How did it augment his argument? Regarding the first question, MacDonald classifies the responses into three groups. One, some believe that though the saying did not originate with Paul, the formula developed within the Pauline sphere of influence. The saying is consistent with Paul's overall understanding of the transformative power of the gospel.[33] Two, the formula derives from Jesus community members outside of Paul's direct influence. Wayne Meeks proposes a scenario where Paul uses a tradition with which he is not completely comfortable agreeing with the "reunification of the sexes and return of the divine image," but not with the possibility of present attainment.[34] Three, scholars, including Walther Schmithals, claim that the formula is "pure Gnosticism."[35] Yet the farther afield that the formula moves from Paul's understanding of the gospel, the more difficult it is to appreciate why Paul would include such a saying.

---

30. MacDonald, *There Is No Male and Female*, 2-5.
31. Ibid., 5.
32. Ibid., 9.
33. Ibid., 9-10; Cf. Bruce, *Galatians*, 187.
34. Meeks, "Image of the Androgyne," 197.
35. MacDonald, *There Is No Male and Female*, 13.

From this listing of views regarding the origin of Gal 3:28 and use that Paul made of the formula, it is evident that there is agreement over the importance of the passage for social and interpersonal roles within the early Jesus groups. Disagreements surface in regards to issues of origins of the formula, extent of Paul's agreement with the formula, and ways that the formula was interpreted by the different Jesus communities. Can a model of eschatological asceticism assist informed readers to make sense of the Paul's words and discourse?

"Neither Jew nor Greek, neither slave nor free . . . neither male and female" (RSV) is embedded in a larger argument found in 3:26–29 where Paul argues for the equality of both Jews and non-Jews based on the fact that now that Christ has come, faith in Christ Jesus allows all to be sons of God (v. 26)—unity leads to equality. The central point that Paul presses here is that both Jew and non-Jew are Abraham's heirs according to the promise (v. 29) because they are united in Christ since they are both Abraham's "seed."[36] This is an important point as it is another step in his argument to establish equality in Christ grounded on family relations by means of adoption so that all are children of God.[37]

An Eschatological Ascetic Model

Paul's calling by God triggered a re-evaluation, a reconstruction of his self-identity (Gal 2:20–21) which also caused him to re-evaluate his social identity. He does not stop being a Jew, but his calling caused him to devalue any human construct that makes distinctions, limiting access to Christ, whether ethnicity, gender, and thus as sources of social identity construction (1 Cor 9:20–21). So on his way toward arguing for equality among Jew and non-Jew, he incorporates a common community tradition that de-emphasizes distinctions between Jew and non-Jew. Yet because of his imminent future eschatological perspective, he does not feel uncomfortable with broadening the categories to include slave relations and gender relations. Paul's de-emphasis of ethnic differences is grounded in his relativizing of ethnic identity markers such as circumcision. He can say, "for in Christ Jesus neither circumcision nor 'uncircumcision' is of any avail, but faith working through love" (5:6, RSV; cf. 6:15). Paul's eschatological views are also embedded in his ascetic outlook heightening the tension involved with his apostolic expectations. For instance, in Gal 4:11, Paul states, "I fear you (φοβοῦμαι ὑμᾶς) lest I have labored over you in vain" (my translation).

---

36. Heitanen, *Paul's Argumentation*, 134–38.
37. Atkins, *Egalitarian Community*, 180–90.

Translations like the NASB misrepresent Paul's intent as a fear for his converts. Rather it is a fear of his converts lest their poor performance impact his own outcome.[38] Similarly in 1 Cor 7:17–28 Paul understands these three pairs as linked "in a thought-pattern which represented Paul's understanding of a 'break-through' in Christ."[39] Paul's eschatological outlook propels his insistence that the human distinctions should be relativized as soon as possible. Paul's ascetic proclivity followed a coenobitic path of communal relationships with all likeminded followers of Jesus—a community of individuals united in their endeavor to deemphasize culturally generated social constructions of importance. Later monastic communities established rules of order that functioned as negotiations that held ideals and practices in tension. In his correspondences Paul is working out rules of order to negotiate the tension between life/freedom in the Spirit and living in a community/house church setting. In 1 Corinthians 14, Paul gives what amounts to ad hoc communal rules to negotiate the tension between freedom of the Spirit/use of charismata and forming/maintaining interpersonal relationships. Many commentators comment on Paul's restrictions on some female behavior when the community gathers, but what is not noticed as frequently is the fact that the women are only one of three groups that Paul calls out to admonish.[40] He is not theologizing on the women issue, but seeking to establish rules that when practiced will maintain the opposition-in-tension that all the members were struggling with in their gatherings.

Constructing and using models and categories carries with it both strengths and weaknesses. The value of any comparative project rests upon at least two factors: the ability of the models or categories to make sense of the most data while at the same time not occluding other difficult or problematic data. As a heuristic category, I have attempted in this essay to construct a category called eschatological asceticism as a way of making sense of one aspect of Paul's interaction with his first-century eastern Roman culture. Whether such a category helps to make sense of Paul's relations with his converts, fellow Jews and non-Jews, it is clear that he is a multifaceted and composite person involved in a complex ministry of establishing Jesus communities composed of both Jews and non-Jews throughout the eastern Roman Empire. His self-identity, his religion, his circumstances, and his career were all comprised of values, beliefs, and rules that demanded difficult

---

38. Gundry-Volf, *Paul and Perseverance*, 266. While most English translations follow the NASB in interpreting Paul's fear as for the sake of the Galatians, but there is a significant number that follow the KJB and ASB interpreting Paul's fear as fear for his own positionality.

39. Bartchy, *First-Century Slavery*, 174.

40. This is a point that was pointed out to me by Bartchy in private conversation.

choices and negotiations when they were brought together and implemented in the real world. The process of implementation is what I have sought to study through the category of eschatological asceticism.

Works Cited

Ashton, John. *The Religion of Paul the Apostle*. New Haven: Yale University Press, 2000.
Atkins Jr., Robert A. *Egalitarian Community: Ethnography and Exegesis*. Tuscaloosa: University of Alabama Press, 1991.
Aune, David E. "Eschatology (Early Christian)." In *ABD*, 2:594–609.
Bartchy, S. Scott. *ΜΑΛΛΟΝ ΧΡΗΣΑΙ: First-Century Slavery and the Interpretation of 1 Corinthians 7:21*. SBLDS 11. Missoula, MT: Scholars, 1985. Reprinted, Eugene, OR: Wipf & Stock, 2003.
Becker, Jürgen. *Paul: Apostle to the Gentiles*. Translated by O. C. Dean Jr. Louisville: Westminster John Knox, 1993.
Betz, Hans Dieter. *Galatians*. Hermeneia. Philadelphia: Fortress, 1979.
Bruce, F. F. *The Epistle to the Galatians: A Commentary on the Greek Text*. New International Greek Testament Commentary. Grand Rapids: Eerdmans, 1982.
Castelli, Elizabeth A. *Imitating Paul: A Discourse of Power*. Literary Currents in Biblical Interpretation. Louisville: John Knox, 1991.
Dunn, James D. G. *The Theology of Paul the Apostle*. Grand Rapids: Eerdmans, 1998.
Ehrensperger, Kathy. *Paul and the Dynamics of Power: Communication and Interaction in the Early Christ-Movement*. LNTS 325. London: T. & T. Clark, 2009.
Engberg-Pedersen, Troels. *Paul in His Hellenistic Context*. Minneapolis: Fortress, 1995.
Fitzmyer, Joseph A. *The Dead Sea Scrolls and Christian Origins*. Grand Rapids, Eerdmans, 2000.
Fredriksen, Paula. "Judaizing the Nations: The Ritual Demands of Paul's Gospel." *NTS* 56 (2010) 232–52.
Gundry-Volf, Judith. *Paul and Perseverance: Staying in and Falling Away*. Louisville: Westminster John Knox, 1991.
Hack-Polaski, Sandra. *Paul and the Discourse of Power*. Biblical Seminar 62. Sheffield: Sheffield Academic, 1999.
Harpham, Geoffrey Galt. *The Ascetic Imperative in Culture and Criticism*. Chicago: University of Chicago Press, 1993.
Hay, David M., ed. *Pauline Theology*, Vol 2: *1 & 2 Corinthians*. Minneapolis: Fortress, 1993.
Hietanen, Mika. *Paul's Argumentation in Galatians: A Pragma-Dielectical Analysis*. LNTS 344. New York: T. & T. Clark, 2007.
Hogan, Pauline Nigh. *No Longer Male and Female: Interpreting Galatians 3:28 in Early Christianity*. LNTS 380. London: T. & T. Clark, 2008.
Kittredge, Cynthia Briggs. *Community and Authority: The Rhetoric of Obedience in the Pauline Tradition*. Harvard Theological Studies. Harrisburg, PA: Trinity, 1998.
Kloppenborg, John S. "Making Sense of Difference: Asceticism, Gospel Literature, and the Jesus Tradition." In *Asceticism and the New Testament*, edited by Vincent L. Wimbush and Richard Valantasis, 149–56. New York: Routledge, 1999.
Kraemer, Ross S. *Her Share of the Blessings: Women's Religions among Pagans, Jews, and Christians in the Greco-Roman World*. New York: Oxford University Press, 1992.

Kwon, Yon-Gyong. *Eschatology in Galatians: Rethinking Paul's Response to the Crisis in Galatia*. WUNT 2/183. Tübingen: Mohr/Siebeck, 2004.

LaSor, William S. *The Dead Sea Scrolls and the New Testament*. Grand Rapids: Eerdmans, 1972.

Longenecker, Richard N. "Is There Development in Paul's Resurrection Thought?" *Life in the Face of Death: The Resurrection Message of the New Testament*, edited by Richard N. Longenecker, 171-202. McMaster New Testament Studies. Grand Rapids: Eerdmans, 1998.

———. *Life in the Face of Death: The Resurrection Message of the New Testament*. McMaster New Testament Studies. Grand Rapids: Eerdmans, 1998.

Lull, David John. *The Spirit in Galatia: Paul's Interpretation of Pneuma as Divine Power*. SBLDS 49. Chico, CA: Scholars, 1980.

MacDonald, Dennis R. *There is no Male and Female: The Fate of a Dominical Saying in Paul and Gnosticism*. Philadelphia: Fortress, 1987.

Marchal, Joseph A. *The Politics of Heaven: Women, Gender, and Empire in the Study of Paul*. PCritCon. Minneapolis: Fortress, 2008.

Meeks, Wayne A. "The Image of the Androgyne: Some Uses of a Symbol in Earliest Christianity." *History of Religions* 13 (1974) 165-208.

Murphy-O'Connor, Jerome. *Paul and Qumran: Studies in New Testament Exegesis*. Chicago: Priory, 1968.

Ridderbos, Herman. *Paul: An Outline of His Theology*. Grand Rapids: Eerdmans, 1975.

Roetzel, Calvin J. *Paul: The Man and the Myth*. 1998. Reprinted, Minneapolis: Fortress, 1999.

Schüssler Fiorenza, Elisabeth. *In Memory of Her: A Feminist Theological Reconstruction of Christian Origins*. New York: Crossroad, 1983.

Stendahl, Krister. *The Bible and the Role of Women: Case Study in Hermeneutics*. Facet Books 15. Minneapolis: Fortress, 1973.

Valantasis, Richard. "Competing Ascetic Subjectivities in the Letter to the Galatians." In *Asceticism and the New Testament*, edited by Leif E. Vaage and Vincent L. Wimbush, 211-29. New York: Routledge, 1999.

———. "A Theory of the Social Function of Asceticism." In *Asceticism*, edited by Vincent L. Wimbush and Richard Valantasis, 544-52. New York: Oxford University Press, 1998.

Vaage, Leif E., and Vincent L. Wimbush. "Introduction." In *Asceticism and the New Testament*, edited by Leif E. Vaage and Vincent L. Wimbush, 1-10. New York: Routledge, 1999.

Wimbush, Vincent L., and Richard Valantasis, eds. *Asceticism*. New York: Oxford University Press, 1998.

Ziesler, J. A. *Christian Asceticism*. Grand Rapids: Eerdmans, 1973.

15

Fresh Screwtape Revelations
How to Bash Gays with the Bible

John H. Elliott

A Bartchian Homage

Our honoree and I, along with other colleagues of the Context Group, have long pondered the appalling ways in which the Bible has been misused to justify gay-bashing and contempt for gays, lesbians, and transgendered folk. I have published on the issue of homosexuality and the Bible and have lectured on the topic to college audiences around the country.[1] For over a decade I served as a member of the Extraordinary Candidacy Project of the Evangelical Lutheran Church of America, which interviewed and approved gay and lesbian candidates for the holy ministry. This undertaking was at first independent of cooperation and approval of the ELCA and its official policy of non-ordination of gay and lesbian candidates. This position in the meantime has been modified to now approve such ordinations. So this topic is close to my heart and to my own pastoral ministry as well as the object of my theological research.

As a jazz artist of extraordinary style and perception, Scott, I hope, will dig the C. S. Lewis-like riffs on the subject.[2] I offer this piece of theological

---

1. Lectures at Pacific Lutheran University, Tacoma, Washington, 2/24/2007, and St. Olaf College, Northfield, Minnesota, 3/8/2011, lie behind the present essay.

2. More prosaic exegetical scores of mine on this theme are Elliott, "No Kingdom of God for Softies?"; and Elliott, "Hunting for Homosexuals at Corinth."

satire in celebration of Scott's retirement this year from full time teaching at UCLA, and with great appreciation for his work over the years as inspiring teacher, generous and supportive colleague, intrepid advocate of social justice, and loyal friend. *Ad multos annos*, lieber Freund!

Introduction

"There are some things that if you don't treat them with humor you would weep," the late famous journalist and renowned Texan, Molly Ivins (August 30, 1944—January 31, 2007) once remarked. Molly was an American newspaper columnist, political commentator, author and humorist supreme. Before Molly, a famous Oxford don during the Second World War took the same tack of gentle humor to address the evils of his day. So for this essay I will take my inspiration from Molly Ivins and C. S. Lewis as I reflect about hermeneutics, the Sacred Scriptures and bashing gays with the holy book.

As the topic of an essay to honor my good friend Scott and to reflect my own work as exegete and pastor over the past 48 years, I thought it should concern the issue of the Bible and hermeneutics, the Bible in culture and community, and use of the Bible today in addressing the challenging spiritual and moral questions of the day. How does one engage the questions of what the Bible *says* and what it meant 2000 years ago? How does one proceed from the Bible's meaning *then* to its meaning *now*—assuming that it has any meaning at all today? How does one determine what guidance these sacred scriptures have for the pressing issues of our time? Why is it essential to the canons of scientific interpretation to examine these texts in the light of their original contexts (historical and ecological and economic and social and cultural contexts)? How does the study of these ancient yet theologically canonical texts relate to the broader enterprise of a university and its study of religion in conversation with all dimensions of the human quest for knowledge and wisdom, and moral engagement with the world, the earth, the universe that are *our* context?

As I pondered a focus for these remarks, a gift landed in my lap beyond my wildest dreams. Amid the latest batch of Wikileak documents was a letter from an old source whose recent silence had misled us into thinking he was no longer an operating agent. Now we discover that he and his minions are indeed alive and kicking and up to their usual devilish skulldugery. This letter writer is a denizen of the Underworld with the moniker "Screwtape." He is an undersecretary of the Lowerarchy of the Infernal Regions. He is writing to his nephew, Wormwood, an apprentice demon and junior Tempter on an urgent issue of the moment. But before I share with you this latest communication from the Underworld, it is perhaps best if I give you a little background and put this communication into context.

Over half a century ago, in the midst of the Second World War, an Oxford University don in Great Britain by the name of C. S. Lewis published a modest little volume entitled "The Screwtape Letters." His full name was Clive Staples Lewis (29 November 1898—22 November 1963), but was commonly referred to as C. S. Lewis and known to his friends and family as "Jack," a marvelous moniker. As Britain struggled with its very survival under attack from Germany's relentless *Angriff*, and as an entire world at war anguished over the fate of humanity and ultimate questions of good and evil, Lewis imagined what evil might look like from the vantage point of the Underworld and the demonic forces of evil themselves. So he gave us a series of letters purportedly written by a certain demon named Screwtape, an undersecretary of the hellish Infernal Regions. Screwtape addressed these letters to his nephew, Wormwood, an apprentice demon and junior Tempter just learning the ropes. The correspondence offered unholy advice on methods for leading astray a gullible humanity and winning them over to the cause of sulfur, stink, corruption and evil. Christians and religious types come in for heavy mention. They are such easy targets of corruption, Screwtape reminded Wormwood. They are so focused on the sins and shortcomings of others that they have little awareness of their own addictions to evil and weakness to temptation.

Lewis's masterpiece has since become a classic and for decades was on the "must read" lists of books that challenge and change your life. More recently, however, it seems to have dropped off college recommended reading charts. Perhaps the newly discovered correspondence I share with you now will reintroduce some of you to an old acquaintance and entice others of you to the library and the C. S. Lewis section of the collection.

Now among the trove of material recently released by Wikileaks, it turns out, is a new letter from Screwtape to Wormwood. After all these years, we discover that these Underworld agents didn't vanish or give up the ghost, so to speak, but were operating and communicating under the cloak of secrecy and non-transparency as usual, much, let us say, like the American NSA or CIA. Screwtape, we learn, never totally quits the scene but just takes breathers for time to "reload," as he puts it. His latest missive to his nephew shows how he has kept abreast of the times and the issues of the moment. This latest instruction concerns the hot issue of gay-bashing in the public square, the military, Congress, and the churches, along with savvy advice on sexual issues in general and how to trap religious types in webs of lies and hypocrisies.

FRESH SCREWTAPE REVELATIONS

Discovery of this demonic advice is so timely since in recent months and years deep-seated opinions and attitudes toward gays, lesbians, bisexual and transgendered persons have slowly begun to change, at least among those of the younger generation. Even institutions are moderating policies and laws. But anti-gay prejudice continues to simmer unabated among the hoi polloi. Around the country and across the denominations, anti-gay fear and animosity show no sign of disappearing. Three years ago the Lutherans in general assembly reversed their policy banning gays and lesbians from ordination to the ministry, but anti-gay attitudes and battles over the Bible still fester, same sex marriages are still forbidden, and scores of congregations across to country are quitting their national church bodies over this issue. The situation in the Episcopal and Anglican communions is even more dire and threatens to permanently divide North American from African churches. In Uganda, gay-bashing urged on by fundamentalist Western missionaries has led to gay-hunting and the rampant murdering of gays. In the U.S., preachers and politicians continue to rail publicly against "faggots" and "dykes" and same-sex marriage, while many of them are devoured by deep-closeted self-hate. Despite polls of the military indicating an overwhelming desire to retire the policy of "don't ask, don't tell," the Pentagon drags its feet with worry about shower rooms and unit cohesion.

In view of these developments here in the U.S. of A. and abroad, it is quite fortuitous—dare we say divinely directed?—that a new Screwtape letter should turn up providing us with revealing inside information on how the demonic denizens of the Underworld have been working overtime in stirring the anti-gay pot and keeping fear and loathing alive. Thanks to Wikileaks we now know that this exchange of correspondence never was terminated and that over the past seventy years the Underworld has kept close tabs on the doings of Earthlings and their recent history of conflicts and wars, ethnic hatreds, bigotries, hypocrisies, and even how they use and misuse their sacred documents—from federal constitutions to holy scriptures—to push their own personal interests, stereotype and demean their opponents, and bash innocent victims in the name of God, the Bible, motherhood, and apple pie.

And now to the letter itself—a fresh communiqué from Screwtape—but also a fantasy on biblical hermeneutics, rhetorical satire in the vein of Scared Scriptless, and theological bigotry offered in the spirit and whimsy of C. S. Lewis.

Screwtape to Wormwood

My dear Wormwood,

I now wish to take up an issue, that, since my last correspondence, has begun to dominate the scene in those English-speaking countries that I previously mentioned. It is the matter of homosexuality, more specifically of homosexual persons and how they have become a rallying point of American fear-mongering and finger-pointing. The churches, I am happy to report, are leading the cause and even some African bishops of the Church of England are joining the fray. The big bugaboo for the churches is what to do about homosexuals seeking ordination, marriage, and an equal place in the political and ecclesiastical sun. Our interest, I remind you, is to fan the fires of ignorance, fear, and bigotry—and on this topic of gay, lesbian, bisexual, and transgender folk in the churches, to urge use of the Bible to denigrate, discriminate, and pontificate. Corralling Christians for the cause of discrimination and fear-mongering is especially gratifying since so many of them are pompous hypocritical liars who love to point judgmental fingers at others while secretly engaging in the very sins of which they accuse others—lavatory sex, hiring boy lovers, hiking the Appalachian trail, abandoning wives on their death beds—the happy list is endless. It is these hypocritical Christians who are among the most effective agents for illustrating the rot of religion and the phoniness of Jesus followers.

Now I know some of our novice demons have been asking why gays are being targeted as hideous sinners and why now. This is the kind of troublesome question we want to discourage and squash. Some humans link gay-bashing with the growing militarization and machofication of human society. Homos stand out as wimps and effeminates in the testosterone wars. Others think that when societies undergo lots of stress and strain, humans yearn for order and stability. They get nervous about people who don't fit the conventional categories and who defy traditional roles and rules. So they fear gays, lesbians, bisexuals, and transgender persons who seem to be neither complete males nor complete females but anomalies in between, neither fish nor fowl, like the unclean animals and unclean food, and other unclean persons of the Bible. Still others think that when homosexuals seek to marry and function in the church or the military like heterosexuals, marriage as an institution will collapse, ordained gays will run amok in parishes abusing children, and military fighting units will lose their precious unit cohesion. Actually, this is the latest in a long line of enemies of society that Americans have constantly manufactured over the centuries—native American so-called "savages" and "redskins," African slaves, Southern white trash, robber barons, immigrants, commies, pinko labor unions, Arab terrorists, Bible-thumping fundamentalists. My, how those Americans love to create outsiders and point the judgmental finger!

But never mind the question of why gays are under attack and why now. This is the kind of question our team wants to avoid. For allowing humans to raise it would only encourage them to think *rationally* about the issue. And that's something we want to head off at all costs. What we, the team from hell, want to do is to keep fueling the emotions over this matter and block rational thought as much as possible. This issue, furthermore, is really useful for diverting attention away from other human attempts to improve the human condition, such as curtailing pollution of the planet, reducing poverty and hunger, providing health care for all, and turning swords into plowshares.

The question that interests *us*, Wormwood, is how can we exploit this hunt for enemies and this antipathy toward gays—however irrational it might seem—for our demonic purposes; namely winning ever more souls for our infernal Father. How can we fan the fires of fear? How can we heat up the battle between gay-bashers and gay-boosters? How can we keep accusations from degenerating into rational discussion and respectful discourse? How can we subvert those claiming to follow the Prince of Peace and Teacher of love into wanting to kill faggots for Christ? How do we keep the hairy bipeds at one another's throats, remembering that ignorance, duplicity, division, and despair are Satan's fondest goals for humanity and that our job is to give our infernal leader what he wants.

An out-of-the-closet gay soldier once said, "I killed a man and they gave me a medal. I loved a man and they threw me in jail." This is the kind of confusion and irrationality we want to encourage, not just in the military but in the churches as well. Once homosexuality was called the "the sin that dare not speak its name." Now we want to redefine it as "the problem that never goes away."

Now when gays and lesbians, bi-sexuals and transgendered folk are seen as a "problem" rather than a fact of life, Wormwood, reference generally is made to only two authorities for assessing this so-called problem: natural law and biblical law. Homosexuality, its opponents have said, is forbidden by the Bible or it is against nature and violates nature's laws. The second claim is a fascinating one, but I am going to reserve it for another letter. It is regularly mentioned in Roman Catholic circles and only more recently by Protestants as well. In this communiqué, however, I'll focus on the Bible and how it can be used among Bible believers as a weighty club for bashing gays and fomenting strife in the pews. As far as the Christians and Jews are concerned, their Bible and their fuzzy thinking about Scripture is a wonderful instrument with which we can torment and confuse our patients and keep the fires of hatred glowing. This always takes Demonic jiu jitsu and hermeneutical dipsy-doodle on our part, but what a payoff!

As for the Bible itself, we don't want to poke fun at it or sneak it away from the Bible readers. Liberals and progressives have made this mistake and as a result millions of Bible believers have simply written them off as mockers of God's holy word. Instead, we want to encourage readers to love this book as the completely inspired and infallible and inerrant word of God, written in God's own language, English, and worthy of memorization and application to any and all daily situations. Still better, let it be celebrated as the *only* reliable source of information and wisdom—better than history books and science texts and egg-headed professors who are mostly doubting Thomases and atheists anyway. Let this holy book be put on a pedestal removed from all other literature and treated like a unique piece of writing dropped straight down from heaven and hot off the divine press, directed at 21st century Americans, with no historical or cultural conditioning whatsoever. No need for Hebrew dictionaries or Greek lexica or grammars. Let the Bible be viewed as pristine in its purity and absolute in its authority, applicable to each and every age and all circumstances. Let us support those who claim that whatever is in the Bible is absolutely true, and what is not in the Bible is not worth knowing. If readers think that God spoke to Adam in English or German or Spanish, all the better. Get people to understand "literal" as meaning "literalistic," which leaves no room for poetry, metaphor, native idiom, or cultural figures of speech. Have Bible instructors talk about the "heart" of Scripture or its "core message" and then let them pass off their own pet notions and peeves as being the heart and core of the Bible. Support the illusion that the Bible just needs to be read and followed, not "interpreted." Try to have all so-called biblical critics stigmatized as godless heretics, relativists messing with the sacred text and distorting it for their own liberal purposes.

Let us of the Underworld also encourage the notion that all biblical laws are eternally valid and to be enforced today, except where this is not the case. And don't let people figure out the difference. Prohibition of adultery, stealing, lying, murder—strictly verboten. But sex during menstruation, eating pork or shrimp, mixing wool and flax, dishonoring parents, committing adultery and divorce—let readers claim that these laws are antiquated and suspended—no problem. But intercourse between persons of the same sex—no way! Let Bible readers also think that all the Bible's values, even including institutionalized slavery, inferiority of females, and the physical beating of children, are biblical family values that should prevail today.

So rather than demean the Bible, we want to have it divinized. Get Bible enthusiasts to pit Scripture against science and find the latter wanting. Support their notions that the Genesis myth of creation is a piece of science and superior to the wacky "man-made" view of Darwin and his supposed atheistic theory regarding the origin of the species. Biblical devolution rather than evolution is the real name of the game, for the Bible says that all peters out and gets shorter or smaller since the great beginning; the earth is flat and the center of the universe; it is the sun that moves. Copernicus, Keplar and Galileo be damned, so to speak.

Here we can tap into that deep American prejudice against eggheads and intellectuals, science and rigorous theology. We want to convince the churchgoers that everything to do with sex is either obvious or dirty, and the less one knows in detail the better. This ostrich approach has worked marvelously when the issue has been war and politics, Iraq, Iran, and Afghanistan, Palestine, the 9/11 demolitions of the twin towers and building seven, not to mention clergy abuse and all other "secrets" Americans prefer not to know about. This attitude of selective ignorance is even easier to foist on Americans in the realm of sex. The principle of the know-nothings is to allow as little information as possible and no discussion in the classrooms and pulpits. This works out perfectly to our advantage, since an absence of clear thinking and a dimming of wits means lots of souls for Satan. The greater the ignorance, the better the confusion, and the more uncertainty, fear, and resistance to change in the status quo.

It's curious that American Christians seem never to have solved the Bible puzzle. They claim to "rightly interpret the word of God," and that they're really serious about not only the Bible but also the best rules and methods of interpretation. Despite the historical-critical method, which that monk from Wittenberg introduced—what's his name? I'm having a senior demonic moment—Martin Luther, I think—Protestant lay folk and many pastors never have gotten beyond a literalistic reading of the text. How lucky for our side! We just have to nurse along this biblical illiteracy. We do this by blurring the difference between a literal and a literalist reading of texts. A *literal* reading of the Bible, I remind you, Wormwood, acknowledges its prose and poetry, history and metaphor. On the other hand, a *literalistic* reading of the Bible leaves no room for symbolism and metaphor, and no place for historical or cultural conditioning. We want to support the literalists and their claim that they alone respect the Bible as the word of God and that they alone represent orthodoxy. And that all others demean the Bible and are mushy-minded liberals who have sold out to the secular culture.

Remember, the chief objective of our devilish endeavors is to make evil look like good, to co-opt rather than confront, to masquerade darkness as light, to divide in the name of unity. With respect to the Bible-thumping Christians, our aim is to get them to confuse "evangelical" with "fundamentalist," to deny history and change, to view their precious gospel as law, to wield their inspired Bible as a club, to employ their means of grace to enforce boundaries of division, to pass off their phobias as God's will.

The ultimate value for us of this battle over gays, ordination, and marriage is the hatred, rage, and despair it arouses in the humans and the splendid damage it does to communities, congregations, entire church bodies, military systems and the society as a whole. It is far bigger than how humans read and use the Bible. But the Bible as an instrument of religious and even cultural authority does have its useful divisive role to play and we should exploit this to the hilt.

Now in regard to the topic of homosexuality and the Bible, we need to do some fancy infernal footwork. One problem we face is that the words "homosexuality" and "homosexual" never appear in the original Hebrew and Greek texts of the Bible because they weren't invented as concepts until the end of the nineteenth century. So we need to keep Bible readers away from the original texts and totally reliant on modern translations that introduce these terms. The translations, too, are a problem since they don't agree among themselves, The result is that some translators of certain biblical texts opt for the rendition "homosexuals" where others read "sodomites," or "catamites," or "effeminates," or "softies," or "sexual perverts," or "sinners against nature," or *Lustknaben* or *invertidos*. With all these different terms, a savvy bible reader is likely to suspect that homosexuality might be more in the eye of the translator and beholder than in the original text.

Still another problem we are up against is that the biblical authors had no knowledge of what the modern humans call "sexual orientation." For the ancients, all acts were intentional conscious choices, not preferences due to sexual orientation. So even if there are Bible passages that speak of intercourse between persons of the same sex, the biological and psychological assumptions are radically different from modern views. Therefore it is best for us, Wormwood, to cover up all this distressing information, and to promote the view that the Bible speaks of homosexuality all over the place, and that specific terminology is just not that important. Even this ploy, however, runs into statistical problems, since of the 31,095 verses of the Bible only six verses have been mentioned as even remotely connected with same-sex sexual relations, and even these six are vague in their terminology and unclear in their meaning. Jesus never once referred to same-sex sexual relations; in the New Testament Paul is the only who does. I mention these distressing facts, dear nephew, just to let you know how tricky our manipulation of the Bible will have to be in order to shape it into an effective gay-bashing weapon. That said, let's look at the six usual suspects.

First off, you should also know, Wormwood, that the story about Lot and the city of Sodom in Genesis 19 isn't relevant at all. This story about Sodom being burnt to a crisp by the Heavenly Enemy is actually a problem for gay-bashers. For it is a horror story not about voluntary sexual relations among homosexuals, as claimed by some. It is rather about strangers arriving in the city of Sodom seeking hospitality and encountering instead residents who wanted to overpower and gang-rape them. Instead of receiving the aliens warmly, as the sacred code of hospitality dictated, the Sodomites sought to humiliate and emasculate the aliens. It was the violation of the sacred code of hospitality that was the sin of the Sodomites, not gay sex, and all the other references to Sodom in the Bible make this clear. A similar story of inhospitality and violence to strangers occurs in the biblical book of Judges (19:1–29). So with regard to this bogus Genesis text, Wormwood, just urge people to repeat the words "Sodom" and "Sodomite" as synonyms for "homosexual," with no questions asked. Since "Sodomite" today points both to gay sex and anal intercourse, we can create marvelous confusion with this passage and kill two birds with one stone, making people think that the story is really about God's punishment of gays and any persons, married or not, engaging in anal intercourse.

The word "abomination" is another great mantra and terrific tool for stigmatizing gays. The Bible readers get this term from two parallel verses in the Old Testament book of Leviticus, Lev 18:23 and 20:13. These verses forbid a male from "lying with a male the lyings of a female. It is an abomination." Leviticus is the biblical book about priests, animal sacrifice, and temple matters and the big issues of holiness and unholiness, clean and unclean, purity and pollution—categories into which Israel divided its people and animals and food and society. A major section of the book insists on the holiness of Israel and the difference between their holy conduct from the unholy customs of surrounding peoples, the Egyptians and the Canaanites. The two passages about male intercourse with males occur in sections prohibiting incest, sexual intercourse with females during their periods, sacrificing children to the god Molech, not eating unclean food, not cross-dressing, not copulating with animals, not consulting wizards and sorcerers and kinky stuff like that. Today, none of the Christian churches pay much attention to these primitive prohibitions—except for the taboo against male same-sex intercourse. The meaning of the words is not at all clear: "A male shall not lie with a male the lyings of a female. It is an abomination." Is this about *how* one lies, or *with whom* one lies. That astute theologian Jerry Seinfeld once said, "'A man shall not lie with a man as with a woman.' No man does that. When a man lies with a man, he lies about how much sex he's had. When a man lies with a woman, he lies about how much money he makes." But you, Wormwood, remember that it is the word "abomination" that gay-bashers glom onto here and that they apply to homosexuality today all the time. By all means encourage this selective way of using texts and particular words. Have Bible readers ignore issues of purity and pollution and all the other obsolete cultural prohibitions, and focus only on the two same-sex passages of Leviticus and the word "abomination." This juicy label can be used liberally to put down anything people don't like or approve of. Here's a wicked secret. Those of us in the know are aware that the word *abomination* in the Greek Bible, *bdelygma*, is what linguistic experts call an explosive and onomatopoetic term. It derives from *bdeô*, meaning "to fart." So the word *bdelygma*, translated "abomination," likely means a fart, a loathsome smell in the nose of God, or as they say today, "it stinks to high heaven." Your task, Wormwood, is to have the humans turn "fart" into a spiritual term for anything they imagine repugnant and offensive to their God. Then promote its use in denouncing gays and whomever else the nice people don't like—sinners and abominators one and all. This tactic works as well with liberals as it does with reactionaries.

The anthropologist Mary Douglas has taught the humans to study whatever is dubbed "abominable" in terms of the classifying system in place and anomalies that don't fit in this system. The sexual relations prohibited in the book of Leviticus are abominated because they do not fit the classification system, which presumes that sexual relations are for producing offspring and that males should not be using other males as passive females. Humans created with penises necessary for penetration are not to reduce themselves or other males to the condition of receptive females lacking penises and serving as objects of penetration. So intercourse between male partners of the same sex is anomalous, transgressing the system, and hence abominable. It poses great danger to the social order while simultaneously being a fart in God's nose. Now listen up, Wormwood, do not let the humans think along these anthropological lines, lest they consider actually changing the classification system they themselves have invented. Make them rather feel bound to all the rules and regulations of Leviticus and its ancient holiness code as an absolute and external expression of God's word and will. Of course, as I mentioned before, they will have to overlook and forget all the exceptions they make such as eating the unclean food of pork and shrimp and mixing linen with wool, and males wearing female clothes in stage productions and church liturgies, but you can surely help them with their hermeneutical amnesia.

As far as the New Testament is concerned, there are only three passages that critics of gays and lesbians have found for their cause. One is in Paul's first letter tot the Corinthians where he is criticizing the Corinthians for tolerating cases of immorality, incest, and injustice in the community (chapters 5–6). In the process, Paul gives a list of unjust persons who will not enter the kingdom of God: "immoral persons, idolaters, adulterers, thieves, greedy persons, drunkards, revilers and robbers" (1 Cor 6: 9–10). In this list he also includes *malakoi* and *arsenokoietai* (1 Cor 6:9). Sorry for the Greek, Wormwood, but it is not clear how these terms are to be translated and what activities they mean or imply. There's no agreement among the Bible translations which range from "softies" to "homosexuals" to "callboys" and "pederasts" to "catamites" and "abusers" to "effeminates," "Weichlinge," and *invertiti*. Our goal is to keep the Bible readers in the dark about these uncertainties of meaning, have them overlook the differences among translations and bible commentators, and just imagine that the terms refer to homosexuals and queer sex, and to stop with all the exegetical hair-splitting. The same word *arsenokoietai* occurs in a similar list of vices in the letter of 1 Timothy (1:9–10). In both lists, let your patients imagine that the actions of *malakoi* and *arsenokoieitai* are worse than all the other vices and are especially offensive to God. Nothing in the biblical texts indicates this, but the readers are so easily deceived since they know so little about how to read the Bible in context.

In his letter to the Romans, Paul, that turncoat who was once on our side, begins with a condemnation of *all* humans for alienating themselves from the heavenly Creator. As an instance of this alienation he paints a lurid picture of Gentile males burning with lust for one another and Gentile females doing the same. His point is that this excessive passion is punishment from God for their engaging in idolatry. This is a recurrent stereotype that Israelites had of Gentile outsiders—they were idolaters and slaves of sexual degeneracy in the practice of their idolatry. When Paul states that this behavior is also contrary to nature, he introduces another stereotype of what is natural and unnatural. In his world, "nature" was a flat and immovable earth around which a circling sun revolved. "Nature," for Paul and the biblical authors, created aggressive, dominant males and modest, subordinate females; male penetraters and female penetratees. "Natural" was moderation, not excessive passion. "Unnatural" was males growing long hair, shaving their legs, and dressing and acting like females, and females with uncovered heads, mouthing off in public and dressing and acting as males. "Unnatural" was blurring gender identities and transgressing the boundaries demarcating males and females, clean and unclean, Israelites and Gentiles. Gay-bashers can't get too far today on the argument from nature, since nature or rather, the humans' understanding of nature, is always changing. Much of what was considered natural two thousand years is no longer regarded as so today. Arguments based on nature rest on constantly shifting sand.

In these six Bible passages, Wormwood, it is likely that some kind of sexual activity between males was involved and in one case sex between females as well. But what kind of sexual activity, how it was performed, and why, is anybody's guess. In some instances, it is likely that abuse of boys by older males was the issue, but this is not certain. In any case, none of these texts is speaking of sex as a voluntary expression of love between committed persons of the same sex. Since this is the nature of the relationship under discussion in the churches *today*, the six usual Biblical suspects have no relevance. Their only significance today is to support the condemnation of any acts—sexual or otherwise—that involve the abuse and degradation of humans. This is the opinion of many exegetes, theologians and ethicians, Wormwood. But we have to get this opinion suppressed as an egghead argument out of line with tradition and the thinking of literalist believers everywhere.

A further problem of these texts for critics of gays today is not only their unusual and unclear terminology but also the biological, psychological, and social premises upon which the prohibitions are based. Since modern humans no longer share the premises, they can't really use the texts as moral guidelines today. Well, actually they do, even though it makes little sense. And that is just the way we want to keep it. Our best response is to delude our Bible-loving patients into thinking that a literalist reading of the Bible is holy and orthodox; then in literalistic fashion to read texts in terms of the present not the past. So Sodomites become homosexual lovers of anal intercourse, the abominations of Leviticus are equated with gay sex; the soft persons of Paul and males lying with males become homosexual perverts; and acts considered unnatural in the first century become crimes and psychological disorders today. Much of this wonderful distortion is incorporated in modern Bible translations and laws of states like Texas and Georgia. So encourage Bible readers to prefer arbitrary translations and take them as references to gay and lesbian partnerships today. Assure them that the historical, social and cultural differences distinguishing the modern age from the biblical period have no bearing on this topic.

Where same-sex sexual acts are mentioned in lists of vices, have your readers ignore the other sins and concern themselves only with supposed homosexual acts. Cherry-picking biblical texts to support subjective opinions has a long history among Bible readers, and is most useful with this topic as well. Also keep the discussion on homosexuality and the Bible focused on laws and rules understood as eternally valid. It's crucial that discussions and studies not wander off into areas of Scripture like the Sermon on the Mount, or Jesus' and Paul's teaching on love and compassion and new creation, and building the body of Christ, and viewing all moral issues through the lens of Jesus's death and resurrection. This will only lead gay-bashers to question the rightness of their position and possibly open the way to dangerous dialogue. Gayboosters, on the other hand, can be rapturously confused by the question of how to read those legal texts. So we want to keep all the biblical marbles in play while at the same time confounding the exegetical rules. Proof-texting, another form of cherry-picking, is also a usefully deceptive practice. Have people first decide what behaviors they don't like and then let them search the Bible for passages that support their prejudice. Let them hone in on sexual sins and avoid the accompanying condemnations of dishonesty, greed, envy, arrogance, hypocrisy, fear-mongering and hatred.

If gay-bashers abuse the Bible by subjecting it to a literalistic and absolutistic reading, gay-boosters often abuse the Bible in another way by abandoning the Bible altogether and finding other supports for their position. Our demonic team wants to encourage both tendencies. Let us help the bashers fine-tune their manipulation of Scripture, and let us assure the boosters that trying to find moral guidance in the Bible is a lost cause.

Have your patients, when beating their biblical drums, use a lot of German and Latin phrases that most people don't understand but make the speakers sound learned—like *scriptura ipsius interpres* or *sola scriptura*, or *vox populi vox Dei*, or *non illegitimi te carburendi* or *hier stehe ich, ich kann nicht sitzen*. Using foreign phrases is always an effective way of giving a scholarly veneer to simplistic opinions and biblical proof-texting. When the Bible quoters run into hard rational opposition, let them claim that their arguments are "clear to anyone who doesn't hate the Bible," and that their conclusions are "obvious to anyone with an open mind" or to all who are "open to the Spirit's guidance." "Divine Spirit" always trumps dictionaries and grammars in the war of religious wits.

By the way, Wormwood, also encourage belief in the notion that Jesus hung out only with men and never women—the Roman popes got this one straight—but that he nevertheless was a robust male with a circumcised penis (which, however, he never used for sexual purposes). Also get people to buy the notion that Paul the widower was rather a life-long celibate who hated sex and despised faggots. Anti-sexual sentiments on the part of Jesus and Paul go a long way toward fueling the healthy flames of sexual Puritanism and homophobia.

Now, nephew, let me review some general Hermeneutical Hints for Confusing the Issue, Compounding Conflict, and Muffling the Gospel. I have focused my foregoing remarks on the Bible because that's where the ammo is for most Protestant gay-bashers. Their marvelously simplistic mantra is "if it's in the Bible it's God's truth, and if it ain't there, I don't want to hear about it." You must aid them in keeping the Bible the central issue, along with its literalistic interpretation. Let them dismiss any scientific research into sexual orientation and any differentiation between orientation and act as unproven or scientific sophistry contrary to the Bible. For if sexual orientation is a biological given and genetically set, then the heavenly Enemy bears the blame for creating gays in the first place and the Bible prohibitions lose their punch. So we've got to seriously downplay all this unhelpful talk about "orientation," and instead support the idea that gay sex is always a free choice like the Bible assumes, and that it can even be reversed with psychological counseling. Congregations and Bible study groups are excellent venues for fostering this delusion.

Of course it is well-known in demonic circles that the opposition of straights to gays and lesbians is not ultimately about Bible texts, but about straights feeling threatened and endangered by gays. On this anthropologists like Mary Douglas have had something to say. The Bushmen of the Kalahari believe that if a man sits on the female side of the residence, his virility will be weakened. That's the sentiment we want to encourage when straights face gays today. Similar to the fear about AIDS, many straights fear "catching gayness" through physical contact. They fear becoming gay if in the company of gays. Hence their denial of the existence of gays in their congregations. Macho athletes like basketballer Tim Hardaway fear the shriveling of their cojones if in the locker room with queers. Through the presence of gay soldiers, military leaders fear the loss of "unit cohesion." Through the ministry of ordained gays, the churches fear the corruption of their children, as though gayness had anything to do with pedophilia! Through the marriage of committed gays and lesbians, congregations fear the crumbling of male to female marriage, as though their flood of divorces hadn't already undermined that institution! Our infernal propaganda program has been fantastically effective in planting seeds of fear and distrust everywhere. This fear-mongering has had unparalleled success for us in the U.S. of A. to compel cooperation and acquiescence with the Patriot Act and whatever is cooked up in war-intoxicated Washington. And it works well with church folk in the hinterland as well. You, Wormwood, have got to do your part in hyping this hysteria. So jack up that high fear alert and make no room for reasoned thought.

Concerned churchgoers and military families need to worry that the fundamental danger posed by gays and lesbians is not the things they do with one another, but a much larger danger—namely a collapse of the social order and the natural distinction of male and female, superior men and inferior women, those in charge and those taking orders. Gays and lesbians challenge these distinctions that give structure to the whole social system and natural order. Effeminate males and macho females, male pansies, fairies and sissies parading around like queens, dykes on bikes—they all threaten the order of conventional society, which church folk equate with nature and the will of God. These boundary-crossers evoke a visceral fear beyond the reach of reason. Bi-sexual and transgendered persons are viewed as even greater violations of the natural order. Again, these are the phobias that we want to feed and foster.

Gotta love that ostrich-head-in-the-sand approach of the military and its "don't ask, don't tell" policy—what a brilliant demonic maneuver! How exquisitely dishonest and hypocritical! And for several years, thanks be to Satan, the Christians have taken it over as well. Bully again for our side. There's nothing like dissimulation and prevarication for stoking the fires of confusion and animosity.

Speaking of the military, the language of combat and battle is a wonderful antidote to the saccharine sounds of love and compassion oozing from the bleeding hearts. So keep the accusations peppered with lingo of military shock and awe: "battling the evil of homosexuality"; "waging war against gays"; "liquidating enemy faggots"; "killing dykes for Christ." As for those claiming to be liberal or politically correct, let them keep repeating murky expressions like "tolerance" or "the right of individual choice" or "celebrating one's sexuality" but without ever asking what might be troubling the gay-bashers and Bible thumpers about in-your-face lifestyles and dangerous sexual choices. In other words, see to it that language is used not to convey the truth but to confuse meaning, not to articulate but to prevaricate.

See to it that the delicious joke about celibacy remains in force among those flip-flopper Lutherans. One of the Enemy's more notorious henchman, that *verückter* German from Saxony back in the sixteenth century—called for a reform of the church because of Rome's requirement of celibacy of the clergy. When Lutherans required celibacy of gay pastors in the twentieth and twenty-first centuries I could hardly stop laughing while Luther was probably revolving in his grave. Dear Wormwood, isn't that a tasty irony?

"Whenever a strict pattern of purity [like celibacy for priests or gays] is imposed on our lives," notes Mary Douglas in her famed study on *Purity and Danger*, "it is either highly uncomfortable, or it leads into contradiction if closely followed, or it leads to hypocrisy" [1984 ed., 163]. In the Lutheran church until very recently we have seen all three: personal uncomfortability, theological contradiction, and public hypocrisy. Another score for our side.

By the way, my compliments to your team of recruiters in Washington, DC. In Congress they have been turning out an awesome gaggle of gay-bashers for years now. These bashers haven't been as extreme as good ole Rev. Fred Phelps and his family who have been picketing liberal churches and U.S. soldiers' funerals with signs reading "Fag troops" and "God hates fags." But they have been most effective in stalling attempts to secure what the misguided call "gay rights" in the military, schools, and businesses. Some deserve extra credit for combining hypocrisy with lying. "I did not have sex with that woman" was a good start, even though Mr. Clinton's lie was about straight sex, however he defined "sex." Other Washington types, however, have raised sexual mendacity to a new laudable level—though it was quite nasty of Max Blumenthal in his expose, *Republican Gommorrah: Inside the Movement that Shattered the Party,* to have spilled the beans.[3] I am referring to such hypocrites as Senator Larry Craig of Ohio, the closeted gay and his sexual escapade in a public bathroom; and to gay-bashing Senator David Vitter of Louisiana and the exposure of his sex parties with high priced hookers and S & M dungeons. Then there is Newt Gingrich of Georgia who abandoned his dying wife for another lover; and Bob Livingston, short-lived speaker of the House, and Mark Foley of Florida, chairman of the House Caucus on Missing and Exploited Children—both of whom resigned in disgrace from office due to the uncovering of their own sexual adventures. Add to this list gay-bashing Senator Rick Santorum of Pennsylvania whose name is now being used in association with anal sex; and South Carolina Governor Mark Sanford who lied about his extramarital affair by saying he spent the weekend "hiking the Appalachian Trail." And then there are other closeted gays in Washington, like Jeff Gannon and Matt Sanchez., who have been outspoken against homosexuality. Then beyond Washington there is Ryan Dobson, divorced son of family-values spokesman James Dobson; and Rev. Ted Haggard, head of the National Association of Evangelicals, exposed by his gay lover; and Navy Captain Owen Honors of the USS Enterprise who showed films on his ship to his captive naval audience that demeaned and put down gays. What a splendid array of lying hypocrites in the halls of power! They all deserve places of dishonor in our infernal hall of shame. Our strategy for undermining respect for religious folk is paying great dividends—keeping the anti-gay preachers like Phelps and Haggard screaming and then seeing them exposed as self-righteous hypocrites. They bring wonderful discredit to the churches and suggest that all followers of Jesus are as hypocritical and mendacious as they are.

On the other hand, watch out for some of those Christians, who, like Luther and that guy who thinks of God as the Ground of Being, prattle on about paradoxes of saint and sinner, doubt and leaps of faith, cross and resurrection, sinning boldly and other drivel, which often lead to humility,

---

3. See Blumenthal, *Republican Gommorrah.*

toleration, compassion and compromise. Wormwood, have your patients eschew paradox and keep issues a matter of black and white. Black vs. white thinking promotes our agenda of moral absolutes with no grey areas. This, in turn, fosters illusions of orthodox certainty which then reinforces intolerance and judgmentalism—all hellish vices beloved by Headquarters.

Encourage the use of derogatory labels and slurs like those used by Anne Coulter and her ilk: "faggot, queer, sissie, pansy, dyke, bitches, hoes, sluts"—whatever offends most and does the most psychological damage given the situation. Also pump up the flow of vitriol and boorish behavior as gay-boosters and gay-bashers attack each other. This kind of incivility is great for inhibiting communication and forestalling mutual empathy. Always let supposed commitment to principle and to the Bible trump compassion and solidarity with sufferers.

The wonderfully devilish thing about this controversy is that both sides of the debate have their hands dirty. The gay-boosters often are as prejudiced and narrow-minded as the gay-bashers. In the churches each side declares the other to be depraved heretics who have taken leave either of their faith or their senses or both. We must do all we can to keep it that way. Above all, this means that we must vigilantly hinder any attempts on the parts of straights and gays, gay-bashers and gay-boosters, to move from accusation to conversation, to be willing to listen compassionately to one another with open minds and open hearts. When this happens, gays can hear where the Bible-lovers are coming from personally and not only theologically. And the Bible-lovers are led to feel the hurt and shame heaped on gays as they hear their personal stories. This is a typical ploy of the heavenly Enemy—to use compassionate listening to undermine prejudice and ignorance and to melt stony hearts. Parents hearing from their gay children their tearful fears of rejection, parishioners witnessing the courageous proclamation of good news by their out-of-the-closet gay and lesbian pastors, straight people witnessing how profoundly homosexuals can love one another—these are the dangerous moments that could lead to the disintegration of stereotypes and the healing of divided congregations and churches.

Compassionate conversation can also lead to personal soul-searching and the taking of personal inventories. This is another thing we want to discourage. The less boosters and bashers know about themselves, the less they examine their own fears and motives, the more they remain in the dark about what really motivates their revulsion against gays or their loathing of literalists.

This too could lead to a reading of Scripture with different eyes and with hearts open to words about God's reversing systems of human rules and values, words about a new creation, walls of separation removed, unity in the one body of Christ, and subversive acts of love and random kindness. This different way of reading the Bible would throw a monster monkey-wrench into our demonic project, Wormwood, so we need to keep it from happening. In the name of all that is unholy, fan the fires of prejudice and hate, undermine any attempts at mutual understanding and personal self-examination, and keep the conflict restricted to abstract issues of theology, tradition, and maintaining the status quo.

As I said to you years ago, "the Heavenly Enemy *really* loves the hairless bipeds he has created" and he really seeks the wellbeing and eternal bliss of all of them." The bipeds, however, are far less gracious than their Creator. They can't endure the thought of grace and life for all. They've got to have enemies to fight, feel better than, and condemn to our hot infernal region. Where would we be without such foot-soldiers for the Infernal One?

At the same time, I regret to say, Wormwood, the American public is trending toward condemning gay-bashing as unjust and wrong-headed. Elements of the religious and military establishments are shaping up as our last bastions of anti-gay discrimination and intolerance. So it is evermore urgent for our demonic team to strengthen the gay-baiting of Bible-thumpers and saber-rattlers everywhere. The last thing we want is for humans moved by that Gospel I just mentioned to overcome their fear-driven prejudice and do the right thing. Hell forbid!

If the Christian hairless bipeds are to join us in hell, we can't have them engaging in what their Bible calls "the fruits of the Spirit" such as love, joy, peace, patience, kindness, goodness, faithfulness, self-control" (Gal 5:23), actions that can't be legislated. These are just the kind of actions that undermine the hammering of homosexuals and the warring of gay-bashers and gay-boosters. Rather we have got to keep the religious folk focused on the law, civil and religious, especially its letter rather than its spirit. The more obsolete in its rationale, the better. But this is not too difficult because so many Christians actually prefer laws and rules to principles of morality and what some call the spirit of the Gospel. Rules and laws are much handier weapons for fomenting division and bashing opponents. The Gospel, on the other hand, speaks not in terms of absolute black and white, but, as I have already reminded you, in the language of paradox and ambiguity, of divine reversals of human perspectives and values, of trusting in a God who exalts the despised and enfolds the excluded, who creates physicality and sex not to be feared but embraced. It speaks through prophets like Jesus and Paul who, in addition to integrity and honesty, prized community-building love above all actions. If notions like this should start thriving in the churchly orchards, only the Enemy knows where it could lead. It might actually turn religious nuts into spiritual fruits.

So be ever vigilant, Wormwood, about this subversive Gospel and its fruits of justice, reconciliation, solidarity and peace. It poses a dreadful danger to productive gay-bashing, Bible-muddling, absolutistic thinking, and petrifying fear mongering—not just in the churches but across the cultural board. If not resisted tooth and nail, it could put a fatal crimp in our entire hellish operation. Forewarned is forearmed. And now onward and downward! In the words of one of our most successful above-ground operatives, "don't retreat, reload."

Your ever-sulpherous uncle,

Screwtape

Works Cited

Elliott, John H. "No Kingdom of God for Softies? Or What Was Paul Really Saying? 1 Corinthians 6:9–10 in Context." *BTB* 33 (2004) 17–40.

———. "Hunting for Homosexuals at Corinth: Exegetical Tracking Rules and Hermeneutical Caveats." In *From Biblical Interpretation to Human Transformation: Reopening the Past to Actualize New Possibilities for the Future. A Festschrift Honoring Herman C. Waetjen*, edited by Douglas McGaughey and Cornelia Cyss-Wittenstein, 3–43. Salem, OR: Chora Strangers, 2006.

Blumenthal, Max. *Republican Gommorrah: Inside the Movement that Shattered the Party*. New York: Nation Books/Perseus Book Group, 2009.

15

A House or a Tower?
Honor, Precedence, and the Contrasting Visions of 1 Peter and *The Shepherd of Hermas*

Drake Levasheff

WHEN ENGAGING IN ACADEMIC work the lingering questions often take on more significance than the answers. So it was with my time studying at UCLA, with Scott Bartchy as my doctoral advisor.[1] Whether it was in a tutorial, a seminar, or one of his lectures, I frequently left with fruitful questions that would stimulate my growth and learning.

Among the most poignant and profitable questions he asked me were those related to the early Christian understanding of God. "What do we mean when we use the word, 'God'?" "How do our conceptions of 'God' or 'divine power' compare to early Christian perspectives?" "How did early Christian understandings of divine power compare to that of their contemporaries?" Those fruitful questions inevitably led me to a significantly deeper understanding of the New Testament and early Christian history than I previously possessed.

Bartchy continues to enlighten his students and colleagues with similar questions energized by his conviction that Jesus of Nazareth, Paul of Tarsus,

---

1. When I began working on my doctoral dissertation, Scott Bartchy encouraged me to maintain a notebook of ideas that interested me but were beyond the scope of my project. The purpose was twofold: 1) to help me stay on track and 2) to serve as a repository of topics for future research. The idea for this article originated while I was working on my dissertation and is the fruit of his helpful advice.

and many early Christians believed that the God of Israel, Yahweh, was deeply concerned with the way his followers treated each other; he identifies this perspective as one of the early movement's core distinctives. Indeed, he often describes their understanding of Yahweh as a "community forming power,"[2] in contrast with Greco-Roman perspectives on divine power, which did not attach any relevance to how adherents treated one another. It is therefore fitting that this collection of essays in his honor would focus on one of the New Testament's most succinct and potent expressions of this perspective, found in Paul's letter to the Galatians.

Paul's assertion that in Christ and his community "there is no longer Jew or Greek . . . no longer slave or free . . . no longer male and female" (Gal 3:28)[3] speaks forcefully to the fundamental distinctions found in the New Testament world, presenting a provocative response to dominant cultural values in the Mediterranean world. The third pairing, which reconfigures how men and women relate in Christ, offers equal standing for all and reflects a rejection of patriarchy, which gave fathers unquestioned authority and unparalleled honor in their family. Outside the household, these values expressed themselves in a distinctly Roman hierarchy: elite men competed for the first place in their city from the seat of the Empire in Rome to the furthest province. It was in this environment that Rome's first emperor, Augustus, had assumed the first place in the capital city, at the apex of the Imperial hierarchy, and assumed the title of *pater patriae*; his claims to power and honor were unparalleled.

Paul of Tarsus was not the only one within the nascent movement to confront patriarchy, precedence and the associated hierarchical system that acquired honor and power for those at the top; the challenge did not originate with him, but is well-attested in Jesus' words and deeds. Bartchy has often emphasized that Jesus' emphatic statement of Matt 23:9, "Call no one your father!" represents a rejection of patriarchy.[4] His table-fellowship praxis and teaching were demonstrably anti-hierarchical and honor-sharing.[5]

---

2. Bartchy would often use this label to explain this perspective in his instruction and conversations with students at UCLA. For an example in publication, see Bartchy, "*Agnostos Theos*," 305, 312.

3. A quotations from Scripture are from the New Revised Standard Version unless otherwise noted.

4. Bartchy, "Who Should Be Called Father?" 138.

5. The canonical Gospels present countless examples of this, with Luke demonstrating special concern for the issue. See, for example, Luke 5:27–30 (// Mark 2:13–17; Matt 9:9–13); 7:34 (// Matt 11:7–19); 13:28–30; 14:7–14 (// Matt 23:12; Luke 18:14); 14:15–24 (//Matt 22:1–14); 15:1–2; 19:1–10. Bartchy's own contributions on this topic, "Table Fellowship" in the *Dictionary of Jesus and the Gospels* and "The Historical Jesus and Honor Reversal at the Table," demonstrates that Jesus' table-fellowship praxis and

Jesus of Nazareth's rejection of hierarchy and precedence is perhaps most poignantly expressed in Mark 10:13–31,[6] a passage that both Matthew and Luke appropriate.[7] It begins with Jesus welcoming little children, rebuking his disciples for hindering them, and then blessing the little ones (vv. 13–16) because "it is to such as these that the kingdom of God belongs" (v. 14).[8] Next, a rich man asks him how he may "inherit eternal life"; Jesus invites the man, who clearly had a grasp of the commandments, to follow him on the condition that he first sell all his possessions (vv. 17–22). The teacher then concludes by emphasizing to his disciples the rich's difficulty entering the kingdom (vv. 23–27), the blessings of costly discipleship (vv. 28–30), and the counter-cultural kingdom reality that "many who are first will be last" and "the last" will be "first" (v. 31).[9] Not only does verse 31 complete Jesus' teaching to his disciples about the wealthy and the cost of discipleship, but it serves as an emphatic conclusion to and summary of the passage as a whole (vv. 13–31): the kingdom belongs to infants, who are last in order of precedence (as the youngest) and offer nothing in terms of honor; but the wealthy, Torah-abiding man—who belonged in the first place and was the epitome of honor—goes away sad. Jesus proclaimed and embodied a kingdom that inverted traditional values related to honor and precedence.

As the movement spread throughout the Mediterranean, Jesus' early followers responded to the dominant cultural values of patriarchy, hierarchy, and precedence in a variety of ways. Some writings, like 1 Peter, reveal significant continuity with both Jesus and Paul in this regard. Others, like *The Shepherd of Hermas,* relax the challenge that Jesus and other followers presented by embracing hierarchical and patriarchal assumptions.

Comparing the perspectives of 1 Peter and *The Shepherd of Hermas* is particularly interesting because of the parallels between the two. Rome is the apparent origin of both writings.[10] At the same time, 1 Peter and *The*

---

teaching challenged dominant cultural values in this regard.

6. Jesus' challenge to Judean leaders and elites (see Mark 11:12–25; 12:1–12; Luke 13:31–32; John 3:1–21) and embrace of the insignificant and marginalized (see Matt 9:33–37; 11:18–20; 18:1–5; Mark 2:13–17; Luke 7:24–31) are well-attested within the canonical Gospels; these examples support the authenticity of the passage.

7. Cf. Matt 19:13–30; Luke 18:15–30.

8. This is not the only occasion in the canonical Gospels where Jesus uses children, who were unlikely examples of faith, to emphasize the inverted values of the kingdom (cf. Matt 18:1–5; Matt 9:33–37 // Luke 9:46–48). These examples support the conclusion that Mark 10:13–16 is authentic.

9. For Jesus' other uses of this saying, which seem consistent with his apocalyptic outlook and perspective on social structures, see Matt 20:1–16 and Luke 13:23–30.

10. First Peter makes an implicit claim of Roman origin, sending a greeting from "she who is chosen in Babylon" (5:13). The Roman origin of *The Shepherd of Hermas*

Shepherd of Hermas both employ building metaphors to describe Christian community. Finally, they possess temporal proximity, with both written by the last quarter of the first or the first half of the second century CE.

But, as noted, 1 Peter and *The Shepherd of Hermas* respond differently to dominant cultural values. In particular, while Hermas appears to embrace hierarchy and precedence, 1 Peter follows Jesus' critique of the dominant society's norms in this area, replacing a hierarchical, patriarchal vision of reality with one that offers the same high honor to all of those in Christ.

Shared Honor and the Rejection of Hierarchy in 1 Peter

First Peter's anti-hierarchical vision is first displayed early in the writing. The letter's compelling reimagining of reality begins by describing believers' relationship with Christ, the "living stone": "As you come to him, a living stone which has been rejected by men but is chosen and honorable (ἔντιμον) in God's sight, you yourselves as living stones are being built into a house(hold) of the Spirit (οἶκος πνευματικὸς) to be a holy priesthood offering spiritual sacrifices pleasing to God through Jesus Christ" (2:4–5, my translation). Humans rejected Christ, but he is defined by God's perspective as "chosen" and "honorable." As believers come to him, Peter envisions them as "living stones" that are "being built into a house(hold) of the Spirit." Commentators have disagreed about the meaning of οἶκος πνευματικὸς. The construction ("built" and "stones") and religious ("holy," "priesthood," "spiritual," and "sacrifices") imagery within the passage have led many to conclude that the phrase refers to a "house" that was the special property of God—a temple of the Spirit.[11] On the other hand, John H. Elliott has asserted based on the breadth and variety of domestic imagery within 1 Peter that οἶκος πνευματικὸς should be understood as a household of the Spirit.[12] The

---

is broadly accepted, based both on tradition from the Muratorian Canon and autobiographical details within the writing.

11. While the ritual imagery of the passage directs the focus to a temple, the passage appears to employ οἶκος with a generic temple in view rather than any particular one. Words such as "holy," priesthood," and "sacrifices" (2:5) are employed both in Judean and pagan religious contexts. Likewise, though οἶκος commonly refers to a house or a dwelling, both Judean and pagan sources use the word to describe their temples from time to time. Indeed, this concept of a temple as the dwelling place of a deity is evident in both the worship of Yahweh (McKelvey, *New Temple*, 5) and in Greco-Roman religion (Lanci, *New Temple for Corinth*, 91).

12. See, for example, Elliott, *Home for the Homeless*, 201. As evidence, Elliott lists a number of sections within the writing that emphasize the household metaphor: being built up (οἰκοδομέω, 1 Pet 2:5); household of the Spirit (οἶκος πνευματικὸς, 2:5); household slaves (2:18); live together (συνοικέω, 3:7); household stewards (οἰκονόμοι,

strong evidence for both perspectives has led Karen H. Jobes to conclude that Peter intended the double meaning; his action allowed him to integrate material with sacrificial imagery into a writing that repeatedly employed household imagery.[13] As the audience of 1 Peter came to Christ, the chosen and honorable stone, they were being built up into God's household and a temple belonging to the Spirit; in both cases, οἶκος πνευματικὸς bespeaks solidarity, equality, and mutuality. As will be evident, their membership in God's household, where God is father (1:2), would fundamentally change how they functioned within their own households.

In the verses that follow, Peter employs Old Testament themes to demonstrate that those who come to Christ share his honored status. He first references Isa 28:16, emphasizing that those who trust in Christ the "chosen and honorable cornerstone" would "certainly not be put to shame" (v. 6, my translation). Those who rejected the cornerstone would stumble and fall (vv. 7-8), but Peter's believing audience embraced an honorable identity: "But you are a chosen race, a royal priesthood, a holy nation, God's own people" (v. 9). Peter thus assigns to his audience a series of epithets previously employed to describe Israel; the terms bespeak honorable standing shared by his listeners. The first, "a chosen race," echoes Isaiah 43:20, which emphasizes that Israel's worth came because Yahweh had selected them. The remaining three reference Exod 19:5-6: "a royal priesthood" bespeaks the honor of access to Yahweh; "a holy nation" describes them as set apart for sacred purposes; and "God's own people" emphasizes their worth in relation to Yahweh's election and future vindication.[14]

First Peter's description of Christian community stands in stark contrast with the prevalent patriarchal and hierarchical perspective that dominated Mediterranean culture.[15] The writing envisions believers as a household and temple of the Spirit. Relationship with God the Father (1:1) shaped their behavior and motives, and every member shared the same, high honor; their membership in the family of faith (2:17; cf. 2:4; 4:17) defined them and superseded other attachments. This perspective is evident and sets the tone throughout the remainder of the letter.

This critical passage is followed by the instruction of 1 Pet 2:13-17, which itself provides the framework for the exhortations to slaves (2:18-20), wives (3:1-6), and husbands (3:7) that follow: "Submit yourselves for the

---

4:10); and household of God (τοῦ οἴκου τοῦ θεου, 4:17).

13. Jobes, *1 Peter*, 150.

14. Michaels, *1 Peter*, 109-10.

15. Balch's respected study of the domestic code in 1 Peter, *Let Wives Be Submissive*, illustrates the centrality of patriarchy in ancient Mediterranean discourse about civic and domestic life (21-80).

Lord's sake to every human institution, whether to a king as the one in authority, or to governors as sent by him for the punishment of evildoers and the praise of those who do right. For such is the will of God that by doing right you may silence the ignorance of foolish men. Act as free men, and do not use your freedom as a covering for evil, but *use it* as bondslaves of God. Honor all people, love the brotherhood, fear God, honor the king" (NASB). Since they had exalted status and belonged to God's household (4:18) where Yahweh was father (1:2), they were "free" (2:16) and were no longer defined by patriarchal, hierarchical relationships in their home and city.[16] They were still commanded to "submit" themselves to human institutions, but "for the Lord's sake" rather than as subjects (2:13). Thus, while much of their behavior toward outsiders would not have changed, they were no longer accountable to the same authorities: they were "free" with regard to human institutions (2:15) but were bound by their place in God's household to act as his "bondslaves" (2:16; cf. Mal 3:17, 18). The list of imperatives in verse seventeen outlines expected behavior in light of their high honor in Christ and membership in the household of the Spirit: they were to "honor" everyone, including their emperor; they loved "the family of believers" within God's household; and they feared God. These final four commands reflect a changing situation since everyone, not just the emperor, was to receive honor, and they were members of a new family.

First Peter's household code in the verses that follow reveals how much the situation had changed. While the Epistle's instruction in this area follows the *topoi* of Hellenistic writers and employs an apologetic approach similar to Josephus in *Contra Apionem* as David L. Balch has demonstrated,[17] it diverges from contemporary hierarchical assumptions. The audience addressed provides evidence that those assumptions had changed: whereas Hellenistic writers' household codes were generally written to fathers and masters, the exhortations in 1 Peter also provide instructions to slaves (2:18) and wives (3:1–6), recognizing them as individual moral agents. The admonitions to slaves to "submit" themselves to their masters (2:18) and wives to their husbands (3:1) are to be understood in this light; indeed, the imperatives to wives and slaves find their basis in "the fear of the Lord" (2:18) and God's presence (3:4), rather than the rule of male authority in the home.

---

16. Membership in God's household, where Yahweh was father, fundamentally defined them; the hierarchical, patriarchal relationships that had previously defined them did so no longer. Per Peter's instruction, believers still functioned in an honorable way in household and city not because masters, fathers, and husbands ruled them, but for their Lord's sake (2:13–17).

17. Balch, *Let Wives Be Submissive*, 81–109.

The instruction for husbands provides further evidence that membership in God's household, and not the hierarchy and patriarchy that was embedded in society, defined their actions and assumptions (3:7). Husbands are urged to "give honor" to their wives, behaving in a way that stands in contrast with that of their contemporaries. Significantly, the basis for the command is found in their shared, honorable identity as fellow heirs (συγκληρονόμοις) of eternal life; the assumption is that their relationship as siblings in God's household supersedes the rights a husband would claim over his wife.

Finally, everyone in the community is urged to "clothe [themselves] with humility toward one another" (5:5, my translation); commanding everyone to what was recognized as a notably servile characteristic within contemporary literature[18] assumes an anti-hierarchical perspective. Holistic analysis of 1 Peter indicates that while every member retains his or her role within society, all are instructed to treat each other in ways that reflect the shared, high honor each possesses as fellow heirs and living stones in God's house.

Ultimately, 1 Peter emphasizes that all are worthy of honor and challenges the patriarchy and hierarchy prevalent in the dominant culture; this would have far-reaching implications in society at large, since homes that were well ruled by men served as "a condition of" a well ordered society.[19]

Peter's conclusions about the high honor of every member of the community would have resonated with his audience in Asia. Peter perhaps emphasizes their high honor due to the fact that they were marginalized within their community, which he hints at throughout the letter: he addresses them as "aliens" (1:1; 2:11); he describes them as "scattered" similar to diaspora Judeans (1:2); and he indicates that they have encountered slander (2:12, 15), insults (2:23; 3:9), and reproach (4:14). To an audience who had experienced shame on account of their Christian profession, then, 1 Peter emphasizes that being in Christ was honorable. It is therefore extremely fitting that the writing greets them as "chosen aliens" (ἐκλεκτοῖς παρεπιδήμοις, 1:1, my translation)—an identification that recognizes both the difficulty of their situation and their honor in Christ.

---

18. Reumann, *Philippians*, 308–309. See especially Epictitus 3.24.56 and Josephus *J.W.* 4.9.2, which are among the countless examples provided by Reumann.

19. Balch, *Let Wives Be Submissive*, 35–36.

Honor Precedence in *The Shepherd of Hermas*[20]

Though also written in Rome, *The Shepherd of Hermas* addressed a different situation from that of 1 Peter. Carolyn Osiek's penetrating analysis of Hermas has demonstrated that the writing's intended audience consisted primarily of wealthy freedmen and freedwomen.[21] The narrator Hermas indicates that he was a freedman; the writing appears to have been completed by the middle of the second century.[22]

The Shepherd of Hermas provides its own perspective on Christian community in its third vision, which, like 1 Peter 2, identifies the church with a building. The similarities stop there, however, as *Hermas* envisions a different building, a different response to dominant cultural values, and a different idea of community.

The vision begins with Hermas encountering his guide, an old woman (*Vision* 3.1.2); the encounter provides insight regarding both Hermas and his community. She invites Hermas to sit down, and he first entreats her to have the elders sit first (3.1.8). When again she invites him to sit down, he chooses the place at her right hand, but is rebuffed and told to sit at her left (3.1.8–9). Hermas is "vexed" (λυπουμένου) at this response; his guide explains that the place was not given to him because it was reserved for those who had suffered for the sake of the name (3.1.9).

Hermas' disappointment as a result of the exchange and the final seating arrangement is what we might expect from a Roman male in the second century CE. Table fellowship practices and seating arrangements reflected societal divisions and conformed to the broader social reality.[23] When Hermas suggests that his elders sit first, he demonstrates appreciation of society's order: he was giving the first place to those who had precedence. At the same time, choosing the seat at her right, at the place of honor, is what we might expect of a dinner guest who wanted to enhance his own honor. Hermas' disappointment at being refused the seat of honor

---

20. All translations from *The Shepherd of Hermas* are from Holmes, Lightfoot, and Harmer.

21. Osiek, *Rich and Poor in the Shepherd of Hermas*, 55, 91–132.

22. While an exact origin date is uncertain, scholarly consensus dates it between 70 CE and the middle of the second century CE. Irenaeus' mention of the writing indicates that it could not have originated later than 175 CE.

23. Luke 14:7–14, for example, reflects this reality. In vv. 7–11, Jesus describes men's competition for the most honorable seats at a meal—competition for honor that occurred at table and beyond—and urges them not to exalt themselves through taking the best seats. Verses 12–14 note the role social divisions played in who was invited: Jesus exhorts his listeners not to invite relatives or social equals who could repay them, but rather those without the capacity to return the favor or enhance the host's status.

is also what one would expect: the woman has shamed him, and he feels the sting of this humiliation.[24]

The moment of shame becomes Hermas' teachable moment. The seat of honor is not for Hermas or his elders—those with precedence in his community—but for those who have suffered for the sake of the name (3.1.9). Hermas and so many freemen like him in Rome had their own conceptions of what was honorable, but through this one encounter, his perception of what and who was honorable had been challenged. The vision he was about to see would only reinforce this reorientation by reconfiguring the church hierarchy.

In the distance, the old lady showed him a tower being built upon the waters (3.2.3–5). The stones used and the order in which they are added to the tower define hierarchy within the church in a way that is ultimately consistent with Hermas' prior interaction with the old lady. First, square white stones are fitted together at the bottom, representing apostles, bishops, teachers, and deacons (3.5.1). Stones dragged from the depths are added next, representing "those who suffered for the Lord's sake" (3.5.2). Other, well-polished stones taken from the land and added to the tower represent those who have lived lives of purity (3.5.3). After a few others, round stones—the last ones added to the tower—are finally mentioned: they signify the rich, who are unfit to be added to the building until their wealth is removed (3.6.5–6).

The vision thus presents a hierarchical perspective to Hermas and his audience, but it was an outlook that they would not have expected. Those who suffered shaming persecution were elevated to a place of honor—this was a reality that had already confounded Hermas (3.1.9)! At the same time, the wealthy were the last to be added and that only after their wealth had been removed; they might have hoped to be one of the first, but ended up among the last (cf. Matt 20:16). Ultimately, *The Shepherd of Hermas* presents an ordered hierarchy, giving precedence and greater honor to apostles and church leaders, those who have suffered for the name, and the pure over the wealthy, who were added to the building last and only after their wealth was stripped off.[25]

---

24. While Hermas may have been wise to defer to his elders when first invited to sit down, he would have avoided the vexation he later experienced had he heeded Jesus' advice in Luke 14:8–10 and taken the inferior seat, the one on the left.

25. This perspective reflects the "great reversal" motif, which is evident in the New Testament. However, *The Shepherd of Hermas* diverges from teachings attributed to Jesus, Paul's writings, and, as I argue, 1 Peter, in its continued embrace of hierarchy.

Two Buildings—A Comparison

As noted, common ground exists between 1 Peter and *The Shepherd of Hermas*. Both writings are thought to originate in Rome in the first century of the Christian movement's existence. Both employ building metaphors to challenge dominant society's ordering of persons: 1 Peter rejects hierarchy by representing the church as a temple where every member is a living stone, built into Christ and worthy of the same high honor; and Hermas' fourth vision reorders hierarchy and precedence by revealing the church as a tower comprised of many stones where the wealthy are added to the building only after leaders, those who suffer for their profession, and the pure.

At the same time, 1 Peter and *The Shepherd of Hermas* part ways in the content of their critique of hierarchy and precedence: the former rejects these dominant cultural values while the latter simply reconfigures them.[26] But what accounts for their varying responses? Are these best explained by differences in genre? By the divergent backgrounds of their authors? Or by a consequential shift in perspective?

Comparing passages from different genres is always tricky; this is especially true when one of them is apocalyptic. The vivid imagery and otherworldly occurrences within *The Shepherd of Hermas* make interpretation and comparison especially challenging. How can one be sure that their interpretation of an apocalyptic passage is consistent with the author's intent? And how can a comparison involving one such passage be made with certainty?

Thankfully, in the case of the third vision of *The Shepherd of Hermas*, the guide provides the interpretation and states it explicitly: certain people have precedence over others when the church is constructed. First Peter, as an epistolary writing, is also explicit in the section in question, emphasizing the equal, high standing of those in Christ. The contrast is therefore obvious and the difference in perspectives cannot be explained away based on genre: 1 Peter views the church as a family with shared honor, while *Hermas* imagines it as hierarchical and ordered by precedence.

The question of authorship may shed some light on the differing perspectives of 1 Peter and *The Shepherd of Hermas*. Even if one concludes that the Apostle Peter was not the author of 1 Peter, the language and illustrations employed by the writing indicate that it was written by a Judean.[27] On

---

26. The radical vision of *The Shepherd of Hermas* should not be diminished, however; in a context where wealth was valuable to acquire and retain honor, *Hermas* asserts that wealth actually prevents one from gaining honor in God's eyes and position within the Church.

27. The author not only employs language that suggests a Judean origin (see, for

the other hand, as noted, *Hermas* appears to have been written by a Roman freedman. Such different authors can be expected to bring different assumptions about leadership, power, and community: in particular, while a Judean was part of a religious tradition that gave a place to both the great and the small[28] and called for justice and humility from leaders,[29] the freedman occupied a well-ordered world[30] with powerful fathers and masters, a world that depended on hierarchy and precedence to run smoothly.[31] In light of 1 Peter's rejection and *The Shepherd of Hermas'* embrace of these dominant cultural values, it seems possible that the social background of the writers influenced their response to those values since each writing mirrors the perspective of their culture of origin; the writing that more closely followed Jesus and Paul in challenging hierarchy and precedence is the one whose author shared their socio-religious context.

Conclusion

Jesus of Nazareth and his earliest followers challenged traditional values related to honor, hierarchy and precedence. As noted, one of the more poignant expressions of this is the declaration of Gal 3:28 by Paul of Tarsus that opposed the dominant culture's division of person related to ethnic identity, status, and gender. First Peter presents a similar challenge by emphasizing the shared honor of these early Christians and rejecting hierarchy and precedence; in particular, the metaphor of 2:4–9 describes the writing's audience as possessing high honor by virtue of being built into one temple and household in Christ.

The Shepherd of Hermas responds differently to the dominant culture than Jesus, Paul, and 1 Peter do. Rather than rejecting hierarchy and precedence, *Hermas'* vision of the tower reconfigures social structure: those who suffer for Christ gain honor and priority, while the wealthy are added only at the end after their riches are removed; later explanation of the third vision makes it clear that the wealthy should use their riches on behalf of

---

example, ἐκλεκτός [1:1; 2:4, 6, 9]; παρεπίδημος [1:1; 2:11]; διασπορά [1:1]), but also includes, among other things, allusions to the flood (3:20) and epithets used to describe Israel during the Exodus (2:9).

28. See for example Deut 10:17; 2 Chr 19:4–7; Ps 147.

29. See for example 2 Sam 12; Ps 82; Amos 5; Mic 6:8.

30. Indeed, Hermas would have been painfully aware of just how "well-ordered" society was: as a freedman, though free and no matter how wealthy he was, he could never escape the stigma of having once been a slave.

31. For further discussion of ancient Roman social dynamics, please see Lendon, *Empire of Honor*, or MacMullen, *Roman Social Relations*.

the poor (*Vision* 3.9.2–6).³² Though different from prior, canonical sources, the prophecy does part ways with dominant culture by honoring those who had suffered persecution and shaming those who would have been honored.

Both writings embrace, in continuity with Jesus of Nazareth, Yahweh's concern for community. Everyone was to have a place. Everyone had honor. And the wealthy would not enjoy pride of place over the poor, but were exhorted to use their power in service of the poor. Therein, Scott Bartchy's perspective is apt: in 1 Peter and *The Shepherd of Hermas,* as in so many other early Christian writings, God was concerned with how the members of his churches related and could rightly be described as a "community-forming power."

Works Cited

Balch, David L. *Let Wives Be Submissive: The Domestic Code in 1 Peter.* SBL Monograph Series 26. Chico, CA: Scholars, 1981.

Bartchy, S. Scott. "Table Fellowship." In *Dictionary of Jesus and the Gospels,* edited by Joel B. Green, Scot McKnight, and I. Howard Marshall, 796–800. Downers Grove, IL: InterVarsity, 1992.

———. "*Agnostos Theos*: Luke's Message to the 'Nations' about Israel's God." In *Society of Biblical Literature 1995 Seminar Papers,* edited by Eugene H. Lovering Jr., 304–20. Atlanta: Scholars, 1995.

———. "The Historical Jesus and Reversal of Honor at Table." In *The Social Setting of Jesus and the Gospels,* edited by Wolfgang Stegemann, Bruce J. Malina, and Gerd Theissen, 175–84. Minneapolis: Fortress, 2002.

———. "Who Should Be Called Father? Paul of Tarsus between the Jesus Tradition and *Patria Potestas*." *BTB* 33 (2003) 135–47.

Elliott, John H. *A Home for the Homeless: A Social-Scientific Criticism of 1 Peter, Its Situation and Strategy: With a New Introduction.* 1981. Reprinted, Eugene, OR: Wipf & Stock, 2005.

Holmes, Michael W., Joseph Barber Lightfoot, and J. R. Harmer. *The Apostolic Fathers: Greek Texts and English Translations.* 3rd ed. Grand Rapids: Baker Academic, 2007.

Jobes, Karen H. *1 Peter.* Baker Exegetical Commentary on the New Testament. Grand Rapids: Baker Academic, 2005.

Lanci, John R. *A New Temple for Corinth: Rhetorical and Archaeological Approaches to Pauline Imagery.* Studies in Biblical Literature 1. New York: Lang, 1997.

Lendon, J. E. *Empire of Honour: The Art of Government in the Roman World.* Oxford: Oxford University Press, 1997.

MacMullen, Ramsay. *Roman Social Relations, 50 B.C. to A.D. 284.* New Haven: Yale University Press, 1974.

McKelvey, R. J. *The New Temple.* London: Oxford University Press, 1969.

Michaels, J. Ramsey. *1 Peter.* WBC 49. Waco, TX: Word, 1988.

---

32. Other sections from the writing, such as the first parable and the parable of the elm and the vine, also urge the wealthy to use their wealth on behalf of the poor.

Osiek, Carolyn. *Rich and Poor in the Shepherd of Hermas: An Exegetical-Social Investigation*. Catholic Biblical Quarterly Monograph Series 15. Washington, DC: Catholic Biblical Association of America, 1983.

Reumann, John. *Philippians*. AB 33B. New Haven: Yale University Press, 2008.

17

Sibling Rivalries
On the Reception of *1 Clement* in Corinth

Cavan W. Concannon

IN THE LATE 1990S, I came to UCLA as a political science major. Not long into my freshman year I enrolled in a large lecture course on the history of religions taught by Scott Bartchy. Little did I know the long-term consequences of this decision! Not long afterward I began majoring in the study of religion, joining a small cohort of students who cobbled together a degree by taking classes in history, anthropology, classics, and other humanities departments scattered across North Campus. At the center of this web of courses was Scott, who helped me to navigate my way through this interdisciplinary introduction to religious studies and many of the strange adventures I have embarked upon since then. From advisor, to colleague, to part of my own fictive kin group, Scott has been one of the most important people in my life and continues to be an example to me of how to live a life dedicated to rigorous scholarship, embodied ethics, and love for all people as siblings and children of God.

One of the things that I associate most with Scott's work on early Christianity is the importance of kinship language.[1] Sibling language is almost ubiquitous in early Christian texts, particularly as a way of describing those

---

1. See, for example, Bartchy, "Undermining Ancient Patriarchy"; and Bartchy, "Who Should Be Called Father?"

who are on the "inside."[2] To explain the emergence of this way of structuring and naming group membership, Scott has noted the importance of Jesus' attacks on patriarchal family structure (e.g., Matt 23:9; Matt 10:34–37 // Luke 14:26) and Paul's rejection of ethnic, status, and gendered difference in Gal 3:28. For the Jesus of Matthew and Luke, only God can be called father. As children of God, those who follow Jesus are invited into a new family where old filial ties no longer hold sway (Matt 12:46–50 // Mark 3:31–35 // Luke 8:19–21 // *Thomas* 99:1–3; Matt 8:19–22 // Luke 9:57–62). For Paul, baptism into Jesus erodes the boundaries that separate Jew from Greek, slave and free, male and female.[3] No longer bound to traditional categories, those in Paul's communities address one another as "siblings" (ἀδελφοί).

In this paper, I want to follow Scott's interest in early Christian siblings and show how it can help us reconstruct the reception of *1 Clement* in second-century Corinth. Writing to the Romans, bishop Dionysios of Corinth mentions *1 Clement* in a quotation that has been used since Eusebius to argue for the use of *1 Clement* in early Christian liturgical practice (*Hist. eccl.* 4.23.11). While I will not dispute the importance of *1 Clement* for a large swath of early Christianity, in this paper I will read (and re-translate) Dionysios's reference to *1 Clement* in his letter to the Romans as part of the complicated kinship diplomacy between Corinth and Rome in the late second century.

Only fragments and summaries of Dionysios's writings survive in Eusebius's *Ecclesiastical History*. Among these fragments, we can see examples of how political, theological, and diplomatic issues between early Christian communities were negotiated using forms of kinship diplomacy. Caught up in a complicated diplomatic exchange with the Romans, Dionysios casts both churches as siblings descended from the same apostolic ancestors. By paying attention to the dynamics of kinship in Dionysios's letter to the Romans, we can see how sibling rhetoric could be deployed by those who were no longer Jew nor Greek, Roman nor Corinthian to resolve complicated disputes and explain longstanding connections.

1 Clement in Early Christianity

Scholarship has long noted that *1 Clement* is perhaps the oldest Christian text that was not eventually included in the New Testament canon, dating

---

2. See Hellerman, *Ancient Church as Family*. In Paul's undisputed letters, for example, ἀδελφ- based words appear 118 times.

3. It should be noted that Paul may not have envisioned the erasure of gender difference "in Christ." See, for example, Martin, *Sex and the Single Savior*, 77–90.

to sometime between 80 and 140 CE.⁴ The creation of the canon was a fluid process that moved at different paces and in different directions in Christian communities throughout the Mediterranean basin.⁵ At various points of time, *1 Clement* seems to have been given the same kind of authority as the texts that ultimately came to be a part of the New Testament. We can see this in a number of places. Hegesippus, an early Christian traveler, knew *1 Clement* and visited Corinth when Primus was bishop (*Hist. eccl.* 3.16; 4.22.1-2). Polycarp makes use of the text in his letter to the Philadelphians.⁶ Clement of Alexandria quotes frequently from *1 Clement* as a source of authority.⁷ Clement operated with a very flexible notion of the texts that were authoritative for Christian theology, which underscores both the importance of *1 Clement* in Alexandria and the fluidity of the canon in the early third century. Eusebius is ambivalent about the authority of *1 Clement*. The text does not make it into Eusebius' list of the materials that he thinks are recognized or agreed upon (ὁμολογούμενος) as authoritative by the churches (3.25.1-7); however, there are several places in the Ecclesiastical History where Eusebius, nonetheless, refers to *1 Clement* as "recognized" (3.16.1; 39.1).⁸ The *Apostolic Constitutions* (47.85) adds 1 and 2 *Clement* to Athanasius' list of canonical books found in his 39th Festal Letter.

First Clement also makes it into a number of biblical codices, where it is included among other New Testament texts. It is included after Revelation (leaves 159-68) in the fifth-century codex Alexandrinus.⁹ A fragmentary Coptic papyrus of the fifth century contains *1 Clement* and portions of James and the Gospel of John. A Syriac codex of the twelfth century includes 1 and 2 *Clement* after the Catholic Epistles. The scribe who copied the manuscript

---

4. On the date, see Welborn, "On the Date of First Clement," 34-54; Welborn, "The Preface to 1 Clement," 197-216; and Bowe, *A Church in Crisis*, 2-3. McDonald notes that 1 Clement probably predates some of the works that were included in the New Testament (*The Formation of the Christian Biblical Canon*, 237).

5. McDonald, *The Formation of the Christian Biblical Canon*. Even after the canon became somewhat fixed in the fourth century CE, Bovon has shown that many early Christian authors retained a category of "useful" books between canonical and rejected books (Bovon, *New Testament and Christian Apocrypha*, 318-22). On this threefold categorization, see Eusebius, *Hist. eccl.* 6.25.

6. Lightfoot, *Apostolic Fathers*, 1.149-52. Ignatius also may allude to *1 Clement* in Rom 3.1.

7. For a list, see Grant and Graham, *Apostolic Fathers*, 5-6.

8. We should not be surprised by such slippages, considering Eusebius is clear that even the disputed writings are considered authoritative by many (γνωρίμων δ' οὖν ὅμως τοῖς πολλοῖς [3.25.3]).

9. This version of *1 Clement* lacks 57:7—63:4.

divides both letters up according to the same lectionary pattern as the rest of the materials found in the codex.¹⁰

From this very rough sketch of *1 Clement*'s reception in early Christianity, it is clear that the letter was widely known and widely used as an authoritative, if not occasionally canonical, text, a testament to the fluidity of the canon itself.

1 Clement in the Letters of Dionysios of Corinth

One of the earliest references to *1 Clement* comes in the letters of Dionysios of Corinth, which have been preserved as summaries and fragments in Eusebius' *Ecclesiastical History* (4.23). Dionysios mentions *1 Clement* in a letter that he has penned to the Romans (4.23.11 [see Fig. 1, no. 2]):

> τὴν σήμερον οὖν κυριακὴν ἁγίαν ἡμέραν διηγάγομεν, ἐν ᾗ ἀνέγνωμεν ὑμῶν τὴν ἐπιστολήν, ἣν ἕξομεν ἀεί ποτε ἀναγινώσκοντες νουθετεῖσθαι, ὡς καὶ τὴν προτέραν ἡμῖν διὰ Κλήμεντος γραφεῖσαν.¹¹

Translators usually render the Greek text in English in such a way as to imply that *1 Clement* is regularly read during worship in Corinth. We can take, for example, the popular translation of Paul L. Maier: "We read your letter today, the Lord's Day, and shall continue to read it frequently for our admonition, as we do with the earlier letter Clement wrote on your behalf."¹² Such translations render Dionysios's letter as evidence for the use of *1 Clement* in church worship in the second century, thereby further extending its authority in early Christianity. These translations are supported, and perhaps also unknowingly influenced, by Eusebius's framing of the quotation. Before he quotes from Dionysios's letter, Eusebius writes that the quotation he is about to list shows that "it had been the custom from the beginning to read [*1 Clement*] in the church" (δηλῶν ἀνέκαθεν ἐξ ἀρχαίου ἔθους ἐπὶ τῆς ἐκκλησίας τὴν ἀνάγνωσιν αὐτῆς ποιεῖσθαι).¹³

In what follows, I want to challenge this reading (and translation) of the quotation by paying attention to the larger context surrounding

---

10. For a discussion of these codices and other early translations and version of *1 Clement*, see Grant and Graham, *Apostolic Fathers*, 3–4; and Ehrman, *Apostolic Fathers*, Vol. 1, 28–30.

11. For the text of Eusebius, I have made use of Eusebius, *Eusebius Werke, Band II, Teil I: Die Kirchengeschichte*. Translations are my own except where explicitly stated.

12. Maier, *Eusebius*, 159.

13. Eusebius elsewhere notes that *1 Clement* was used in churches in many places from earlier times to Eusebius's own (*Hist. eccl.* 3.16).

Dionysios's letter to the Romans. This letter negotiated a delicate diplomatic situation between Corinth and Rome. By paying attention to the tensions between the "siblings" in Corinth and Rome, we will see that Dionysios's mention of *1 Clement* is not actually evidence of the letter's authority and use in second-century Corinth, but an ambivalent reference to an earlier admonition sent from Rome to Corinth.[14]

Looking at the Larger Context

Dionysios was bishop in Corinth in the second half of the second century. During this time, he wrote letters to a number of Christian churches in the eastern Mediterranean, some of which eventually found their way into a collection that Eusebius had in his library.[15] Dionysios's letter to the Romans is the only letter from the bishop's collected writings that Eusebius quotes.[16] The three quotations (4.23.10–11; 2.25.8) help us to understand something of the complicated kinship diplomacy that the letter addressed. In Figure 1, I have listed the three quotations as they appear in Eusebius.

From these fragments, we can learn a few things about the rhetorical situation to which the letter was addressed. First, Dionysios sent the letter to the Romans during the time in which Soter was bishop (4.23.10). This places the letter sometime between 165 and 174 CE.[17] Second, in the

---

14. This argument should not be read as a critique of the prevailing opinion that *1 Clement* was an important and widely used early Christian text. The development of the Christian New Testament was never a linear process nor was its eventual form ever predetermined. *First Clement* did make it into some New Testaments, was used as an authoritative texts in other places, and was seen as helpful and important by a broad swath of early Christians. On the importance of looking at the broader context when assessing fragments of ancient writings, see Magny, "Porphyry in Fragments," 515–55.

15. Of the letters that were found in this collection, seven were addressed to cities (Sparta, Athens, Amastris, Nicomedia, Gortyna, and Knossos) and one to a woman named Chrysophora (*Hist. eccl.* 4.23). A testy letter in reply to Dionysios and penned by the bishop of Knossos, Pinytos, was also found in the collection available to Eusebius. For more on Dionysios and his letters, see Nautin, *Lettres et écrivains chrétiens des IIe et IIIe siècles*, 13–32; Kühnert, "Dionysius von Korinth," 273–89; Noethlichs, "Korinth—ein 'Aussenposten Roms'?," 232–47; and Concannon, "Ethnicity, Economics, and Diplomacy in Dionysios of Corinth," 145–69.

16. A fourth quotation from Dionysios (*Hist. eccl.* 4.23.12) is often assigned to the Roman letter, but I think it more likely this was lifted by Eusebius from the cover letter to the collection, explaining why it was put together in the first place.

17. On the date of Soter's career as bishop, see *Hist. eccl.* 4.22.1-3 and Irenaeus, *Haer.* 3.3.3. Lightfoot, *Apostolic Fathers*, 155, suggests 166–174 CE as rough dates for Soter's career. So also Lampe, *From Paul to Valentinus*, 397–406. Carrington, *Early Christian Church*, 2.192, suggests 166–178 CE.

letter Dionysios thanks the Romans for a gift that was sent to Corinth (ἐφό-δια [4.23.10]) and also praises Soter for his role in organizing the collection. Why the Corinthians needed this financial gift from the Romans is unclear;[18] however, the letter and the gift that it references show that there had been earlier interactions between Corinth and Rome. We can envision this interaction in four stages. First, the Corinthians experienced some event or found themselves in a situation in which they needed financial help. Second, word reached the Roman churches, either through an embassy sent from the Corinthians or through other intermediaries, of the Corinthians' need. Third, a collection was raised and sent to Corinth along with a letter from the Romans. Fourth, Dionysios wrote a letter back to the Romans thanking them for their gift and responding to the contents of their letter. It is the letter sent by the Romans, of which we have no summary or quotation, that Dionysios compares to *1 Clement*.

Though the contents of the Roman letter are unknown, Dionysios offers us a vital clue to its contents in the word that he uses to parallel it with *1 Clement*. Dionysios describes the Roman letter as an "admonishment" (νουθεσία [*Hist. eccl.* 2.25.8]; νουθετέω [4.23.11]). Though it came with a generous gift, the Roman letter evidently sounded similar to the harshly worded attack on Corinthian strife in *1 Clement*. To reimagine the Roman admonishment, we thus have to go back to *1 Clement* and its intervention in Corinthian affairs.

First Clement addressed itself to what the Roman church at the end of the first century saw as dissension in the Corinthian church, namely, that several of the church's presbyters had been expelled.[19] Clement took the position that the church in Corinth needed to reinstate the presbyters and learn humility and obedience (1–3; 44:1–6; 57:1–7; 63:1). Though the deposed presbyters are the specific issue addressed in the letter, *1 Clement* is more concerned with the dangers of stasis in the community.[20] *First*

---

18. See Concannon, "Ethnicity, Economics, and Diplomacy," 155–62, for discussion about possible reasons the Corinthians needed help from Rome.

19. Welborn, "Clement, First Epistle of," argues that the text is a piece of deliberative rhetoric that offers counsel (συμβουλή) (58:2). Welborn notes that the opening of *1 Clement* stages a fictive *captatio benevolentiae*, where the author attempts to position himself and his community alongside the Corinthians in dealing with similar problems of strife. As Welborn rightly notes, this is probably fictive, allowing *1 Clement* to offer a harsh judgment on Corinthian strife while pretending as if this admonition ought to apply equally to both communities.

20. Bowe, *A Church in Crisis;* van Unnik, "Studies on the So-Called First Epistle of Clement," 115–81. To this end, the letter offers counsel through exhortation (προτροπή) and warning (ἀποτροπή), in keeping with the standard forms associated with deliberative rhetoric (Welborn, "Clement, First Epistle of").

Clement describes its goal as an "admonishment" (νουθεσία [7:1]), which is designed to show the Corinthians that their actions were the result of jealousy, envy, strife, and sedition (3:1) and elicit repentance and the readmission of the banished presbyters. Though the letter begins with attempts to show Roman sympathy with the Corinthians, by the end the rhetoric encouraging concord and unity becomes more threatening. In 59:1, the author suggests that those who do not take his advice are transgressing and in danger. The Romans have even sent three witnesses to ensure that their advice is followed (63:3; 65:1).[21] As Barbara Ellen Bowe has argued, *1 Clement* perceives the situation in Corinth as a dangerous theological problem: "The actions of the Corinthians are sinful; they transgress God's law; they invite eternal damnation; and finally, they bring blasphemy upon themselves, and even upon God."[22]

Though it was originally addressed to a situation of perceived ecclesial *stasis*, those who read *1 Clement* later saw it as directed toward larger ends. Irenaeus, noting the context of Corinthian *stasis*, summarizes the main content of the letter: "The church in Rome sent a most suitable writing to the Corinthians, which instructed them toward peace, renewed their faith, and announcing the tradition which he had recently received from the apostles" (*Haer.* 3.3.3, following the Greek text quoted in Eusebius, *Hist. eccl.* 5.6.3).[23] Irenaeus reads *1 Clement* as both an intervention against stasis *and* as a primer on ecclesial harmony, faith, and apostolic tradition. As an admonishment, it is possible that the Roman letter to the Corinthians may have struck similar themes to *1 Clement*.

While *1 Clement* deployed deliberative rhetoric to persuade its Corinthian audience, Dionysios focuses on its claim to offer admonishment (7:1) when comparing it with the Roman letter. To bring out the way in which Dionysios compares the two letters, I suggest an alternate translation that conveys the subtle resistance that I will argue constitutes the major thrust of Dionysios's letter to the Romans: "Today we passed through the Lord's holy day, in which we read your letter. When we read it we will always have

---

21. Bauer, *Orthodoxy and Heresy in Earliest Christianity*, 95–129, suggested that these witnesses came with money to help grease the wheels in Corinth. Welborn, "The Preface to 1 Clement," 213–16, shows that this procedure was a regular activity for arbitration in the ancient world.

22. Bowe, *A Church in Crisis*, 32.

23. ἐπέστειλεν ἡ ἐν Ῥώμῃ ἐκκλησία ἱκανωτάτην γραφὴν τοῖς Κορινθίοις, εἰς εἰρήνην συμβιβάζουσα αὐτούς, καὶ ἀνανεοῦσα τὴν πίστιν αὐτῶν, καὶ [ἀναγγέλλουσα] ἣν νεωστὶ ἀπὸ τῶν ἀποστόλων παράδοσιν εἰλήφει. The addition in brackets is based on the Latin version, which remains extant and which uses the term *annuntians* here. The Greek is only extant in Eusebius's citation, which ends more abruptly than the Latin and likely cut out the participle governing the last phrase.

an admonishment (νουθετεῖσθαι) as also with the former [letter] written to us through Clement" (*Hist. eccl.* 4.23.11 [Fig. 1, no. 2]). We learn from this quotation that when it was received the Roman letter was read in public when the Corinthian assembly gathered together for its regular meeting on the Lord's Day. Dionysios describes the Roman letter as an admonishment similar to that which one would read in *1 Clement*, the content of which was familiar to the bishop. Admonishment remained on Dionysios's mind since elsewhere in his letter he again describes the Roman letter as an admonishment (νουθεσία [*Hist. eccl.* 2.25.8, see Fig. 1, no. 3]). *First Clement* is not an encouraging letter, but a harsh and long-winded rebuke of what it perceives as Corinthian strife. That the Roman letter reminds Dionysios of *1 Clement* can give us some sense of the harsh tone that it must have taken, even as it accompanied a gift that showed the generosity of the Roman churches.

A letter of admonishment written to the Corinthians from Rome would have placed Dionysios in an awkward position. On the one hand, the gift that the Corinthians had just received made Dionysios and the Corinthians clients to Roman patronage. Second, the admonishment itself posed a threat to Dionysios' leadership and authority, since implicit in the overall stance of the Roman letter was the idea that Rome could and ought to intervene in the affairs of other churches. By paying close attention to Dionysios' rhetoric, we can see how he navigates this complicated rhetorical situation.

Dionysios employs two interconnected strategies in his response to the Roman letter and gift. First, he stresses the interdependent, familial relationship between Corinth, Rome, and other Christian communities, thereby making the Corinthians' "debt" a family affair and not one between a patron and client. Second, he emphasizes the parallel apostolic origins of the Roman and Corinthian communities, which places the two sees on equal authoritative footing. For Dionysios, the Corinthians are obligated neither to treat the Romans as their patrons nor to cede theological and political authority to them.

Dionysios frames the Roman gift within a history of Roman benefaction. According to Dionysios, the Romans have "from the beginning" (ἐξ ἀρχῆς and ἀρχῆθεν) acted as benefactors (εὐεργετεῖν) to many of their "siblings" (ἀδελφοί) in other cities (*Hist. eccl.* 4.23.10 [Fig. 1, no. 1]). The Roman tradition of benefaction is described in specifically financial and material fashion. The Romans have, through their actions, relieved the poverty of those in want (τὴν τῶν δεομένων πενίαν ἀναψύχοντας). The gifts that they provide are described as ἐφόδια, which has a distinctly financial and material resonance.[24] Dionysios also mentions Roman provision of supplies to the siblings

---

24. While the term can describe provisions provided to armies or ambassadors for

in mines.²⁵ In each case it seems that the Roman church has been known to provide monetary and material support to other churches. Peter Lampe may be right in suggesting that "Rome apparently had the largest budget and the most members able to donate" of the earliest Christian churches.²⁶

The language of benefaction places the Roman collection within the discourse of patronage, but Dionysios quickly moves to shift the discussion to a Roman *ethos*. The phrases ἐξ ἀρχῆς and ἀρχῆθεν frame the benefactions of the Roman church as practices that they have engaged in since the beginning. Not only that, the recourse to origins is meant to indicate that such benefaction is a continuing practice that defines the community's relationship to other Christian communities. These disparate communities, spread out over the geography of the empire, are linked together by Roman benefaction.

Their financial links are described in the language of kinship, particularly the term "siblings" (ἀδελφοί), which Dionysios uses three times.²⁷ Though a common label in early Christian writings, the title of "siblings" implies a measure of equality between the Corinthians and the Romans. As siblings, the transfer of capital would not fall so cleanly within the confines of patronage. The various Roman gifts to other communities become, not acts of benefaction that create clients for a patronal Rome, but acts through

---

sustenance during travel (as in Josephus, *Ant.* 6.47, 176, 243, 254; 9.251; 14.362; *J.W.* 1.267; Deut 14:15 (LXX); Philo, *Heir* 273), it can also refer to provisions necessary for the maintenance of life (as in Demosthenes, *Tim.* 67; Aeschines, *Tim.* 172; Plutarch, *Arat.* 6.5; Josephus, *J.W.* 6.194, quoted also by Eusebius in *Hist. eccl.* 3.6.17).

25. The reference to Christians in the mines is puzzling. Harnack, *Mission and Expansion of Christianity*, 2.255 n.1, took this reference to refer to Christians in the mines of Sardinia, since Hippolytus (*Ref.* 9.12) mentions that there were Christians who had been punished by being sent there during the bishopric of Victor (189–99 CE). Hippolytus himself was said to have similarly been sent to the mines in Sardinia, according to the Liberian Catalogue, where he is listed as a martyr. Whether we can read this later situation back into Dionysios's time is unclear. Dionysios seems to be referring to something that has become a common practice and also seems to imply that Roman disbursement of funds for Christians in the mines could be distributed through local communities (Osiek, "The Ransom of Captives," 380 n. 38). Whether these practices were aimed at aiding Christians condemned to the mines or freeing Christian slaves who worked in the mines is also unclear. If the former, it is possible that funds like those given by the Romans could be used to secure the release of condemned Christians through bribery, as, for example, in the case of Callistus in Hippolytus, *Ref.* 9.12. The example from Hippolytus is discussed in Osiek, "Ransom of Captives," 380–81. On Roman mines and their administration, see Greene, *Archaeology of the Roman Economy*, 146–48. On the history of sentences to work in the mines into Late Antiquity, see Gustafson, "Condemnation to the Mines," 421–33.

26. Lampe, *From Paul to Valentinus*, 101.

27. A fourth instance of the term occurs in *Hist. eccl.* 4.23.12, which may or may not have been part of the Roman letter.

which siblings generously share resources with one another. The Romans have not just given to the Corinthians but to siblings throughout the world and they have done so, not out of particular political interests, but because this is what they have always done.

This ancient practice of Roman benefaction is presented as an ἔθος of the Roman community. As such, by giving money to the Corinthians, the Romans "have guarded the custom (ἔθος) of the Romans handed down from their ancestors."[28] The work that bishop Soter, as minister of external affairs, put into organizing the collection has added to (ηὔξηκεν) this legacy,[29] making him analogous to an affectionate father with his children,[30] a clever reference to 1 Cor 3:6–7 and 4:15.[31] The ancestral custom of the Romans dictates that they must give to their siblings in need, making the Corinthian gift one of many acts of euergetism that the Romans are obligated to perform.

The rhetoric that Dionysios employs constructs the Roman church as a group whose euergetism is rooted from its very foundation in a particular ethos. The Roman gift is both praised and normalized. Further, in giving to others the Romans give to siblings, communities of equal standing and status. Even more, because they are given to siblings, the gifts sent out by Rome do not make the Romans patrons of client churches. Such behavior is praiseworthy but it is also the kind of thing one ought to do for family members in need. That Soter is likened to a benevolent father underscores the point: he deserves praise for going above and beyond what was required and is a father only insofar as he works to help others and provide hospitality. Soter is less a patron because of the gift than a good example of what Gerd Theissen long ago called "love patriarchalism."[32] What appears as flattery is a subtle insinuation that

---

28. πατροπαράδοτον ἔθος Ῥωμαίων Ῥωμαῖοι φυλάττοντες (*Hist. eccl.* 4.23.10).

29. Literally, the verb refers to making a plant flower, as Paul uses it in 1 Cor 3:6–7.

30. ὡς τέκνα πατὴρ φιλόστοργος (*Hist. eccl.* 4.23.10). The "fatherly" character of Soter is also potentially related to his hospitality toward Christian siblings who come to Rome from abroad.

31. As Lampe, *From Paul to Valentinus*, 402–3, notes, Soter's actions indicate a self-confidence in the authority of his position, in that he increases the foreign aid of the Roman church. Dionysios himself seems to recognize the increasing importance of the bishop in charge of the Roman church's external relations, calling him both a father and an "honorable bishop" (μακάριος ἐπίσκοπος [*Hist. eccl.* 4.23.10]). But, like other bishops before Victor (189–99 CE), Soter is probably still only one among many bishops in Rome. This is in contrast to Bauer, *Orthodoxy and Heresy*, 114, who thought that Soter was the first monarchical bishop of Rome.

32. Theissen, *Social Setting*, 107. Theissen writes, in reference to what he sees as the appearance of this ethos in the writings of Paul, "This love-patriarchalism takes social differences for granted but ameliorates them through an obligation of respect and love, an obligation imposed upon those who are socially stronger. From the weaker are required subordination, fidelity and esteem" (107).

the Roman church ought to continue to give such financial assistance to other siblings in imitation of the traditions of their forebears.

Having argued for the appropriateness of the economic interdependence between siblings, Dionysios constructs a shared history of the Roman and Corinthian communities as a means of asserting Corinth's apostolic heritage (*Hist. eccl.* 2.25.8 [Fig. 1, no. 3]). In this quotation, Dionysios constructs a shorthand account of the legendary founding of the Corinthian and Roman communities by Paul and Peter, which he no doubt draws from the suggestions in 1 Cor 1:12, 3:22, and 9:5 that the Corinthians were familiar with Peter's ministry.[33] Drawing on Paul's image of the planter in 1 Cor 3:6–8, Dionysios stresses the unity of Peter and Paul in their founding of the Corinthian community and in the teaching they offered there. It is this same teaching that was delivered later by both Paul and Peter in Italy before their martyrdoms.

In his work on kinship diplomacy in the ancient world, C. P. Jones argues that the "wandering hero" as founder of cities was an important theme deployed in kinship diplomacy.[34] Dionysios follows these widespread diplomatic conventions in his use of Peter and Paul. If read in the broader context of diplomacy and economic exchange, the letters and the gift between the Roman and Corinthian communities are akin to the "renewal" of kinship common in ancient diplomacy.[35] It was common in proclamations of the συγγένεια (kinship) between cities to "prove" kinship through recourse to common ancestors and cults.[36] Peter and Paul are said to be "planters" of both communities and each is said to have taught in both as well. The focus on teaching and doctrine, which for the Christians is a crucial part of their cult and identity, serves a similar role here.[37] The proof of their kinship is

---

33. Of course, Paul himself claims to have been the only founder of the church in Corinth (1 Cor 4:15). Pervo, *Making of Paul*, 146, thinks it likely that Soter had attempted to bolster his authority by claiming Peter and Paul as dual founders of the Roman church. So also Carrington, *Early Christian Church*, 198. It may be that, rather than making an explicit claim to Peter and Paul as founders, the letter from the Roman church had noted the dual martyrdoms of Peter and Paul in Rome as part of a statement on Rome's authority and position. Dionysios, in response, accepts this claim, but then adds to it a claim of greater antiquity for Corinth. Heussi thought that Dionysios was announcing his exegetical discovery that Peter had been a part of the founding of Corinth as well as Rome (Heussi, *War Petrus in Rom?*, 54, cited in Goguel, *Primitive Church*, 206).

34. Jones, *Kinship Diplomacy*, 12. It is interesting to note that Corinth was singled out by several ancient writers as a city with two founding, patronal deities: Helios and Poseidon (Favorinus, "Corinthian Oration," §11–15; Pausanias, *Descr.* 2.1.6).

35. See Jones, *Kinship Diplomacy*, 24.

36. Battistoni, "Rome, Kinship and Diplomacy," 77–78.

37. Hall, *Ethnic Identity*, 25, notes that ethnic groups often share notions of

in their common ancestors and in the common teaching that both received and guarded.

This construction of the apostolic history of both Corinth and Rome is politically useful for Dionysios. On the one hand, Dionysios gives Corinth a more ancient claim to apostolic priority, since Peter and Paul taught in Corinth first before going to Rome.[38] On the other hand, Dionysios deflects the criticism that must have come from the Roman "admonishment" by noting that both communities have received the same teaching from Peter and Paul. The Corinthians are able to determine for themselves what proper teaching and doctrine looks like without Roman "help."[39]

Ultimately, Dionysios asserts the authoritative status of Corinth with respect to Rome.[40] Corinth and Rome share founders and teachings. They differ only in that Peter and Paul came to Corinth *first,* and then went to Rome to be martyred. The repetition of the language of equality and sameness is striking (and can only be rendered awkwardly in English): "For also both, having planted in our Corinth, equally taught us, and equally also, having taught in the same place in Italy, they were martyred at the same time."[41] Dionysios places Corinth and Rome at least on equal footing as apostolic sees, if not giving Corinth the advantage between the two.[42]

---

common ancestry, shared history, and shared culture (following Smith, *Ethnic Origins of Nations*, 22–30). Buell, *Why This New Race?* 35–62, argues as well for the role of religion as a marker of ethnic identity. Taken together we might think of the claim to a shared and stable set of theological and dogmatic teachings as a means of marking identity alongside recourse to founding ancestors. One can see a similar set of concerns around Spartan invocation and practice of the "Lycurgan Laws" into the Hellenistic and Roman periods (Cartledge and Spawforth, *Hellenistic and Roman Sparta*, 190–212). Though the practices associated with these laws were continually changing, the city continued to use the practice of the Lycurgan laws as a means of demonstrating that Sparta remained faithful to its ancestral laws and customs. Something similar is at play in Dionysios's letter, where the "teachings" of the initial founders of both communities serve as a means of demonstrating how both communities remain faithful to the traditions that have been handed down to them.

38. Pervo, *Making of Paul*, 146, also notes the temporal primacy that Dionysios's phrasing implies. See also Ferguson, "Church at Corinth," 170.

39. In another fragment found in Eusebius, Dionysios claims that it was actually the nefarious editing of the apostles of Satan (*Hist. eccl.* 4.23.12) that brought about the impression that his theology had deviated into heresy.

40. This was noted by Goguel, *Primitive Church*, 182, who saw evidence for both Corinth and Ephesos vying with Rome for leadership among the various churches.

41. ἄμφω, ὁμοίως (twice), ὁμόσε, κατὰ τὸν αὐτὸν καιρόν (*Hist. eccl.* 4.23.10).

42. There is a similar invocation of shared ancestors in the letter to the Athenians, where Dionysios dwells on the apostolic connections shared by both communities through Dionysios the Areopagite (*Hist. eccl.* 4.23.2–3; 3.4.10).

Conclusion

As Pierre Nautin has rightly argued, Dionysios's letter is full of "subtle nuances and insinuations" that both affirm a connection to Rome while asserting Corinth's right to be governed by its own traditions.[43] Though we only have fragments of the letter itself, it is clear that Dionysios is playing a complicated and subtle game with his Roman "siblings." Seen in this larger context, the mention of *1 Clement* by Dionysios cannot be read, as Eusebius perhaps wishes, as a simple statement of *1 Clement*'s usefulness and use in early Christian churches. Rather, Dionysios equates *1 Clement* with an unwanted Roman intervention in Corinthian affairs. *First Clement* is remembered in Corinth as an admonishment sent from siblings living abroad. It is when Rome tries to make Corinth into a client and subject it to admonishment that *1 Clement* comes to mind. This does not change the fact that *1 Clement* was an exceptionally important, influential, and (occasionally) scriptural authority in early Christianity; however, Dionysios' letter to the Romans suggests that the descendants of the original recipients may have viewed the letter ambivalently. Ultimately, siblings, even early Christian ones, did not always get along.

Fragments of Dionysios's Letter to the Romans	
1. ἐξ ἀρχῆς γὰρ ὑμῖν ἔθος ἐστὶν τοῦτο, πάντας μὲν ἀδελφοὺς ποικίλως εὐεργετεῖν, ἐκκλησίαις τε πολλαῖς ταῖς κατὰ πᾶσαν πόλιν ἐφόδια πέμπειν, ὧδε μὲν τὴν τῶν δεομένων πενίαν ἀναψύχοντας, ἐν μετάλλοις δὲ ἀδελφοῖς ὑπάρχουσιν ἐπιχορηγοῦντας· δι' ὧν πέμπετε ἀρχῆθεν ἐφοδίων, πατροπαράδοτον ἔθος Ῥωμαίων Ῥωμαῖοι φυλάττοντες, ὃ οὐ μόνον διατετήρηκεν ὁ μακάριος ὑμῶν ἐπίσκοπος Σωτήρ, ἀλλὰ καὶ ηὔξηκεν, ἐπιχορηγῶν μὲν τὴν διαπεμπομένην δαψίλειαν τὴν εἰς τοὺς ἁγίους, λόγοις δὲ μακαρίοις τοὺς ἀνιόντας ἀδελφούς, ὡς τέκνα πατὴρ φιλόστοργος, παρακαλῶν. (4.23.10)	For from the beginning this has been a custom for you, always acting as a benefactor to siblings in various ways and sending financial support to many assemblies in every city, thus relieving the poverty of those in want and supplying additional help to the siblings who are in the mines. Through the financial support which you have sent from the beginning, you Romans keep the custom of the Romans, which was handed down from your ancestors, which your honorable bishop has not only maintained but also added to, by providing an abundance sent across (from Rome) to the saints and encouraging with honorable words the siblings from abroad, as a devoted father.
2. τὴν σήμερον οὖν κυριακὴν ἁγίαν ἡμέραν διηγάγομεν, ἐν ᾗ ἀνέγνωμεν ὑμῶν τὴν ἐπιστολήν, ἣν ἕξομεν ἀεί ποτε ἀναγινώσκοντες νουθετεῖσθαι, ὡς καὶ τὴν προτέραν ἡμῖν διὰ Κλήμεντος γραφεῖσαν. (4.23.11)	Today we passed through the Lord's holy day, in which we read you letter. When we read it we will always have an admonishment, as also with the former [letter] written to us through Clement.
3. ταῦτα καὶ ὑμεῖς διὰ τῆς τοσαύτης νουθεσίας τὴν ἀπὸ Πέτρου καὶ Παύλου φυτείαν γενηθεῖσαν Ῥωμαίων τε καὶ Κορινθίων συνεκεράσατε. καὶ γὰρ ἄμφω καὶ εἰς τὴν ἡμετέραν Κόρινθον φυτεύσαντες ἡμᾶς ὁμοίως ἐδίδαξαν, ὁμοίως δὲ καὶ εἰς τὴν Ἰταλίαν ὁμόσε διδάξαντες ἐμαρτύρησαν κατὰ τὸν αὐτὸν καιρόν. (2.25.8)	By these things you have united through such an admonition the planting from Peter and Paul among the Romans and the Corinthians. For after both planted among us in our Corinth and likewise also in Italy, and also taught in the same place, they were martyred at the same time.

43. Nautin, *Lettres et écrivains*, 31. Noethlichs, "Bedeutung des Bischofs Dionysius," 247, n. 85, offers a similar estimation of the historical situation, arguing that Corinth and Rome stood in tension with one another as opposing apostolic sees into the early third century.

Works Cited

Bartchy, S. Scott. "Undermining Ancient Patriarchy: The Apostle Paul's Vision of a Society of Siblings." *BTB* 29 (1999) 68–78.

———. "Who Should Be Called Father? Paul of Tarsus between the Jewish Tradition and *Patria Potestas*." *BTB* 33 (2004) 135–47.

Battistoni, Filippo. "Rome, Kinship and Diplomacy." In *Diplomats and Diplomacy in the Roman World*, edited by Claude Eilers, 73–98. Mnemosyne Supplements 304. Leiden: Brill, 2009.

Bauer, Walter. *Orthodoxy and Heresy in Earliest Christianity*. Edited by Robert A. Kraft and Gerhard Krodel. Philadelphia: Fortress, 1971.

Bovon, François. *New Testament and Christian Apocrypha*. Edited by Glenn E. Snyder. Grand Rapids: Baker Academic, 2009.

Bowe, Barbara Ellen. *A Church in Crisis: Ecclesiology and Paraenesis in Clement of Rome*. Harvard Dissertations in Religion. Minneapolis: Fortress, 1988.

Buell, Denise Kimber. *Why This New Race?: Ethnic Reasoning in Early Christianity*. New York: Columbia University Press, 2005.

Carrington, Philip. *The Early Christian Church*. 2 vols. Cambridge: Cambridge University Press, 1957.

Cartledge, Paul, and Antony Spawforth. *Hellenistic and Roman Sparta : A Tale of Two Cities*. 2nd. ed. States and Cities of Ancient Greece. London: Routledge, 2002.

Concannon, Cavan W. "Ethnicity, Economics, and Diplomacy in Dionysios of Corinth." *HTR* 106 (2013) 145–69.

Ehrman, Bart D. *The Apostolic Fathers*. Vol. 1. LCL. Cambridge: Harvard University Press, 2003.

Eusebius. *Eusebius Werke, Band II, Teil I: Die Kirchengeschichte*. Die griechischen christlichen Schriftsteller der ersten Jahrhundrete. Berlin: Akademie, 1999.

Ferguson, Everett. "The Church at Corinth Outside the New Testament." *Restoration Quarterly* 3 (1959) 169–72.

Goguel, Maurice. *The Primitive Church*. Translated by H. C. Snape. London: Allen & Unwin, 1963.

Grant, Robert M., and Holt H. Graham. *The Apostolic Fathers: A New Translation and Commentary. Vol. 2, First and Second Clement*. New York: Nelson, 1965.

Greene, Kevin. *The Archaeology of the Roman Economy*. Berkeley: University of California Press, 1990.

Gustafson, Mark. "Condemnation to the Mines in the Later Roman Empire." *HTR* 87 (1994) 421–33.

Hall, Jonathan M. *Ethnic Identity in Greek Antiquity*. Cambridge: Cambridge University Press, 1997.

Harnack, Adolf von. *The Mission and Expansion of Christianity in the First Three Centuries*. 2 vols. Gloucester, MA: Peter Smith, 1972.

Hellerman, Joseph H. *The Ancient Church as Family*. Minneapolis: Fortress, 2001.

Heussi, Karl. *War Petrus in Rom?* Gotha: Klotz, 1936.

Jones, C. P. *Kinship Diplomacy in the Ancient World*. Revealing Antiquity 12. Cambridge: Harvard University Press, 1999.

Kühnert, Wilhelm. "Dionysius von Korinth: eine Bischofsgestalt des zweiten Jahrhunderts." In *Theologia Scientia Eminens Practica: Fritz Zerbst zum 70. Geburtstag*, edited by Fritz Herbst and Hans-Christoph Schmidt-Lauber, 273–89. Vienna: Herder, 1979.

Lampe, Peter. *From Paul to Valentinus: Christians at Rome in the First Two Centuries*. Translated by Michael Steinhauser. Edited by Marshall Johnson. Minneapolis: Fortress, 2003.

Lightfoot, J. B. *The Apostolic Fathers*. Vol. 1, *S. Clement of Rome*. London: Macmillan, 1890.

Magny, Ariane. "Porphyry in Fragments: Jerome, Harnack, and the Problem of Reconstruction." *JECS* 18 (2010) 515–55.

Maier, Paul L. *Eusebius: The Church History*. Grand Rapids: Kregel Academic, 1999.

Martin, Dale B. *Sex and the Single Savior: Gender and Sexuality in Biblical Interpretation*. Louisville: Westminster John Knox, 2006.

McDonald, Lee M. *The Formation of the Christian Biblical Canon*. Peabody, MA: Hendrickson, 1995.

Nautin, Pierre. *Lettres et écrivains chrétiens des IIe et IIIe siècles*. Patristica II. Paris: Cerf, 1961.

Noethlichs, Karl Leo. "Korinth—ein 'Aussenposten Roms'?: Zur kirchengeschichtlichen Bedeutung des Bischofs Dionysius von Korinth." *Jahrbuch für Antike und Christentum. Ergänzungsband* 34 (2002) 232–47.

Osiek, Carolyn. "The Ransom of Captives: Evolution of a Tradition." *HTR* 74 (1981) 365–86.

Pervo, Richard I. *The Making of Paul: Constructions of the Apostle in Early Christianity*. Minneapolis: Fortress, 2010.

Smith, Anthony D. *The Ethnic Origins of Nations*. Oxford: Blackwell, 1986.

Theissen, Gerd. *The Social Setting of Pauline Christianity: Essays on Corinth*. Translated by John H. Schütz. Philadelphia: Fortress, 1982.

Unnik, W. C. van. "Studies on the So-Called First Epistle of Clement. The Literary Genre." In *Encounters with Hellenism: Studies on the First Letter of Clement*, edited by Cilliers Breytenbach and Laurence L. Welborn, 115–81. Arbeiten zur Geschichte des antiken Judentums und des Urchristentums 53. Leiden: Brill, 2004.

Welborn, L. L. "Clement, First Epistle of." In *ABD*, 1:1055–60.

———. "On the Date of First Clement." *Biblical Review* 29 (1984) 34–54.

———. "The Preface to 1 Clement: The Rhetorical Situation and the Traditional Date." In *Encounters with Hellenism: Studies on the First Letter of Clement*, edited by Cilliers Breytenbach and Laurence L. Welborn, 197–216. Arbeiten zur Geschichte des antiken Judentums und des Urchristentums 53. Leiden: Brill, 2004.

www.ingramcontent.com/pod-product-compliance
Lightning Source LLC
Chambersburg PA
CBHW061431300426
44114CB00014B/1639